AF328655

CONTEMPORARY BRITISH CERAMICS

beneath the surface

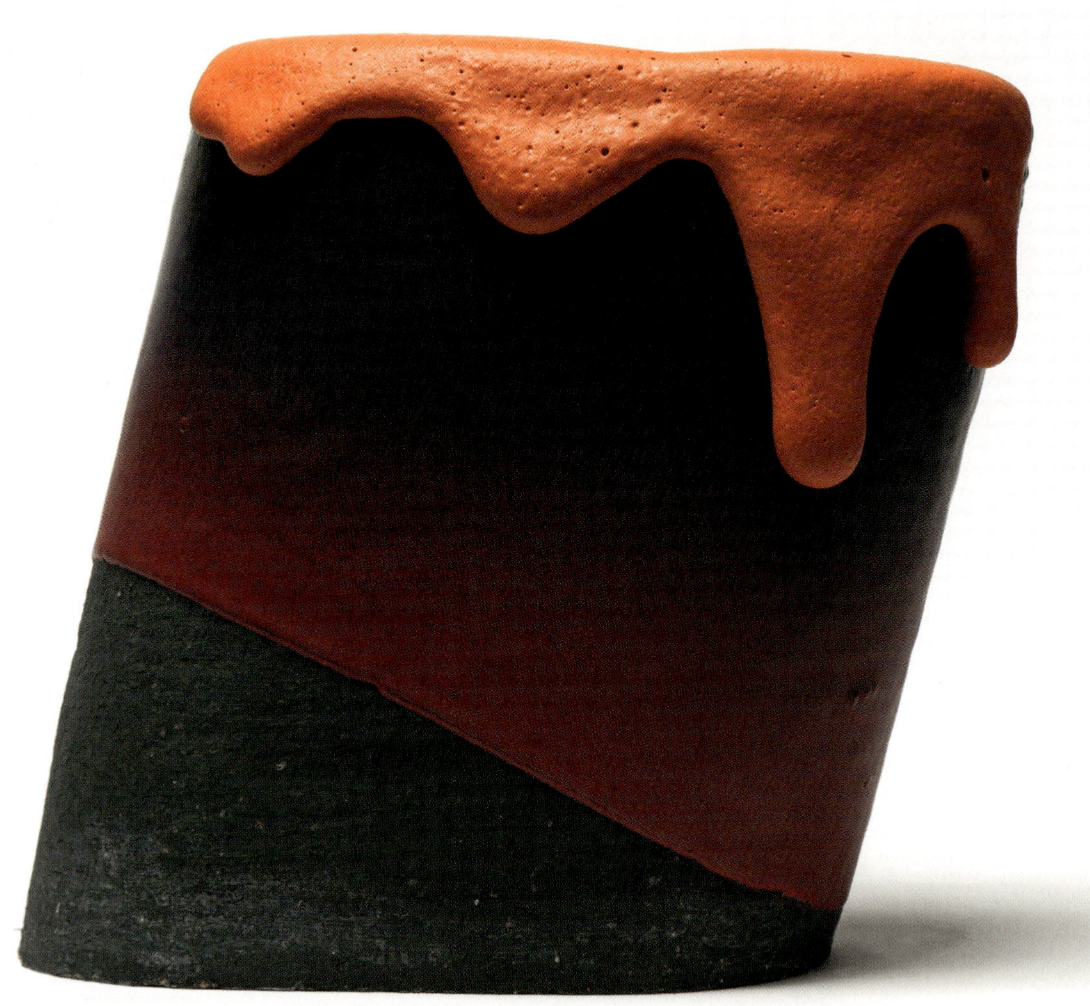

CONTEMPORARY BRITISH CERAMICS

beneath the surface

Ashley Thorpe

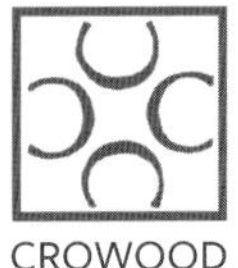

CROWOOD

First published in 2021 by
The Crowood Press Ltd
Ramsbury, Marlborough
Wiltshire SN8 2HR

enquiries@crowood.com
www.crowood.com

British Library Cataloguing-in-Publication Data
A catalogue record for this book is available from the
British Library.

ISBN 978 1 78500 888 7

Frontispiece
Merced, California, Pam Su, 2018.
(Photograph by Chao Wang)

Cover design: Kelly-Anne Levey

Typeset by Kelly-Anne Levey
Printed and bound in India by Parksons Graphics

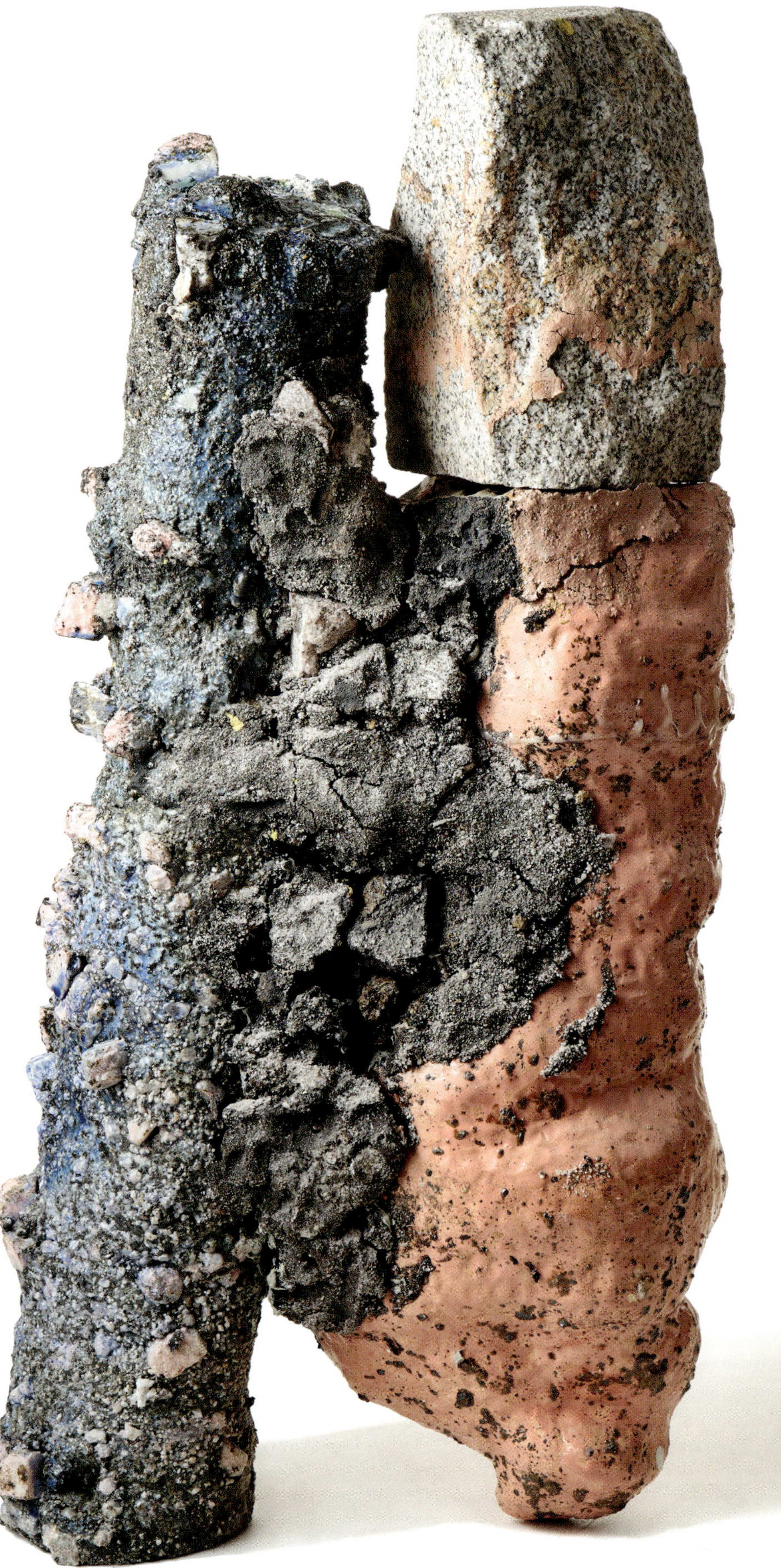

Contents

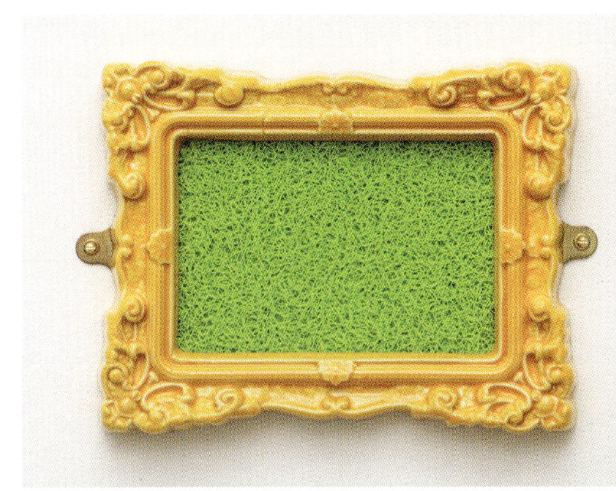

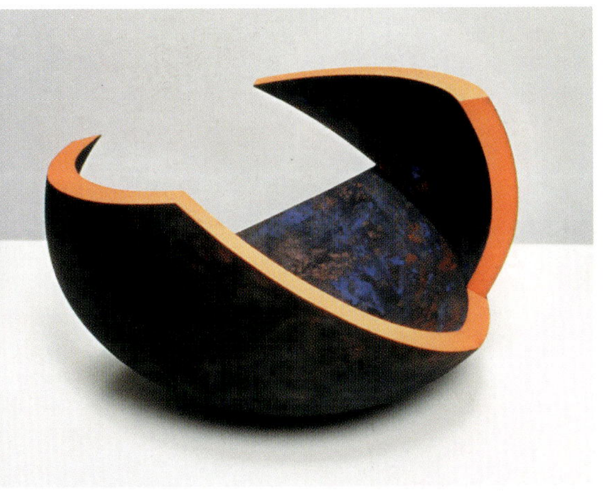

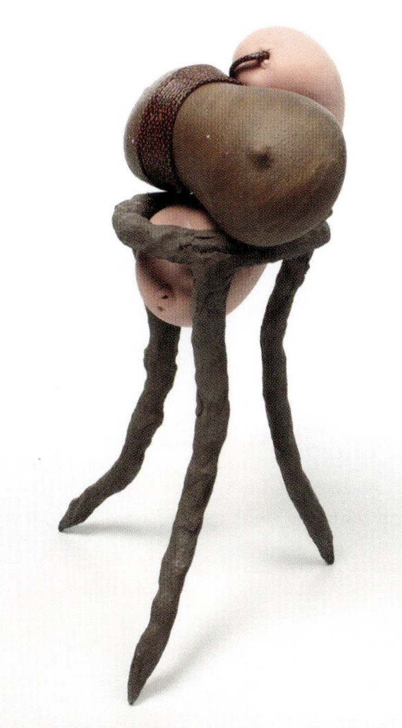

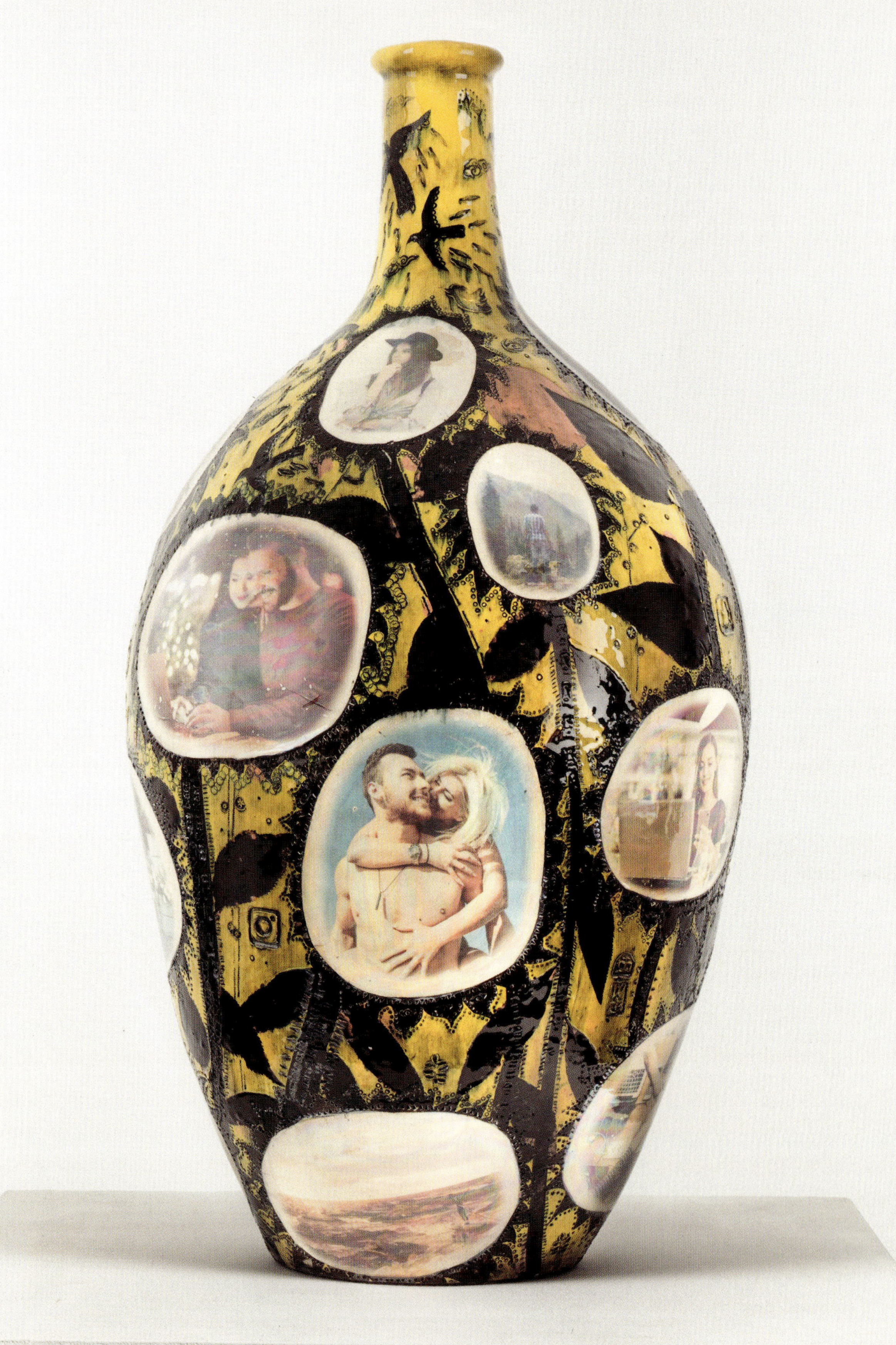

Introduction

The Collector's Eye

I have called this introduction 'The Collector's Eye' in response to *The Maker's Eye*, a Crafts Council exhibition consisting of some 500 objects – textiles, ceramics, paintings, wood, metal and glass – chosen by fourteen craftspeople, held in London in 1982. In the year before the exhibition opened to the public, the Crafts Council published an accompanying catalogue. Selectors were arranged in the volume alphabetically by surname, and essays by two ceramicists with seemingly antithetical views were serendipitously placed next to each other. In the first essay, Alison Britton noted how her selection of works moved beyond utility. She observed how each object gave more than was asked of it, offered reflections on ideology as much as function, and existed in a space somewhere between craft and art. In contrast, in the second essay Michael Cardew asserted functionality as key for the consideration of ceramics as craft, a term he felt needed to be defended from the emergence of a new hierarchy that prioritized ceramics as 'fine art'.

My relationship with ceramic practice rests entirely on the fact that I am a collector rather than a maker. Looking back at *The Maker's Eye* catalogue exactly forty years after its publication, I am struck at how much has changed, and how much seems to have stayed the same. In some ways, ceramics as a discipline seems more at ease with itself. The impassioned debates about whether ceramics can or should be 'art' have perhaps been settled. Ceramics is an incredibly varied set of practices and ideologies, which includes anything from the most unpretentiously utilitarian bowl through to the most recent developments in fine art sculpture and site-specific performance. The British Ceramics Biennial, launched in 2009, has showcased the array of approaches that exist, and offered a platform of encouragement for recent graduates and established talent alike. Commercial galleries have focused on specific but varied types of work: some showcase more functional ware, others ceramic art and sculpture, and a handful of others exhibit both. Some artists exhibit with craft shops, others with fine art galleries.

Many collectors embrace this range of possibility. Others, I have observed, are much more resistant to it. Pots are an easier sell, and they certainly command the highest prices at auction. Names such as Hans Coper (1920–81), Lucie Rie (1902–95), Edmund de Waal, Jennifer Lee and Grayson Perry all achieve the eye-watering prices previously reserved for oil paintings and bronze sculpture (in 2018, a Coper vase sold for £318,000). Perhaps people know where they are with a pot; the familiarity of containment, however nominal, is reassuring.

If we look elsewhere, such as in the US, we find a much longer tradition of abstract and sculptural ceramics, and where such work is more readily regarded as contemporary art. In the mid-1950s, whilst Rie and Coper were crafting tea and coffee sets in Albion Mews, Peter Voulkos (1924–2002) was already working with the likes of John Mason (1927–2019) and Ken Price (1935–2012). These artists were pivotal in redefining what ceramic as a material could do. Utilizing techniques derived from Modernist, Abstract and Expressionist art, they successfully freed clay from its associations with domestic utility.[1] The exhibition *The Ceramic Presence in Modern Art*, held at Yale University Art Gallery in 2015, demonstrated how these artists were deeply integrated with the wider milieu of the American avant-garde. In the US in the 1950s, fine and ceramic art circles were conjoined, and larger works by these artists now command tens of thousands of dollars at auction.

The 2015 Yale exhibition also included work by Rie and Coper. In discussions of line, volume and tone, it can be argued that some of their output contributed to a shift in ceramic practice in the US, and the UK, though in the latter perhaps as much, if not more, through their teaching.[2] Certainly, the tone adopted by the curators for these artists was much more benign. It was noted, for instance, how Rie and Coper were resolutely tied to the realm of British pottery.[3] Whilst the influence of continental modernism to Lucie Rie, and the sculptures of Henry Moore to Hans Coper, revealed connections to the wider preoccupations of fine art, the exhibition made absolutely no attempt to claim that they were as enmeshed into fine art circles in Britain as their counterparts were in America.[4] And that is, quite simply, because they were not. At least, not until the late 1980s and early 1990s, by which point Coper had died. Is this a problem? Yes and no. 'Pottery' is not a dirty word. Though I sometimes wonder whether British ceramic artists who do not make pots are overlooked for doing so, whilst also being snubbed by fine art galleries for using (what some art collectors might perceive as) a 'craft' material. Things are changing, but progress seems to me to be slow. Why?

There are undoubtedly many nuanced and complex reasons as to why the US and UK should have different aesthetic emphases. We could look, for example, to the different socio-economic and cultural impacts of the Second World War. We could recognize the legacy of mass-produced tableware in cities such as Stoke-on-Trent for framing expectations around ceramic practice as essentially vessel based. We might also look at the pervasive influence of Bernard Leach (1887–1979), and his belief that the Anglo-Oriental approach was *the* way to unify utility with art. We could explore the impact of Leach's criticism of artists such as William Newland (1919–88) and James Tower (1919–88) who, by making work influenced by Pablo Picasso in the 1950s, were derogatorily termed 'the Picassettes', further cementing a divide between 'fine art' and 'craft art'. We could consider the status of Rie and Coper as immigrants, and the fact that they initially had to situate their modernism within the prevailing Leach aesthetic. There is also the role of government institutions in promoting certain ideologies around craft, and the significance of museum acquisition policies privileging certain practices over others. All of this, and undoubtedly a great deal more, has played a part.

In recent decades, there have been significant attempts to communicate to a wider public how contemporary ceramic artists work across forms, practices and approaches. The ceramic galleries of the Victoria and Albert Museum in London, for instance, have sought to challenge perceptions with a host of temporary exhibitions and artistic residencies, many of which are not rooted to the vessel. A number of the artists featured in this book have participated in this scheme. Similarly, the Centre of Ceramic Art in York has mounted exhibitions of ceramic sculpture by Gillian Lowndes (1936–2010) and, by holding examples of work purchased by the collector Anthony Shaw on long-term loan, brought sculptural work by the likes of Ewen Henderson (1934–2000), Sara Radstone and Eileen Nisbet (1929–90) to new audiences.

Yet, the problem with any public gallery is that it has to classify its collections according to material. Ceramics in a dedicated gallery is a double-edged sword: it necessarily highlights ceramics as a practice and enables stylistic changes within the discipline to be observed. However, it is also more difficult to perceive its connections with other artistic movements, and perhaps risks clay being determined as a rather

> If anything surprises me about the forty years since *The Maker's Eye*, it is that the mingling of 'art' and 'craft' has not become a more commonplace approach in exhibition curation.

self-referential medium. Disappointingly, the exhibition *A Secret History of Clay: from Gauguin to Gormley*, held at Tate Liverpool in 2004, emphasized fine artists who engaged with ceramic practices (the approach of fine artists perhaps demonstrates less understanding of the history of ceramics than those who studied it at art college). It included only a handful of ceramic artists moving into fine art (two with pots, one with tiles), and rather overlooked the vital interconnections between painting, sculpture and ceramics.

If there is a 'secret' history of clay, it is that studio ceramics has been a fertile area of enquiry precisely because it has always brought together different arts practices. Yet, this is nothing new. Japanese Jōmon (14000–300 BCE) and Chinese Majiayao (3300–2000 BCE) cultures made both ceramic pots and sculptures using carving, sculpting, hand-building, drawing and painting skills. Contemporary British ceramic practice as described in this book is doing nothing more than flexing the ancient muscles of the medium.

If anything surprises me about the forty years since *The Maker's Eye*, it is that the mingling of 'art' and 'craft' has not become a more commonplace approach in exhibition curation. It is particularly surprising because a number of contemporary makers continue to draw, paint and make prints. But it also helps to illuminate what is going on in terms of dialogue. As an ideological platform, *The Maker's Eye* empowered Alison Britton to convincingly describe a significant mutation in British ceramic practice. Britton herself has been inspired by the US artist Betty Woodman (1930–2018), whose work sits in between ceramics, sculpture and painting.[5]

This amalgamation of disciplines has also been important for Britton's own practice, as demonstrated in the essay on her work included here. To my mind, Britton, and others (Richard Slee in particular) have engaged with the opening out of perspectives offered by ceramic abstraction from the US as much as, if not more than, the modernist and sculptural impulses of Coper and Rie.[6] Perhaps by offering an alternative to Michael Cardew's validation of the Leach doctrine, Britton's essay in *The Maker's Eye* gave words to a conceptual space that a number of British artists already inhabited, but which had not otherwise been formally articulated. Her essay continues to be relevant because it argues for the unification of intellect, artistry, skill and playfulness beyond the constraints of utility. As I look across this volume, I find such unification in abundance.

Nevertheless, sculptural ceramics is not new to Britain. The brilliant *The Art of the Modern Potter* by Tony Birks, first published in 1967, documented works by Ruth Duckworsth, Ian Godfrey, Bryan Newman and Anthony Hepburn. All of these artists, especially the latter, sought out new sculptural vocabularies for clay that seem contemporary even now. Over the past few decades, the likes of Jill Crowley, Kerry Jameson, Claire Curneen and Bryan Illsley have created a compelling body of abstract and figurative sculptures. My riposte to any naysayers who are dismissive of work beyond the vessel is that ceramic art does not have to look like a pot to be a container. Ceramic sculptures might not be designed to hold water, but they certainly hold ideas. They carry liquid meanings: our desires, fantasies, dissatisfactions, memories and passions.

I am very aware that, with the exception of some works by Martin Smith, there are no throwers included in this book. It is not that I dislike thrown pots, feel they are lesser, or consider them devoid of interest. As a collector, I love all forms of ceramics, and it is the malleability of the material that stimulates me most. It is more that I have had to implement criteria to make the volume feasible. Paul Rice's *British Studio Ceramics* (2002) focuses exclusively on the vessel, much of it thrown, and so I have sought to offer something of an alternative here. I have also chosen to concentrate on artists who are still active, meaning the work of luminaries such as Nicholas Homoky, Rupert Spira, and the late Janice Tchalenko (1942–2018) and Robin Welch (1936–2019) are regretfully omitted. Other important names – Gordon Baldwin, Claire Curneen, Edmund de Waal, Walter Keeler, Magdalene Odundo, Grayson Perry and Julian Stair – have been written about elsewhere.[7] In any case, this book was never meant to be a comprehensive survey. Rather, I have sought to offer a deeper reflection on the work of specific artists, and interweave established names with emerging makers, some of whom have never been written about before.

In this respect, I am most influenced by the structure of *The Art of the Modern Potter*. Any volume reflects the tastes of its author, and in what might seem like a blindingly obvious statement (but one that is often glossed over), I have only written about work that I like and when I feel I have something to say. For artists nearer the start of their careers, and who are still in the process of discovering their voice, I have responded to what I perceive as exciting discoveries in their work, even if these prove to be transient. For more established artists, I have tried to find a new angle on their practice.

Although Britain is the focus for this volume, this particular constraint should not be regarded as an endorsement of nationalist insularity. If anything, British ceramics seems more international than ever. British artists regularly exhibit abroad, both in solo and group shows. In fact, some artists find it easier to exhibit abroad than they do in Britain, a sad and rather telling indictment. Social media has enabled artists from around the world to share their work and comment upon it, and British artists can participate in international discussions about practice without even leaving their studio. The artists explored here demonstrate an interest in, and a response to, work from Europe, the US, Japan, and elsewhere. This influence is not just confined to the field of ceramics, but also extends to wider fine art and sculptural practice, as well as the critical writing that accompanies it.

From the outset, I wanted this book to be critically engaged, accessible, and a good thumb-through. I also knew I did not want a lot of section headings. Some books bracket artists together through shared themes or approaches, such as 'materiality', 'space', the 'abstract' etc. I understand the value of this approach, but equally I am often left confused as to why one aspect of an artist's work, such as 'material', has been deemed more important than another, say 'space'. Why must artists only appear in one category in a book when their work is out of necessity much broader? There is a risk, I think, of distorting what the work actually is in order to meet the demands of a particular thesis.

Neither did I want this volume to follow the educational approach. This proposes that if artists trained at the same institution, perhaps under the same teacher, it follows that their work must be broadly similar. Not everyone who studied ceramics at Camberwell, the Royal College of Art, or wherever else, produces work according to the same aesthetic ideals. This is not to say that artistic genealogy does not have its place. There can, however, be an over-emphasis on education as the primary determinant. In saying all this, I am not anti-theory, or anti-history. It is simply that, in this volume, I have sought to approach contemporary ceramics in Britain in a slightly different way.

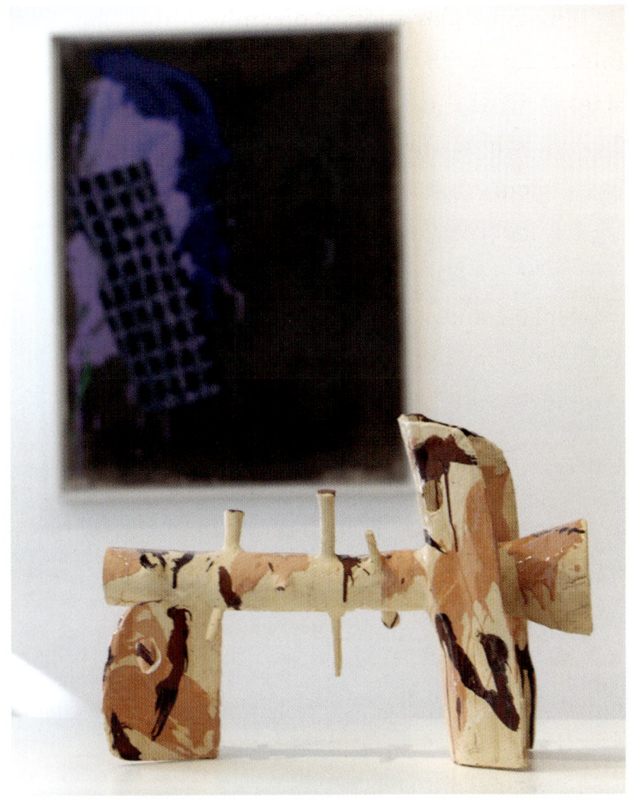

Bryan Illsley, *Hoarse*, featured in *Fun and Games,* his 2014 solo show at Marsden Woo Gallery.
(© Philip Sayer. Courtesy of Marsden Woo)

The guiding principle in this volume has been remarkably simple: treat each work as its own object in the world. By framing the analysis in this way, I have tried to think about what these pieces evoke as works in their own right. How might they make us feel? How does ceramic relate to other arts? How might one aspect of an artist's work resonate with another? These essays stand as records of my perception of the work and its meaning as expressed in the examples I have selected. It is entirely subjective. My approach to each chapter has also been quite uniform. I have formulated my ideas, usually in relation to an existing concept, and then approached each artist to seek permission to write on them. I have then tested out my thinking, either

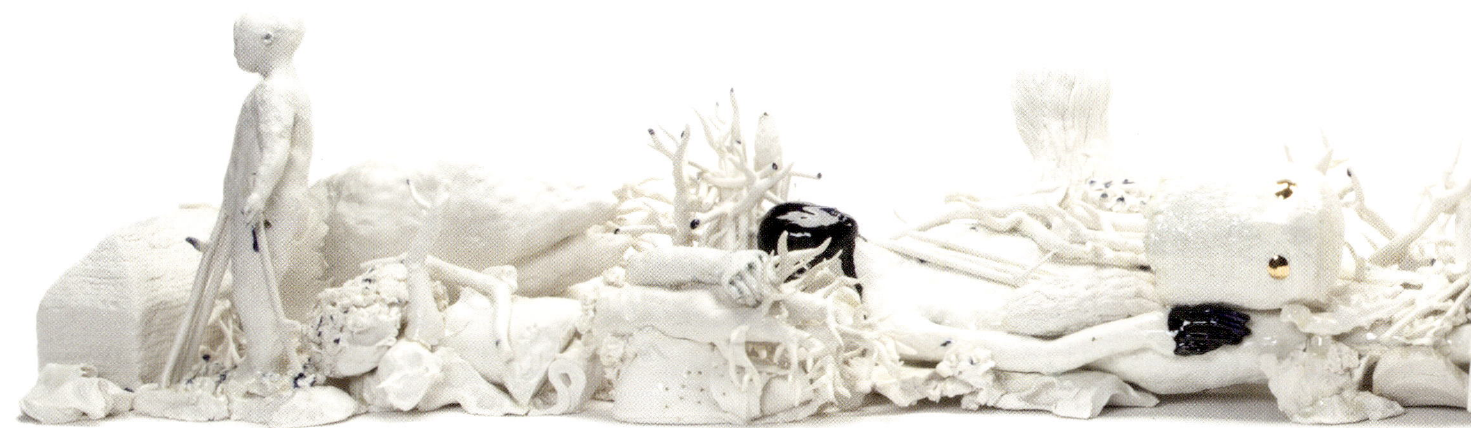

by meeting the artist and discussing their work in person, or by sending them the writing for a response, or, more often, both.

You will, of course, be approaching this book with different motives and priorities. For some, flicking through the pages to look at the images will be the main concern. This is how it should be. Certainly it always is for me: why else would you buy an art book? In structuring the accompanying text, I have tried to account for different approaches to its reading. Each chapter is self-contained, enabling you to dip in and out the book as you see fit. For those who decide to read the book chronologically, I have placed artists in close proximity where there is a shared vocabulary or point of reference. This is not so much putting work into conceptual boxes; more curating it into echoes and synergies, as well as very real and significant differences. For this reason, I do not consider the lack of sub-sections in this book to be a critical retreat. Quite the opposite, in fact.

There is a definite logic suspended in the progression of the essays. Moving from the first to last chapter, there emerge questions concerning the rela-

tionship of ceramics to painting, drawing, memory and emotion, ecological disaster and the environment, place, architecture and space, identity, and history. These categories are not exclusive: the essays speak to many of these concepts in different ways. The critical perspective I offer here is to state categorically that thematic relationships are more complicated and nuanced than sub-sections can ever hope to convey. Should you journey through the book from beginning to end, the themes will mutate as you progress, and you will find the strongest conceptual synergies between essays in proximity. However, the first and last essays should not be regarded as end points in a spectrum. Rather, these chapters – focusing upon the work of Richard Slee and Neil Brownsword – explore how work sits amongst and between the categories of 'fine art' and 'craft'. In this sense, the volume has a very circular structure; you can read chronologically from any chapter and end up back in the same place.

I have to admit that when I look back on the process of writing this book, I cannot help but wonder what each artist made of me when I marched up to them and brazenly responded to their work. But I

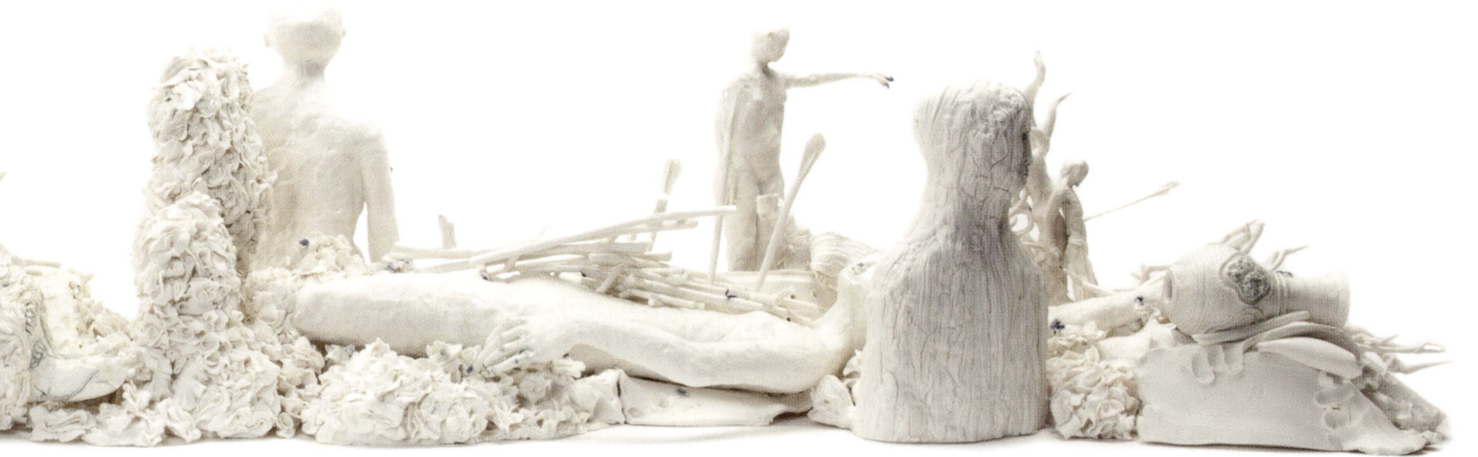

have been consistently amazed at the generosity of their response. I remain indebted to all of the artists included here for their time, tolerance and support in responding to the writing, and in liaising with their equally generous photographers to enable pictures of their work to be reproduced. Each essay has been read by the artist prior to inclusion. Some made suggestions, others did not, but in all cases the writing remains my own response to their work. There is a short biography for each artist at the back of the volume, but there is otherwise no statement by them on their practice. This, I think, is important to viewing their work in the world: that is, as works that are discovered without a need to validate responses through biography, the artist's own thoughts, or technical processes.

As someone who is not a maker, I only have a rudimentary understanding of clays, glazes, and firing temperatures. I have not asked artists to supply this information in detail, and I accept that this might be frustrating for some readers (and perhaps some artists too). For me, there is an element of mystery in how these pieces are produced, and I feel this

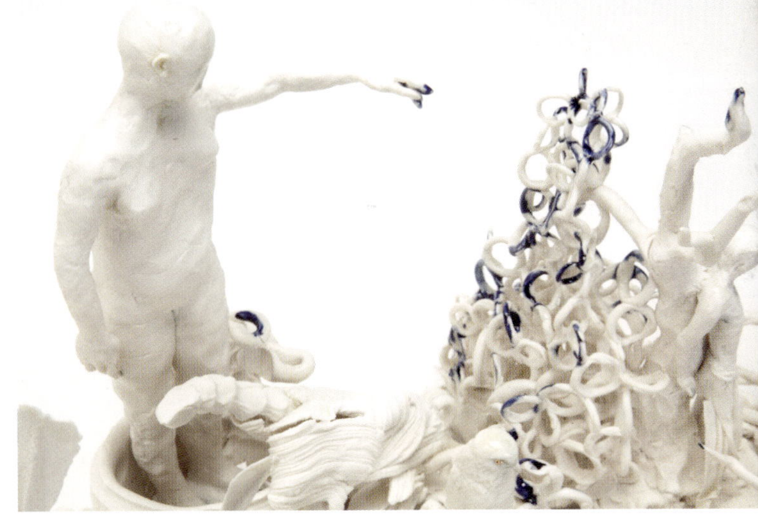

Claire Curneen, Detail of *Tending the Fires* (2016).
(Photograph by Dewi Tannatt Lloyd)

has equivalence in discussions of other arts. Fine art criticism, for instance, does not tend to focus on technical details at the expense of other kinds of analysis, even if it includes reference to conventions (e.g. the golden ratio in painting). Certainly, painters are rarely asked to document the five pigments they mixed together to get the shade of green they used

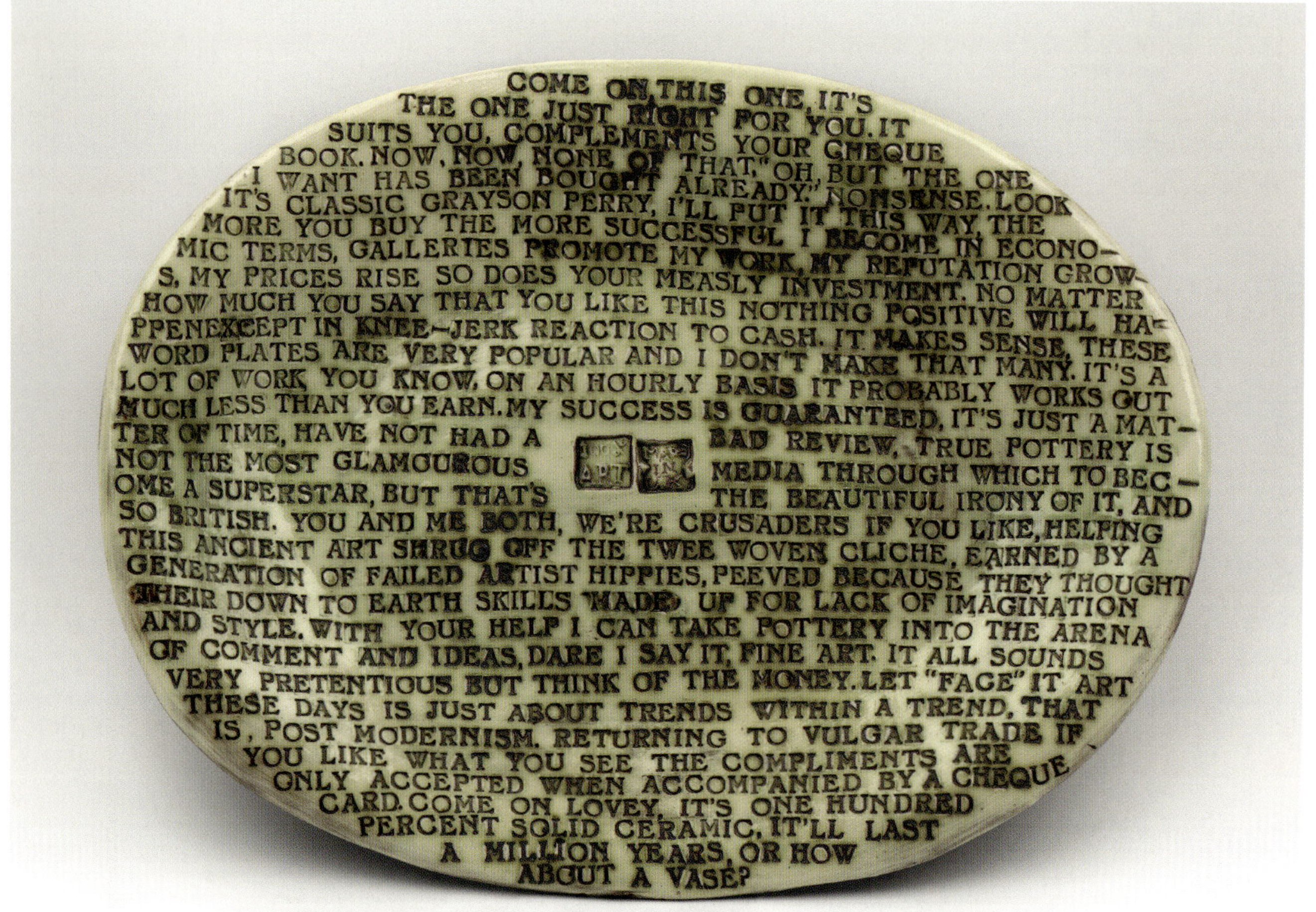

Grayson Perry, *Sales Pitch* (1987).
(© Grayson Perry. Courtesy the artist and Victoria Miro)

for blades of grass in an oil painting. It is not the point. In accepting that ceramics is its own medium, has its own needs, languages and perspectives, I still do not feel compelled to include technical data. There are plenty of books about this already. The focus here is on the work produced and its impact; how it got into the world is of less importance to me than the fact it is here at all.

These essays, then, represent my honest responses to the work, written from the heart as much as the head. For me, ceramics have become tied to every-day experience in distinctive ways. What might seem like mundane or trivial incidents can sometimes trigger a particular way of responding to an artist's work. If parts of this volume seem autobiographical, this arises simply from the fact that the works I have selected are sewn into the fabric of daily life. I am sure that an artist, dealer, curator, historian or critic would have a very different take on the questions I have explored in this introduction, and which rever-berate across the book. But I am not pretending to be something I am not. I am a collector, and I speak from that position, with respect, affection and con-viction. What follows is nothing more than a view from the collector's eye.

Richard Slee

Frames of Reference

> *Art* [...] differs from *handicraft*; the first is called *free*, the other may be called mercenary. We regard the first as if it could only prove purposive as play, *i.e.* as occupation that is pleasant in itself. But the second is regarded as if it could only be compulsorily imposed upon one as work, *i.e.* as occupation which is unpleasant (a trouble) in itself, and which is only attractive on account of its effect (*e.g.* the wage).[8]

This rather snobby division between art and craft – of art exhibiting a playfulness and love of beauty for its own sake, whilst craft simply being a highly skilled imposition that earns a crust – was proposed by the influential German philosopher Immanuel Kant (1724–1804). In *The Critique of Judgement* published in 1790, Kant sought to understand how it was possible for us to recognize and experience beauty. Kant's analysis has been developed, and critiqued, but has remained a highly influential theory. Indeed, I regard it as a useful frame of reference for exploring the work of Richard Slee. In 2018, Slee held an exhibition, *Framed*, at the Crafts Study Centre in Farnham, Surrey. The exhibition consisted of twenty-five wall-mounted works, many of the pieces taking the form of found objects edged by ceramic frames. The exhibition raised questions about the divide between art and craft, the nature of the boundaries, and the possibility of their blurring.

In order to understand the implications of the divide between art and craft, and the challenge Slee's work offers to it, we first need to explore Kant's ideas in more detail. Kant offered four observations, a kind of criteria, about how we experience beauty and, in turn, how we come to recognize fine art. His first assumption was that:

> *Taste* is the faculty of judging of an object or a method of representing it by an *entirely disinterested* satisfaction or dissatisfaction. The object of such satisfaction is called *beautiful.*[9]

For Kant, there was an important distinction between things that we produce because we need them to survive, and things we make simply because they give us pleasure. For an object to be beautiful, it cannot be functional. Indeed, Kant argued that producing an object was not a remarkable thing in itself; all livings things produce what they need to survive. Bees make honey, spiders make webs to catch flies; only humans produce things that they do not actually need. For Kant, this was the first requirement for an object to be beautiful, and by extension, to be art; it must have no industrial benefit, no utility, no need beyond its own existence. Thus, when we look at art, we are not looking at it in an interested way (that is, in terms of how we can use it to help us survive), but what Kant describes above as a 'disinterested' way. We contemplate the object simply for its own sake. If we look at an object in this disinterested way, and find it to our 'satisfaction', we find it beautiful. If it gives us 'dissatisfaction', we do not.

> The beautiful is that which pleases universally, without a concept.[10]

Secondly, if everyone can feel pain, Kant observed, then everyone can feel pleasure, and so beauty must exist as a universal phenomenon. For something to be beautiful it must be liked by more than one person. Whilst taste varies between individuals, an object will not be validated as beautiful if only one person thinks it is; beauty is a socialized phenomenon.[11] Furthermore, Kant suggested that in the aesthetic contemplation of an object, we look 'without a concept'. What he means is that when we look at something in a disinterested way, our imaginations go into overdrive, and we open up a number of different conceptual understandings about what we see: there is not one correct interpretation. Kant called this appreciation of an object without a concept 'Free Play'. Free Play is a crucial mode of analysis that our minds enter into when we make aesthetic judgements about beauty.

> *Beauty* is the form of the *purposiveness* of an object, so far as this is perceived in it without *any representation of the purpose.*[12]

Thirdly, Kant argued that for something to have beauty, it has to set out to be beautiful in the first place, but it cannot look like this is what it is setting out to do. This might seem self-evident, but he argued, for instance, that a flower is beautiful to us simply because it was grown and made (its 'purposiveness') to be beautiful. Bees could not find a flower beautiful, assuming they could have such a judgement, because their interest was in a practical search for nectar. Similarly, in art, a painting can be beautiful because it is designed and made to be beautiful: this is its sole purpose. Yet, when we contemplate art, we do not want to feel that we are being manipulated into appreciating beauty. If we become too aware of the artist's labour, we look at a painting in terms of how it elicits our feelings, that is, we focus on the labour of the artist's technique. In such instances, our own 'disinterested' aesthetic experience is lost; rather, we become 'interested' in how the artist achieved the work, and view the painting as a kind of skill or craft, and not as art.

The *beautiful* is that which without any concept is cognised as the object of a *necessary* satisfaction.[13]

Finally, Kant argued that beauty rests upon supplying us with some kind of aesthetic satisfaction. Again, this seems self-evident, but it is nevertheless an important point. If an object does not satisfy us (give us 'necessary satisfaction'), we will not find it beautiful.

The significance of Kant's ideas to the analysis here rests upon recognizing that we apply certain kinds of criteria to help us distinguish art from other kinds of object. We make art 'special'. How? When we want to experience and appreciate art, we go to special buildings (galleries), into special rooms (exhibitions), to look at paintings on a white wall free of other visual distractions, and which are made even more important by being marked out by a picture frame. All of this facilitates, as observed by Kant, a disinterested way of looking at an object. We dismiss the practical and look for the aesthetic. By going to a gallery, we actually make a physical effort to separate ourselves from the daily lives of work and family, to stop thinking about what we need to do to survive, and to instead immerse ourselves in a search for beauty. Indeed, art, for most of us at least, is not a daily experience; it is a special activity. The hushed environment of a gallery, should we happen upon it, assists us in our search for aesthetic enlightenment by reinforcing our temporary removal from the humdrum of the daily grind.

If we follow Kant's ideas, ceramics, as a craft practice, is concerned with function, and so it cannot be art. A pot is designed to be a useful container: it cannot be pure beauty. The judgement we make about a pot fundamentally rests upon whether it can do the job of holding a liquid properly. We do not need to go to a special gallery to experience ceramics. In fact, they are such a fundamental part of our daily lives that we need go no further than the kitchen. All of this rests, of course, on the assumption that

a theory from 1790 still holds water. It seems to me that many contemporary ceramic artists have overturned some of these assumptions. Richard Slee is certainly one of them.

How does a pot become art? Context demands from the spectator a very particular way of seeing. Marcel Duchamp (1887–1968) understood this only too well when he famously took a readymade ceramic toilet urinal ('not art'), and, stripping it of its possible function, put it in an art gallery in 1917 (now 'art'). Equally, Grayson Perry has shown that the unassuming shape of a pot – bound up with the daily, the disposable and the domestic – is the perfect vehicle for smuggling unsettling imagery into the fashionable galleries of the contemporary art world.[14] Once a pot is in a gallery, people are forced to look at it differently, as art, and not wonder about whether it will leak if filled with liquid. Such shifts in context are crucially important when considering the artworks (note the term) of Richard Slee. *Framed* brought together a number of different worlds – craft techniques, the handmade, the readymade – and, in what stands as a strong riposte to Kant, quite literally reframed these things into fine art.

There remains something mischievous about putting an art exhibition on in a craft centre. Slee designed the exhibition specifically for the Craft Study Centre, and so the politics of this decision is very resonant. The Crafts Study Centre originated at the Holburne Museum in Bath, where it opened in 1977, before moving to Farnham in 2000. It includes an extensive archive about, and numerous world-class examples of, studio ceramics, calligraphy, wood, furniture and textiles. It holds some works on paper, but it is by no means an Art Gallery. In *Framed*, Slee showed that the divisions between art and craft are very tenuous, if not ultimately irrelevant. At least half of the overall material on display was ceramic, but since the works were all designed to be fixed to the wall, there were no

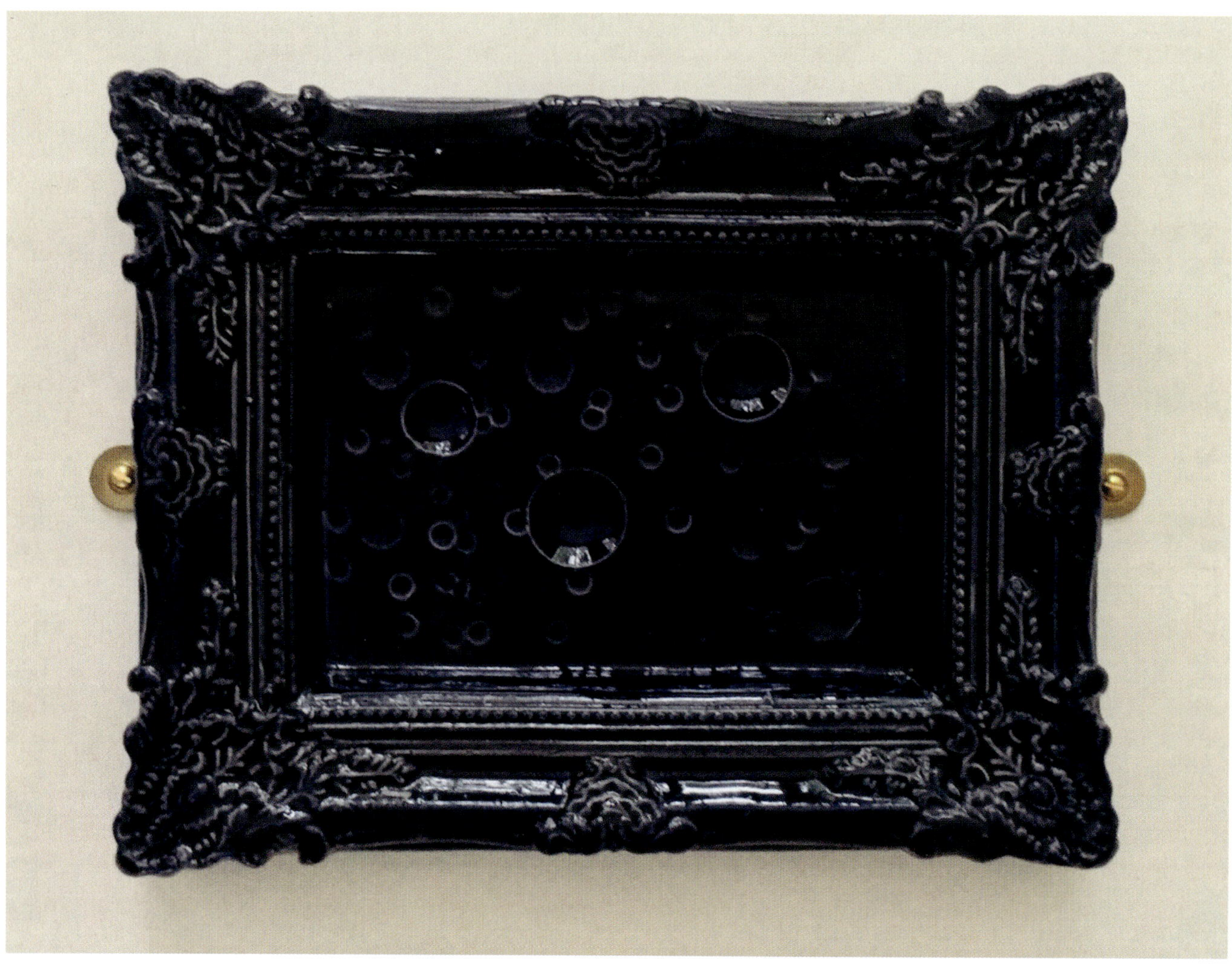

Space (2015).
(Photograph by Richard Slee)

plinths or shelves. The exhibition space was designed to perform like an art exhibition. Slee seemed to be provoking his audience: if you come to a craft gallery to see a ceramics show, and are confronted by a fine art experience, you will be tested against your own preconceptions. Look for craft and you will see craft. Look for art and you will see art. Look for both and you will find the work of Richard Slee.

The pieces in *Framed* were made entirely from found objects, processed by Slee in particular ways. During one of his adventures around pound shops, Slee came across a range of baroque-style plastic picture frames. There is an interesting conceptual tension in these objects that no doubt aroused Slee's interest. In these frames, the baroque style – the ornate grandeur of the seventeenth and early eighteenth centuries – has been mass-produced in plastic and sold, at profit, for only one pound. They capture a wider sense of collapse between high art and mass consumerist culture. More people have seen Leonardo da Vinci's *Mona Lisa* (1503) as a digital image, a poster or a postcard, than in the flesh as an oil painting. Of those who have made the pilgrimage to The Louvre, many will simply have been jostled past it

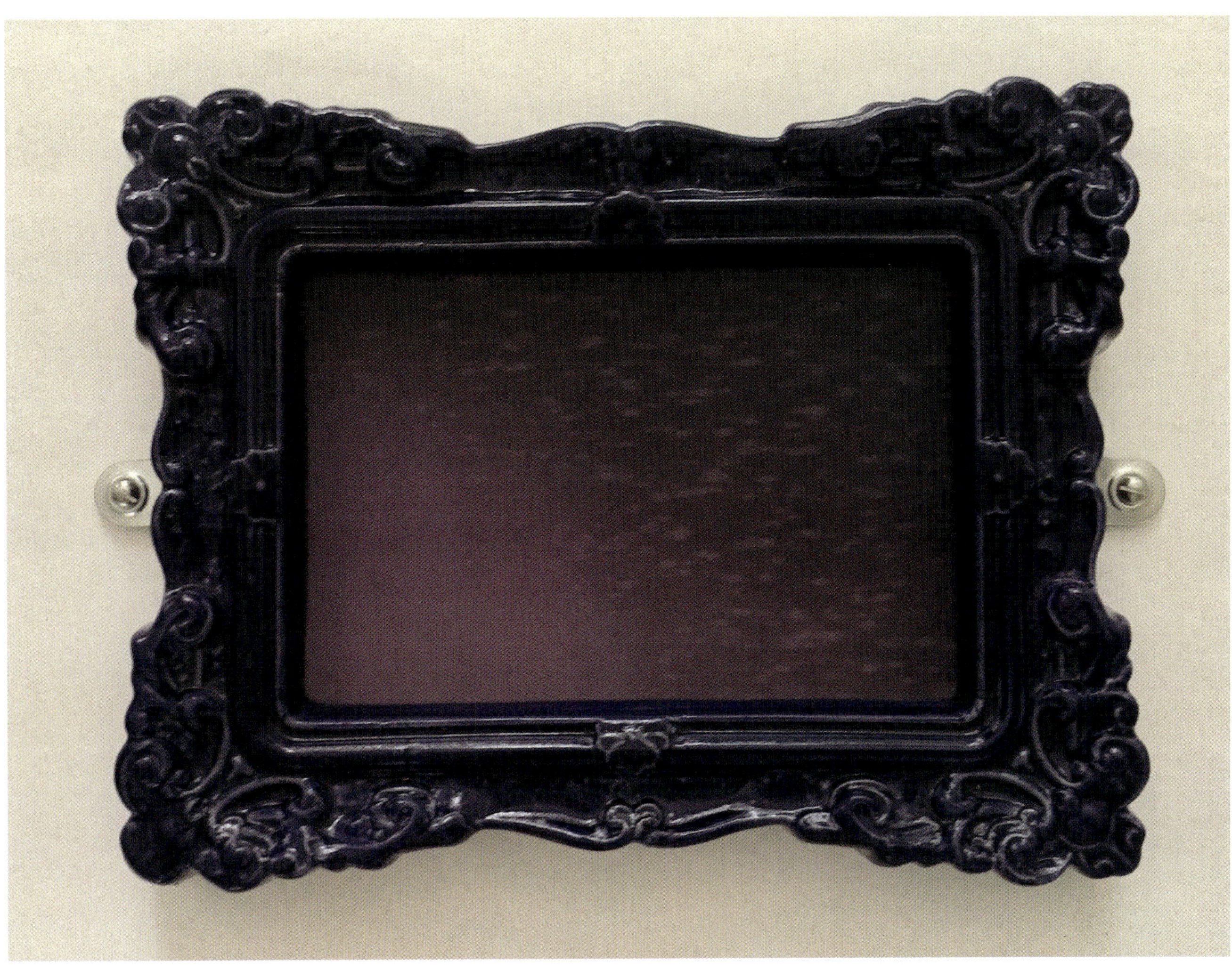

Deeper Space (2015).
(Photograph by Richard Slee)

by the crowds. So much for the quiet contemplation of beauty. Kant, one imagines, would disapprove. Slee's engagement with these picture frames relates to wider questions of cultural value, the impact of mass production, and the increasingly topsy-turvy relations we have with the concept of high art.

Slee created plaster moulds from the plastic frames and used press-moulding techniques to create his ceramic copies. The frames were populated with other treasures from pound shops: lenticular prints, fablon, and sections of plastic and metal. If the baroque plastic frames brought high art into the consumer market, Slee's decision to frame these bargain objects in the exhibition elevated them from the cheapest art commodities into the subject matter of high art. Slee's trademark style – the bright colours and glossy sheen – make the frames appear cartoon-like, implying his awareness of the transactional changes in value he has initiated. As art works by Slee, these frames are now worth far more than they cost to source and make. Yet, such upcycling is in keeping with the broader concerns of Slee's practice. From the late 1990s to the early 2000s, he produced a number of sculptural works that featured miniature ceramic figures; some sourced from a collection his daughter had discarded, others bought from charity shops (see, for example, *Landscape with Hippo*, 1997, now in the ceramic collections of the Victoria and Albert Museum). Slee's work has long brought the 'mass-produced' into the domain of 'the unique sculpture as artwork'. In so doing, he has blurred the divisions between art, craft, and the mass-produced.

It is clear that *Framed* sits in between the art/craft divide when focusing on specific pieces. The subject matter of each work can be categorized in numerous overlapping ways. Some of them focus on astronomical space to consider questions of pictorial space. *Space* (2015) is an entirely ceramic work created in the same colour. Here, a sense of space is contingent on a lip creating a visual separation between the image and the frame that surrounds it. Yet, these two elements are mutually dependent: without the frame the picture is not delineated and thus it does not exist. In *Space*, the frame, usually considered supplementary to the image, actually creates the main image. Thus the frame is given visual equivalence

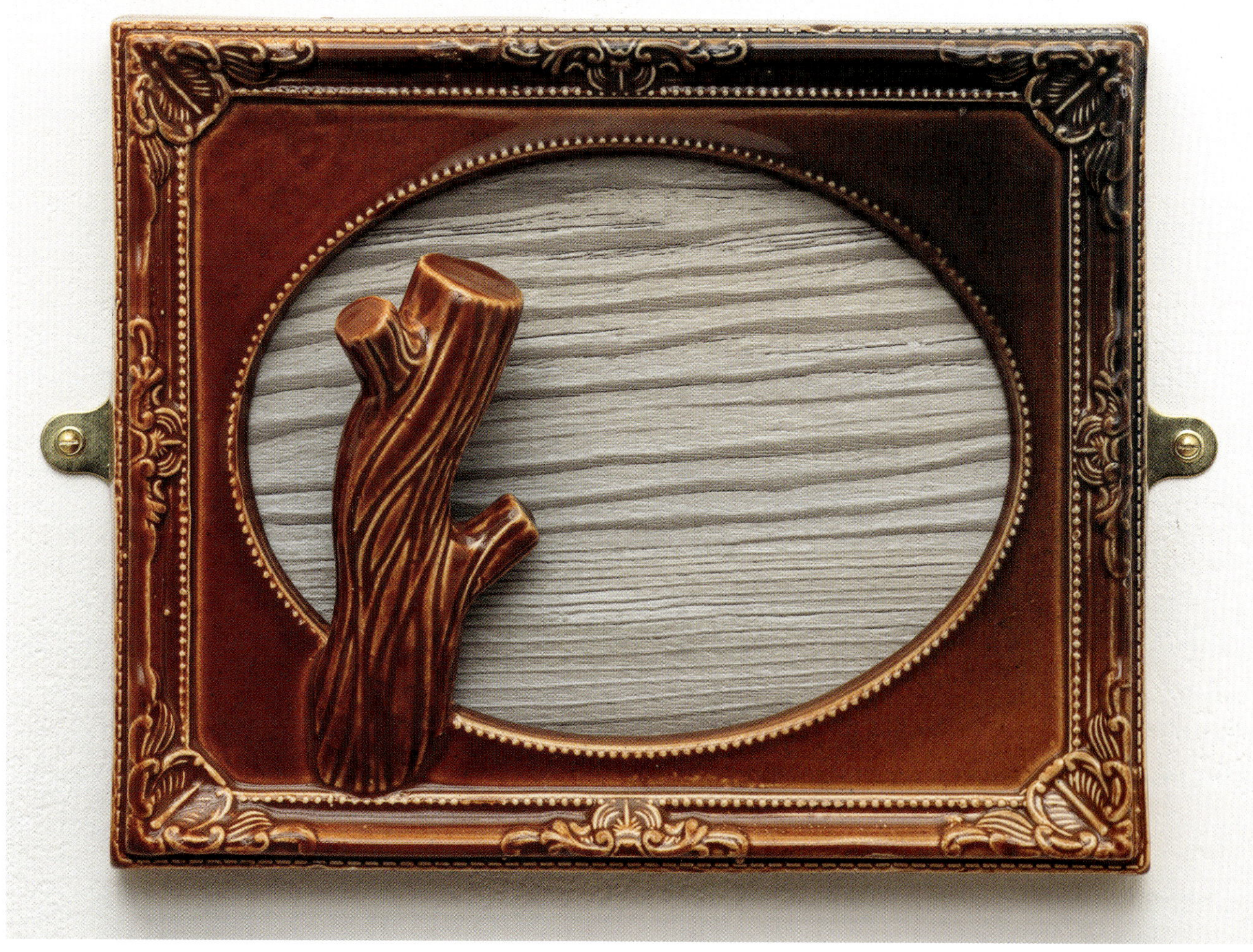

Wasteland (2018).
(Photograph by Damian Griffiths, courtesy of Hales Gallery)

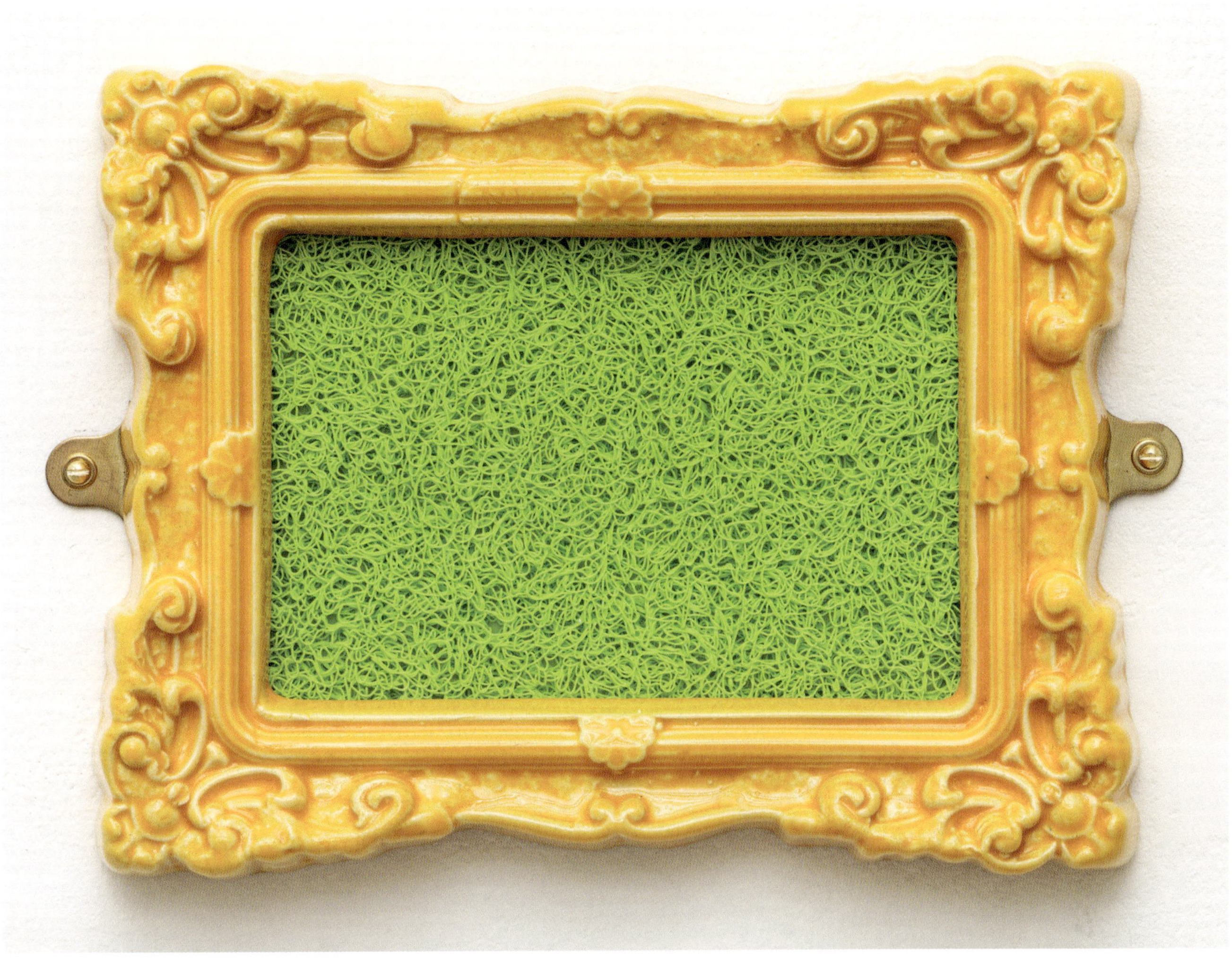

Green Field (2015).
(Photograph by Damian Griffiths, courtesy of Hales Gallery)

to the picture by creating both in the same material and colour. The perception of depth arising from the frame lip is extended in *Deeper Space* (2015), where the same colours are deployed as in *Space*, but a lenticular image deepens the spatial perspective. The three-dimensional image is at odds with the flattening effect of the frame, and in turn, the frame's relationship with the wall.

Other works referenced fine art landscape painting. Frame and subject were again fused in *Wasteland* (2018), where a dead tree was modelled into the structure of the frame itself. A tile, chosen because it has a kind of horizon line, was placed behind the tree to form the pictorial space. The frame activates the tile – a found object – into a landscape. This complex and clever work demonstrates Slee's understanding of the power of framing, in both a literal and conceptual sense, to our perception of objects. Recontextualizing an everyday object profoundly alters our experience of it. In the same way, *Green Field* (2015) frames green plastic grass to offer a witty evocation of a field.

Reference to fine art also included specific movements and styles. In *Impression* (2018), Slee used

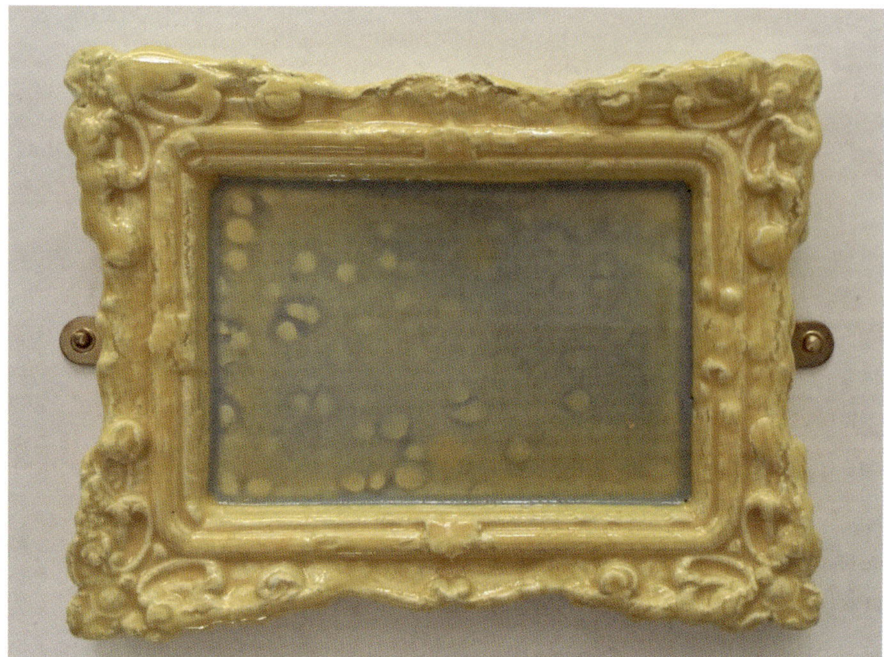

Impression (2018).
(Photograph by Richard Slee)

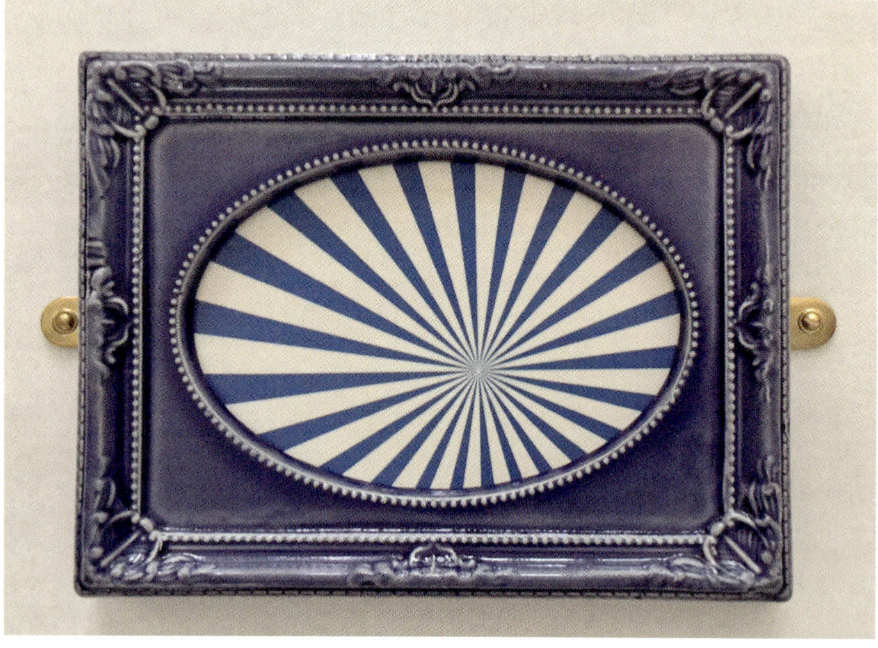

No Title (2018).
(Photograph by Richard Slee)

glaze across a flattened plane to evoke the impressionist strokes of Monet's paintings. *No Title* (2018) could easily have been a print by Victor Vasarely or an early work by Bridget Riley, but it is in fact a found piece of printed plastic (plastic also being a medium used by op-artists). *Abstract* (2018) is self-evidently abstract art, whereas the diptych *Something to Think About* (2018) offers a humorous take on conceptual art, where the title simultaneously directs and obscures the meaning of the work.

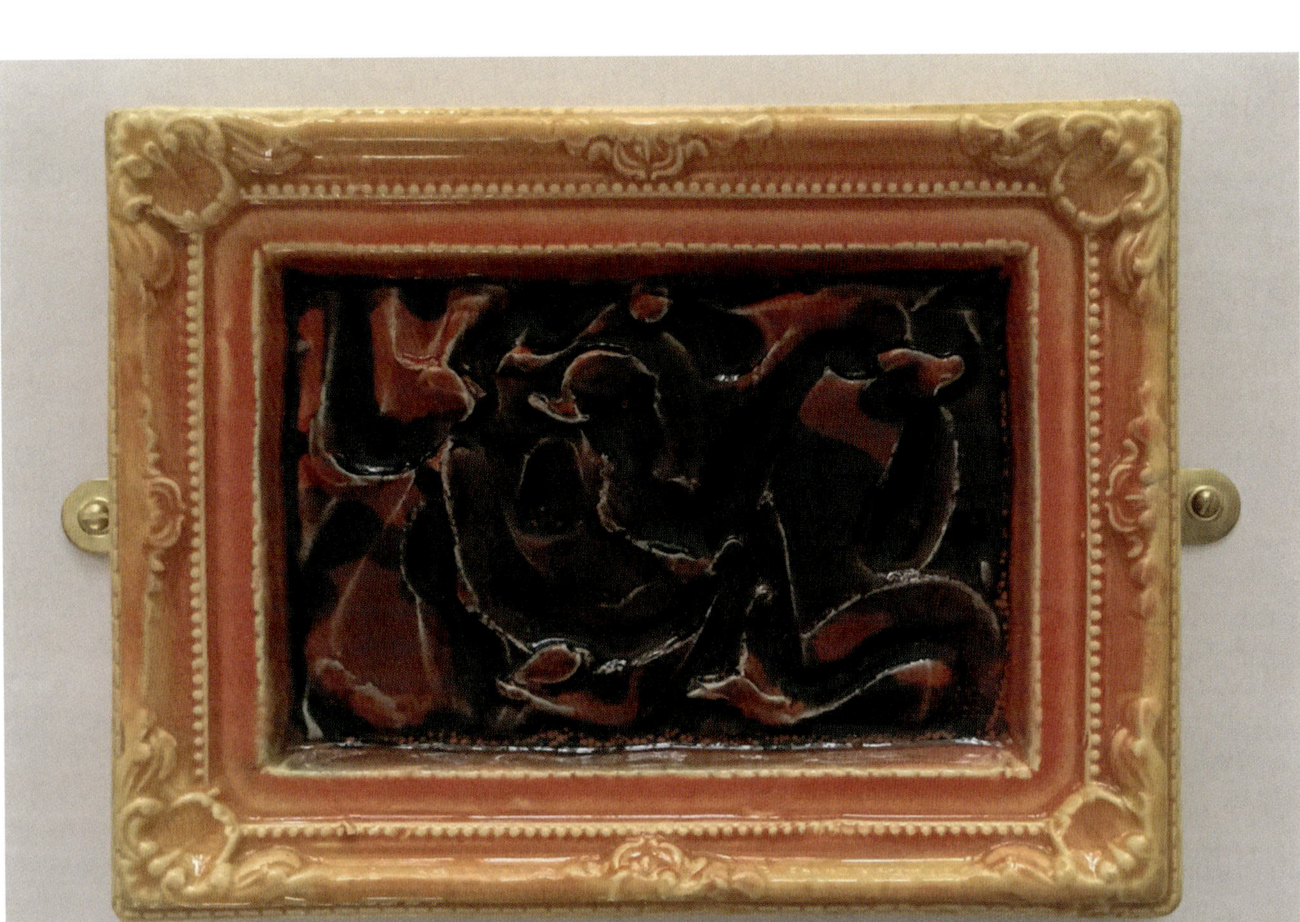

Abstract (2018).
(Photograph by Richard Slee)

This is not to suggest that *Framed* is not conceptual art. As a body of work, it absolutely is conceptualized, and skilfully so. Slee works, not in series, but in relation to constraints that require specific kinds of answers.[15] Here, picture frames offered a literal and theorctical constraint within which to work. They enabled him to consider how readymades are recontextualized into art through the device of framing at a literal, institutional and conceptual level. Yet, they also document a more straightforward joy in colour, shape, texture and rhythm discerned in the objects of the everyday. There is obvious delight in finding an object in a bargain shop, releasing it from its historical meaning and daily use, and placing it into a new context where it only refers to itself. *Something to Think About* and *Purple Grill* (2018) aptly demonstrate this. Indeed, the plastic in these works has greater resonance with Abstract Expressionist artists like Roy Lichtenstein than the everyday object. Yet, there is no attempt to disguise the fact that these are found objects. In fact, the works are contingent upon the spectator recognizing their duality as found objects altered into the status of fine art. Each work thus has a triple subject: the frame, the framed, and the relationships between the two. We are able to see how Slee is using the frame to shift, even reframe, our perception of each object as art, but also how there is potential for art all around

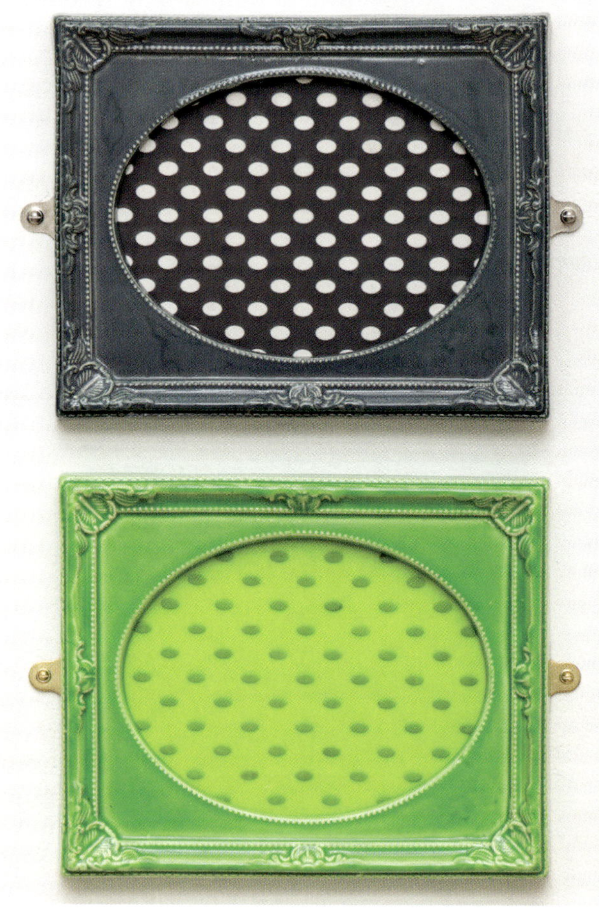

Something to Think About (2018).
(Photograph by Damian Griffiths, courtesy of Hales Gallery)

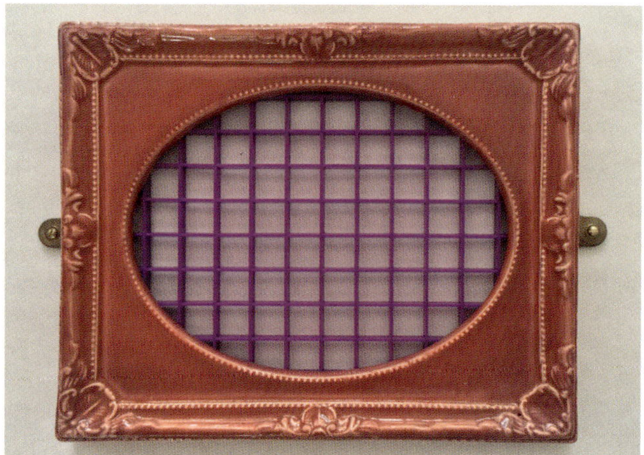

Purple Grill (2018).
(Photograph by Richard Slee)

us in our daily lives if we choose to look for it. The key to unlocking this lies in imagination and play.

Kant proposed that art has to be regarded 'as if it could only prove purposive as play, *i.e.* as occupation that is pleasant in itself.' Craft, however, 'is unpleasant (a trouble) in itself, and which is only attractive on account of its effect (*e.g.* the wage).'[16] Slee's ceramics are a product of play, of labour, and of craft skill. Indeed, if the pursuit of aesthetic beauty is predicated on looking at something in a 'disinterested' (that is, non-utilitarian) way, then Slee's reframing, repurposing and even dis-functioning of found objects means they have to be regarded as art. In fact, Kant's notion of Free Play is clearly at the heart of everything Slee does.

Framed asks us to look at how we see things, how we frame things, and challenges us to reconsider what we view as important. This is proven by the fact that in *Framed*, there was a particular and knowing inversion of the fine art hierarchy. In an art gallery, frames are always of secondary importance to the artwork they surround. I am willing to wager that very rarely, if ever, will visitors to the Tate walk out of the gallery commenting on the aesthetic merits of the picture frames they saw. Yet, in *Framed*, this was precisely the point. Picture framing, a craft skill, was elevated to be the subject of an art exhibition.

At the other end of the spectrum, it seems possible that some audiences were unimpressed that the readymade, the mass-produced and the pressmoulded ceramic object should be given a platform at the Craft Study Centre. Where is the skill of the craftsperson? Where can one discern the imprint of the artist's technique? Ceramicists may feel that the argument as to whether ceramics can be art or not was settled by the mid-1990s. Perhaps for artists it was. Whether fine art collectors are prepared to buy more than a few well-known names in ceramics remains to be seen. As a swipe at any fundamentalists

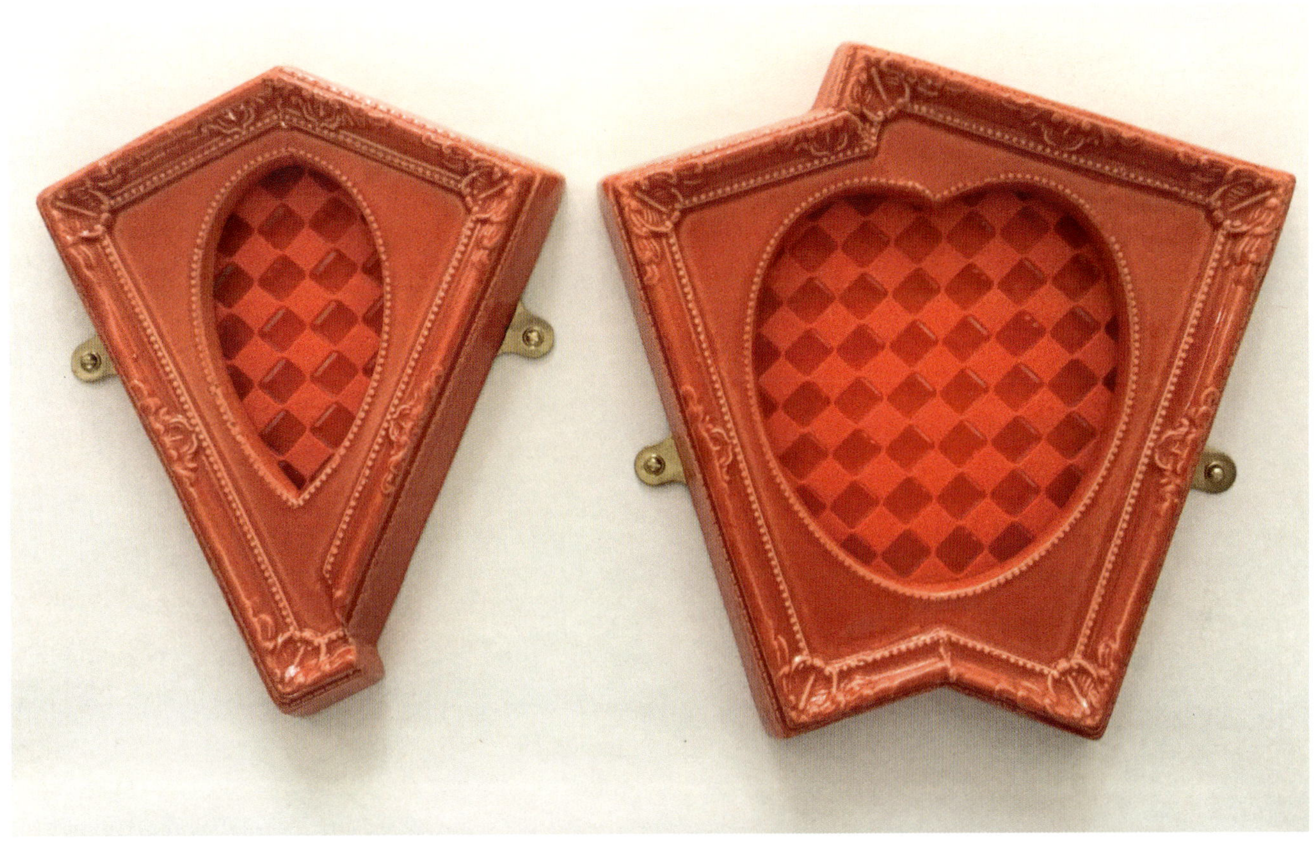

ABOVE: *Pair* (2015).
(Photograph by Richard Slee)

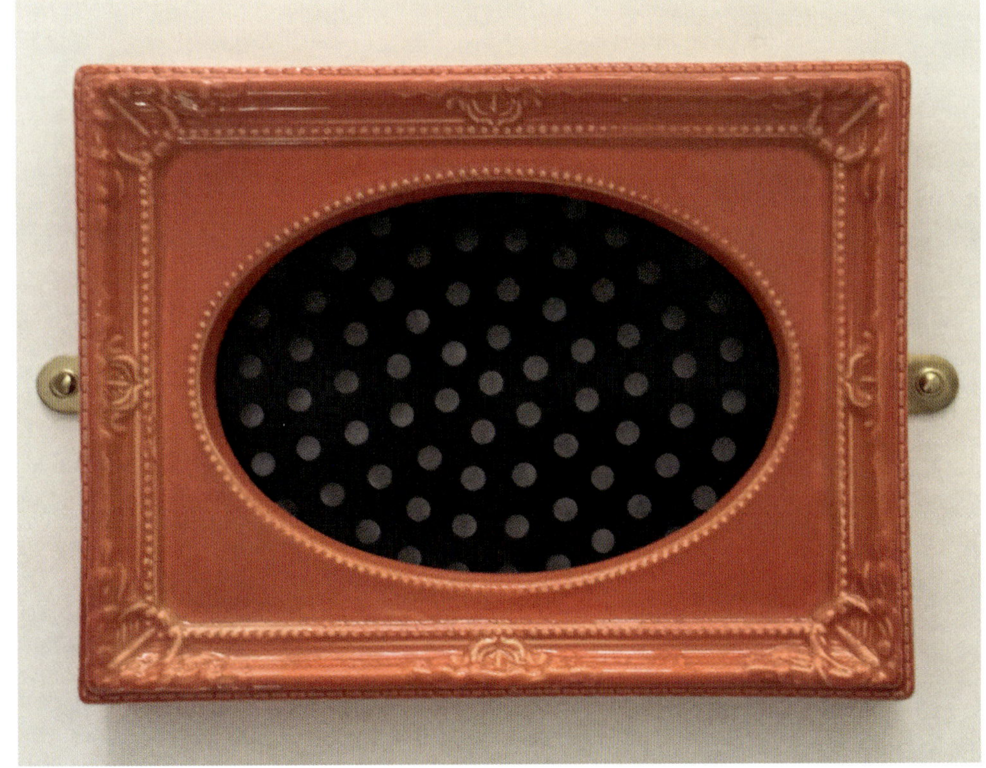

Black Holes (2018).
(Photograph by Richard Slee)

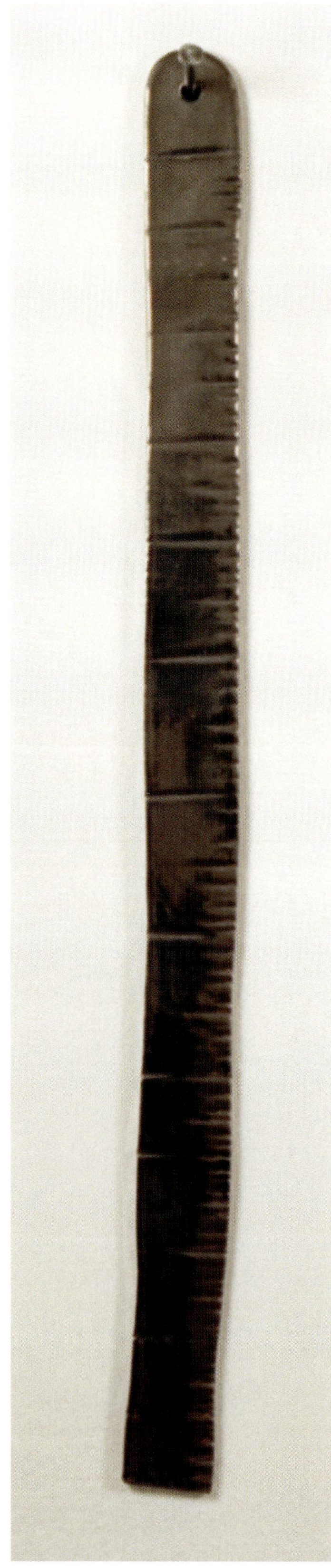

LEFT: *Craft Rule* (2016). (Photograph by Zul Mukhida, courtesy of Richard Slee)

who might have huffed and puffed as they made their way around the exhibition, Slee included the work *Craft Rule* (2016), a large glazed ceramic ruler that featured no marks for measurement, was not straight, and was hung on the wall like an overgrown phallus. Situated directly opposite the entrance of the exhibition, this was the first piece that visitors encountered. As a useless yardstick for the measure of success, *Craft Rule* offered a barbed satirical portrait of anyone walking around the gallery with conceptual narrow-mindedness.

Slee's skill lies in his ability to ingeniously play with conceptual categories. His work sits in between and amongst notions of art and craft; he is neither artist nor craftsman, but wholly both. In this respect, *Eye* (2018), stands out for me as a signature piece in the exhibition. This surrealist work consisted of a small letterbox-like frame, with an eye-shaped hole surrounded by false eyelashes cut into the middle. Almost like a portrait, *Eye* stands as an 'I', a subject in the world that perceives things from a particular point of view. *Framed* invites us to reassess ourselves in light of our own prejudices, and to breakdown any residual parochialism on either side of the art/craft debate. Slee asks us to look again through new frames of reference.

BELOW: *Eye* (2018). (Photograph by Richard Slee)

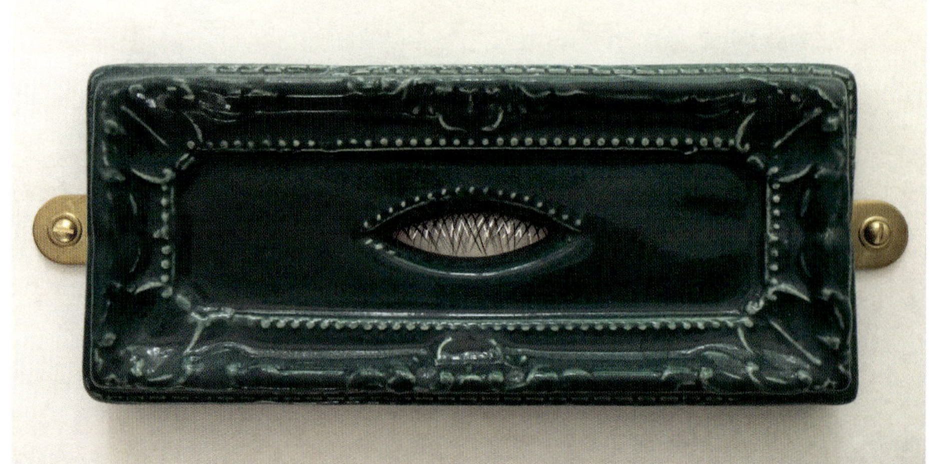

Alison Britton

In Between

Work: an effort directed to an end; employment; to make efforts to achieve or attain anything; to be occupied in business or labour; to be in action; to operate, function: to produce effects.

Play: to engage in pleasurable activity; to perform acts not part of the immediate business of life, but in mimicry or rehearsal or in display; to amuse oneself.

Chambers Dictionary

Work is serious; it requires effort, design, and is laborious. Play is aimless, frivolous, light and humorous. They are antithetical. Early on in her career, John Russell Taylor described the pots of Alison Britton as 'genuinely playful, with a spirit of freewheeling fantasy. The first impression one gets from these pots is of enjoyment: they are made by someone who enjoys handling clay, playing with clay, trying ideas out just to see what develops.'[17] If Britton's pots emerge from 'play', how can she have exhibited 'work' in ceramics for over forty years? So much has been written about her practice;[18] indeed, much has been written by her.[19] How has she achieved this commanding career in ceramics through play?

The anthropologist Victor Turner argued that the division between work and play was invented during the Industrial Revolution. A separation between work and leisure time was introduced and rigorously enforced to ensure the workforce had sufficient rest to efficiently manufacture goods. In contrast, Turner suggested that pre-industrial societies merged play and work to produce periods he described as 'liminal', that is, in a state of being 'in between' different positions, statuses, shapes or thresholds. 'In liminality,' Turner argued, 'people "play" with the elements of the familiar and defamiliarize them. Novelty emerges from unprecedented combinations of familiar elements.'[20] To make pots that are in between work and play is thus, it seems, to re-connect contemporary ceramics with pre-industrial concerns, to be 'in between' states, both ancient and modern, and to elide contemporary categories.

Indeed, Britton's impact as a maker was immediate precisely because she interwove what were then seen as distinct areas of practice in Britain: pottery and fine art. In *Alison Britton in Studio*, Peter Dormer highlighted the significance of painting, specifically Jackson Pollock, to Britton's mark-making. He suggested that

> What is transferable and what Britton owes to Pollock is the principle that decoration can achieve a coherence without relying on geometry and without being predictable: what Pollock offers is the ultimate asymmetrical non-narrative decoration. [...] Finally, however, we must be clear that Britton's 'abstract' pots are not about painting; they are decorated pots.[21]

Are Britton's pots not about painting? Are they non-narrative? I am not so sure. Whilst Britton has acknowledged her excitement in encountering Pollock's work, it seems untrue to suggest that Britton's work has neither geometry nor, in the sense of ceramic technique at least, predictability. Geometry may be taken to mean mathematical symmetry; but the basic terms of geometry – planes, angles, curves, surface, manifold, length, area and volume – could easily be applied to a Britton pot. It is true that Britton's approach has relied upon an instinctive response to the situation at hand; for some works, marks are first made on flat slabs of clay, and the nature of the marks provide hints as to how

the form might evolve. However, this is not a uniform approach: in others, the marks are only made once the piece has achieved something of its form. Writing in 1980, John Houston suggested her work had 'an informal, improvised quality, "made-up" on the spur of the moment of making'.[22] But there is also the repetition of formal concerns, shapes and lines. Britton's pots always look different, yet they always look like *hers*. As Linda Sandino highlighted in an essay investigating a new group of work exhibited in 2000,

> Gestural marks of the Pollock/Britton kind have come to stand for 'pure' artistic expression. [...] That there is no such thing as unmediated expression is clear, but we have come to see this as the conventional sign of 'pure expression'. Nevertheless, to simply see the dots and splashes as imitation Pollock is to misunderstand the significance of what these marks mean within Modernism, and in ceramic history. Applied art, as design, is the result of planning and this has been one of the key distinctions between design and art.[23]

There is enormous control in Britton's output, yet this is not to imply stasis, deny spontaneity, nor the ability to surprise. Is it work, or is it play?

Perhaps her important statement in *The Maker's Eye* exhibition catalogue, published in 1981, offers a conceptual map for this 'in betweenness'. In her essay, Britton seemed to put her finger on the pulse of a shift in ceramics in Britain, where an object (such as a pot) could imply function without supplying it. Some of the objects she chose for the exhibition consisted of those that were, as she herself suggested,

> about life and still life at once. They *can* be used, but their function is partly frozen in reflection about themselves. [...] Objects such as these fill the gap between prose and poetry, between ordinary and breathtaking, combining both. [...] Two-faced objects

such as I have described are giving more than was
demanded of them.[24]

This observation was to resonate for decades, and to
be regarded as applicable not only to the work of Britton herself, but to contemporaries such as Jacqueline
Poncelet, Janice Tchalenko, Carol McNicoll, Elizabeth Fritsch, Nicholas Homoky, Jill Crowley, Angus
Suttie (1946–93), Andrew Lord and Martin Smith.
Might this insightful statement have cast too long a
shadow, and obscured mutations in her own practice? Tanya Harrod, writing a decade later in *Alison
Britton: Ceramics in Studio*, seemed to think so:

Although Alison Britton has continued to reiterate
the ideas she so eloquently expressed in *The Maker's
Eye*, those ideas are no longer strictly relevant to her
own work. [...] Instead they are merged with a sense
of grand inevitability. In fact the bowl and jug qualities
do not seem to be the key to what is going on here.
[...]. Perhaps unsurprisingly, the collectors of these
late pieces own them in lieu of sculpture and demand
from them all the problematic resonances that only
sculpture can provide.[25]

Equally, Dormer suggested that there was greater separation between utilitarian ceramics and Britton's own
work than her essay in *The Maker's Eye* suggested:

While I think we can agree with her illuminating analogy
of prose and poetry, and the notion that the desirable
pot is the one that has leanings towards both, I do not
think it reasonable to take the criteria that one uses to
judge a thrown bowl and use it to judge, say, Britton's
own work. There is a definite sense in which she and one
or two other studio potters are out on a limb.[26]

Perhaps these statements are of their time. It is not
so much that they are necessarily untrue, more that

they come to stand for one facet of a body of work
that demands to be in between. To describe Britton's output as sculpture is to deny its implied utility,
and this seems an integral element of the expressive
capacity of the work. The pots offer a potential commentary on actions, on flow, giving, receiving, or
denying. These are domestic actions in the sense
that they are fundamental to human relationships;
to deny the implied domesticity of the form is to
decontextualize the work and diminish the emotional force of the statement. They are sculptural,
but they are also pots. Can they not be both, and
therefore, as a hybrid, more than the sum of their
parts? Interestingly, in 1985 Britton argued 'the fact
that pots are three-dimensional has misled people
into making claims for sculptural connections with
ceramics. The more essential connections,' she suggested, 'are with painting.'[27] And so we return to the
two-dimensional, and a gentle counter-assertion to
Dormer that 'Britton's "abstract" pots are not about
painting; they are decorated pots.'[28]

Each selector in *The Maker's Eye* exhibition brought
together ceramics, glass, metalwork jewellery, textiles
and fine art that expressed something of their view
of contemporary practices. Britton's selection, which
was perhaps the most discursively coherent, included
a number of paintings. Of her choices, two stand out
as significant in light of the prose/poetry, 'two-faced',
arguments made in her essay. The first is *Three Mugs*
(1944) by Ben Nicholson, which was borrowed from
the collection of Kettle's Yard in Cambridge. In this
image – one of a series of still lives – two mugs interweave in a Cubist-like composition; their outline is
suggestive of two-dimensional illustration, but carefully applied shading simultaneously renders them as
three-dimensional volumes. The second is William
Scott's drawing *Aegean Suite No. 2* (1968), which
depicts vessel-like forms flattened and abstracted
into shapes. Anchored to a horizon line, the eye is

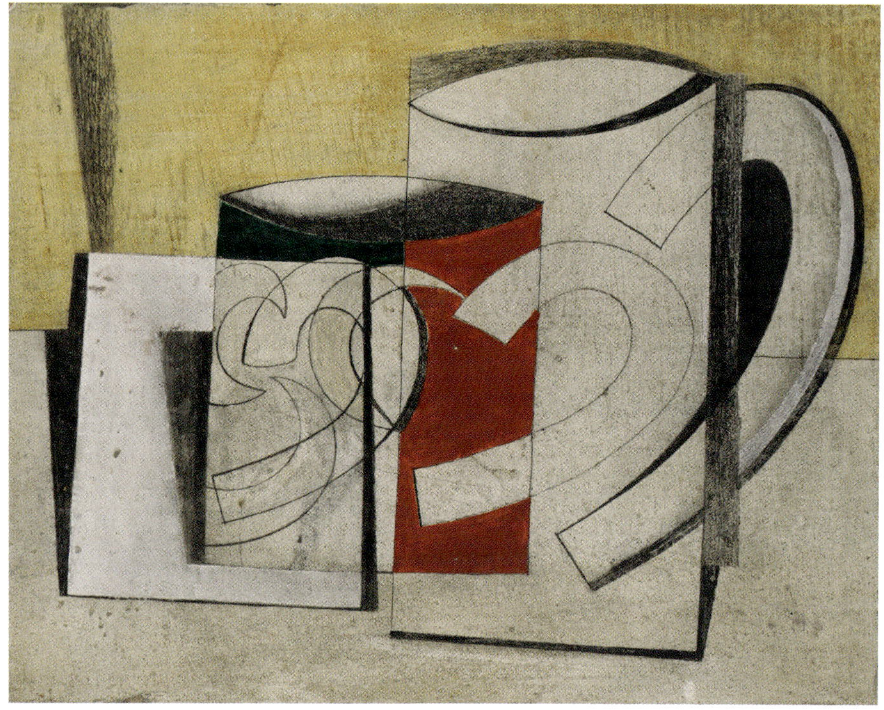

Ben Nicholson,
Three Mugs (1944).
(Kettle's Yard University of Cambridge/
Bridgeman Images. © Angela Verren
Taunt. All rights reserved DACS 2020)

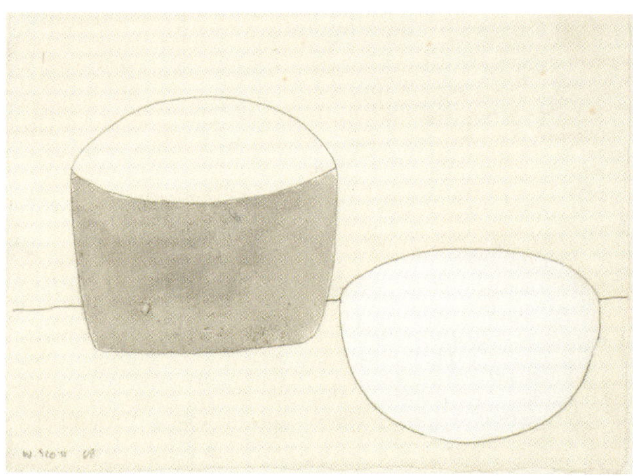

William Scott, *Aegean Suite No. 2* (1968).
(© Estate of William Scott 2020)

compelled to read these shapes as two-dimensional renderings of three-dimensional volumes. These images can be understood as demonstrative of Britton's essay, as fine art expressions of the 'two-faced object'.

Given Britton's statement that ceramics should be regarded as closer to painting than to sculpture, might the choice of these works assist with a consideration of how Britton herself approaches 'in betweenness' in form and mark-making in her own work? I am not, of course, suggesting that Britton is necessarily influenced directly by Nicholson and Scott, more that her choice of these artists for inclusion in *The Maker's Eye* should be considered as more than a comment on form alone. Exploring these works through the prism of both form and mark-making affords an opportunity to consider how a synchronous exploration of two and three dimensions are a fundamental aspect of her work.

Her earliest work was often in the form of the flattest: the tile. This immediately connects with painting because a tile provides a pictorial plane, a ceramic canvas with clear edges. *Two Dogs* (1977), held in the collection of the Crafts Council, offers an interesting exploration of interplay between perspective and form. It typifies Britton's work of the period as exploring aesthetics derived from ancient Egypt (and speaks to a broader interest in non-European practice of the time, echoed, for instance, in Elizabeth Fritsch's 'ethnic' pots of the same period). Britton's source is of interest because it exhibits a 'two-faced' quality arising from the axiality (the tension between shoulders facing front and limbs in profile) found in Egyptian drawing. The application of the border to the panel of the tile further brings an interplay between two and three dimensions into the work: the viewer looks through a border window (representing civilization) onto a scene (representing nature), which both the dog in the lower part of the frame, and the hill to the right, disappear behind. These shifts in dimensionality, of being realistic and representational at the same time, not only echo the work of Ben Nicholson, but also the latter's interest in primitivism as a means to realize a new aesthetic. Even in Britton's early work, form and applied decoration are arranged in tension with one another but are nevertheless resolved to form a coherent statement.

A comparison between Nicholson and Britton offers a new lens through which to approach her work. Indeed, some of the discussion of Nicholson's still life works resonates with Britton's essay in *The Maker's Eye*. The following analysis of Nicholson could easily stand for a description of a Britton pot:

> The distinction between abstract and representational elements becomes irrelevant. The curve of the bowl or the shoulder of the bottle act as the outlines of the solid forms and, in their own right, as tense rhythmic elements across the surface of a decorative composition.[29]

The outline of solidity in the form, such as that found in Nicholson's *Mugs*, structures the rhythmic interplay of lines. If this is applied to Britton's work, one can see that there is reciprocal significance in form and mark: neither is more important than the other. In fact, the 'two-faced' nature of Britton's work is predicated on interpreting all lines as spatial in *both* a decorative and sculptural sense.

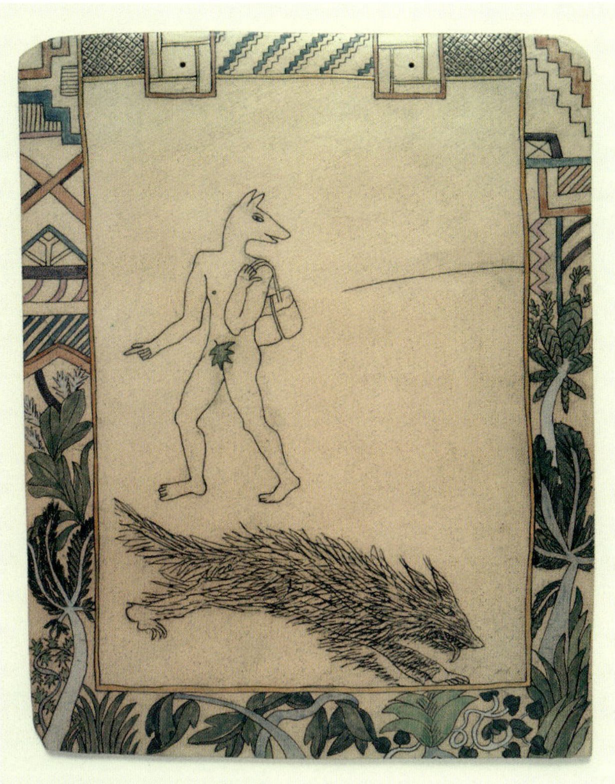

Two Dogs (1977).
(© Estate of David Cripps)

In some works, the skeleton of the object is reinforced by applied marks that conspire to draw attention to each other. In early work, such as *Man/ Lady Jug* (1978), the body of a jug may be defined *as* a body, with an outstretched arm pointing to the spout and a curved arm highlighting the handle. In later work, such as *Blue Pot with Holes* (1991), this motif was abstracted, and black lines direct the eye across the work. These lines shoot through the form but perish at its extremities. In such compositions, the centrality of work can be found at its edges; for it is the edge that delimits the potential for expressive marks, just as the frame did in Britton's tile *Two Dogs*. Sculpted lines delineate the edges of the work, but they also provide a rhythmic plane *within* the work, giving formal and marked lines a dynamic equivalence.

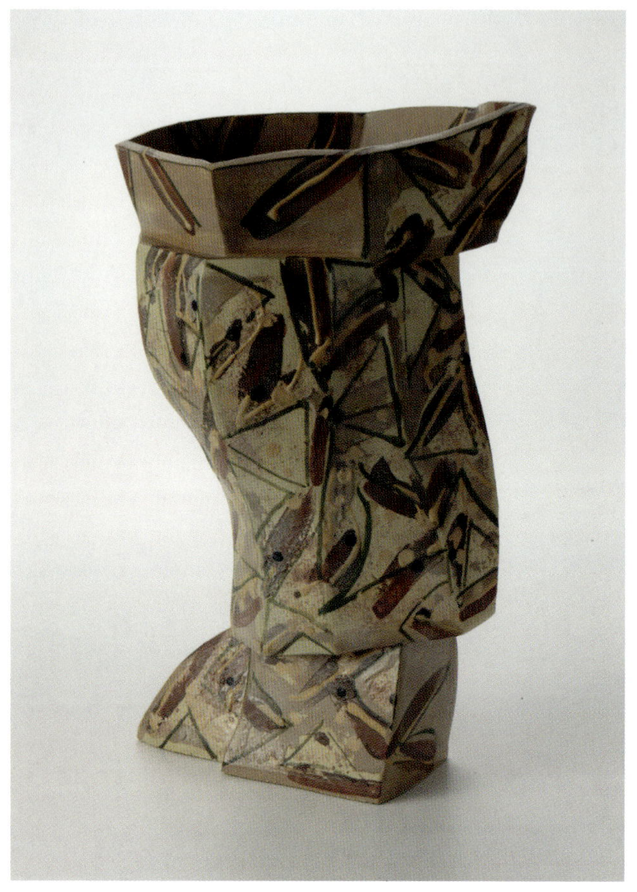

Pot with Green Triangles (1984).
(Photograph courtesy of Shigaraki Museum, Japan)

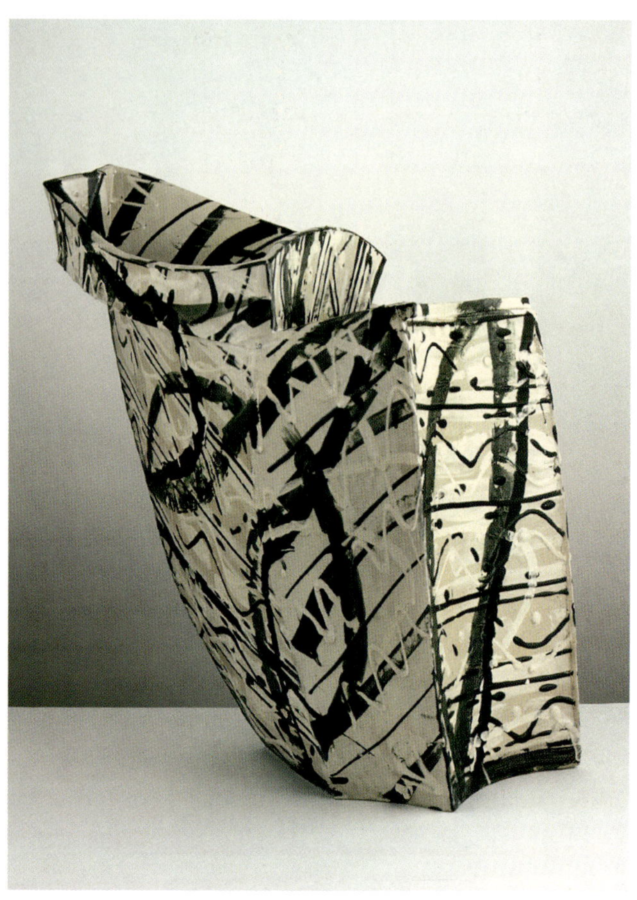

Leaning Black and White Pot (1985).
(© Estate of David Cripps)

This is exemplified in an analysis of sculpted and applied lines in pieces taken from different moments in Britton's output. The axiality of the Egyptian torso in *Two Dogs* is reflected in the sculptural lines of *White and Brown Pot, Big Spout* (1990), shown on page 34. The twist in the middle of the pot echoes the 'S' shaped line of Anubis, from his left (pictorial right) foot, up the leg, into the spine, and then into the head which peers behind. Balance is achieved by the placement of the right leg (pictorial left), which is echoed in the pot by the lower left section. *White and Brown Pot, Big Spout* is thus, in a sense, a three-dimensional drawing.

Examining Britton's work as three-dimensional drawings highlights how she achieves compositional tension. *White and Brown Pot, Big Spout*, for instance, places spatial and applied lines in counterpoint. There is equivalence in form between the triangle in the lower left, and in the upper right, as well as the triangular space to the interior marked out by the spout. In terms of marks, the ovoid towards the left finds balance in the circle upper right, as well as the interior carved by the form of the main body. Of course, as three-dimensional objects, Britton's work engages across a number of rotating spatial planes. It is in the interplay between different facets of each work, how space is delineated between two- and three-dimensional lines, that compositional complexity is achieved. She takes sides, pushes them as far as they might go, and recombines them with compositional virtuosity.

Space, as two- and three-dimensional, is an important feature of William Scott's paintings. Scott himself stated the importance of translating one form into another context, and of animating space as dynamic:

> Sometimes the object disappears and takes on a new meaning. It is during this moment of transition when I feel I realize most completely my intentions. Apart from the subject, which I can do nothing about, what interests me in the beginning of a picture is the division of spaces and forms; these must be made to move and animated like living matter.[30]

While the idea of 'transition' speaks to Britton's notion of the 'two-faced' object, Scott's emphasis on the division of space and form as a means to animate the picture resonates more forcefully. Dynamism, specifically expressions of containment and release, are repeated across Britton's output. Indeed, exploring space across two and three dimensions is the perfect medium for the expression of these ideas. It is Britton's ability to prise open and close down space that creates force and expression in her work. Where lines intersect and cross, the eye finds an interplay between space and surface. Rhythms can appear to be more regular, offering a sense of solidity to spatial structure (a kind of decorative prose to the three-dimensional frame of the work), or they can add fluidity to a surface as lines pursue a spatial flow only to disband, and to be picked up by another series of marks (a kind of decorative poetry across the three-dimensional frame).

This complexity perhaps suggests that Britton's work has to be carefully planned out (and the inclusion of a handful of doodles as the frontispiece for Harrod's *Alison Britton: Ceramics in Studio* might support such a view). What room is there for chance and instinct in this spatial intricacy? William Scott said of his own practice that

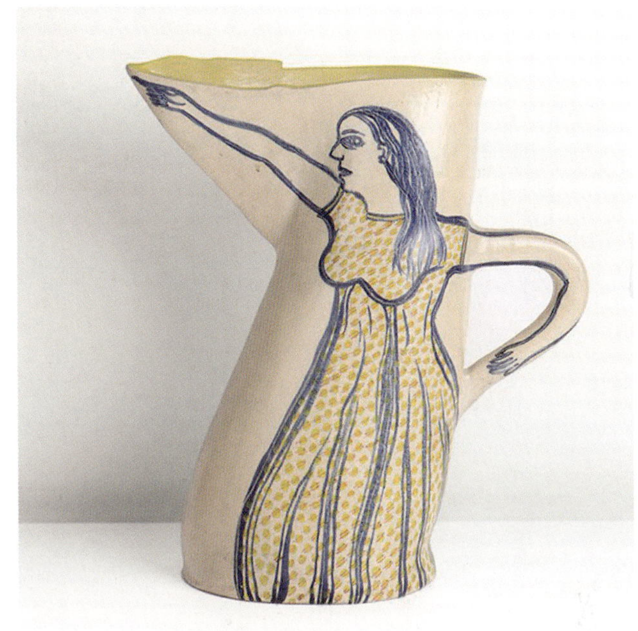

Man/Lady Jug (1978).
(Photograph courtesy of MAAK London Ltd)

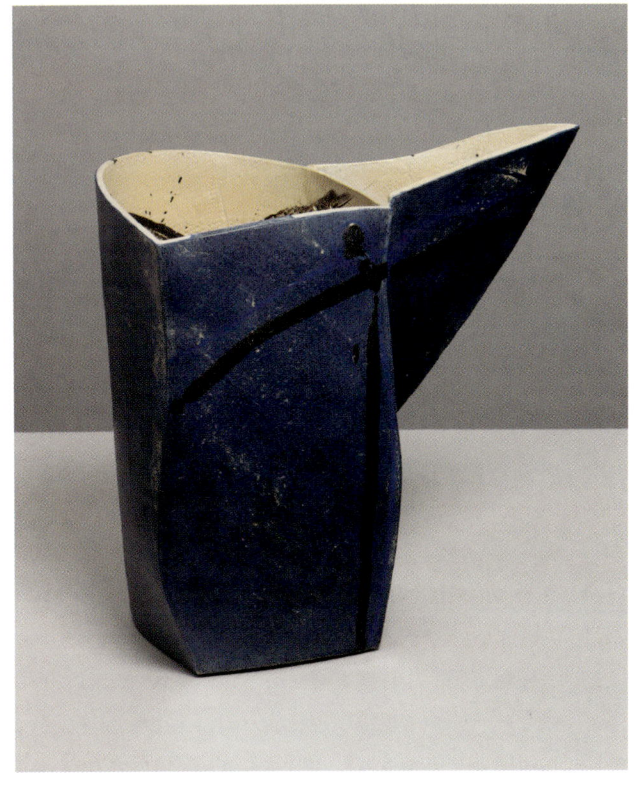

Blue Pot with Holes (1991).
(Photography by Marcus Leith for Corvi-Mora)

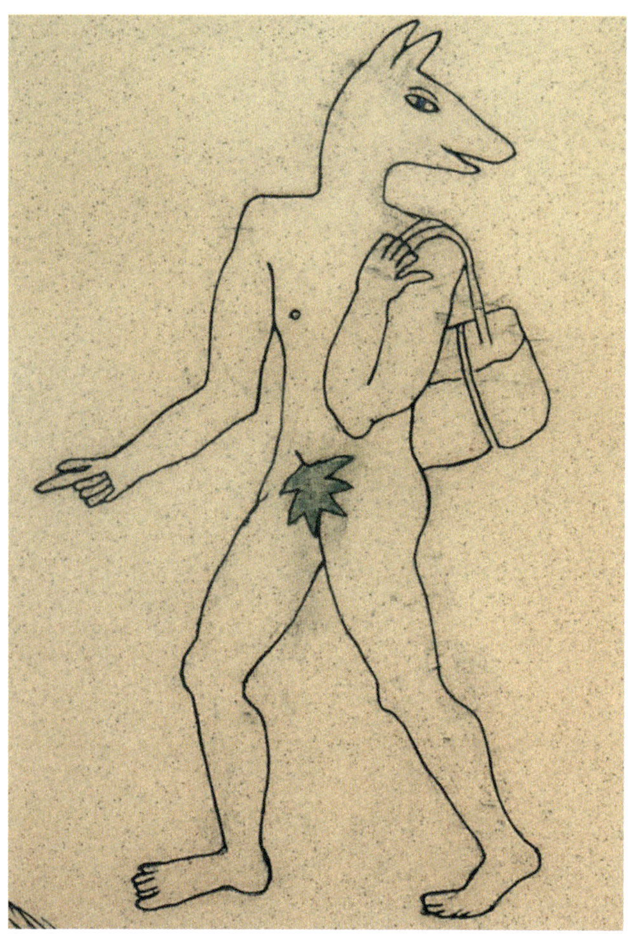

Detail from *Two Dogs* (1977).
(© Estate of David Cripps)

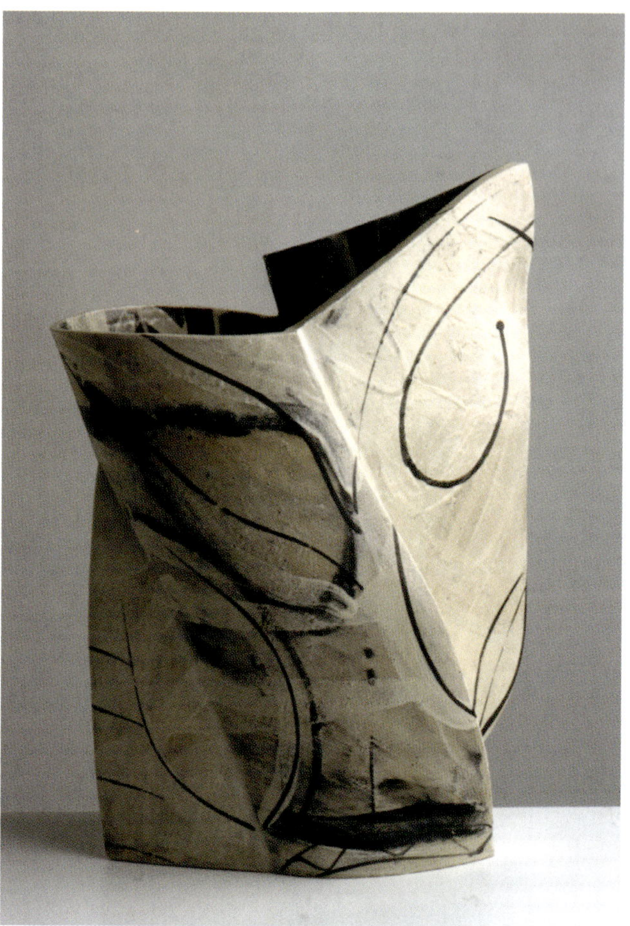

White and Brown Pot, Big Spout (1990).
(Courtesy of Alison Britton)

To have a too clearly conceived idea before beginning a work is for me a constriction; it is in the act of making that the subject takes form, it is in the adding, stretching, taking away and searching for the right and exact statement that a tension is set up.[31]

Adding, stretching, and taking away seem to me to be a fundamental aspect of Britton's approach and, in particular, in developing new avenues for exploration. As an example, a significant change in direction occurred in 2010, when a new body of work emerged that followed a consistent approach of creating the form first and then applying the marks. Of course, this was not the first time Britton had worked this way, but this series was distinctive. Coloured slip was poured onto the work before its first firing, and then glazes, some coloured though transparent, were poured before a second firing. As a series of pieces, there is a particular communion between form and mark.

The series, shown in an exhibition titled *Standing and Running* at the Marsden Woo Gallery in London in 2012, documented how chance does not diminish the relationship between form and mark. Rather than being applied with a brush, coloured slip, and later coloured glaze, was mostly poured on. The contours of each piece directed the runs, of course, providing a tension between marked and unmarked areas. This, in turn, suggested different speeds. Glaze darts across the vertical planes providing a flash of colour, which finds contrast with the stasis of the non-marked spaces. Indeed, the non-marked spaces are not 'empty'; they are simply charged with a different energy. In these works, gravity demanded an interplay between form and mark, for the application of glaze had no choice but to yield to the curvi-linearity of form. These works were quieter, perhaps more introspective – certainly a change in dynamic, but consistent with previous investigations in two- and three-dimensional spaces.

Her recent work has embraced yet another direction, whilst still investigating the relationship between form and mark, two and three dimensions. In works such as *Flotsam* (2017) and *Crater* (2018),

reproduced on page 38, flattened planes evoke a return to the ceramic tile explored at the start of this essay (indeed, these works are made for the wall). However, they have a three-dimensional linear vig-our. Space is shaped by lines; some consist of thin coils added to the surface, others are carved into it through sgraffito marks. Colour may be confined by three-dimensional lines, or spill over them. Yet, the eye is forced to read in between the two- and three-dimensional as integral to the composition.

Is it appropriate to locate a discussion of form and mark in Britton's work around a discussion of Modernist painting? To explore her choice of painting in *The Maker's Eye* through the prism of form alone seems, to me, to be missing the point. In the same way that Nicholson explored the possibility of rendering

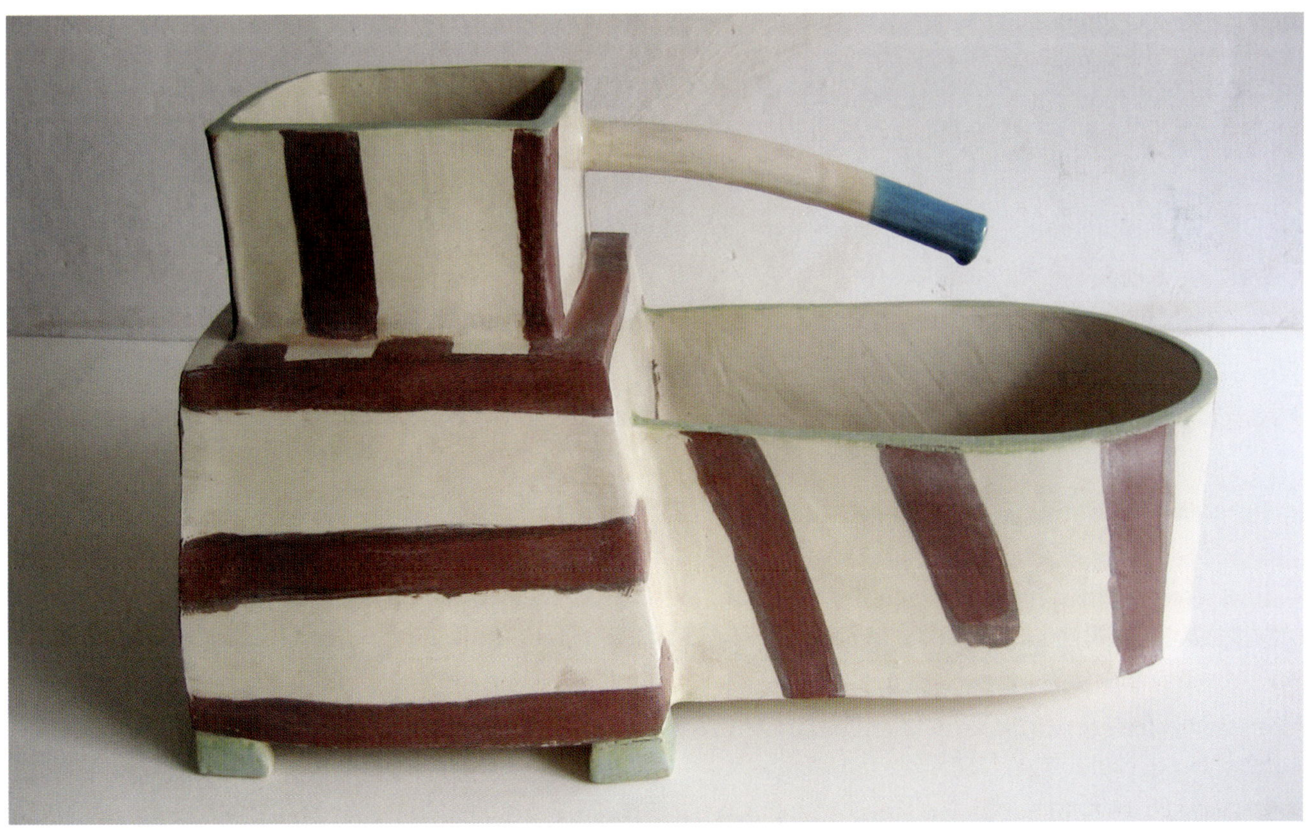

Sluice (2007).
(Photograph by Alison Britton)

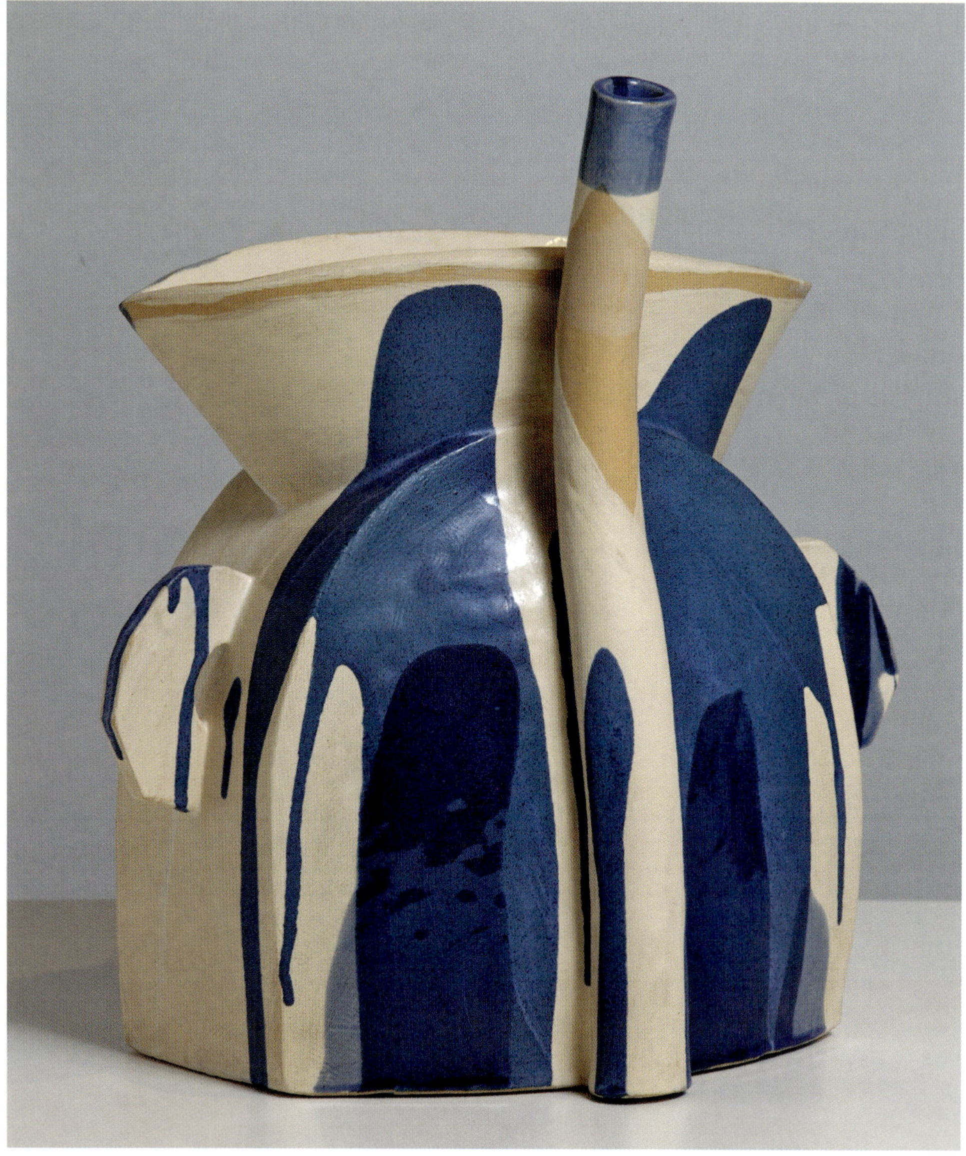

Cave (2012).
(Photograph by Philip Sayer)

a still life through the combination of perspectival and non-perspectival means, and Scott explored the three-dimensionality of space as a rhythmic form in two dimensions, Britton masterfully interweaves the plastic possibilities of clay as a spatially three-dimensional and pictorially two-dimensional practice.

Through a series of ever-startling innovations into the possible relationships between form and mark, Britton has opened up a distinctive, and consistently original, domain for the vessel as concept. She has asked many provocative questions about what vessels are, and perhaps critics have sought to stabilize themselves by anchoring her output to certain pre-existing discourses in ceramics or fine art. For someone like me, who feels an outsider to these narratives, they obscure rather than assist. For me, her works are not sculpture, neither are they domestic ceramics. They are not fine art painting, but her work seems more than a 'decorated pot'. In the same way that her work exists in between two and three dimensions, so she operates

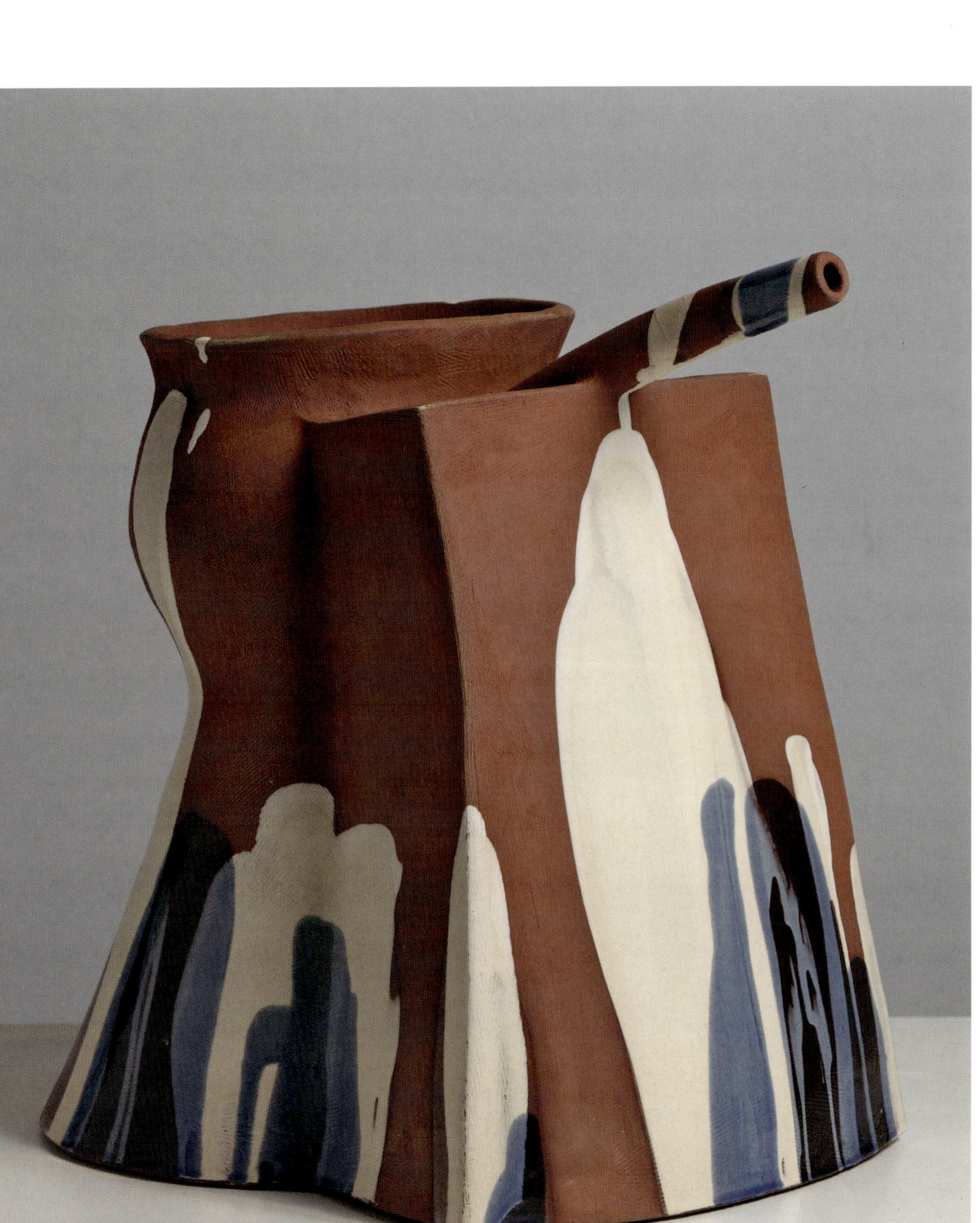

Watershed (2012).
(Photograph by Philip Sayer)

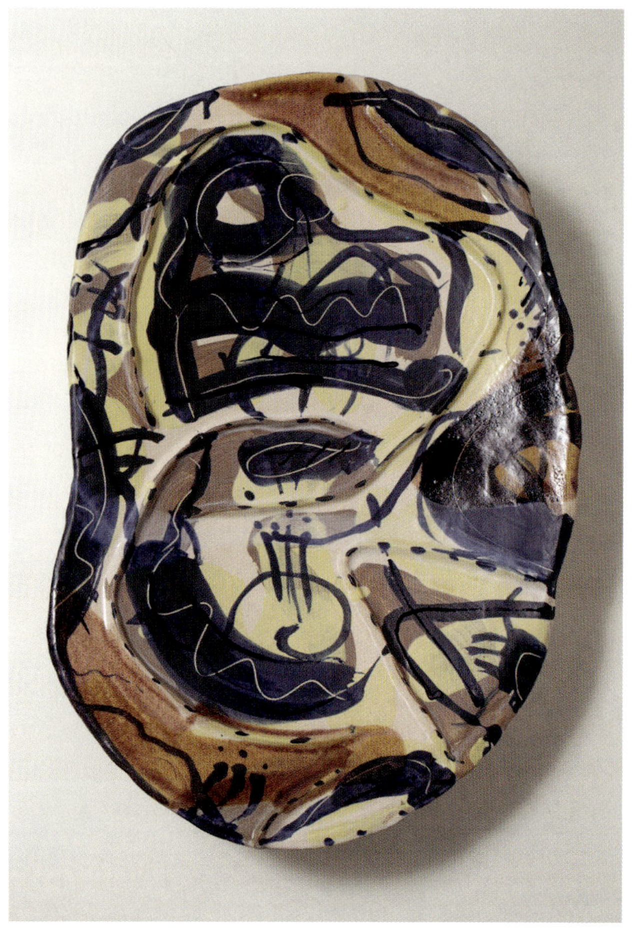

Flotsam (2017).
(Photograph by Philip Sayer)

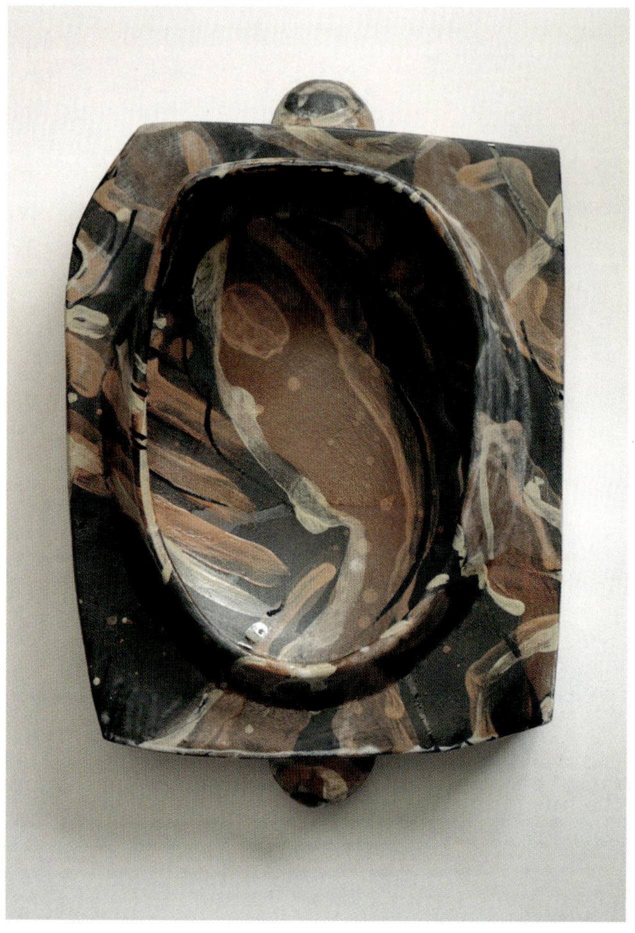

Crater (2018).
(Photograph by Jack Cole)

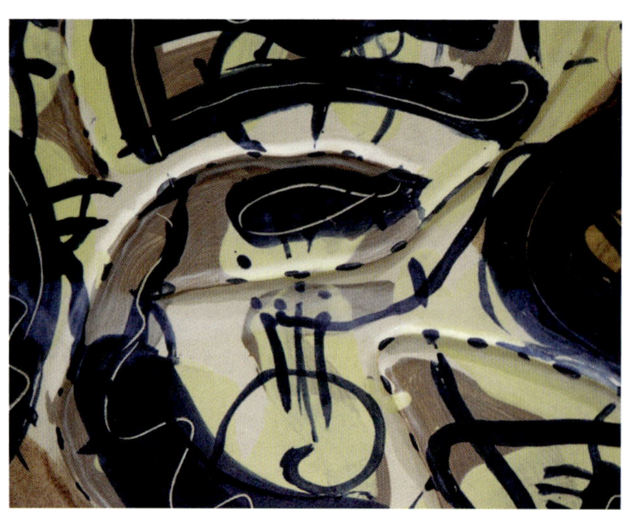

Detail of *Flotsam* (2017).
(Photograph by Philip Sayer)

at the interstices of genre. To claim her work as one thing or another – for ceramics as sculpture and fine art, or as a mere mutation of the domestic pot – is to distort what she does. There are no sides of an argument to take: her work is liminal, it is 'in between'.

Yet, despite all the words, theories, and commentaries, what stimulates me most in Britton's work is the sense that she herself is excited by the discoveries she makes. Her work is both intellectual and emotional, playful and serious. Perhaps this is an important element of her work as a female maker, but we should balk at generalizations. Indeed, Britton's work has taught us this.

Jennifer Lee

Drawn Together

In her essay for Jennifer Lee's 2011 exhibition *Falls the Shadow* at Galerie Besson, Tanya Harrod noted how 'before Lee embarks on another piece, she records the finished work in large exquisite drawings in pencil and crayon or in ink in a parallel series of (A3) volumes'. These sketches, Harrod suggested, 'are both *finis* and continuity, suggesting that her work is not taken directly from nature but depends upon accumulated knowledge, on work gone before'.[32] Since 2006, alongside these sketches, Lee has produced full drawings specifically for exhibition as stand-alone works. Because they can only be completed once the pots are finished, it is tempting to consider this strand of Lee's practice as a secondary activity. This is not the case. In fact, I propose that they are vital drawings offering a significant insight into Lee's approach.

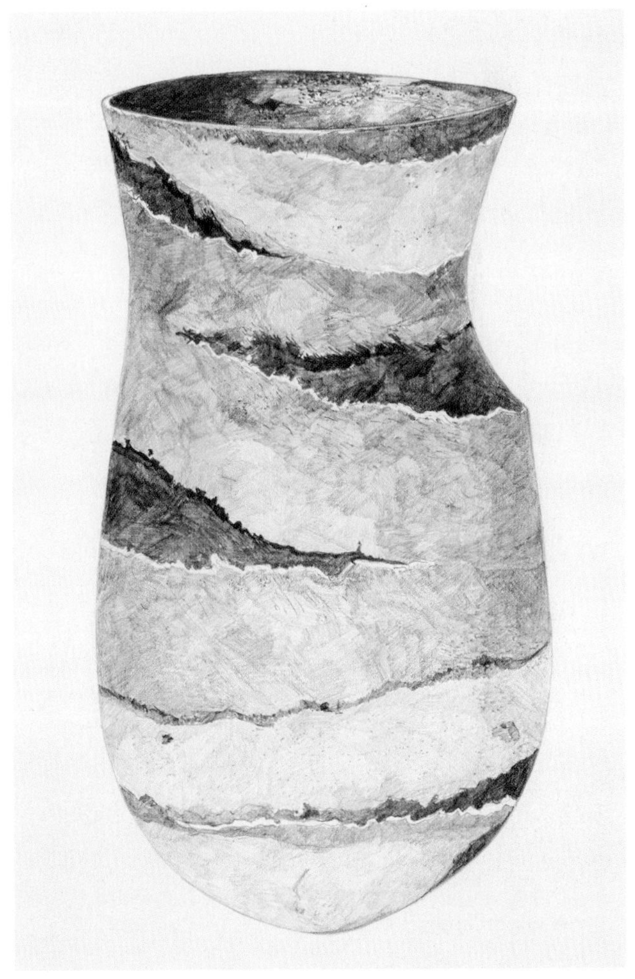

JL900 (2018).
(Courtesy of Sokyo Gallery)

In preparing his 2009 installation *Signs and Wonders* for the Victoria and Albert Museum in London, Edmund de Waal observed that:

Sometimes if you look at something intently and look away there is an after-image left behind. It can be very intense. A profile or a fragment of pattern can feel as if it is burning on your retina.[33]

Drawing is a practice predicated upon intently looking and recording the after-image. Unless the artist is able to observe the subject and draw without looking at the paper, the image must be internalized, suspended in memory, and committed in a new context. If drawing is fundamentally about the creation of after-images, Lee's drawings are after-images produced out of self-reflection. More than *a posteriori* records of accrued knowledge, they are visual essays detailing how the artist perceives her own practice.

To reverse the emphasis, that is to consider the drawings as the primary referent through which to approach the pot, is an invitation to approach Lee's work through her own line of sight. The drawing *JL900* (2018) (of *Banded olive, peat, sand, haloes, flashing*), reproduced on page 39 for instance, highlights the central significance of form in space. Here, as is usual, the vessel is placed towards the middle of the paper with no foreground or background. Lacking any definite anchor to the floor, the pot looks as though it might lift up and float away, just as her work

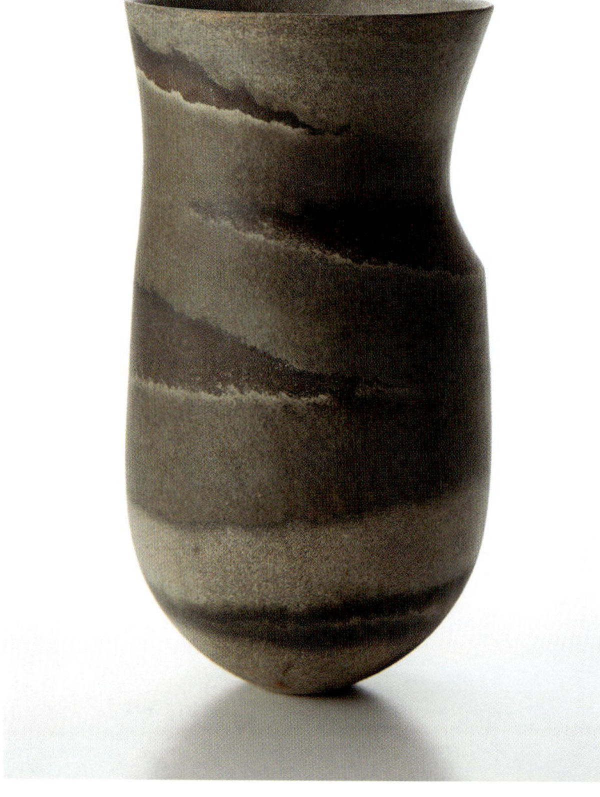
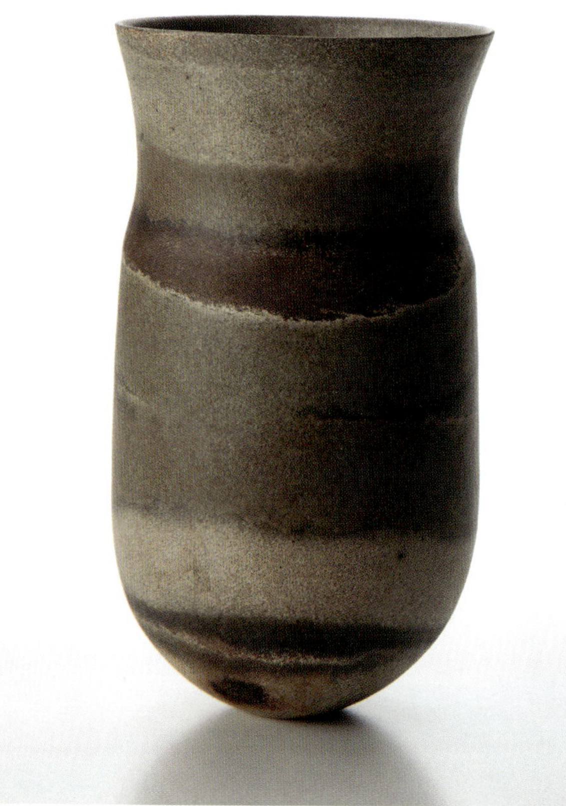

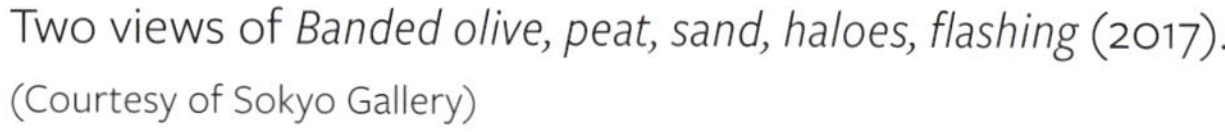

Two views of *Banded olive, peat, sand, haloes, flashing* (2017).
(Courtesy of Sokyo Gallery)

did when Issey Miyake placed her pots on a shimmering pool of water for an exhibition in Tokyo in 2009. Yet, there is also the steeliness of a critical gaze. There are no background distractions: no anchoring the pot in three-dimensional depictions of studio paraphernalia to produce a still life. In the drawings, Lee confronts the nakedness of her own pots as objects that must make their own way in the world.

One notices how the rim is drawn to be rigorously exact, with the three-dimensional turn fashioned by a combination of delicately placed shading and brilliantly empty curves of paper. There is close attention to the dynamic rhythms of the interior of the pot; the rim is constructed out of a vibrant interplay between interior and exterior textures. As the eye moves down the drawn body, the addition of shading to the right-hand side suggests curvature, but the emphasis on gradations of texture flattens perspective. Three dimensions become two as the eye glides across the drawn surface, almost as if observing a landscape from the air. Pencil shading swirls around the pot like wind through a wheat field. Yet, moving out from close observation to take in the entire form once again, the two-dimensional outline is lost to a three-dimensional rhythm. Darker tones hang like clouds in an evening sky, and a sense of depth emerges. Pulsations of shading give the drawing intense movement; the three darker sections across the top half drift apart and outwards on a soft white underlay, straining at the moorings imposed on them by the pot's edges.

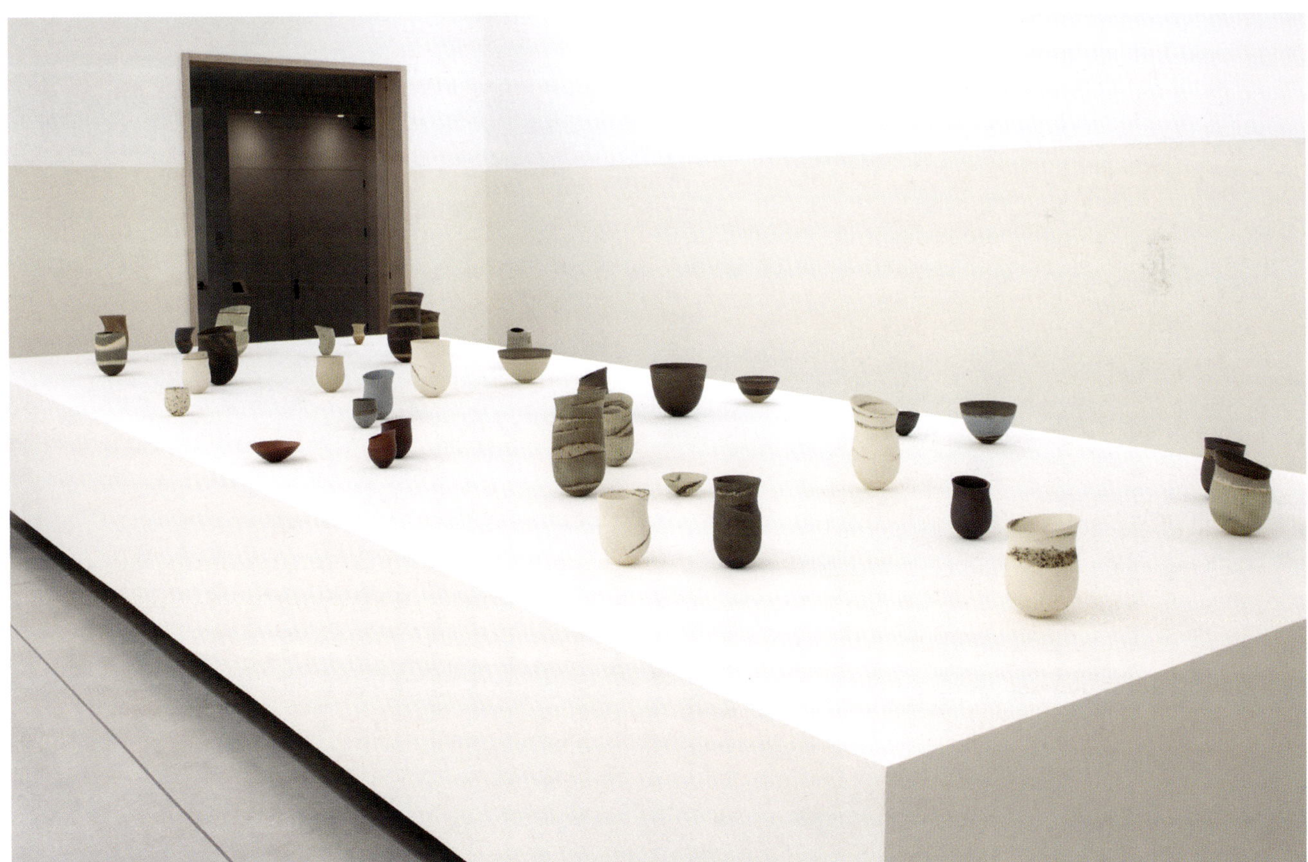

Installation shot of *the potter's space*, Kettle's Yard (2019).
(Courtesy of Kettle's Yard University of Cambridge. Photograph by Stephen White)

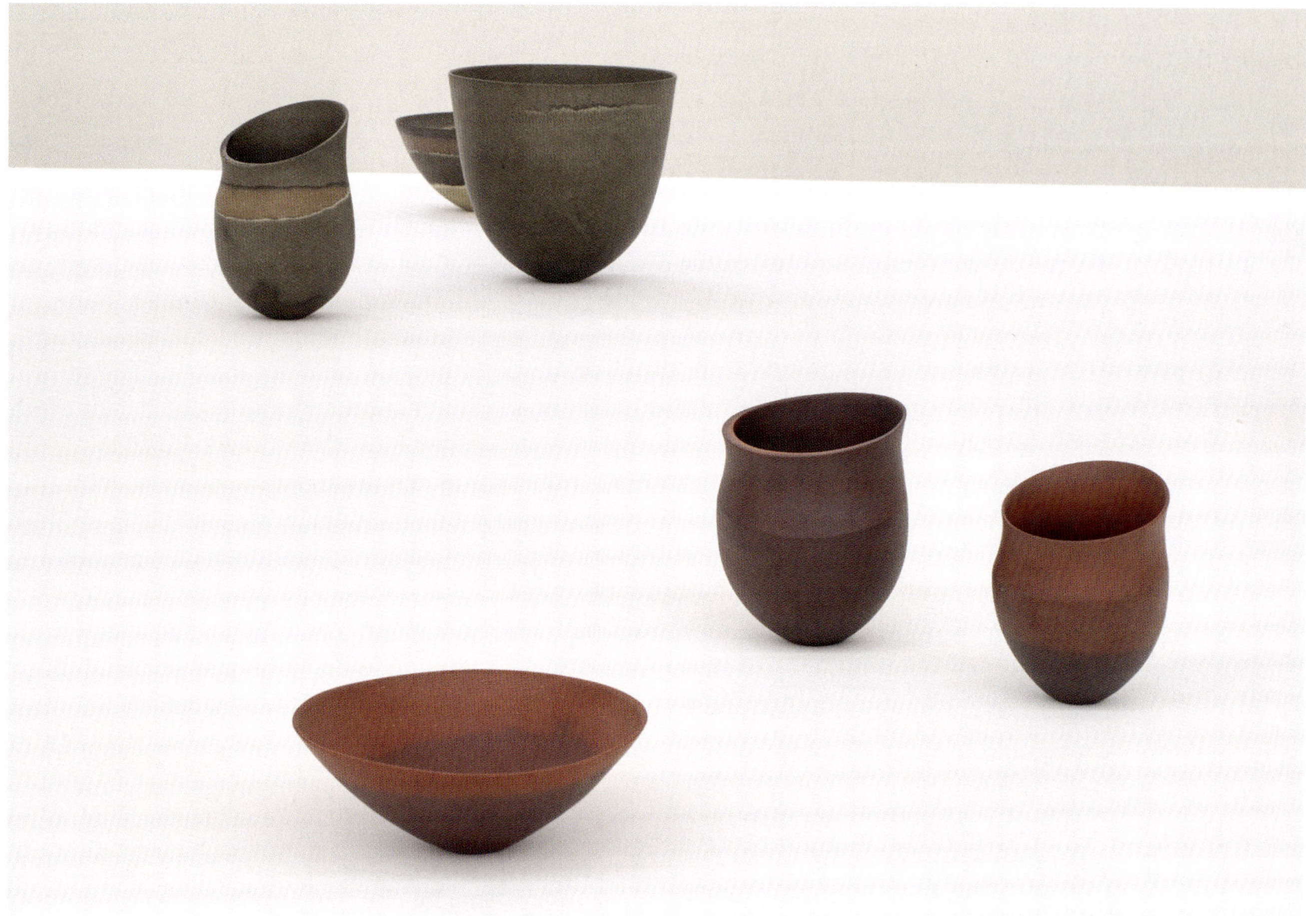

Installation shot of *the potter's space,* Kettle's Yard (2019).
(Courtesy of Kettle's Yard University of Cambridge. Photograph by Stephen White)

Approaching the subject through its portrait, for me at least, enables greater comprehension of her achievement in ceramics. In the pot *Banded olive, peat, sand, haloes, flashing* (2017) shown on page 40, the emerging swirls have equivalent buoyancy to the drawing, except the eye is able to pursue their course around curved horizons. Her pots now become three-dimensional drawings, where axis, line, volume, tone, form, balance, edge, rhythm, blend and texture – all terms used in drawing – are deployed with precision for maximum aesthetic impact. Yet the fluctuations between two and three dimensions observed in the drawing are also evident here: viewed from a certain perspective, the pot foreshortens, the surface appearing flatter than it actually is.

This subtle effect is, in fact, evident in many of Lee's pots. The exhibition *the potter's space,* held at Kettle's Yard in Cambridge in 2019, consisted of forty-nine of Lee's ceramic works and drawings from a forty-year period. The central part of the exhibition was formed of thirty-six pots placed on a white platform – situated at the same height as Lee's own work bench – in the centre of an off-white room. The impact of the design was to situate the pots in a similar context to her drawings; the off-white background seeming to match the colour of the paper used in her drawing. Upon walking around the platform, pots situated at close and medium distance seemed to foreshorten, to exist in between two and three dimensions even as they rotated in space.

For me, the effect was delicate but significant. Lee is not known for exploring questions of volume in the same way as, say, fellow Royal College of Art graduates Elizabeth Fritsch or Alison Britton. Indeed, such conceptual questions are not Lee's primary concern. Some might consider her work to be an expression of organic abstraction; her aesthetic connected with geology rather than with other kinds of art practice. Made from different coloured clays, some of her pots do evoke layers of strata, but they are hardly mimetic descriptions of rock. They also bear little relationship to the work of other ceramic organic abstractionists: not the rough textures of Ewen Henderson, nor the boulder-like forms of Gordon Baldwin. Rather, the conceptual edge I find in her work comes not from the earth but from the body, from the eye and, specifically, from drawing.

The drawing *JL506* (2019) (of *Pale, speckled, emerging rim*) demonstrates how form enables surface texture via light and shadow. The picture captures many of the elements that are important to Lee's work:

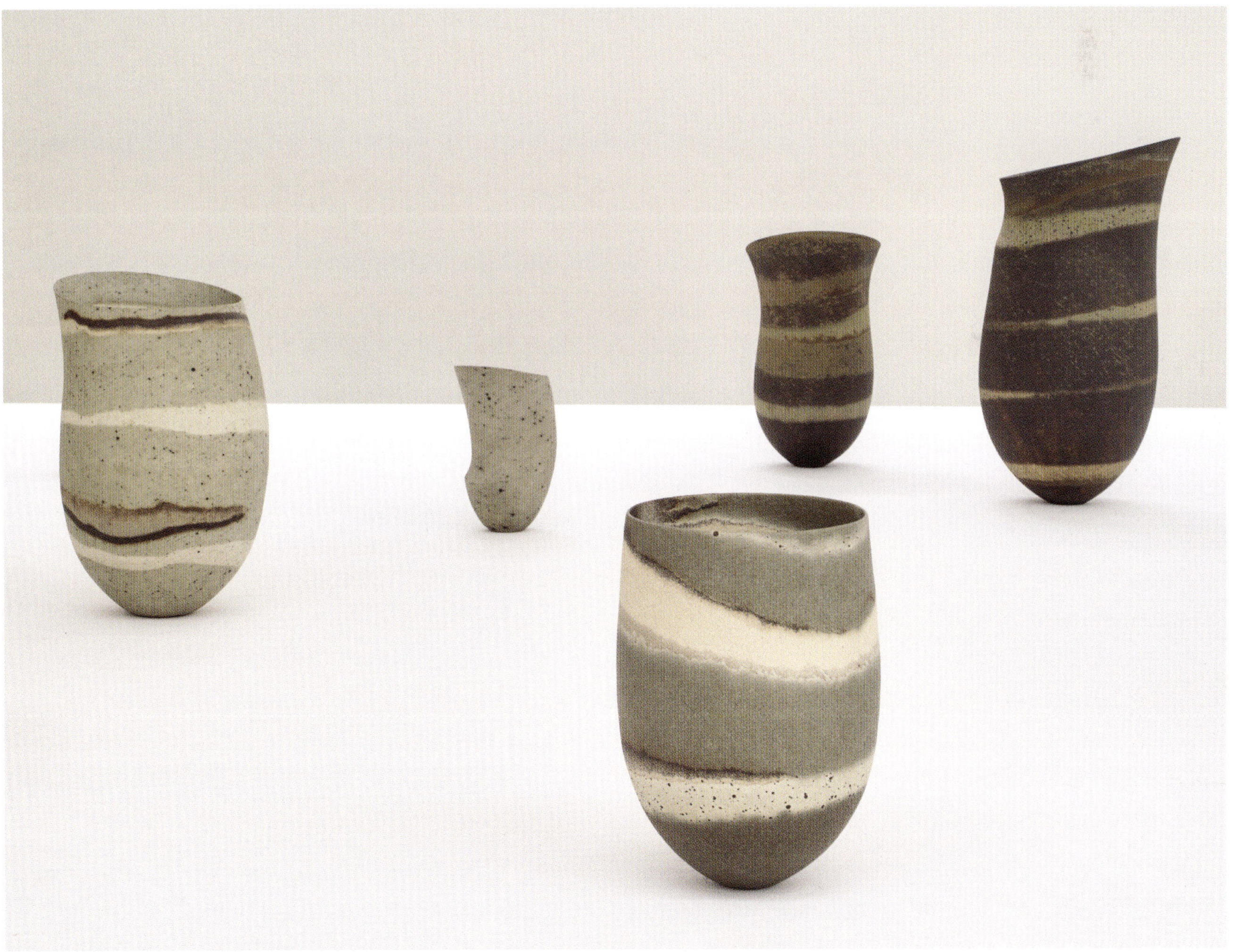

Installation shot of *the potter's space*, Kettle's Yard (2019).
(Courtesy of Kettle's Yard University of Cambridge. Photograph by Stephen White)

rim, interior, spatial rhythm, line, and, of course, form. Here, however, the texture of the body exudes a soft shading that highlights the sinuousness of the exterior. With its dots and dynamic shape, the upper section seems antithetical. Yet the darker shelf upon which the rim rests, delineated by both shading and unmarked paper, functions as a rhythmic connective between the two. This enables the drawing to depict a strong sense of emergence to the rim, a compositional aspect that was evidently essential when fashioning the original pot.

While Lee is renowned for her meticulous hand-building, she has also made a series of small thrown pots. These pots have also been the subject of drawings, implying that they remain serious works despite the difference approach to making. The drawing *SH-34–14* (2018) (of *Shigaraki 34–14*) aptly demonstrates the interest throwing holds for Lee. Form, rim, interior and exterior surface are as present in these drawings as those of her hand-built pots, but there is a different energy. The shading captures the turn of the wheel, a sense of a pot rising up to take its shape. This rotating energy takes the eye from the base up to the depiction of the rim, where the detail of the interior brings the movement to a close. The rim becomes a full stop and the form is complete. These drawings express a pleasure

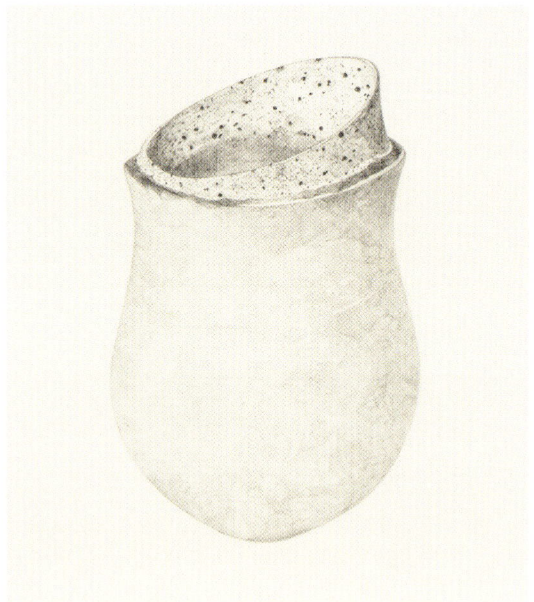

JL506 (2019).
(Photograph by Michael Harvey)

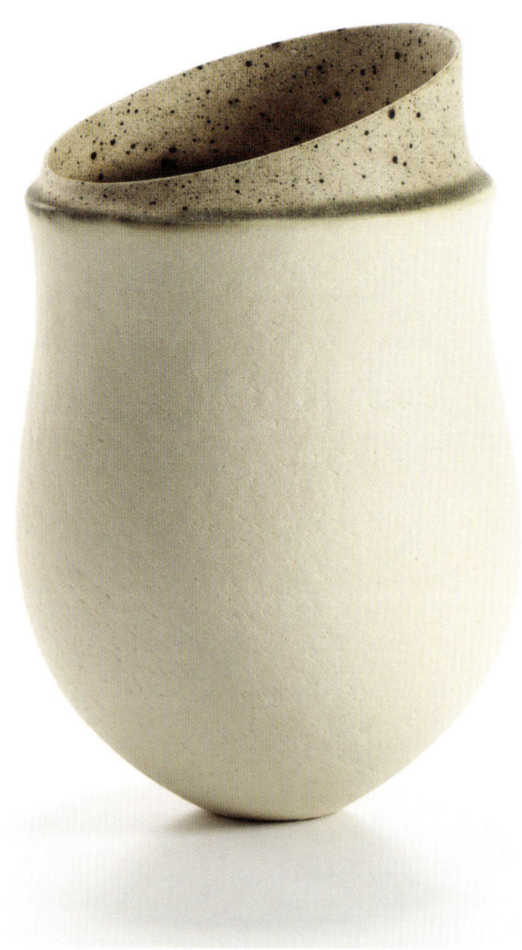

RIGHT: *Pale, speckled, emerging rim* (1997).
(Photograph by Michael Harvey)

in throwing, but they also reveal the extent to which Lee scrutinizes her work. The use of different clays in these thrown pots capture the speed of the wheel, but they also evoke the same stately qualities found in her hand-building. Presence is created in the tension between speed and stasis.

Knowing when and how to stop – how to avoid saying more than needs to be said – is key in Lee's drawings and in her pots. In the graphite depiction of texture and pattern, there is a kind of caress, the remembrance of the hand touching the pot as it is built, of the eye stroking the pot with satisfaction after a successful firing, and of the pencil imbuing these emotions onto paper. Multidirectional shading threads together a patchwork of descriptions, particularly of the coloured clays that are her trademark. The pencil burnishes the paper as drawing, building and throwing collapse into one activity. Lee's drawings reveal how she perceives her work, but they also lead me to believe that her pots are as drawings, and her drawings are as pots. These different aspects of her work are, like the different clays she uses, wholly fused.

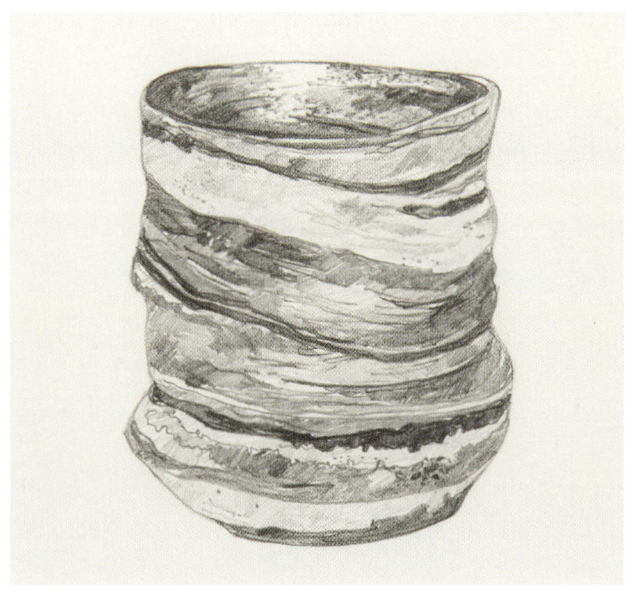

SH-34-14 (2018).
(Courtesy of Sokyo Gallery)

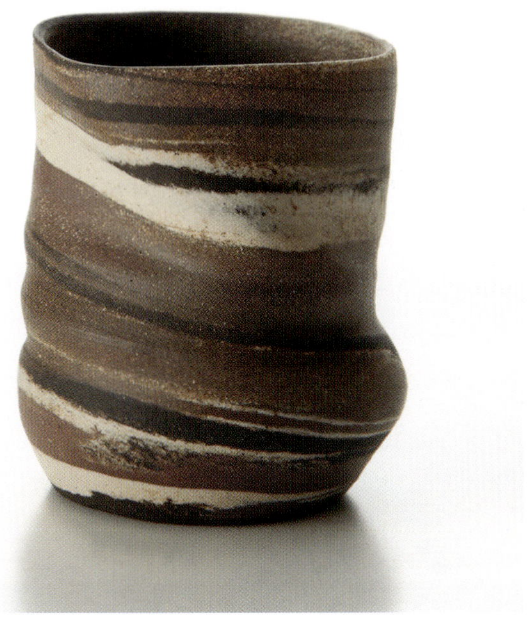

Shigaraki 34-14 (2014).
(Courtesy of Sokyo Gallery)

Carol McNicoll

Montage Notations, Bricolage Citations

人	+	木	=	休	
rén		*mù*		*xiū*	
person		wood		rest	

休	+	口	=	咻	
xiū		*kǒu*		*xiū*	
rest		mouth		to call out; jeer	

The ideographs of the Chinese language are sometimes straightforward symbols of the things they represent. A person (*rén*), for instance, is depicted by strokes that look like two walking legs. The character for 'wood' (*mù*) almost seems like a tree. A person leaning against this 'tree' must be having a rest (*xiū*). However, this person evidently has time on their hands, for when they open their mouth (*kǒu*) they call out or jeer (*xiū*) at a passer-by. In this way, each individual character takes on a new and more specific meaning once it is placed into a relationship with another.

This, claimed the highly influential Soviet filmmaker Sergei Eisenstein (1898–1948), 'is exactly what we do in the cinema, combining shots that are depictive, single in meaning, neutral in content – into intellectual contexts and series'.[34] Eisenstein considered montage – the bringing together of images to create symbolism – as fundamental to the art of theatre and cinema. In his writings, he began by identifying the basic action of a theatrical scene as an 'Attraction', a form of shorthand for the molecular structure of a particular moment. These 'Attractions' were then placed together in a form of theatrical collage that constituted the entire performance: what Eisenstein called a 'Montage of Attractions'. As he moved away from theatre and into film, Eisenstein developed his theory to consider how 'Attractions' could be subjected to five distinct but overlapping approaches in the editing of sequences:

Metric: shots in a sequence all last the same length of time, giving it a definite metrical rhythm.

Rhythmic: a pattern is produced through similar compositional choices in each shot (e.g. marching along a street, with movement across the frame from left to right in each shot).

Tonal: shots are arranged to elicit a particular emotional reaction akin to the use of major and minor scales in music.

Overtonal: the interplay of metric, rhythmic, and tonal montage to produce a specific audience response.

Intellectual: the introduction of metaphoric shots to facilitate symbolic commentary.[35]

His ideas have exerted considerable influence on filmmaking and are referenced in some of the most acclaimed films of the twentieth century: Alfred Hitchcock's *Psycho* (1960), Francis Ford Coppola's *The Godfather* (1972) and *Apocalypse Now* (1977), and John G. Avildsen's *Rocky* (1977), to name but a few.

The bound sketchbooks of drawings by Carol McNicoll are, for me, a kind of cinematographic montage. This reading stems from the fact that McNicoll has always had a strong interest in film. When she studied Fine Art at Leeds Polytechnic in the late 1960s, she produced a postmodern response to *The Sound of Music*, a 16mm film called *Musical* that was completed in 1968.[36] Alternatively,

perhaps it simply comes from looking across her many sketchbooks in one sitting, the absorption of correspondences between images as I moved across a substantial and impressive body of work.

I find that McNicoll's drawings exhibit a keen sense of cinematography. Perhaps this arises from the 'when' and 'why' McNicoll is drawn to her sketchbook. Despite attending some life-classes with Ewen Henderson in the early 1990s,[37] the majority of drawings are undertaken when she is on holiday and finds herself in need of a creative task to keep herself occupied. This motivation is crucial to the kind of drawings she makes; they are often

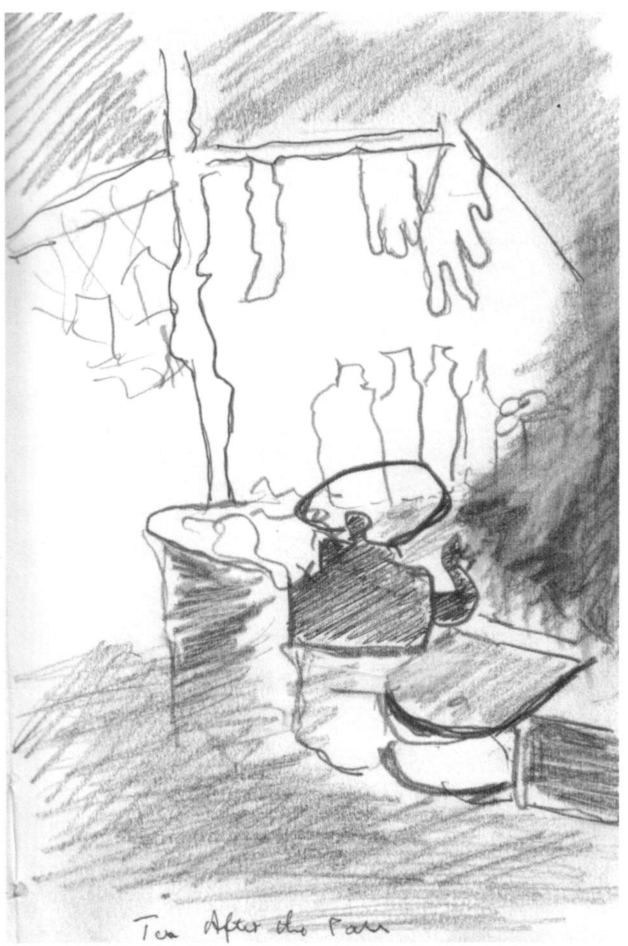

Tea After The Pass.
(Photograph by Carol McNicoll)

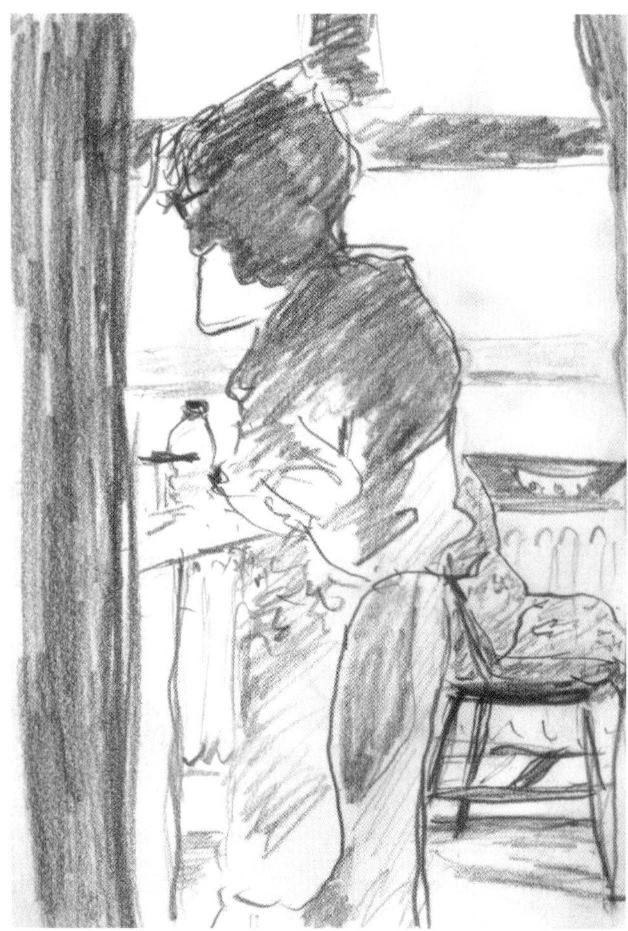

Untitled (*Kitty in her Kitchen*).
(Photograph by Carol McNicoll)

uncontrived depictions of fairly unremarkable moments. Undoubtedly, these would have been lost to time if it were not for the artist's creative impulse. McNicoll's drawings document moments such as someone reading a book, people talking on the beach, an aunt making a cup of tea. Yet, they are truthful documents of life, captured by McNicoll's strong visual memory and processed into a single image on the paper despite the passage of time. They present like stills from a film. Taken together, they form a kind of 'Montage of Distractions'.

Tea After The Pass was the first sketchbook drawing that McNicoll ever made. It was completed while she was on holiday in the Indian Himalayas in the early 1990s. The subject is almost a scene of British domesticity – a steaming kettle ready to make tea following a trek in the mountains. The light beyond the tent is so bright that the landscape is obscured; the fabric roof evidently provides welcome relief from the scorching sun. There are no people in the scene; whoever put the kettle on has either left or has been left alone. The lack of detail in the exterior space increases this sense of isolation. Steam from the kettle merges with smoke from the stove. As it billows up the side of the tent, the eye is taken on a circular trip around the interior space by the use of pencil shading.

There is a similarly dramatic use of shading in *Untitled (Kitty in her Kitchen)*, a drawing of McNicoll's aunt making tea in her house in Ireland. Kitty's face and shoulders are obscured in darkness, her business in the kitchen lost behind the dark grey shading suggestive of an interior door. Again, the landscape beyond the domestic sphere is absent; this time the lack of exterior suggests not abandonment but safety, a concentrated sense of embrace within a known and comfortable family home. The frying pan in the right-hand background plays a similar compositional role to the kettle in *Tea After The Pass*. It draws attention to the back of the hob, the wall, window frame and door, thus taking the eye on a similar journey of circularity through shading. In bringing these images together, it becomes possible to consider them as a rhythmic montage: the compositional choices elicit similar directions of movement around the image. In this sense, they seem like moments from a film storyboard, even a documentary contrasting notions of domesticity around the world through montage.

A similar juxtaposition can be found in the two drawings *Janice on Wednesday after Lunch* and *Madras Airport*. They share similar compositions –

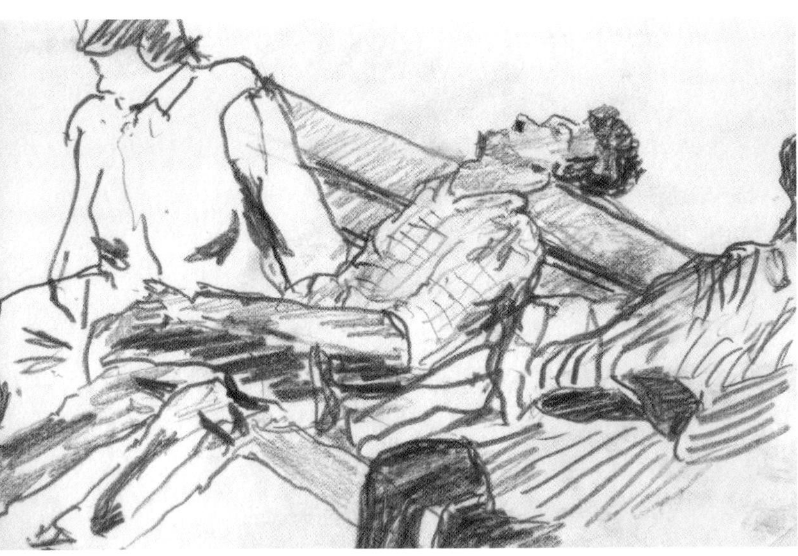

Madras Airport.
(Photograph by Carol McNicoll)

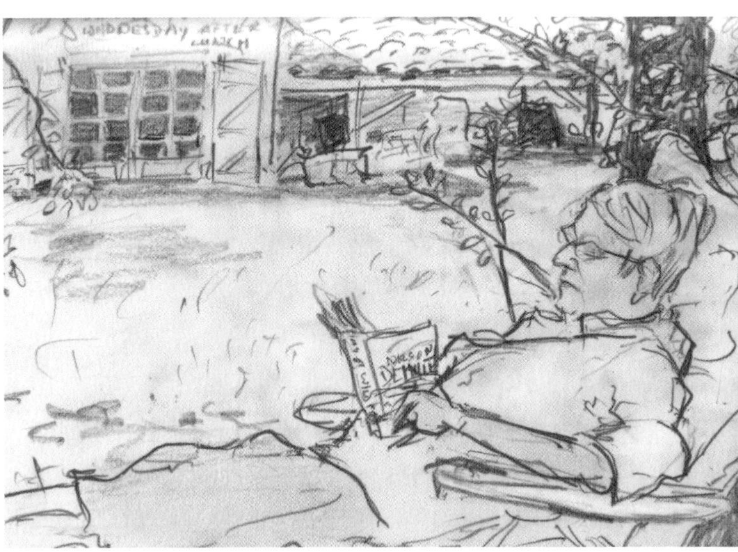

Janice on Wednesday after Lunch.
(Photograph by Carol McNicoll)

the elongated horizontal body, the significance of the forearm of the central figure to the composition, and the diagonal mid-ground captured by the branches and the bench respectively. *Janice on Wednesday after Lunch* is a portrait of the potter Janice Tchalenko (1942–2018). A drawing takes on a different status after someone has gone. Photographs may capture a moment for posterity, but drawings are stronger, deeper remembrances of not just a moment, but an intense mode of looking, and of the act of drawing itself. McNicoll may well have been bored by Tchalenko's absorption in her book when she decided to do the drawing, but the lines demonstrate an intense enquiry into the scene, a meaningfulness behind every mark.

There is similar attention to the man outstretched on the bench in *Madras Airport*. Anyone who has travelled through an airport will be familiar with the sight of an exhausted passenger occupying a seat in a contorted position of sleep. Designed as transitory environments, airports seem to be constructed to keep people on the move; the luxury of

rest only open to those who can afford business class lounges or stopover hotels. *Madras Airport* captures the laborious reality of travel. When this image is juxtaposed with *Janice on Wednesday after Lunch*, the contrast highlights different kinds of labour; one figure is in a state of relaxation and can enjoy travel as holiday, the other relaxes in travel out of exhausted necessity. Taken together as a kind of intellectual montage, these drawings point to wider inequalities in the global distribution of wealth and labour.

There is a strong sense of affection in all of McNicoll's portraits of her close friends. *Janice on Wednesday after Lunch* is indicative of McNicoll's tendency to draw her friends focused on some kind of activity, especially when it is of little interest to her. *Janice on Wednesday after Lunch* is a drawing that expresses a fondness for Tchalenko, but is also fundamentally about being passed over for a book, in this case, the popular detective novel *Wild Fire* (2006) by Nelson DeMille. In *Jacqui and Babs on the Beach*, McNicoll sits apart from her friends, close enough to hear, but far enough away to turn

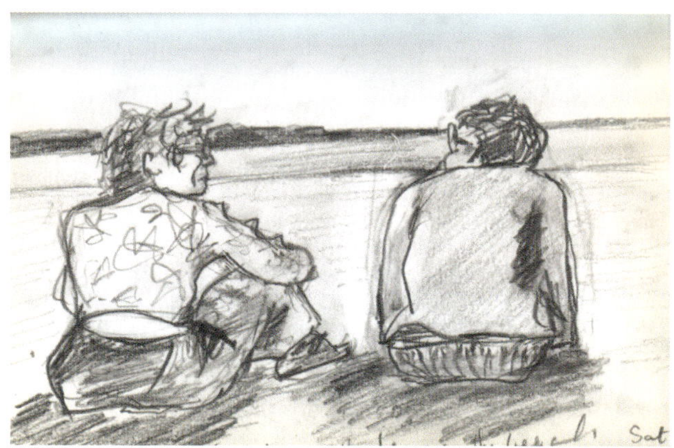

Jacqui and Babs on the Beach.
(Photograph by Carol McNicoll)

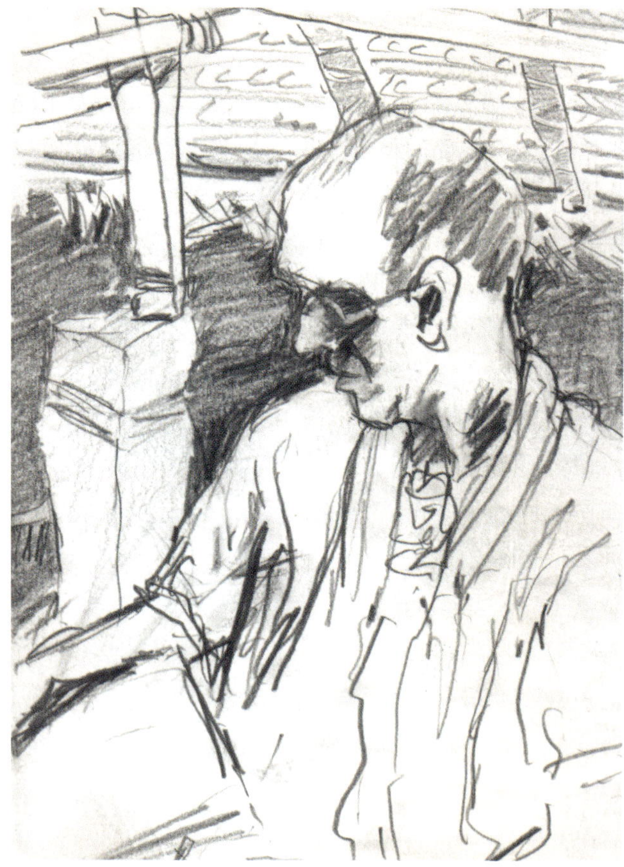

Andrew Painting in the Kitchen.
(Photograph by Carol McNicoll)

them into subjects for a drawing. I find the tension between inclusion and exclusion in this drawing particularly strong. The placing of a cardigan over the artist Jacqui Poncelet's shoulders obscures her body. As we cannot see her face, we are deprived of any visual clues as to the subject matter of the conversation. The Dutch ceramicist Babs Haenen listens intently, the position of her head perhaps also demonstrating an awareness that McNicoll is in the corner of her eye drawing in her sketchbook.

The artist Andrew Logan is painting something, or someone, in *Andrew Painting in the Kitchen*. Shadow falls across his face, his eyes lost to a darkness behind his glasses, his cheeks and lips veiled and somewhat inscrutable, as though his presence has been channelled somewhere else entirely. It is, nevertheless, a very affectionate portrait that implies movement; we almost wait for him to awaken from his creative trance, turn his head upward, and smile. Indeed, as the subjects of these drawings are not looking directly at the viewer (they never do), we cannot help but project onto them an anticipated movement that will further the implied narrative. In this sense, like films, they capture realistic and relatable circumstances. The drawings elevate mundane activities into symbolically and emotionally charged scenes.

There is a sense of cinematography in another important facet of McNicoll's drawings: landscape. Her compositional instinct is always to situate a building amongst its surrounding landscape – a location shot if you will – even if this is evoked symbolically. For instance, in the drawing *Inside Gompa Leh*, the interior of one of the temples of the Indian Himalayan region of Leh is mapped out in a series of loose ink lines. Despite an absence of references to the exterior, traces of it can still be found in the interior of the shrine roof, the marks capturing the intricacy of the shrine structure but also the rugged terrain of the mountainous landscape within which it sits.

A similar composition can be found in the much later drawing *Side of House from Garden*, undertaken at a friend's house in Tobago. Again, undulations across the central axis of the drawing can be discerned. Here, there is the sense of a small hill exemplified in the pitch of the roof. This gives the horizon line a ˏ^ shape. *Inside Gompa Leh* has a comparable horizon line, but it appears in reverse, the roof descending down to and then above the shrine in a ^ˏ shape. These drawings highlight the kinds of compositional structures that interest McNicoll. When considered as an interrelated series, however, they resonate with ideas of film montage.

As a modernist, Eisenstein regarded montage as a means of harnessing the power of new film technologies to imagine and then realize a better world. However, as curators and critics Glenn Adamson and Jane Pavitt argue, modernist collage 'did not entail a radical "undermining" of artistic authorship, or any sense that the avant-garde might need to be replaced with a new set of artistic values'.[38] Eisenstein was the director-as-author of his films, and his emancipatory belief in technology was tied to the formalism of his own approach. In contrast, postmodernism brought about 'an acute self-awareness about medium and mediation, and a radical openness to the world beyond'.[39] In many ways, montage as a modernist concept led the way for the postmodern idea of blending, quoting and recontextualizing. Yet there is an important difference, and this is exemplified in McNicoll's practice. The drawings described above are, themselves, meaningful, and for McNicoll especially so. The juxtaposition of images in her sketchbooks present themselves like a form of modernist montage bound into the linear format of a volume. However, once her drawings are transformed into transfers, they become a resource as readily available as the ceramic moulds that are

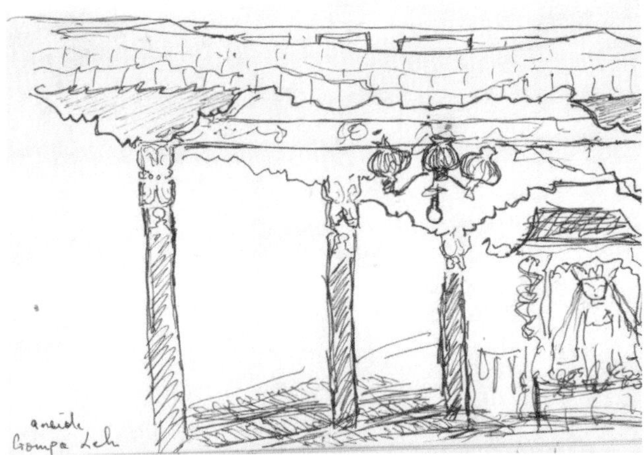

Inside Gompa Leh.
(Photograph by Carol McNicoll)

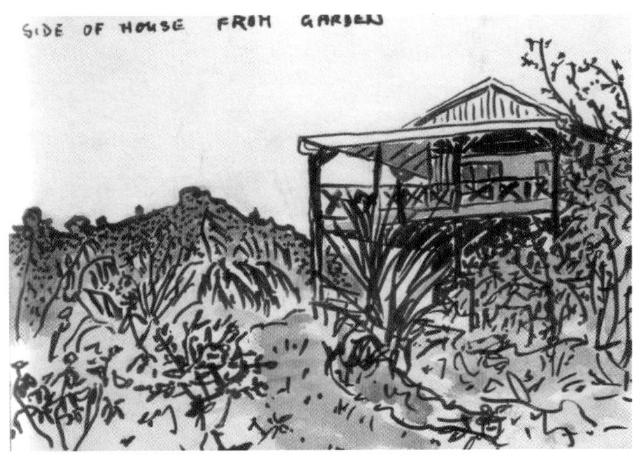

Side of House from Garden.
(Photograph by Carol McNicoll)

used to construct some of her works. As Victor Buchili noted in his discussion of bricolage in *Postmodernism: Style and Subversion, 1970–1999*:

The bricoleur is a 'jack of all trades' who, with cunning and resource, ransacks the 'ready at hand' to create something new. Inherently anti-modern, the bricoleur accepts the world as it is and reconfigures it, rather than anticipating a new world and inventing it. In this respect the bricoleur has a different concept of time compared to the modernist: one that is retrospective, based on the continuous reworking of the received elements of the world, as opposed to prospective and filled with imagined new conditions and possibilities.[40]

McNicoll is certainly a 'jack of all trades': ceramicist, capable visual artist, and maker of clothing. McNicoll's drawings are transformed into 'ready at hand' works once they are printed as transfers. Here, the emphasis shifts from drawing as production towards processes of reproduction, away from the bound montages of the sketchbook and into the bricolage of fine art.

McNicoll briefly used transfers of her own drawings on a selected number of works in the late 1990s, but the cost of commissioned transfer prints was prohibitively high because they had to be screen-printed. Once digital production made them more affordable, transfers of her drawings started to appear on her work as early as 2016. They predominated in the pieces shown at *Cut and Paste*, an exhibition held in 2019 at the Marsden Woo Gallery, London. The ceramic works included in *Cut and Paste* consisted of a range of bowls and jugs that were cast as

sections, conjoined, and then decorated with a variety of transfers. In film terminology, of course, to 'cut' is to edit and splice together shots into a sequence. Whilst some of the transfers applied to the ceramic surfaces were of McNicoll's own drawings, others were commercially available and given to her by friends because they were surplus to requirements. This engagement with techniques of ceramic mass production, particularly in her use of commercially produced as well as bespoke transfers, places her work firmly within the postmodernist frame, the 'cut and paste' identified by Adamson and Pavitt. In particular, her mixing of different types of reproduced image complicates modernist ideas of authorial ownership and negates the possibility of a single meaning.

Renovation People Places (2019), for example, is a bowl consisting of ceramic strips that have been woven together. These ribbons of clay are evocative of strips of celluloid. Eisenstein's formalist approach to montage meant he had no choice but to follow the linear limitations of strips of film to communicate an equally linear narrative. In contrast,

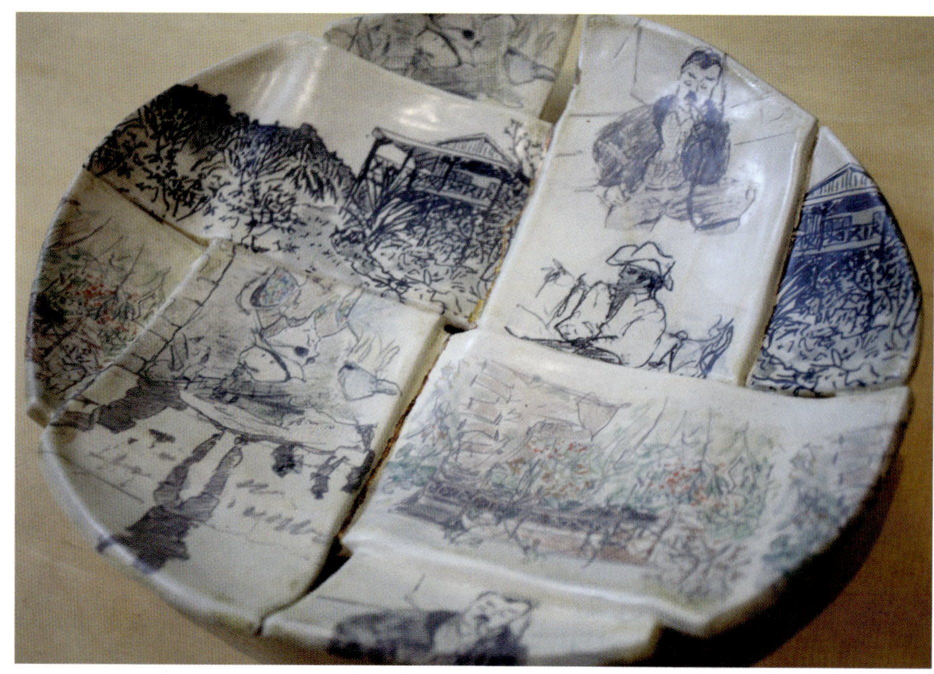

Renovation People Places (2019).
(Photo by Philip Sayer courtesy of Marsden Woo)

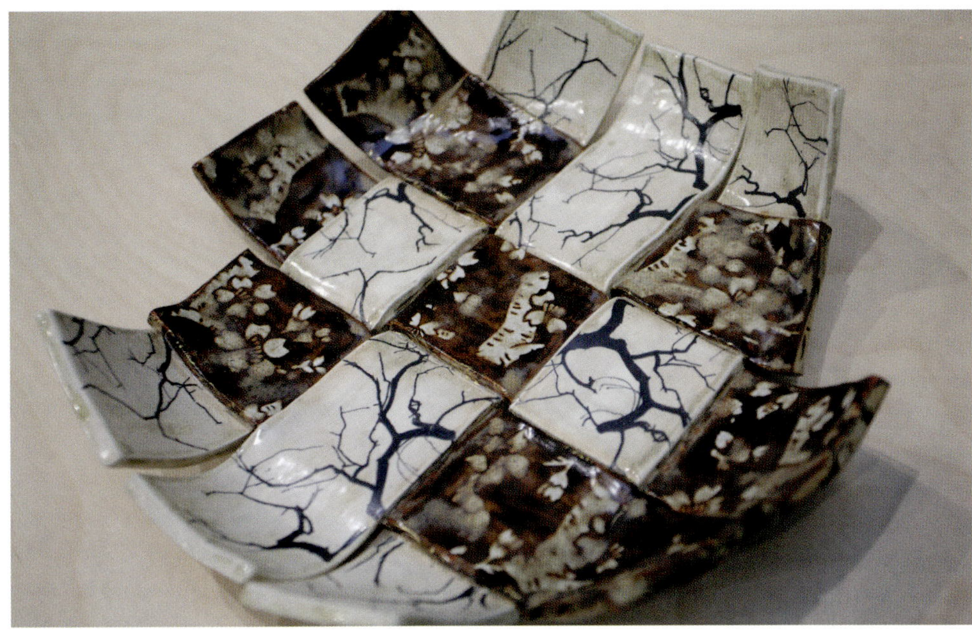

McNicoll's narratives are, like postmodern bricolage films, asynchronous and multiple. There is no clear centre; instead there is a sense of fragmentation, a narrative disintegration that is echoed in the fact that the strips of clay have gaps between them preventing the bowl from being watertight. The drawings, which include reproductions of *Side of House from Garden*, capture the range of her interest in landscape and the figurative. Combined into a mixture of location and interior 'shots', the bowl offers a filmic juxtaposition of multiple images that can be connected in numerous ways to evince different storylines. Considering all the figures, for instance, as connected in some way, or as complete strangers unknown to each other, generates wildly different narratives about the possible relationships between them, as well as the relevance of the landscapes. For me, *Renovation People Places* is a postmodern film in the form of a bowl.

The decoration of other works is entirely comprised of commercially produced transfers. This should not be regarded as a critique; in fact it intensifies the sense of asynchronous postmodern bricolage cinematography. *Walking on the Heath* (2019) offers multiple viewpoints of the same experience. The action of walking is often assumed to be a wholly linear journey from A to B. Yet, when we walk, we take in different vantage points: we look at the ground as we move along, perhaps as much as we take in the scenery around us. Here, the interwoven ceramic strips evoke this fragmented sense of looking, even if the strips themselves take the eye on a linear journey – a kind of walk – across the bowl.

A more dystopic evocation of the natural world can be found in *Nature Jug* (2019), which combines leafless trees with lush flora and fauna. Cute bunnies hop around the jug while insects fly up its handle. This must be the green and pleasant land that constitutes the imagined English rural idyll. But the trees seem to be dead. Is this simply winter, or something more ominous like the destruction of the environment? Is the jug half full or half empty? For me, the lack of narrative certainty across the jug seems to map onto contemporary debates about environmental destruction, the holding of science in dispute, indecision, and of time running out.

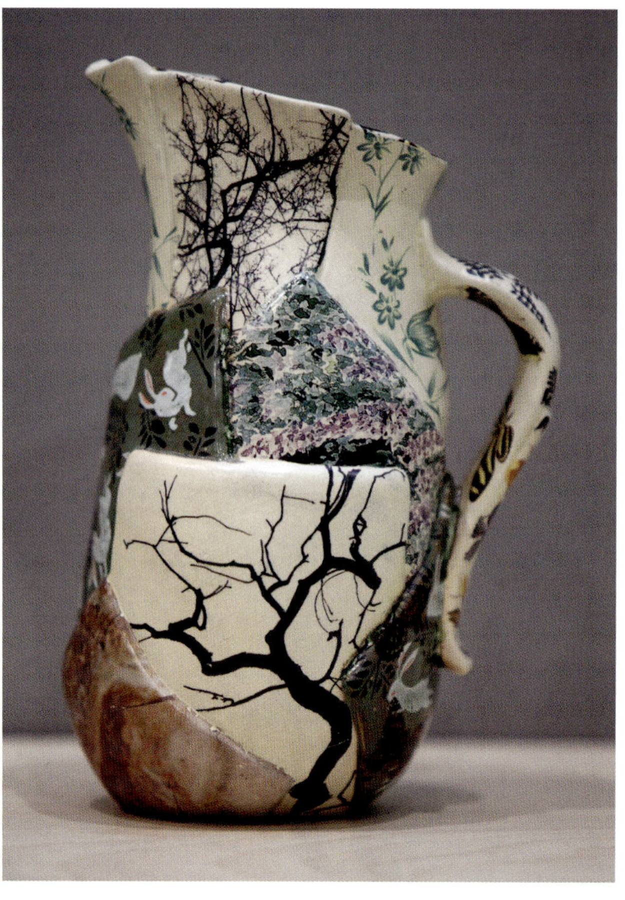

Nature Jug (2019).
(Photo by Philip Sayer courtesy of Marsden Woo)

Fragments (2019) appears to be made from scrap clay, the individual sections looking like torn paper. Each section has a different transfer image: some commercially available, others of McNicoll's drawings. As the title suggests, this work presents as extremely fragmentary. Yet what at first seems chaotic does, in fact, have visual correspondences that are only discovered upon closer scrutiny. For example, the enlarged rose is echoed in tiny blooms that adorn the black and white fragments. These same sections also feature leaves, a shape caught in the wallpaper-like patterns elsewhere. In the midst of these commercial images are McNicoll's drawings of urban landscapes and houses. Strangely enough, this piece is the most evocative of her own sketchbooks which, themselves, bind together multiple experiences as fragments of memory. In particular, it highlights McNicoll's intuitive sense of shape, space and composition; the rough edges of each ceramic fragment evoke the mountains of *Side of House from Garden*, as well as the interior of the shrine roof of *Inside Gompa Leh*.

Of all the works included in *Cut and Paste*, perhaps the most poignant is *Janice Jug* (2019), a moving

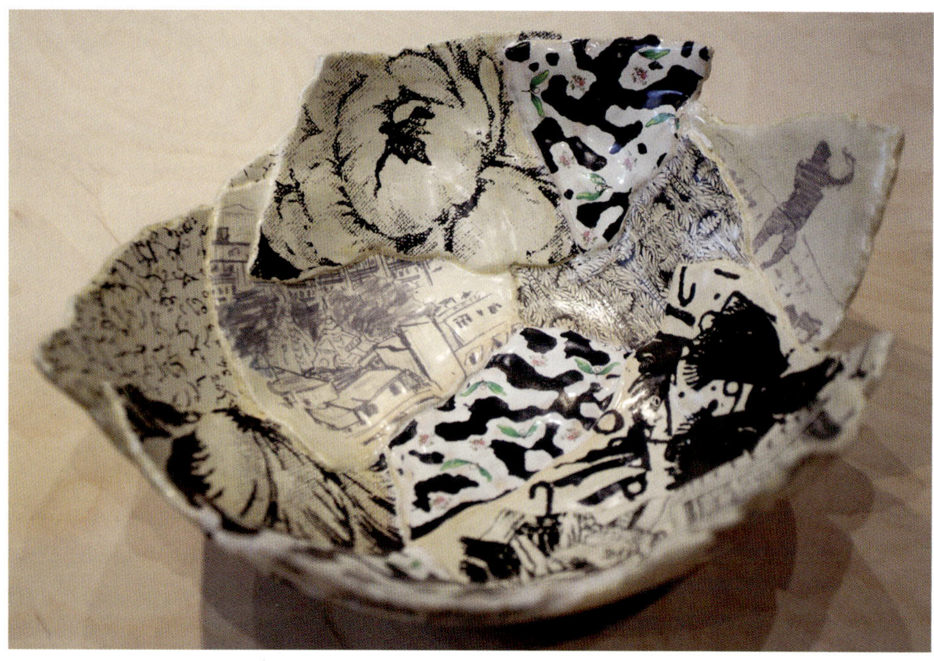

Fragments (2019).
(Photo by Philip Sayer courtesy
of Marsden Woo)

tribute to Tchalenko following her death in 2018. The drawing *Janice on Wednesday after Lunch* is repeated around the body of the jug. Rather than appending the drawing in full, her face is usually the main focus; she seems to peer across and around the other images of street posters, ornate patterns, fragments of buildings and leaf motifs that are all in some way connected with her or her family. Tchalenko is no longer reading her book; she is now surveying the jug itself, taking in the symbolic references lovingly applied by someone who was clearly very close to her. McNicoll could, one supposes, have used a photograph of Tchalenko, but the slower act of drawing is a reminder of a more contemplative time. In the course of remembering the life of and love for another, decades collapse into seconds, memories become snatches; the highlights of joy and the lowlights of regret. Amidst such flashes of memory, drawing stands out as a memorial of what it was to spend time in the company of another. It is for this reason that I always find drawing such an effective and affective medium: to have drawn is to have been with those who have now gone.

When we look back at our own lives, or our relationships with others, we collapse time and space by selectively editing our experiences. Of course, one might liken this to the photo album. Photographs document moments at speed; the mechanical process of photography facilitates an ever-faster responsiveness to fleeting situations. Drawing cannot hope to compete with this, but given that it is an entirely oppositional practice, it seems strange that it should be expected to. Drawing is physical, slow, requires intense looking, and visual imagination. Drawings are not records *of a moment*, they are records of being *in the moment* with another person, fully present, and over a sustained period of time.

Yet, once a drawing is reproduced as a transfer, its status changes. Drawings can be deployed at speed, and onto an endless variety of ceramic forms.

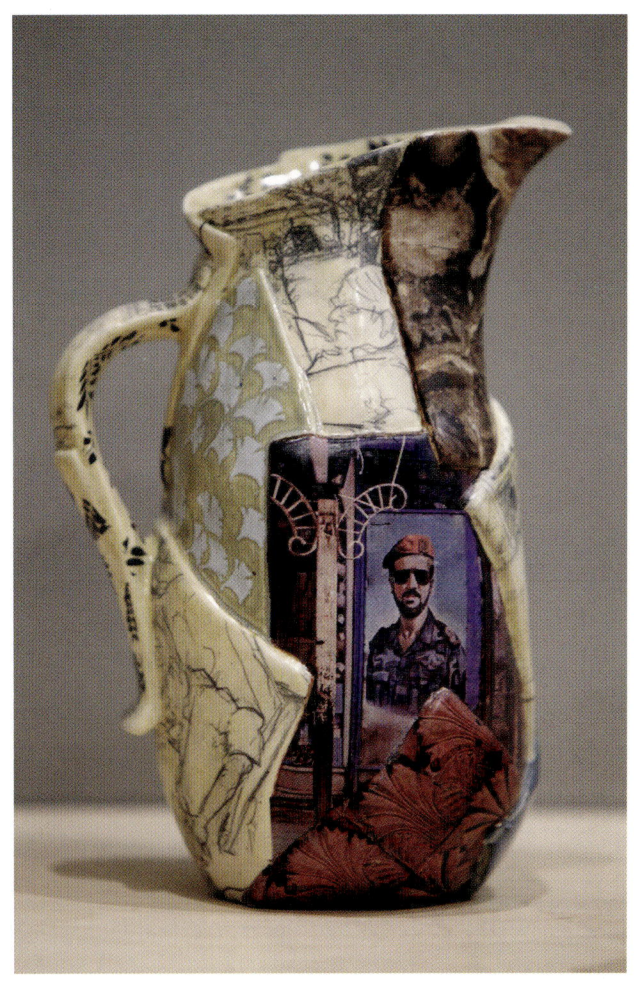

Janice Jug (2019).
(Photo by Philip Sayer courtesy of Marsden Woo)

In the turn towards bricolage, McNicoll acknowledges that memories are partial and fragmentary. Removed from the personal to become metalinguistic symbols in an open-ended visual language, we are asked to navigate our own way through each set piece. As someone who has worked in industrial ceramic production and studio one-off contexts, McNicoll realized early on in her career that 'once you do things for industry, you start undercutting your own market'.[41] By occupying a space between modernist montage and postmodern bricolage, she has resolved the contradiction and carved out her own distinctive space.

Sara Radstone

By Accident and Design

★ ★ ★

Out of fragments comes the whole.

Instinct.

★ ★ ★

Over the course of a four-decade-long career, Sara Radstone has been a singular voice in contemporary British ceramic sculpture. Her work has been connected with organic abstractionists such as Ewen Henderson (1934–2000), as well as the abstract wall hangings of Gillian Lowndes (1936–2010).[42] Both Henderson and Lowndes were working at Camberwell in the 1970s when Radstone was there, and it seems likely that her own approach was stimulated by this environment. However, I do not find her work to be the response to the London landscape, of urban disintegration, nor its regeneration, that some have claimed.[43] Particularly in works from the last twenty years, the landscapes she documents seem more akin to an emotional interior. For me, Radstone is an artist who explores the complexity of personal history and memory as the impetus for her practice. She has developed vocabularies that are at once highly varied and yet remarkably consistent. Her work is uniquely identifiable as her own.

Is it then possible to read each piece as a kind of biographical diary? No. The power of Radstone's work lies in the fact that any reference to her own circumstances is abstracted to such an oblique degree that each piece becomes an open-ended conversation. In this sense, Radstone disappears in her own work; she provides us with nothing except the trace of her touch in the clay. Often her works are untitled, leaving us to figure meanings out for ourselves. Where titles are given, they are often only one or two words (e.g. '*Cradle*', '*Untold*'), hinting at, but never disclosing, the intention behind each piece. This frees her work to respond to the

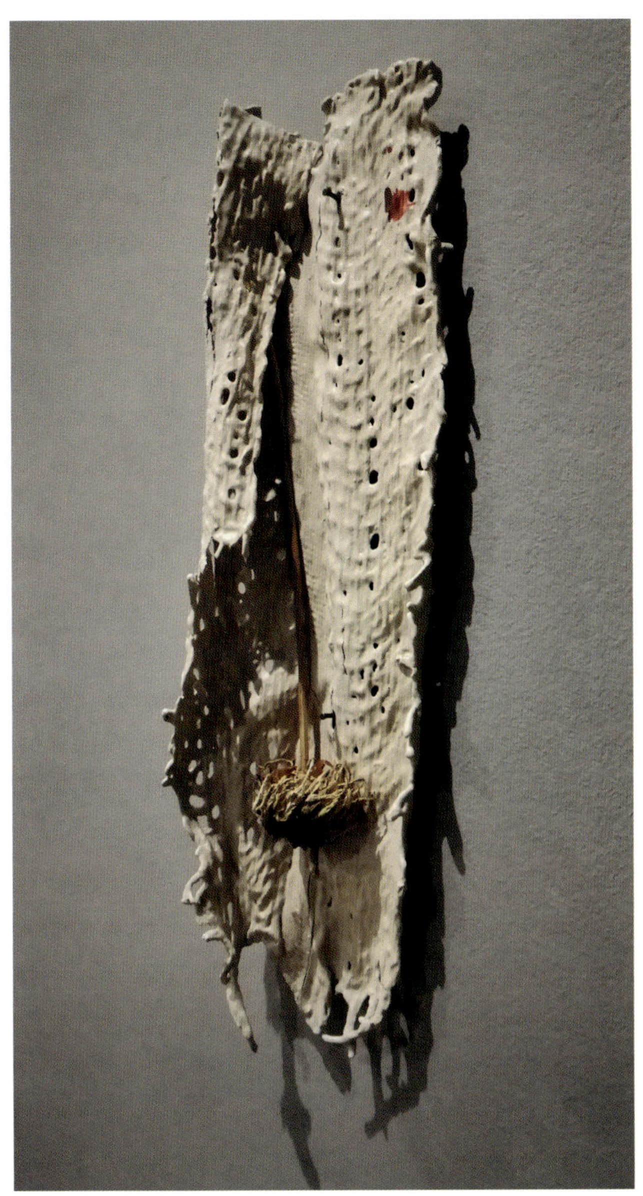

Untitled (2016).
(Photograph by Sara Radstone)

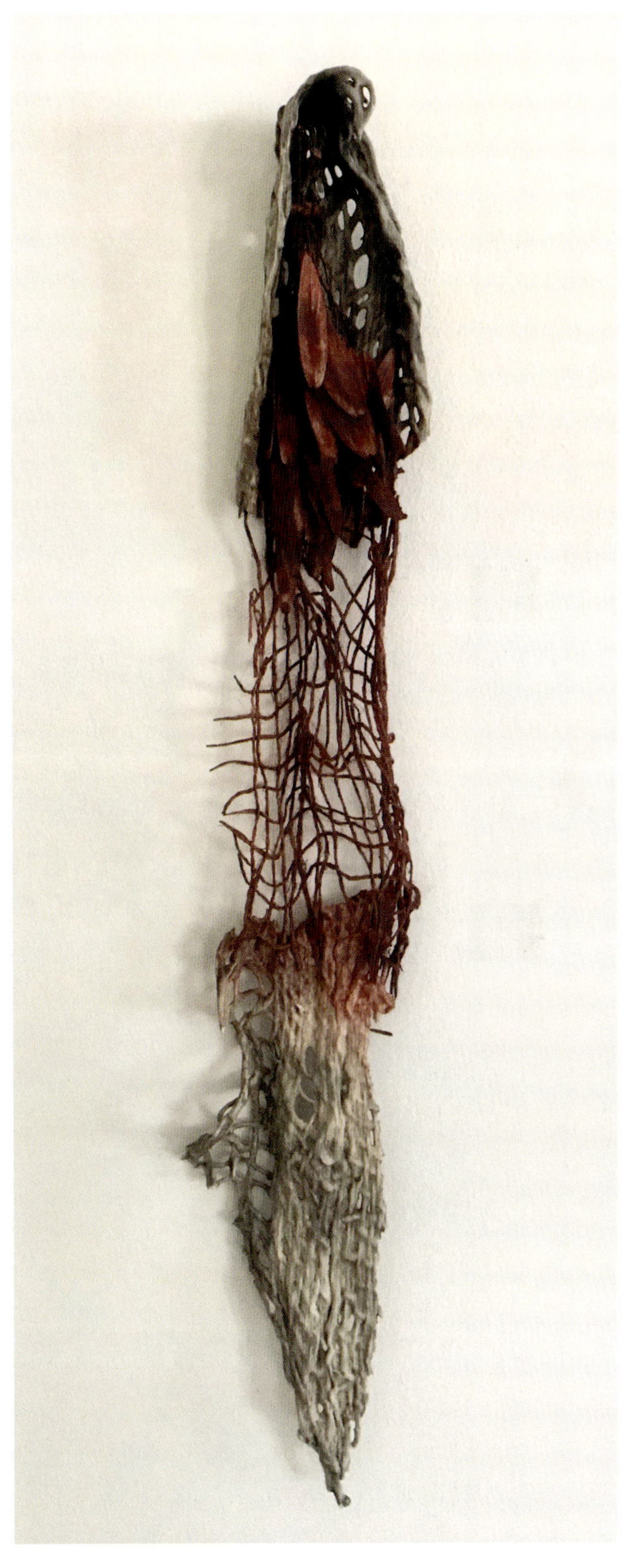

Untitled (2019).
(Photograph by Ashley Thorpe)

particular yet expand towards the general. She directs attention and suggests responses, but they are never authenticated. Nor should they be. To formalize conclusions would be to diminish the impact of her output.

Perhaps some audiences find all this a little demanding. Certainly the searching questions she asks are not easy to answer. They might even ask us to confront challenging moments in our own lives. Yet, this is what makes her so individual. Her work does not confront the world as organic abstraction; it confronts us with ourselves.

★ ★ ★

Explore each piece, let it speak, and see how it resonates.

Crisis, rupture, faith, healing.

★ ★ ★

A close relationship of mine, which had lasted twenty-two years, very suddenly came to an end. A shocked calmness soon acceded to an intense and unshakable grief. As the months wore on, I looked back, saw clues, felt stupid. How was I so blind? Like

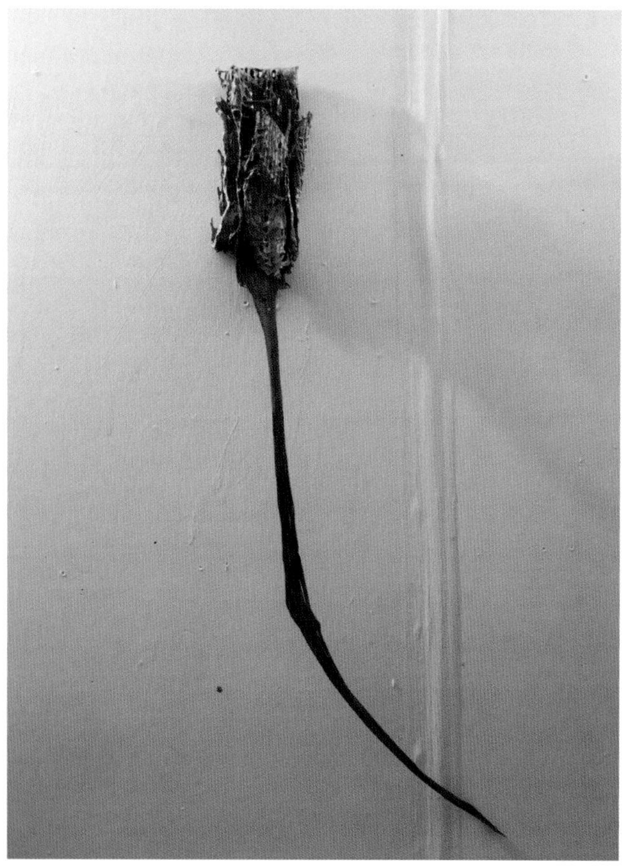

Untitled (2019).
(Photograph by Sara Radstone)

fresh water pouring out of a bottle onto the pavement, I observed my unspent love drain away. I tried to get on with my life as months turned into a year. I kept busy…

Commitment to this 'keep busy' regime took me to more and more exhibitions, including one featuring work by Radstone. I found a small work and committed to buy it. A few days later, I received a very apologetic email informing me that the work had been broken and could no longer be sold. I was fatalistic. To be honest, in the circumstances, it seemed rather apt. A year later, Radstone wrote to me to say that the work had been, not repaired, but reconfigured. The two broken pieces had been connected by red scrim, giving it a quite remarkable new composition: the breakage now an intrinsic part of the work (see *Untitled* (2019), shown on page 57).

As the pain of separation receded into history, I could not help but interpret the work as a symbol of healing. It takes time to recover from the grief of personal loss. We may be left exposed, hanging by a thread, damaged and scarred. Yet, as with a cut to the skin, eventually, our interior wounds heal. The work reminded me that such painful experiences change us in profound and irreparable ways. I told Radstone about all of this when I collected the work. She had no idea, of course. Embarrassment about the whole incident turned into relief and contentment: the process had become truly meaningful for the piece.

★ ★ ★

Strength and fragility.

★ ★ ★

Recent work by Radstone has taken the form of wall sculptures made from both ceramic and organic material. Radstone soaks scraps of scrim in paper clay slip before firing them in the kiln. Many of these structures do not survive the first firing, while those that do

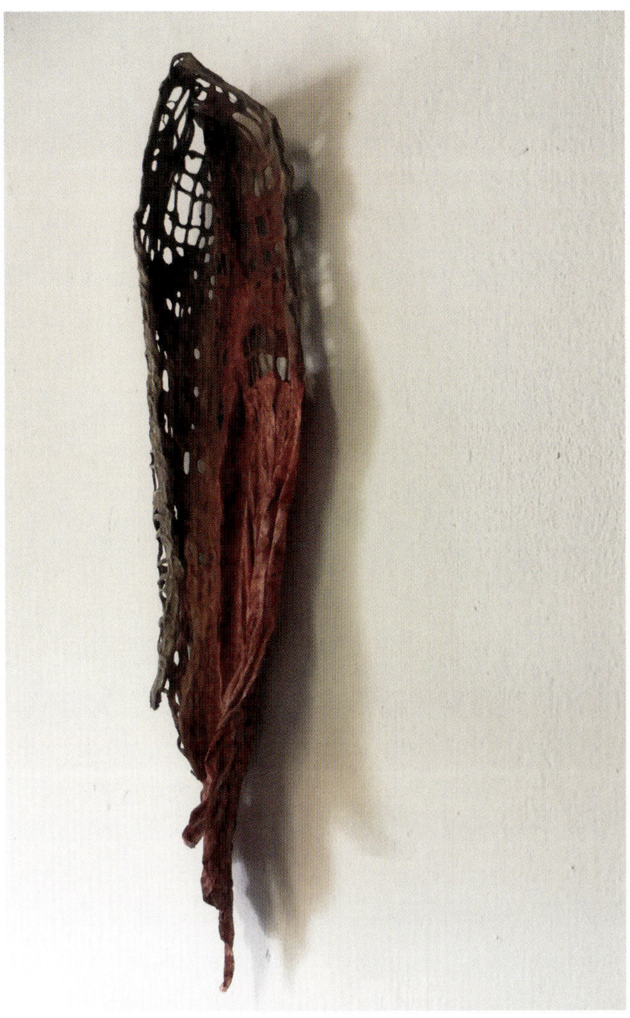

Untitled (2019).
(Photograph by Sara Radstone)

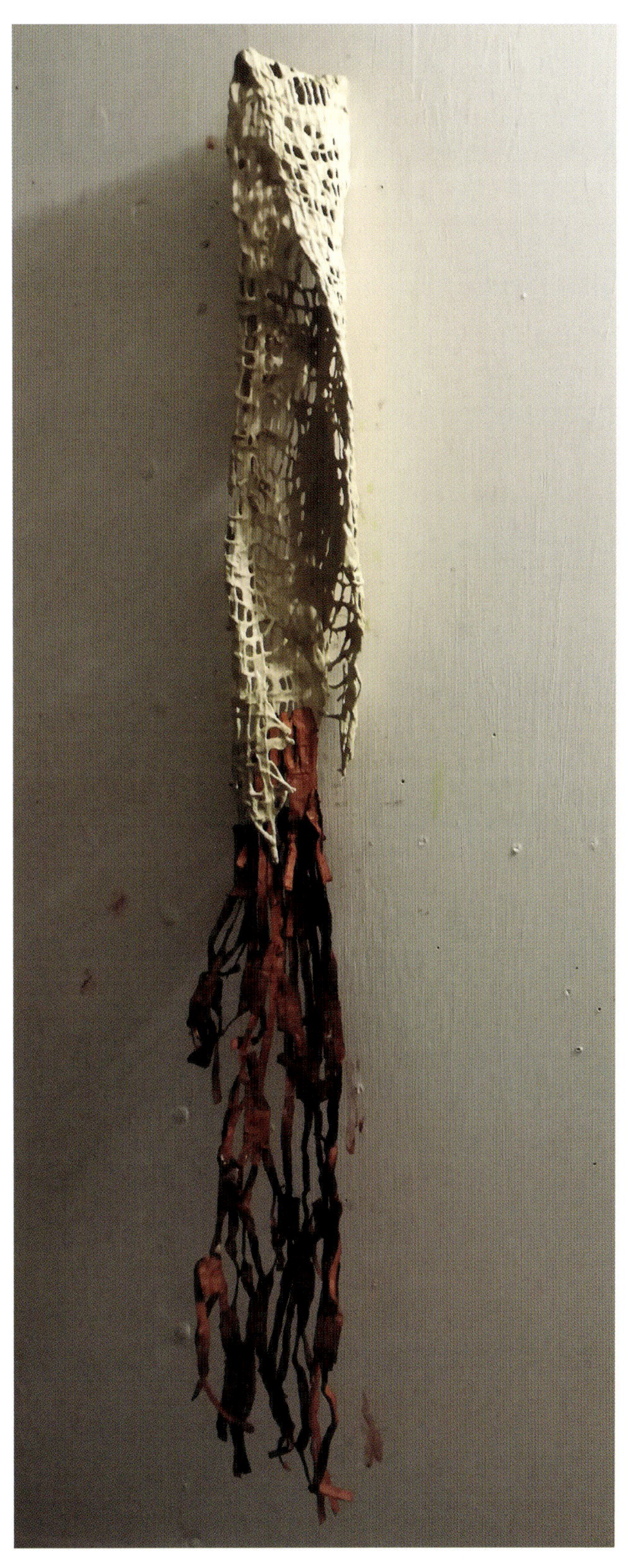

Untitled (2019).
(Photograph by Sara Radstone)

undergo a drastic change as they shrink, bend or crack. The pieces that emerge are placed in a pile in her studio as her raw material for sculpture. She makes connections between different fragments and combines them into a kind of ceramic construction. These constructions are glazed, or re-glazed, and then re-fired until Radstone is satisfied with the result. To these fired constructions, organic material, such as painted dead leaves, scrim or even tissue paper, is often added.

These sculptures capture the enduring fascination of clay as a material. Clay can be made so fluid that it can be absorbed by fabric, yet once fired it can become so brittle that it will snap under pressure. This process of transformation is risky; Radstone is only too aware that each piece will emerge from the firing fundamentally changed. Yet, such faith in destruction is an important element in Radstone's process. If she is not surprised by the outcome, the work is deemed too obvious and pre-determined. She has no interest in identical mass production. Radstone needs to feel challenged, even caught unawares, by the results of her own process. In this sense, her method owes much to chance. Radstone is a technically accomplished maker, however. She knows what she is looking for and strives hard to achieve it. She has an intuitive sense of how to combine different elements to enable each sculpture to impose itself into space, and command interest across internal elements of the composition. Radstone chooses a production process that enables her to realize her intuition. These sculptures are highly thought out on a technical and aesthetic level, even as they are also a product of accident and intuition.

These untitled wall sculptures exhibit structural integrity and collapse. The evidence of clay slip as a wet material is imprinted into the forms as they hang, a ghost of their former life suspended in time by the flame of the kiln. Some of the forms enclose in on themselves, as if shielding their interior from prying eyes. Others are compacted, layer piled over layer, evoking depth and resilience. These are skeletons of fabric, tailors from the afterlife, suggesting something of what it is to exist, and what it is to die. The colours of the ceramic structures – greys and browns – seem autumnal and subdued, a choice that actually draws attention to the intricate and arresting surface detail of each component piece. Paradoxically, the inclusion of dried painted leaves and flowers introduces a strong red colour, evocative of blood and life. The interplay between these elements situates them in a state of tension: of emergent growth or gradual decline, depending on your point of view. For me, their simultaneous strength and fragility makes them remarkably human: a tender portrait of the battle-scarred psyche.

★ ★ ★

Plan to make the unplanned.

★ ★ ★

In 2017, to coincide with the exhibition *More Than Words* held at the Centre of Ceramic Art (CoCA) in York, the collector Anthony Shaw asked Radstone to produce a series of works for inclusion in a special edition of the exhibition catalogue. The fifty or so works on paper that Radstone made in response explored the seemingly limitless variation of a finite number

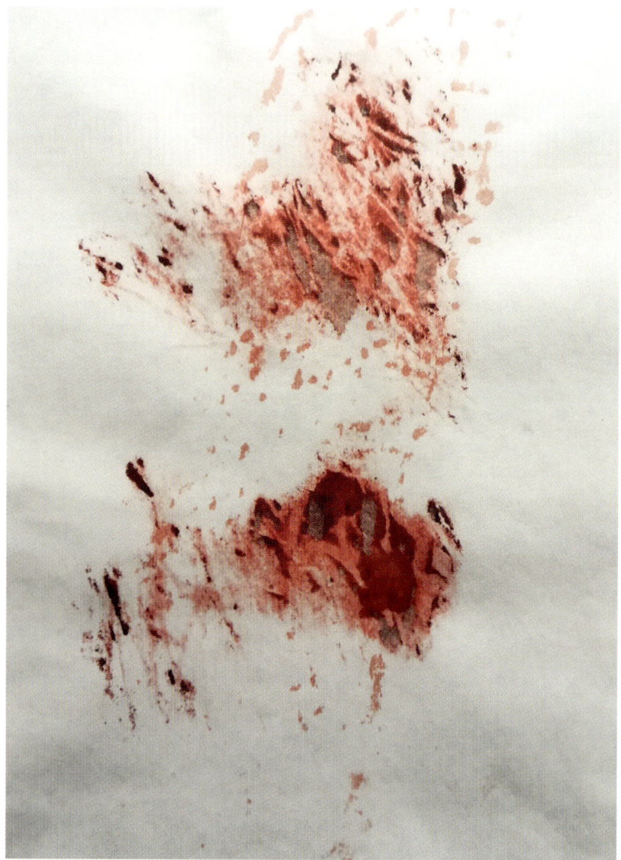

Untitled (2017).
(Photograph by Sara Radstone)

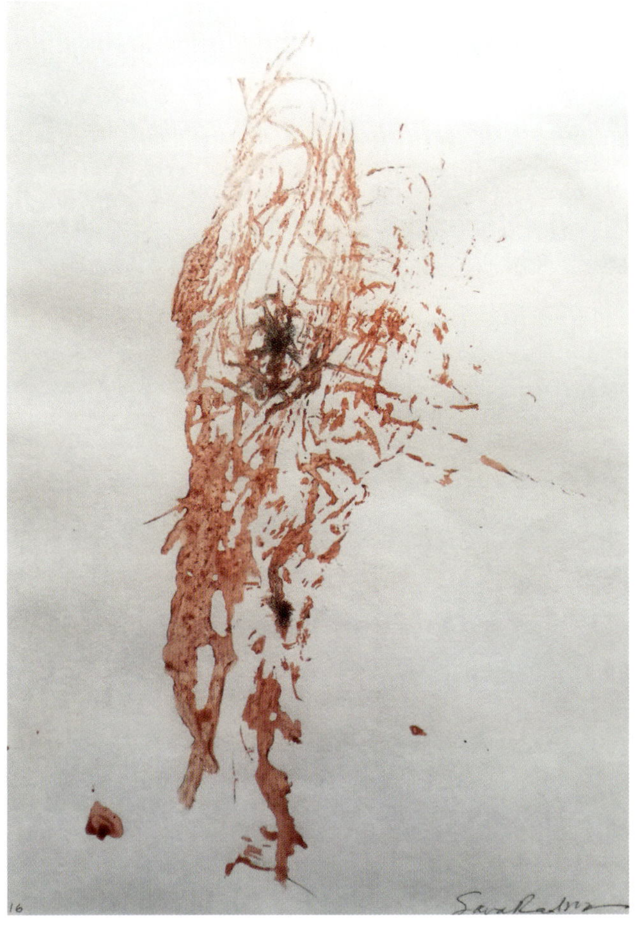

Untitled (2017) [16].
(Photograph by Sara Radstone)

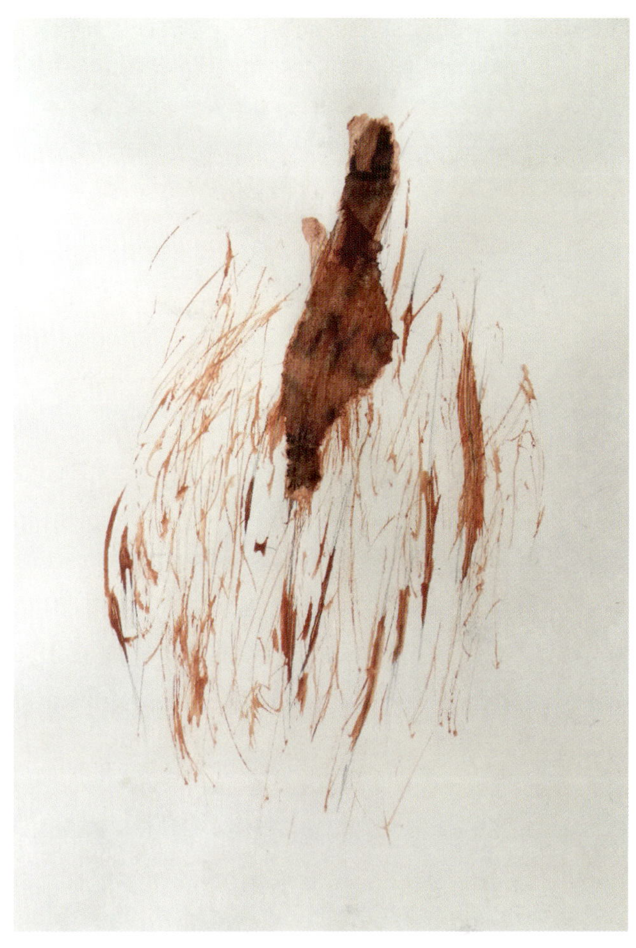

Untitled (2018) [18].
(Photograph by Sara Radstone)

of processes: marks made by newspaper, tissue paper and scrim dipped in red acrylic, fragments of which might also be used in collage, as well as pencil. Although the images might be regarded as peripheral to her ceramic output, the analysis of these works is purposefully placed at the centre of this essay. They draw attention to fundamental ideas in her practice: series, constraint, chance, shape and space.

To work in series is to provide formal constraints around a concept, the focusing of possibilities and the need for constant reinvention. Drawing enables the artist to discern and develop the nature of the composition in the moment, as a response to the unfolding drama playing out before them. This is,

however, just as important to her ceramic practice, where fired elements might be grouped together in new ways, re-glazed and re-fired. Drawing is faster, ceramics is slower, but they are approached by Radstone in fundamentally the same way.

Chance is vital; she is looking for intensity arising out of fluency and intuition. The resulting images have a strong sense of energy and movement. The first work for the series (*Untitled*, 2017), which Radstone considers one of the better images, consists of two island-like marks seemingly dashed across the paper, with elements of torn paper adding texture and depth of colour. It is in one sense a violent image, but it also has a calmness that

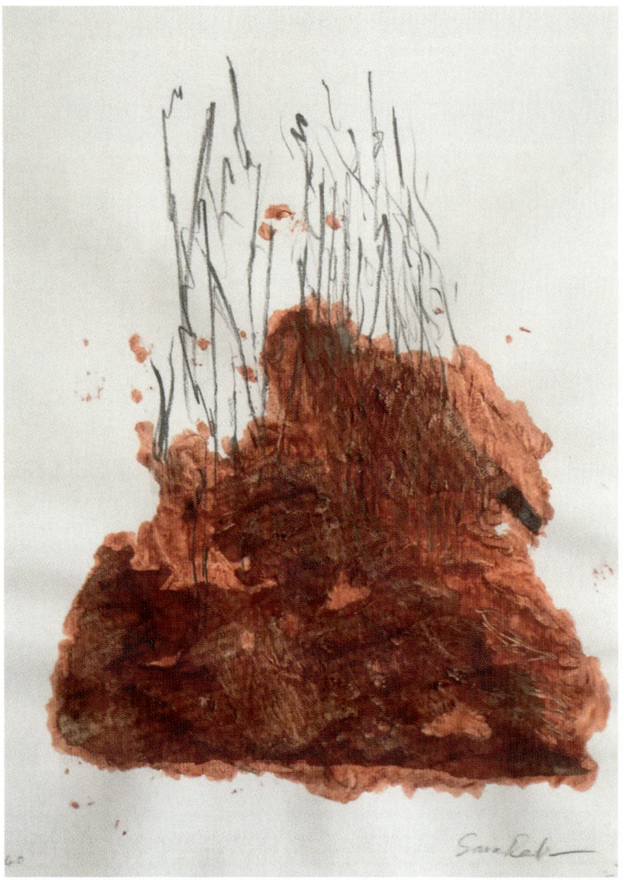

Untitled (2017) [40].
(Photograph by Sara Radstone)

readings. Is this a shadowy figure moving through the grass? Is it a bird flying out of water? These abstract works evoke the Rorschach inkblot tests used in psychological studies: what we see reveals more about us than the actual work itself. The use of collaged newspaper in *Untitled* (2017) [40] gives the work a strong texture that is impossible to capture in photography. Stained red, the still visible newsprint makes the image feel heavier, the grey lines suggestive of movement down (rather than up) the paper.

What is particularly important in these images is the edges of each shape. Radstone's forms carve undulating lines, sometimes brashly so, into space. There are no neat straight lines in her drawings, nor around the edges of her sculptures. This sense of undulation is, perhaps, why some have regarded Radstone as an organic abstractionist, viewing these folds as suggestive of rock formations or mountainous terrain. For me, these lines are more about compositional impact. A jagged form is more commanding in space and less polite. In any case, if these works are reflective of life, undulation feels appropriate. Life rarely moves in straight lines.

★ ★ ★

There is no one way to interpret her work.

Except through experience.

★ ★ ★

One morning, at around 4am, I receive a phone call telling me that my grandmother is acutely ill, and the prognosis is not good. I jump in the car and drive for two hours to the hospital. During the journey, it snows lightly. It is so early that there is little traffic and I recall staring through the empty road and watching the snowflakes hit the windscreen. When I arrive, the shock of seeing a loved one lying motionless with tubes coming out of them, fighting for their life, is colossal. We sit by her bedside. Nothing happens.

evokes Chinese ink painting (*shuimo*). The sense of space in the image is integral. The white of the paper is not 'empty'; rather, it serves to suspend the vigorous action of the marks, enabling the image to become balanced and unified, as well as taut and expressive.

In other works, such as *Untitled* (2017) [16], the use of paint-soaked scrim to create a structural form is given compositional focus by the inclusion of two black pencil dots surrounded by hatching. They remind me of the Spanish painter Joan Miró (1893–1983), whose automatism led to the development of a strong compositional instinct, the painting hinging on a single line or dot. *Untitled* (2017) [18] has an intense sense of action, yet an ambiguity that invites narrative

For hours. Such is the banality of the closing stages of life. We talk but have no idea if she can hear. Eventually, we are asked to leave so that her bed can be changed. Reluctantly, yet weary, we go. We are given a room, sit, try to make chat, drink tea. We've been away too long, have heard nothing, so go back. My grandmother is now in an immaculately made bed. The scene reminds me of how Snow White was laid out after she ate the apple. It is all very surreal. Her breathing is weaker. I catch myself breathing in sync with her.

This is all so painful, yet I recall feeling how fortunate I was to be there, and how I would not want to be anywhere else. Her breathing weakens further. It stops. We freeze. It starts again. We laugh. This happens so many times, what else is there to do? Her breathing stops again. We wait. Nothing. Silence. A doctor is summoned. He shines a torch in her eyes. I catch the retina's flash in the light, but there is no response. I am numb. I have never watched anyone die before. I am held as I collapse into tears. We eventually emerge from the hospital amid dark clouds and a strong breeze. I sit in my car in silence. There is a flash of lightning, thunder, and it hails. It hails with such voracity that it builds up to fill the entire windscreen and I can't see out. Adding to the epic sense of unreality, I feel I have gone from a nightmare *Snow White* scenario to the cleansing rain scene in *Ben Hur*. I think how my grandmother was an extraordinary woman: strong, independent, funny, generous, loving, and somehow always there. She taught me so much. Now she's gone. Her final lesson, I realized later, was to dispel any illusions I had about death.

In the months that followed, I found myself repeatedly looking at two older works by Radstone from 1989. They are two casket forms, each with a long gash running across the top. One of the forms has a gaping hole, almost resembling a mouth. I looked at these vaguely coffin-shaped works and

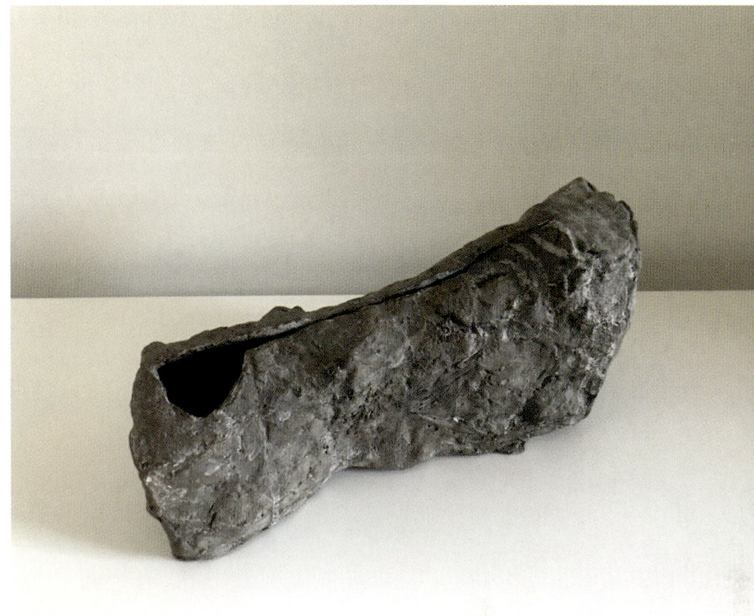

Casket (1989).
(Photograph by Ashley Thorpe)

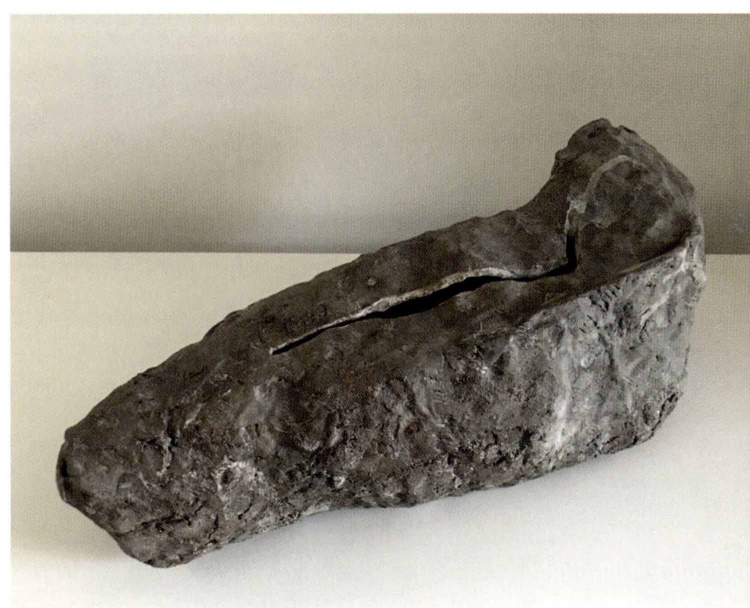

Casket (1989).
(Photograph by Ashley Thorpe)

was reminded of my grandmother's last breaths. They speak of life having escaped; the caskets are the hollow shells of a life now spent. As time danced on, and the grief mutated, I found myself looking at them differently. I no longer saw just exhalation and death, but a reminder that there was life in the first place. The works evoke presence as much as absence. They are reminders that death is one of the few things we all have in common, but also that acknowledging the presence of life is just as important as remembering its passing. One day, as I looked at the pieces, in my head, I heard my grandmother's voice telling me to stop making such a fuss. She giggled in that way she did. I realized her love is still here; grief now mutated into gratefulness. Radstone's works are as much *memento vivere* – a reminder to live – as they are *memento mori*.

* * *

Some of Radstone's sculptures are assemblages of papyrus-like sheets of clay. The forms resemble documents or pages torn from a book. Made from paper clay and oxide-stained paper, these works are glazed, scratched and marked, sometimes over the course of several firings, until they have acquired the depth of colour Radstone desires. *Chart* (2014) is a single piece which, during the process of firing in the kiln, has warped to produce a wonderfully curved edge. They recall Chinese and Japanese painted scrolls, which unfurl to visually describe a long journey

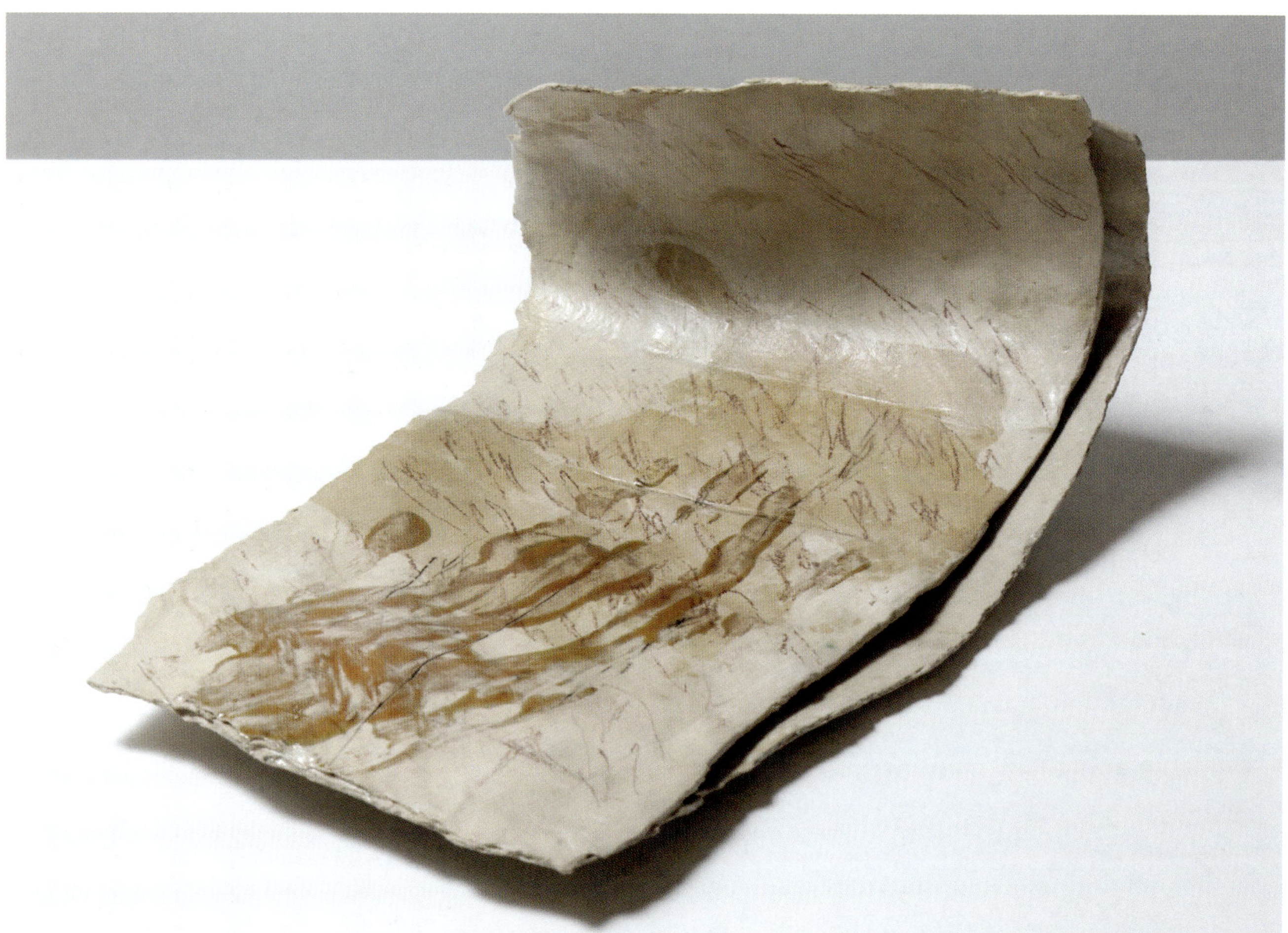

Chart (2014).
(Photograph by Philip Sayer)

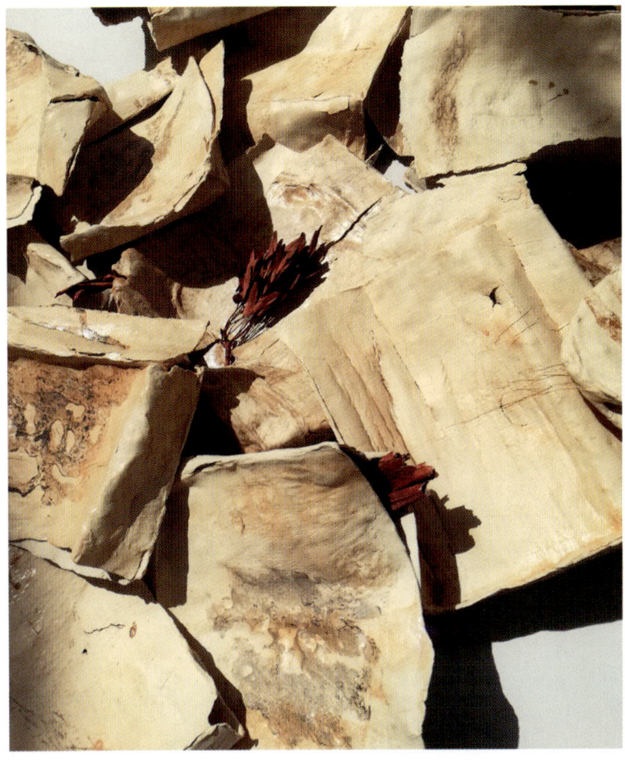

RIGHT: Detail of *Untold* (2017) at the exhibition *More Than Words*, York.
(Photograph by Sara Radstone)

to an important celebration. The abstract marks applied to the surface are not suggestive of any particular landscape or journey, yet the title asks us to consider the work as some kind of map. The striations could be landscape markers, the brown glaze delineating rivers or representing mountains. Ominously, the brown also looks like a hand sliding down the piece; perhaps the last touches of a dying body. Nothing is confirmed of course, and others will, and should, have different interpretations. Yet I find these works powerful because they are so rich in narrative

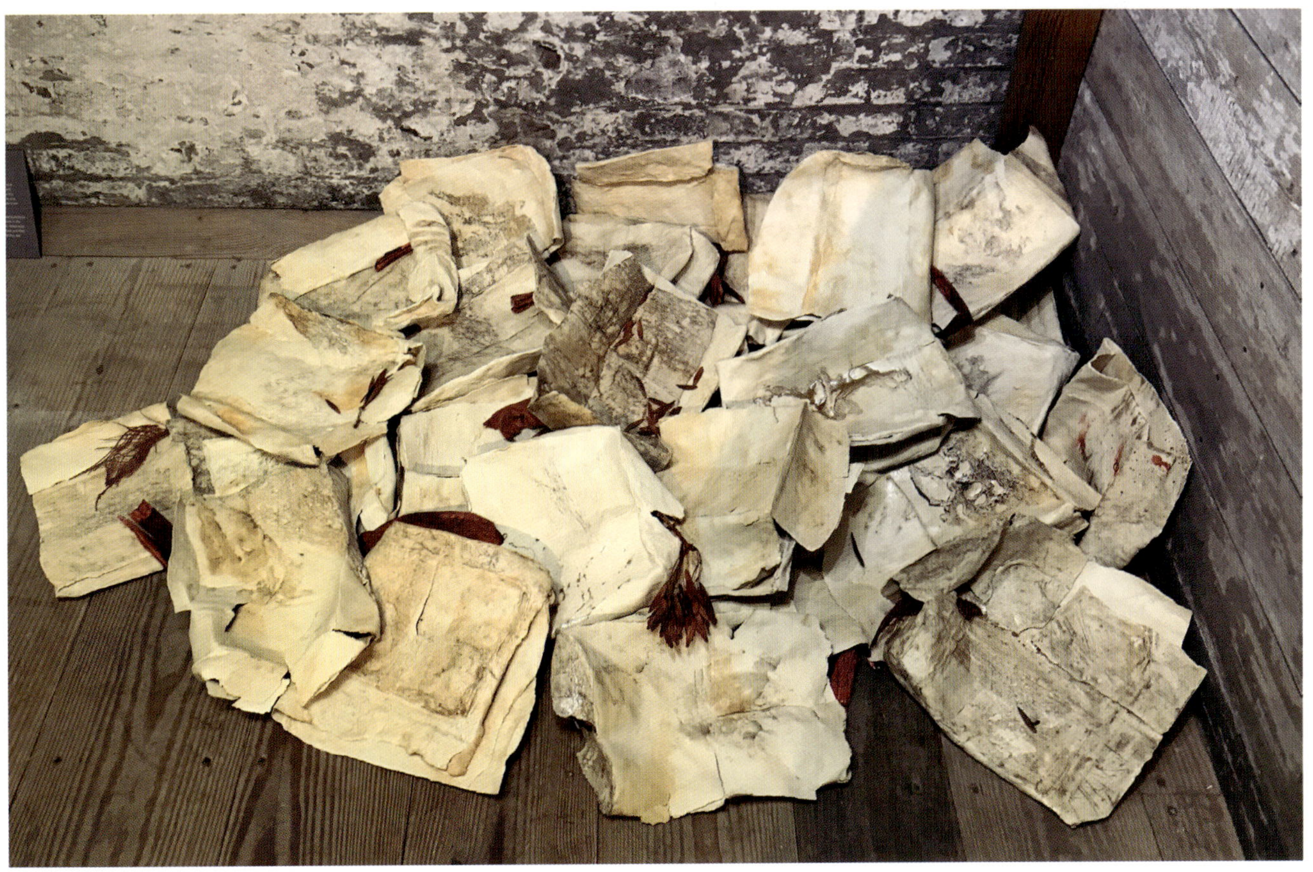

BELOW: *Untold* (2017) at *Unearthed* show, London.
(Photograph by Ashley Thorpe)

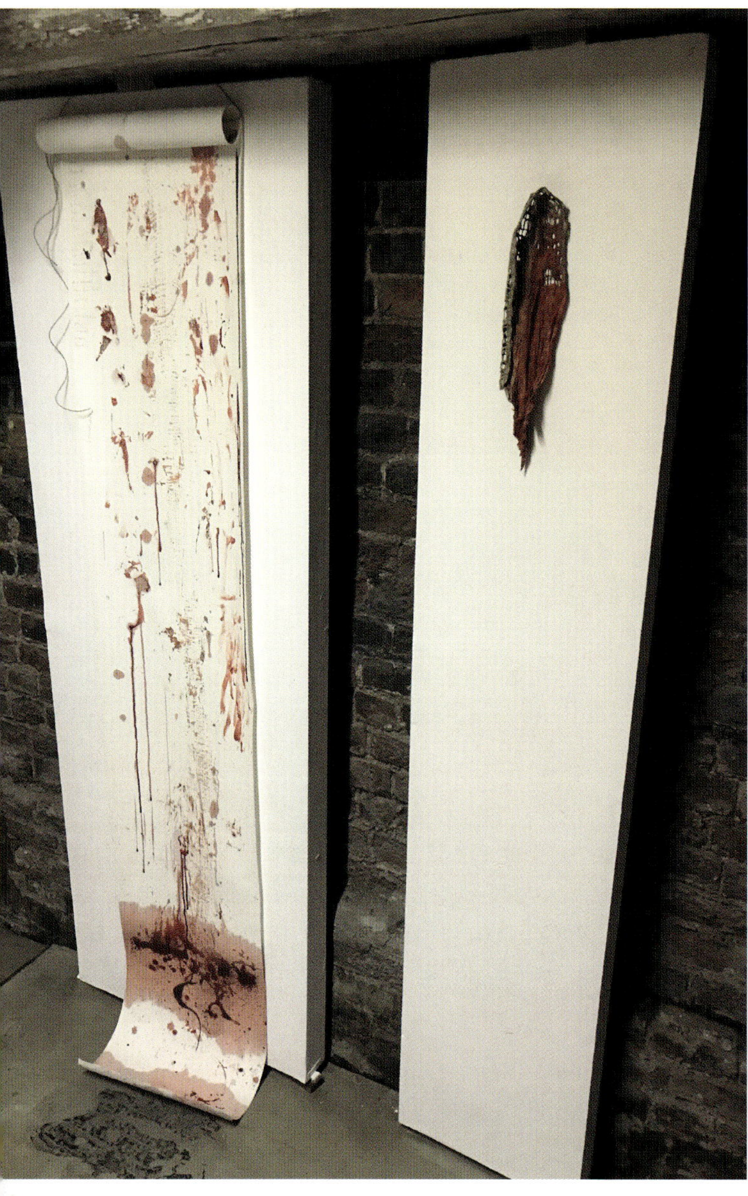

Untitled (2019).
(Photograph by Ashley Thorpe)

possibilities. They tell stories of migration – voluntary and enforced – and map a journey between points, perhaps even between life and death.

A number of such pieces were placed together to make the large work *Untold* (2017), first shown at the York Art Gallery. Here, the piece was placed on a low-level white plinth, enabling audiences to walk around and observe it from different angles. The disjuncture between the clean white plinth and the apparently crumbling ceramic forms highlighted Radstone's ability to handle clay with dexterity, to push it as far as it will go. The constituent forms draw attention to Radstone's love of the robustness and fragility of fired clay. The treatment of surface turns each piece into a kind of landscape. They speak of exile, of crossing landscapes in desperation, but the desire to survive at all costs. They also speak of fascism, the burning of books, the silencing of voices, and the destruction of knowledge.

The work is especially poignant in the wake of the refugee crisis caused by the Syrian Civil War (2011–present). Documentaries such as *For Sama* (2019)[44] brought the devastation and heartbreak of daily life in cities such as Aleppo to the attention of the world. Meanwhile, the news captured the desperate stories of Syrian migrants risking their lives in overcrowded boats to cross the Mediterranean Sea from Libya to Italy. The drowning of men, women and children in capsized boats became a grim, almost daily, headline in 2015 and 2016. *Untold* speaks of the migrants who have been silenced, drowned, stifled by authoritarian regimes, suffocated by chemical weapons, and to whom nations still closed their borders. Despite the absence of text, these 'pages' are far from blank; the writing is in a pictorial language. Radstone's glaze is her ink. Each undulation, mark, torn edge, patch of colouration are words in a sentence of battered hieroglyphs.

Untold was shown again in 2019 at *Unearthed*, a group show held at House Mill in East London. In the latter venue, the walls of the historic eighteenth-century mill house became a frame for the interpretation of the work. The worn wooden floor, side panels and brickwork were echoed in the rough textures of these ceramic sheets. *Untold* could almost have lain there for centuries. The seemingly discarded ceramic pages spoke of a human presence now absent. Dried red flowers suggested memorialization of the dead, while red scrim evoked fishing nets that could have been used on the nearby River Lea. The work captured the decline of labour-intensive manufacturing and stood as a memorial to the histories of the working classes.

★★★

… the existence of nothing (wu 无) as a precondition for bringing concrete things into existence and for their possessing value.[45]

At the 2019 *Unearthed* exhibition, Radstone showed a large work on paper for the first time. Drawing upon the same approach used in the images commissioned by Anthony Shaw, red marks were made onto a long paper scroll by paint-soaked scrim, newspaper or tissue paper. A larger patch of red, accompanied by marks made in a deep burgundy, pooled at the bottom of the work. The scroll form once again evokes Chinese ink painting. The use of empty space speaks to an aesthetics of economy, what art historian Minghua Fan describes in the above quotation as a conceptualized 'nothing'. As Fan further suggests:

artistic creation is not merely the creation of shapes and forms; it must also have a higher metaphysical objective, namely the manifestation of an artistic world. Although art is first and foremost perceptual, meaning it must appeal to the admirer's five senses, it is also transcendent.[46]

The success of Radstone's untitled work rests upon her fluency, the cascading of marks down the scroll that evoke an abstracted waterfall. But this is not a representational painting; nor does it follow the aesthetic philosophies of Chinese art. It does,

however, confront us with visceral sensations, for me, once again, of life and death. Is this the splattering of blood? Is this a journey from birth to death? Or do the marks represent different pathways through life? Like a visual form of music notation, the marks evoke stasis and speed; the lines made by the application of scrim providing a horizontal counterpoint to the otherwise vertical dribbles and splodges. Similar to the vertical wall sculptures, this work depicts transcendental forces: the marks we leave behind when we ourselves have turned to nothing.

★★★

Like the journey of life; a process made by accident and design.

★★★

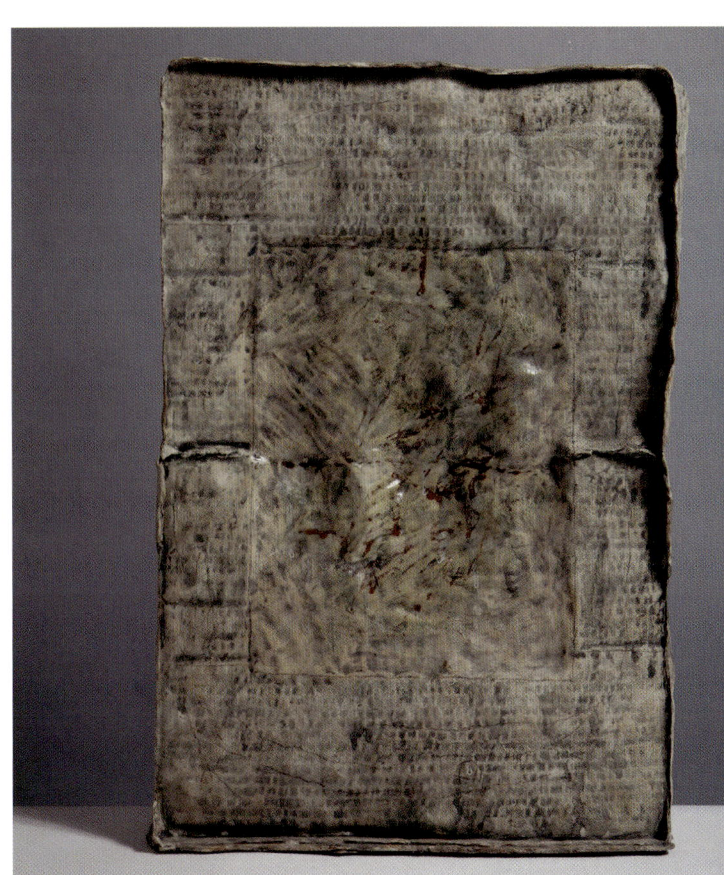

Winter (2010).
(Photograph by Philip Sayer)

Pam Su

Directly Indirect

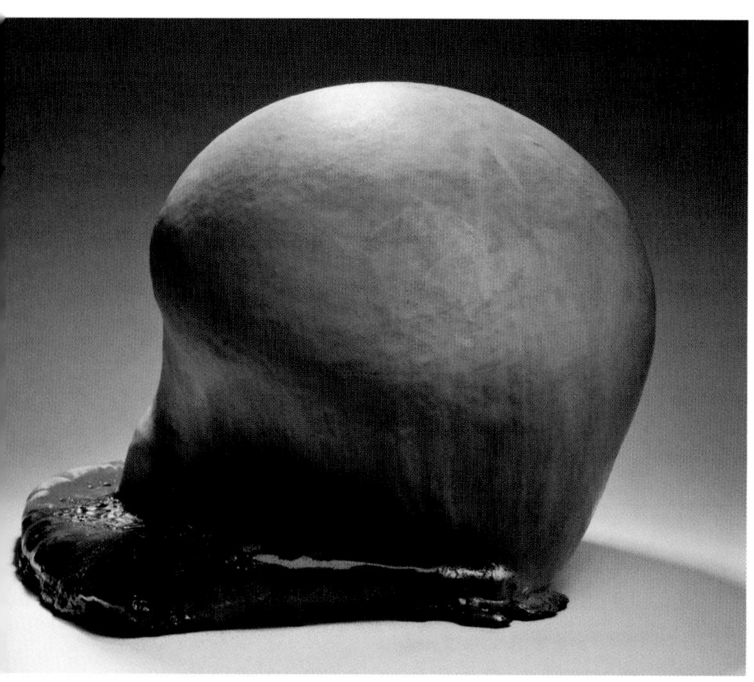

New York I Love You But You're Bringing Me Down (2018).
(Photograph by Ester Segarra)

The sculptural ceramics of Pam Su are raw statements of emotion. The titles of her work, which are carefully thought through, read like diary entries. This directs us to conceive of each piece as somehow representative of a meaningful moment in her personal life. Yet, her work is not concerned with documentary realism, and biography is, at best, obliquely recorded. That we are denied access to the specific events referred to in each title does not diminish the impact of her work, however. In fact, it strengthens it. The gap between title and work can only be filled by the active participation of the viewer. As an audience, we are invited to speculate upon the meaning of her work and form our own interpretation as to its significance.

The essence of a moment, mood, or feeling are rendered through shape, colour, tone and texture. In particular, decisions about colour and texture

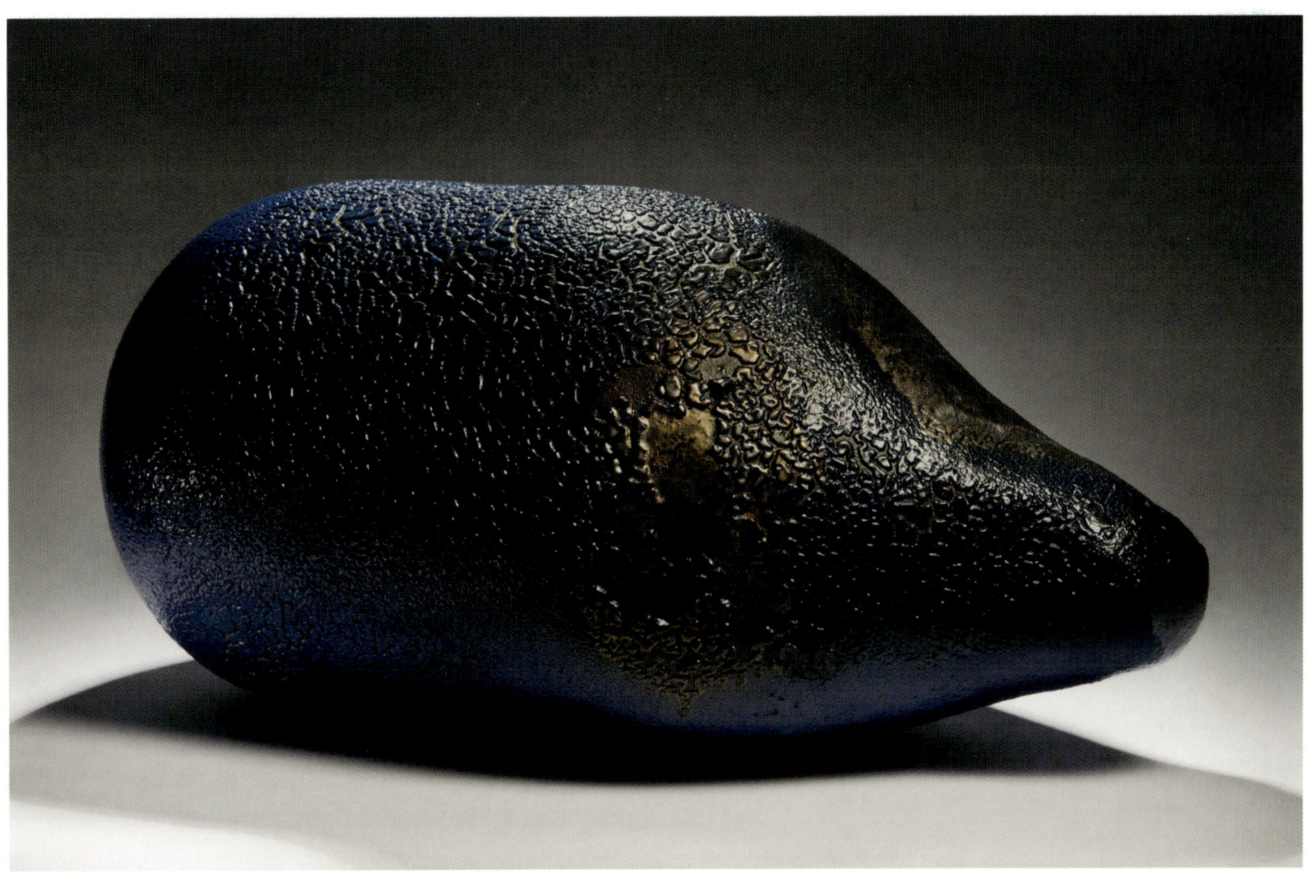

Eating Ice Cream in the Backseat (2018).
(Photograph by Ester Segarra)

are made, and only make sense, in relation to form. The way in which glaze mutates across a work – the top versus the bottom, or one end versus the other – enables Su to express emotional movement, a fleeting action made resonant in clay. In *New York I Love You, But You're Bringing Me Down* (2018), the glaze has pooled at the base in different colours, yet it anchors the glaze across the skull-like head that constitutes the main sculptural body of the piece. The glaze suffocates the form, preventing it from escaping its glazed incarceration. There is, therefore, a sense of entrapment, of being held by a force that is beyond control, of being 'brought down'. In the more celebratory *Eating Ice Cream in the Backseat* (2018), it is tempting to try and use the title as evi-

dence for documentary in the work. Is the sculpture representative of a giant tongue? Or is it an ice-lolly, thus referencing the ice cream of the title? For me these readings are rather reductive. There is something sensuous about the form: a feeling of relish in the opulent glaze. It is not a sculpture representing eating ice cream, more a depiction of how it *feels* to eat a cooling ice cream in the back seat of a car on a hot summer day. In this sense, it seems possible that Su's titles are maps of feelings, and not a guide for literal interpretation.

Did Su make the work first and then apply the title, or make the work as a response to a specific moment? Does it matter? Naming a work posthumously is hardly unusual, and it seems an irrelevant

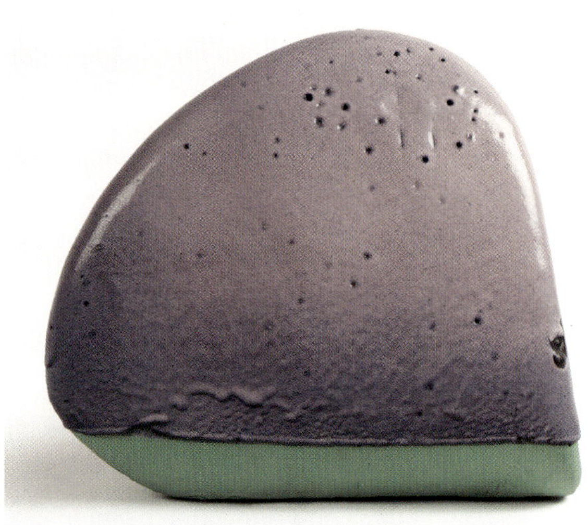

Subway (2018).
(Photograph by Chao Wang)

distinction in any case. That these works are named *at all* is significant, for the act of naming gives each work narrative worth and emotional resonance. Her work is not a foray into the formal possibilities of sculpture alone, but an abstracted representation of the emotions of the everyday.

Recognizing her work as depictions of experience gives it greater conceptual coherence. In *Merced, California* (2018), orange glaze hangs across the top of a red and green body. Will it smother the piece or remain suspended as a weight to be carried? Given that the title of the work relates to a specific location, it is tempting to view it as an expression of the artist's own relationship with place, as an Asian American artist living and working in Britain. How do we carry our identity into our lives and into our

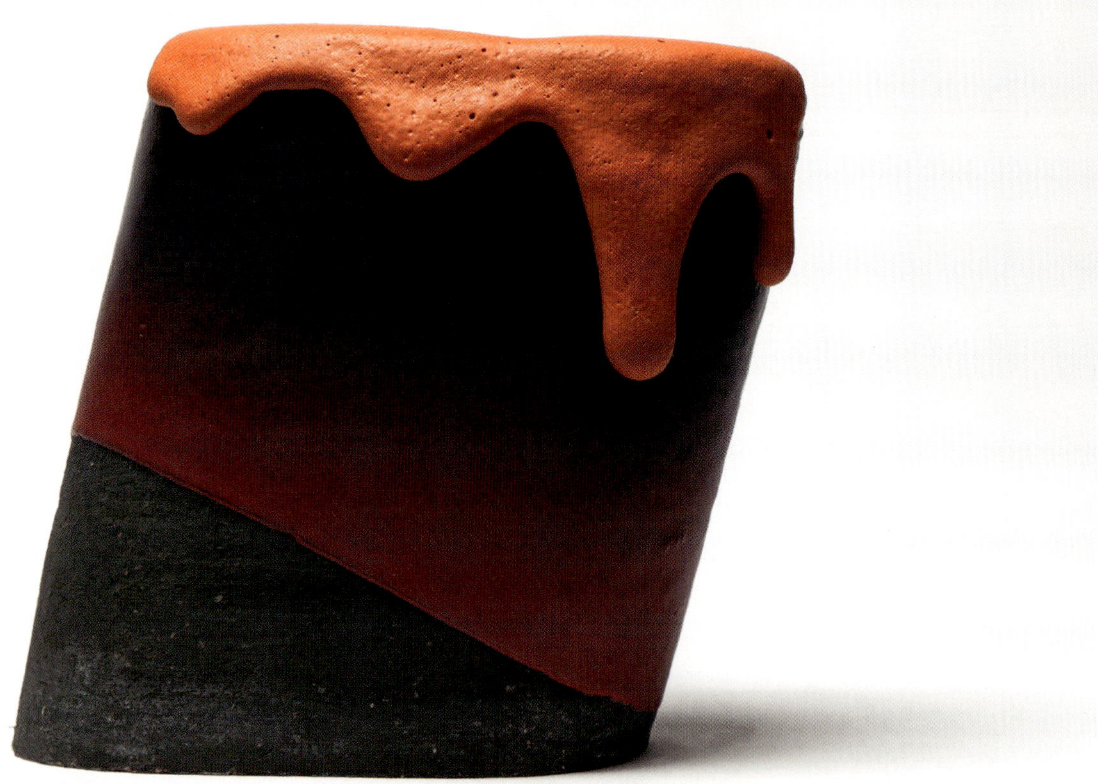

Merced California (2018).
(Photograph by Chao Wang)

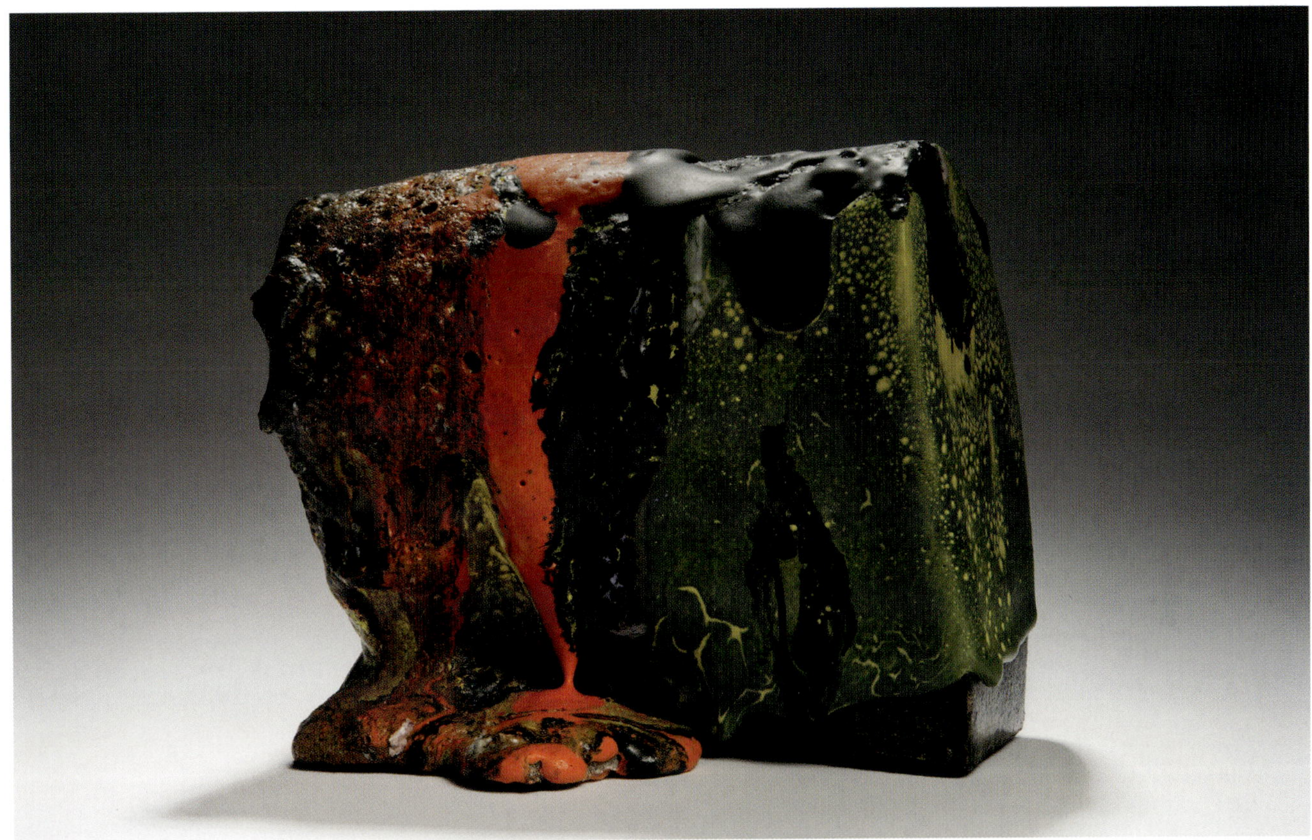

My One-Eyed Cat (2018).
(Photograph by Ester Segarra)

work? How do we express the tensions we might feel about the places in which we have lived, and in which we live now? There is no answer to these questions in Su's work; rather there is a statement of paradox and complexity.

In *Subway* (2018), the lilac glaze has been halted in a neat line towards the bottom of a pale green form. A subterranean world is revealed that would otherwise have been smothered. Perhaps emotions are being blanketed here; a desire to both express and repress feelings turns into a psychological power struggle played out in glaze. If such readings sound grandiose, it should not be forgotten that, above all, these works are beautifully inventive and visually striking. They are vital forms in themselves, whatever narratives they may or may not suggest.

A particularly striking example of this kind of work is *My One-Eyed Cat* (2018), which evokes an entity apparently dissolving into the floor. Su's use of colour is more adventurous here, and the glaze seems to erupt down the form. To achieve such a sense of emergent movement, and fix it in glaze, is a genuine breakthrough achievement. Although one might imagine that her work is closer to the US tradition of ceramics – the likes of Ron Nagle, Ken Price and Brian Rochefort come to mind – her use of glaze in relation to form is distinctly her own. It has a genuinely painterly quality, a style akin to Abstract Expressionism, which is given an enhanced sense of movement by its relationship to form. In *My One-Eyed Cat*, the flattened upper surface of the work, the vertical drop to its side and the pooling of glaze at the

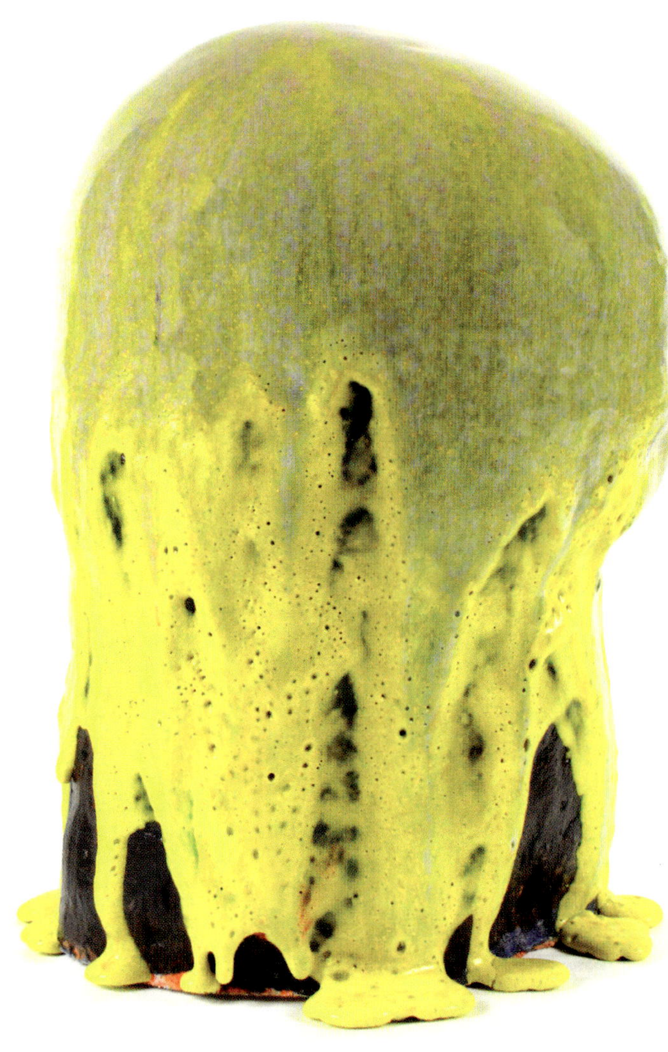

Working Class Hero (2018).
(Photograph by Pam Su)

bottom provide a dramatic sense of movement. The sides of her forms become a kind of refined cliff edge rendered into a highly expressive surface. For me, it is this feeling of movement in the sculpture that makes sense of its title: *My One-Eyed Cat* has the stasis and dynamism of its namesake.

Movement is bought to the fore in two other strong works. The first, *A Perfect Day for Bananafish* (2019), is named after a short story by J.D. Salinger. Published in 1948, the story focuses on the

interweaving nature of relationships, repression, love, violence and depression. As would be expected, Su's sculpture is not a direct sculptural rendering of the narrative, but it does elicit some of the same emotions that Salinger's characters experience.

The top of the sculpture erupts with blood red, which is constrained beneath a bright yellow surface (connecting it with the bright yellow colour of the Banana Fish itself). This mixture pours over the side of the leaning tower to solidify, become darker, and finally pool at the base. The eruption of bright colour at the top of the work, and its diffusion down the sides, symbolizes life and death, love and loss, energy and decay, fused into one statement. It is a masterful work, not only because it has such powerful expression, but also because depicting such a sense of movement through glaze over such a large surface is breaking new ground.

The second, *Working Class Hero* (2019), recalls the 1970 John Lennon song of the same name, and is, the artist tells me, about her father. The piece brings together a number of concerns in her practice. The skull-like head structure of *New York I Love You* is conjoined with the emergent movement of *My One-Eyed Cat*. Here, areas of the base are left exposed by the yellow glaze, giving the form room to breathe. Because of the title, I interpret the sculpture as a kind of concealed head, but nevertheless one that emerges, and, above all, survives. The fantastic yellow glaze, which forms a lilac and silver freckled surface across the top, is wonderfully celebratory. Above all, *Working Class Hero* is a very beautiful work. It seems to stand as a monument to hard-won victories; a parent who has worked hard but is now somehow lost, smothered through time and distance, masked by vanishing memories. It is also a symbol of the painstaking process involved in discovering new kinds of making.

In considering Su's painterly work, I am reminded of the British painter Howard Hodgkin (1932–2017), whose colourful abstract works were formulated as a response to intense emotional recollections of personal events and situations. In an essay written to accompany *Absent Friends*, Hodgkin's last major retrospective (he died shortly before it opened), held at the National Portrait Gallery in London in 2017, Paul Moorhouse (a Senior Curator at the National Portrait Gallery) noted how

> In developing the image, [the artist] seeks equivalence between, on one hand, the original experience, and, on the other, the visual information contained in the painting and the emotions evoked by its expressive character. Equally, however, it is evident that while the artist recognises an equivalence between the painting and its private subject, others may not. When the painting is finished it is put out into the world, at which point it must fend for itself.[47]

Su's work occupies identical territory. Her sculptures are rooted to her own experiences, but they are also abstracted and oblique. Ultimately, it is the viewer who activates the relationship between object, its title, and the artist. As works in the world, Su's pieces must indeed find their own way. Her sculptures may roam, but they are very worthy of being sought.

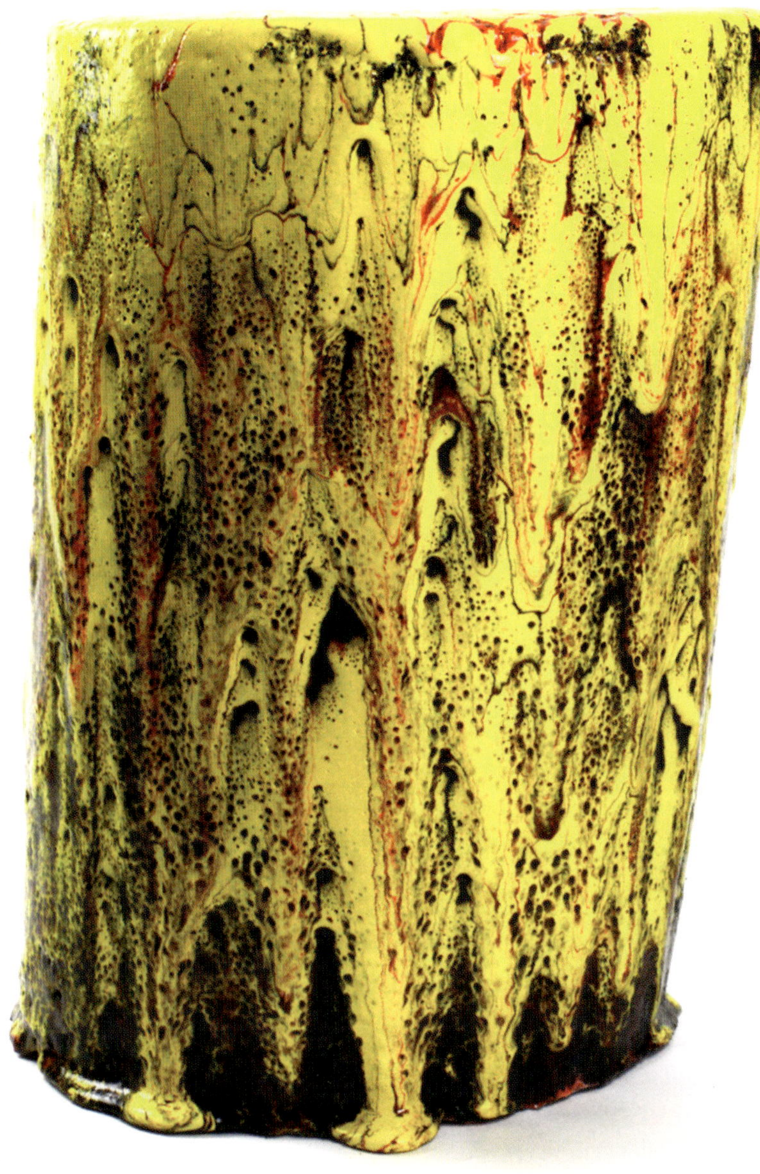

A Perfect Day for Bananafish (2019).
(Photograph by Pam Su)

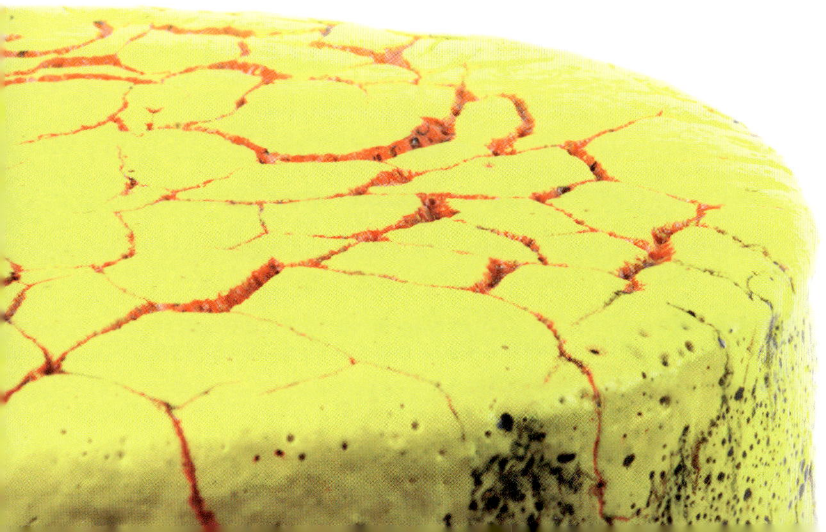

Detail of *A Perfect Day for Bananafish* (2019).
(Photograph by Pam Su)

Benjamin Pearey

Pages from a Diary

Social media affords artists the opportunity to show their work without the intermediary of gallery representation. This is not to demean the significant role that good galleries can play in bringing work to curators, clients and general audiences. However, despite the criticism and the dangers, one of the democratizing side-effects of platforms like Instagram is that they have made unrepresented practice visible. Artists who are nearer the beginning of their career, who are not represented by a gallery, and for whom experimentation is of fundamental importance as they grapple to comprehend their own artistic identities, appear amongst the feeds of their more established peers and mentors. In many ways, this is echoed in the structure of this book.

My first encounter with Benjamin Pearey's work was in the form of a series of social media videos. He dropped heavy objects onto his unfired ceramic sculptures, often architectural and the product of many hours labour, and squashed them. My initial response was bafflement and amusement in equal measure: there was something self-aware, even comic, in being given enough time to read the details of a sculpture, only for a spike or a large wooden pallet to suddenly appear out of nowhere from the top of the frame and puncture it. I wondered if these videos were simply designed to be clickbait. If they were, on me, they worked. But it was only after looking at the photos on his feed, seeing the products of these videos in their final fired state, and watching the style of his work develop at an astonishing pace, that I realized there was more to Pearey than I first thought.

As I write this text, it has not even been two years since he graduated with a BA (Hons) in Ceramics from University of the Creative Arts in Farnham, Surrey. This chapter documents Pearey's stylistic development over a period of only sixteen or so months. During this time, his style has ceaselessly mutated as he has opened up distinctive and innovative lines of enquiry. His work sits in between painting, sculpture, print and ceramics. In this respect, he is emblematic of so many of the emerging generation who find the art/craft debate a conceptual cul-de-sac. As an artist, Pearey does what he does; it just happens to be in clay.

Finding a unified aesthetic within such experimentation is challenging. Perhaps this is as it should be; diversity such as this is testament to an inexhaustible quest for development and reinvention. I have titled this chapter 'Pages from a Diary' for two reasons. The first is that I expect Pearey's work to continue to mutate as it develops. Five years from now it might have diverged significantly from the practice recorded here. It is plausible that revisiting early work for an artist is rather like looking back through a diary, of feeling proud of achievements while also having a nagging feeling that things could have been, should have been, different. This, of course, is how an artist develops: satisfaction is hard won, and when satisfaction finally comes it often demands a new course, a wiping of the slate.

The second reason is that each piece that Pearey makes is a response to a personal event, a feeling, or an impulse. Neither work, nor title, makes reference to what these circumstances might be and Pearey has no interest in divulging them to the public. The work itself is the statement, and in this sense, they are like diaries written in a special code that only the author can understand. To deny autobiography might frustrate those who want to fix the author's intention to an individual piece. But it is also extraordinarily liberating, asking audiences to engage with each work on its own terms and from their own perspective. Pearey's work can be complex, minimal, witty, serious, totemic, abstracted, self-referential of material, demanding, or unassuming. Yet, by insisting that each of his works fend for themselves once they are out in the world, they are also robust and uncompromising.

For his degree show, Pearey produced a range of sculptures that were, in part, a response to the work of Nao Matsunaga (discussed in Chapter 18). Deconstructing and remaking work influenced by another is a natural part of any artist's development, and Pearey was able to explore how

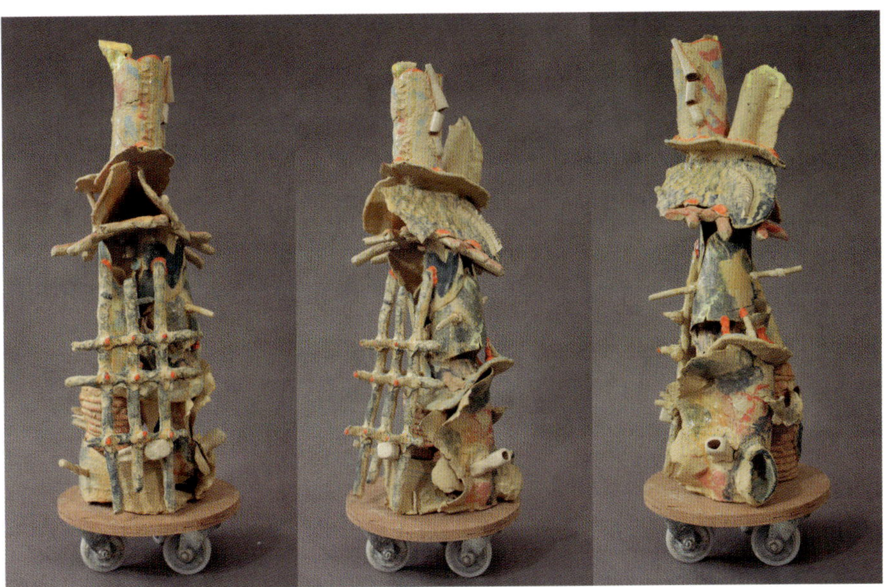

Angry Rabbit (2018).
(Photograph by Georgia Sewell)

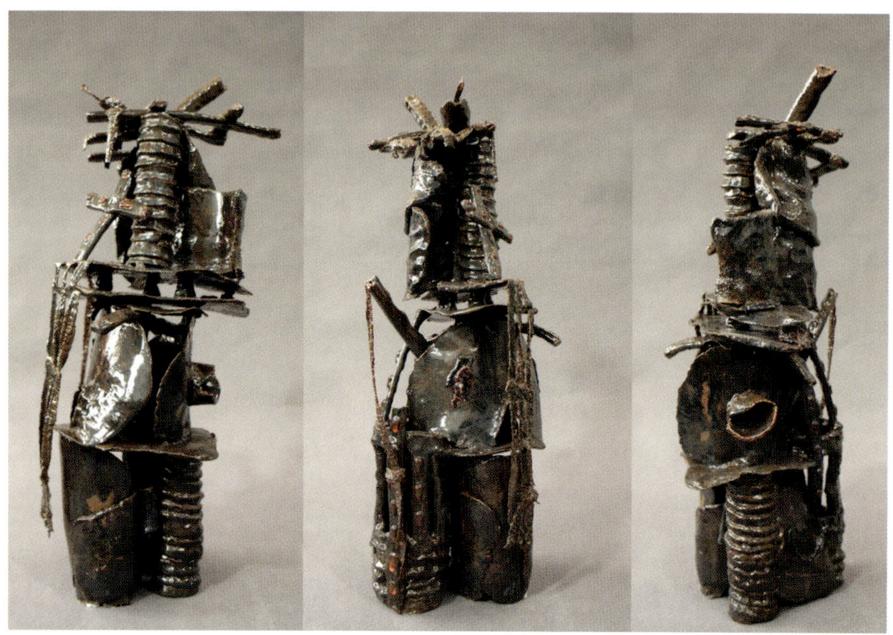

Shiny Dark Thing
(*With Ergonomic Handle*) (2018).
(Photograph by Georgia Sewell)

narratives could be deployed in a language that was indirect and fragmentary. *Angry Rabbit* (2018) has a surface resemblance to Matsunaga's work, but in its totemic structure it is given a psychological narrative all of its own. The ears, head, teeth and stick-like arms render this rabbit as dystopic; a kind of macho reimagining of *Alice in Wonderland's* White Rabbit, replete with penis. What is making the rabbit so angry? There are many possible interpretations, ranging from animal rights to a commentary on twenty-first century masculinity, and it would do the work a disservice to propose only one reading.

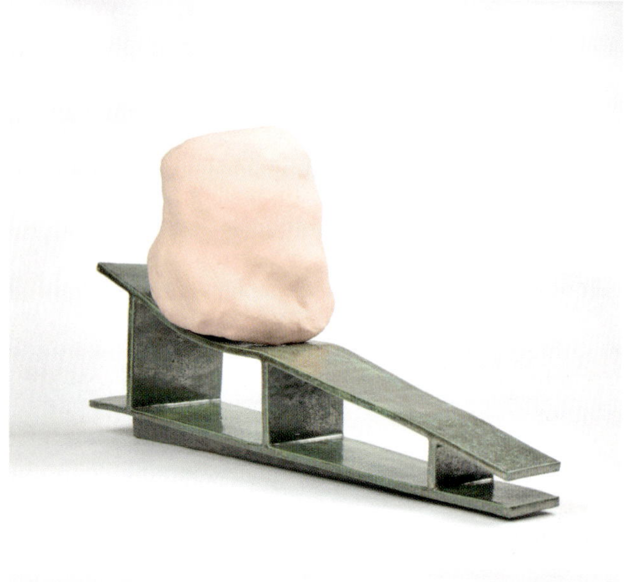

Indestructible Croc (2018).
(Photograph by Benjamin Pearey)

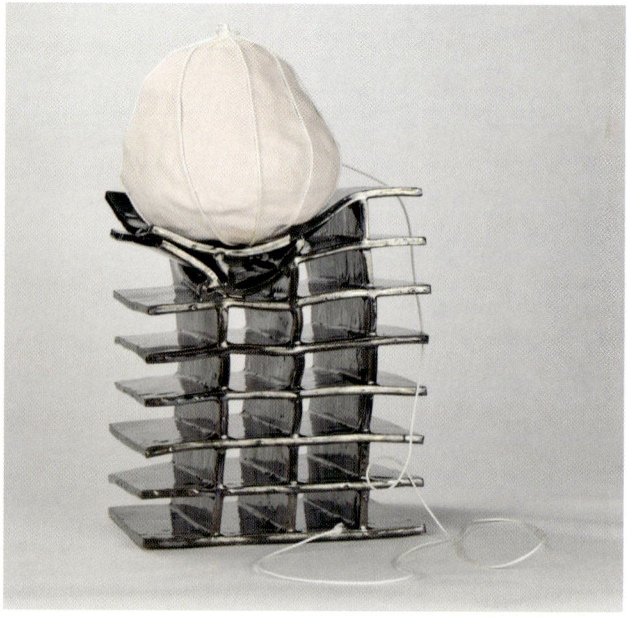

Bon-B (2018).
(Photograph by Benjamin Pearey)

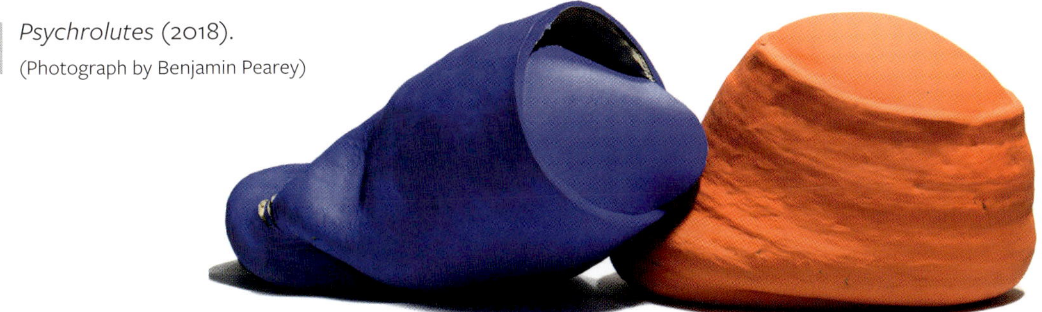

Psychrolutes (2018).
(Photograph by Benjamin Pearey)

Other sculptures in this body of work appear more concerned with sculptural space, volume and presence. *Shiny Dark Thing (With Ergonomic Handle)* (2018) has greater spatial presence by virtue of its silhouette, and the spaces in between segments are as important as the structure itself. At points, the shine of the glaze catches the light, bringing attention to the rounded three-dimensions of individual parts. By opting for a darker surface treatment, these sculptures seem more original, more abstract, and less compromising than *Angry Rabbit*. In them, Pearey uncovered key ideas – structure, intuition, abstraction and monotone colours – that were to be developed over the months that followed.

Bon-B and *Indestructible Croc* (both 2018) were amongst the first body of work Pearey produced after completing his undergraduate studies. Here, structures are sculpted from slabs of clay, which are then damaged by the impact of an object. These works are further investigations into architecture as a means of spatial control, but they also bond robustness with fragility. They become self-referential comments on the physical properties of ceramics, of the strength of the material once fired, but also its disposition to

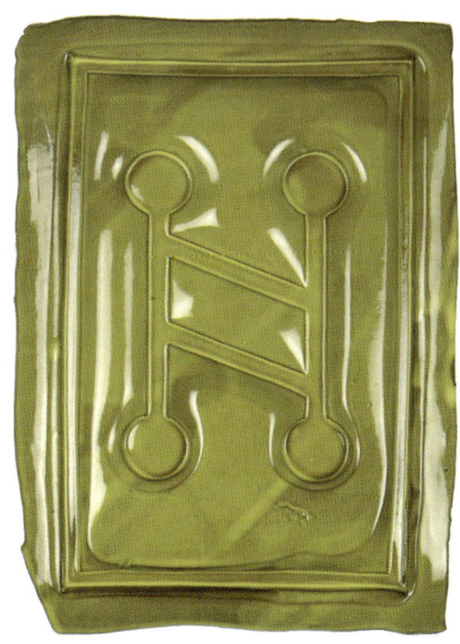

Slab 2 (2019).
(Photograph by Benjamin Pearey)

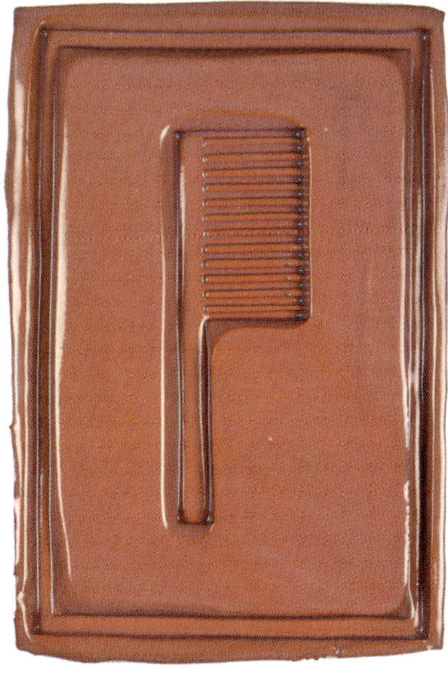

Slab 3 (2019).
(Photograph by Benjamin Pearey)

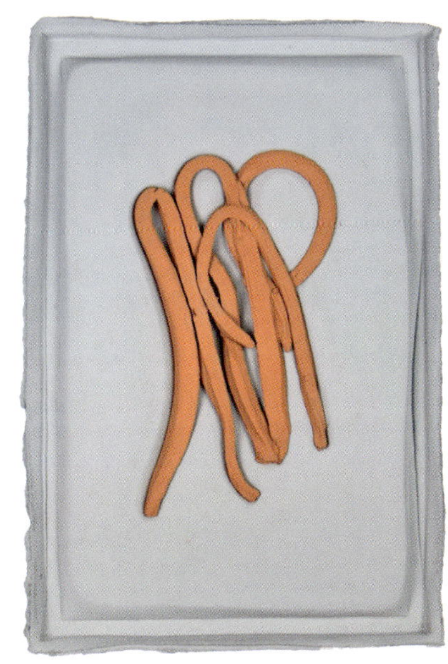

Slab 8 (2019).
(Photograph by Benjamin Pearey)

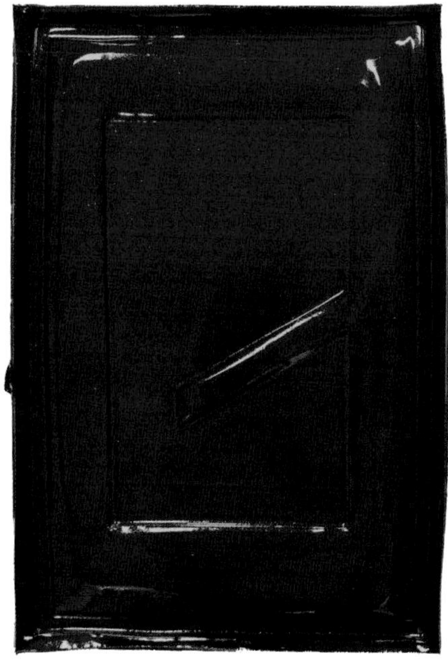

Slab 12 (2019).
(Photograph by Benjamin Pearey)

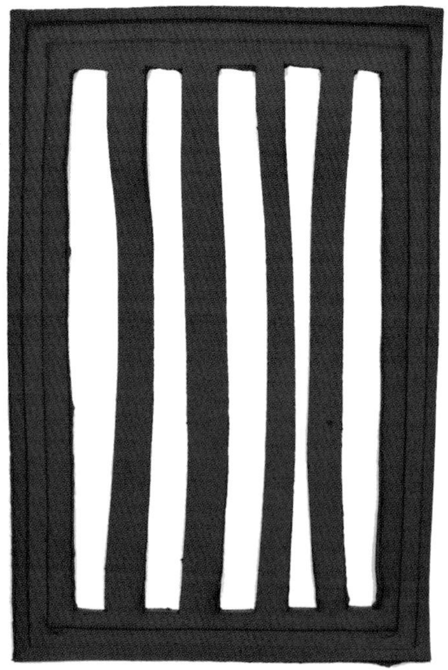

Slab 26 (2019).
(Photograph by Benjamin Pearey)

break through shock. In capturing this double sense, they also express action. The act of dropping objects on these sculptures when they are leather-hard enables each work to describe stasis and movement, structure and anarchy, pattern and spontaneity, in a single statement. Is there an emotional undertone to these works? Perhaps there is a veiled comment on how weight – in the psychological sense – is carried by masculine structures supposed to be stout and strong, but, as before, this can only be supposition. In any case, other works more readily lend themselves to narrative reading.

Psychrolutes (2018) takes its name from a deep-sea fish that has a large, round, protruding head and is known for ambushing its prey. Here, the blue form reaches in, its top open, its lid curved like a repugnant tongue. Quite understandably, the orange form backs away in revulsion.

If these forms document observations and experiences, the slab series of work (2019) are akin to pages from the artist's diary. Pearey frequently set himself the challenge of making one piece a day, to set down in clay what was happening in his life, or how he felt, at a specific moment in time. The resulting slabs were produced relatively quickly by rolling out clay, using a wooden frame to create edges, and then making impressions into the central pictorial space. If the result was considered good enough, the piece would be glazed and fired; if not, it would simply be re-rolled and used again. In this respect, the slabs are the ceramic equivalent of the woodblock print; they are titled as sequential numbers – as a unique series of editions. Because they lack specific titles, the emotional impetus behind each work is obscured and it is up to the viewer to interpret what they might mean. Some of the slabs use objects from the everyday to make impressions into the clay (*Slab 3*), others use shaped pieces of wood to make patterns (*Slab 2, Slab 12*); some have clay additions

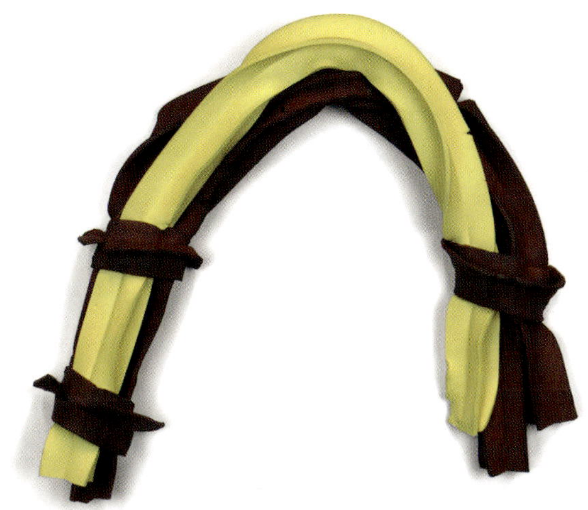

Slab 31 (2019).
(Photograph by Benjamin Pearey)

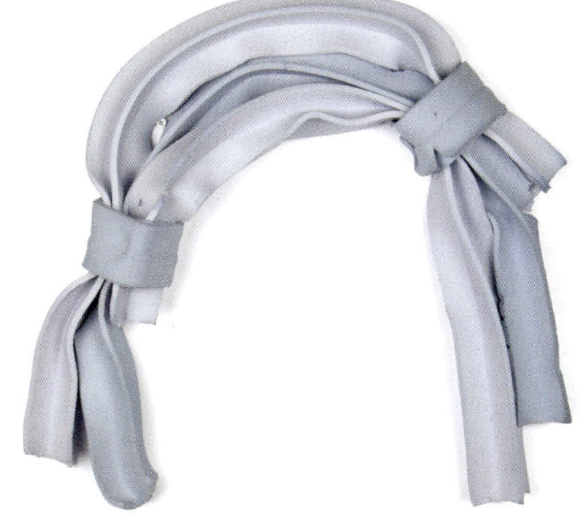

Slab 47 (2019).
(Photograph by Benjamin Pearey)

(*Slab 8*), while others have had sections removed (*Slab 26*). What is the significance of a hairbrush, an image associated with domesticity? What does colour come to symbolize? Are those the bars of a prison? Does *Slab 48* suggest that one person feels isolated, as the odd one out in a group? The slabs hint at states of mind, but nothing is confirmed.

All of the slabs are contoured, but some are more three-dimensional than others. In *Slab 31* and *Slab 47*, clay is shaped and folded into two contoured lines that are fastened by clay strips. In *Slab 31* there are two distinct colours – terracotta and yellow – suggesting two different entities suspended in a relationship. In *Slab 47*, the contoured lines have become the same colour, a light blue. These modifications are suggestive of changes in state, of fusing together. They almost look like fabric curtains tied back, inviting speculations that one is an image of unease, and the other of settled domesticity. Yet, if things start to look straightforward, the entangled lines of *Slab 49* demonstrate complexity. In this slab, the contoured lines are interwoven conveying a sense of flux. The framing device of earlier works

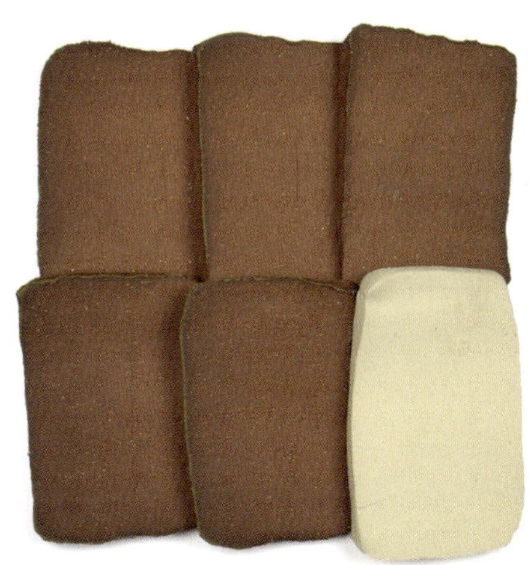

Slab 48 (2019).
(Photograph by Benjamin Pearey)

in the series has vanished, and the sculpture has no obvious base upon which to rest. Certainty has been lost to turmoil; in its place there comes a restless wrestling with something, or with someone.

This sense of uncertainty was further expressed in the named work *Double Bind* (2019). This sculpture has an emergent sense of movement, and demonstrates how Pearey has, through a constant and

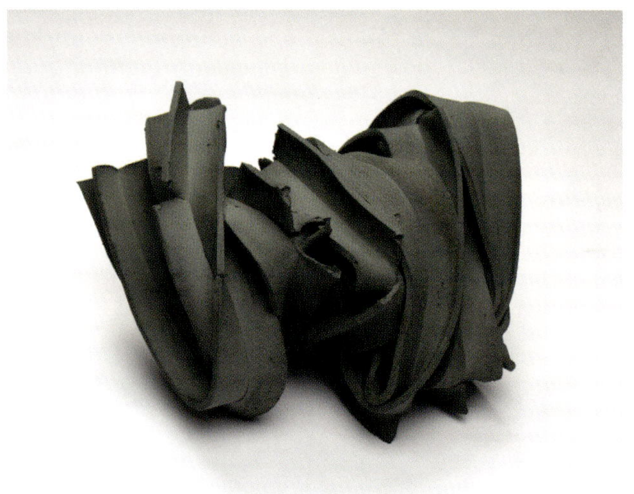

Slab 49 (2019).
(Photograph by Benjamin Pearey)

daily practice, absorbed something from the making of each piece, and relentlessly evaluated his work. The piece has been made by pressing clay through an extruder which, although not especially technically demanding, is difficult to control. Thus, getting the right shape and form is not simple. Working with chance always courts disaster, but Pearey has a strong and immediate reactive instinct that enables

his work to compellingly teeter on the edge of order and anarchy. *Double Bind* is successful because, in keeping with the best of his output, it exhibits states of contradiction. There is a sense of collapse as the clay has landed from the extruder to create the form, but there is also expansion in the upper part of the sculpture, which rears upwards in curiosity towards the top. There is both linearity and circularity in the form, giving the work a strong sense of dynamic movement: it looks like it is being formed in front of our very eyes. Yet it also breaks and folds in on itself, upsetting the clean lines with textural cracks that add a peculiar rhythm to the surface. Ultimately it is a kind of planned spontaneity, a double bind that is the title of the work, but also forms the heart of Pearey's current practice.

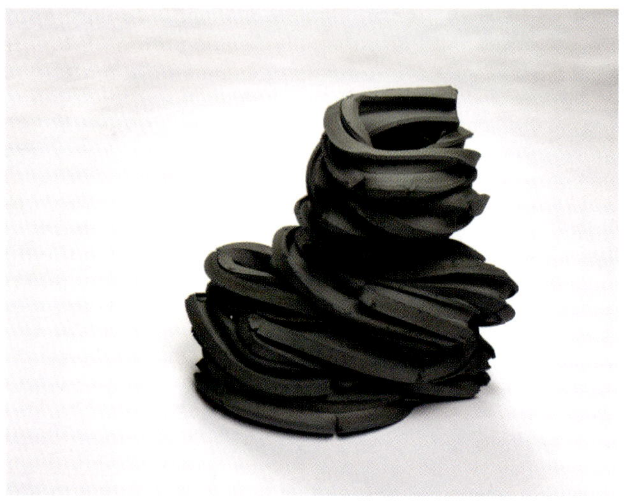

Double Bind (2019).
(Photograph by Benjamin Pearey)

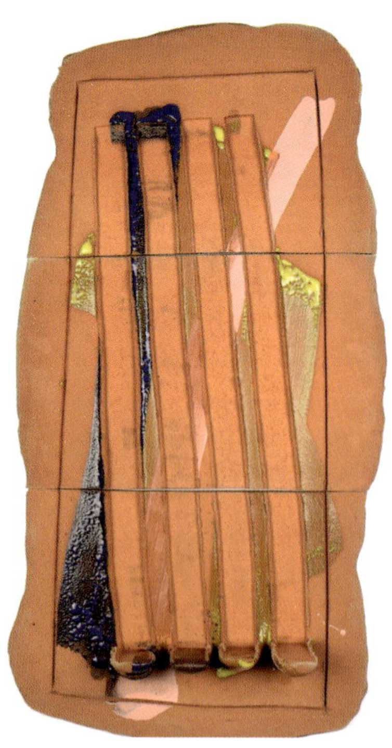

Slab 51 (2019).
(Photograph by Benjamin Pearey)

Aneta Regel

Ceramic Sculptor

<table>
<tr>
<td>

I knock on the stone's door

– It's me, let me in.

I've heard of your vast empty halls,

unseen, barrenly beautiful,

earless, echoless, untrodden.

Admit, even you know little of this.

– Vast, empty halls – says the stone –

but there's no room in them.

Beautiful they may be, but alien

to your beggarly senses.

You may recognize me; but experience me

– never.

My whole surface lies towards you;

my whole interior is turned away.[48]

</td>
<td>

Pukam do drzwi kamienia.

– To ja, wpuść mnie.

Słyszałam, że są w tobie wielkie puste sale,

nieoglądane, piękne nadaremnie,

głuche, bez echa czyichkolwiek kroków.

Przyznaj, że sam niedużo o tym wiesz.

– Wielkie i puste sale – mówi kamień –

ale w nich miejsca nie ma.

Piękne, być może, ale poza gustem

twoich ubogich zmysłów.

Możesz mnie poznać, nie zaznasz mnie

nigdy.

Całą powierzchnią zwracam się ku tobie,

a całym wnętrzem leżę odwrócony.[49]

</td>
</tr>
</table>

The above extract is from the poem *Conversation with a Stone (Rozmowa z kamieniem)* by the 1996 Nobel Prize-winning poet Wislawa Szymborska (1923–2012). The meaning of the poem has been subject to much critical discussion. For some, the stone symbolizes a partner unable to open up to the love of another. For others, the speaker's inability to enter the stone stands

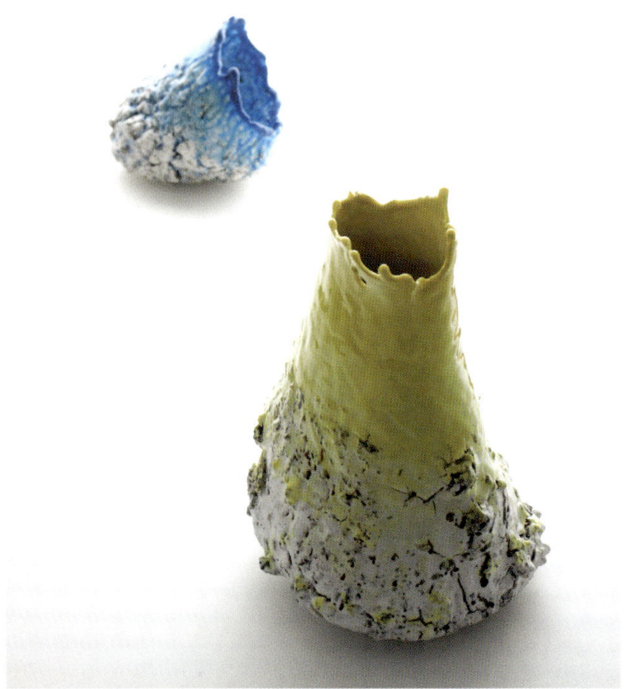

Raining Stones [Yellow and Blue] 2006.
(Photograph by Sylvain Deleu)

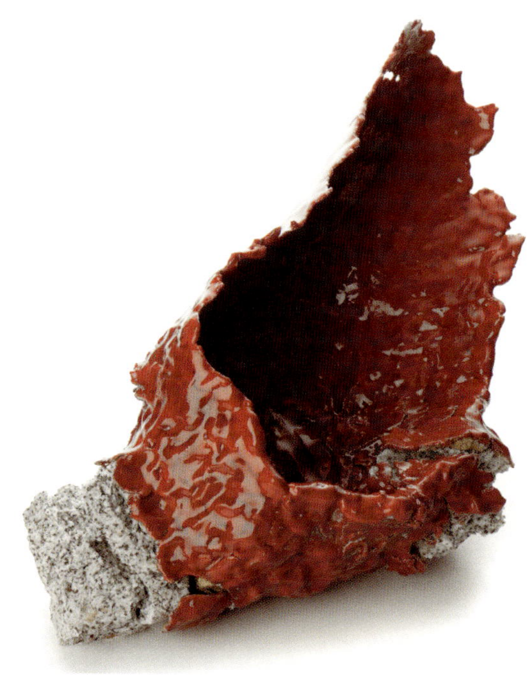

Raining Stones [Red] 2007.
(Photograph by Sylvain Deleu)

for human mortality, even the inability of mortal beings to comprehend the perpetual existence of the natural world.

Regel's sculptures, like Szymborska's poem, explore surface and interior. Inspired by the natural

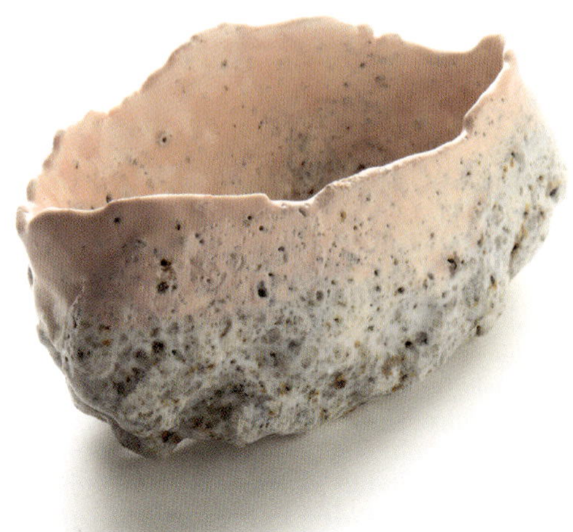

Raining Stones [Pink] 2007.
(Photograph by Sylvain Deleu)

world, Regel's work is concerned with emotional expression, a depiction of interior landscapes through the invocation of exterior terrains. Although Regel has an emotional impulse or conceptual idea behind the creation of each work, this is of importance only to her. Her sculptures are visual poems that do not supply definitive meanings. Trained in her native Poland as a fine artist focusing on sculpture, she has been based in London since she embarked upon ceramics courses at the University of Westminster in 2003, followed by a period at the Royal College of Art, which concluded in 2006. While her early post-degree work was nominally rooted to the form of the vessel, she has since moved towards a freer evocation of natural forms to communicate emotion more intensely. Regel's work revels in what is revealed and what is masked; what the exterior surface will permit us to see, but also what the interior shields from prying eyes.

Some of Regel's sculptures have evolved from individual strands of investigation into series, such as *Raining Stones*. The early vessel-like forms in this series have a strong sense of compositional equilibrium. They balance weightiness with lightness, stony coarseness with planes of smooth porcelain. To name the works after 'stones' is to imply a heaviness; should they strike during descent there would be sharp blows to the skin. Indeed, their granular, weighty bases compel them to the floor; they speak of recent impact even as they sit proudly on a surface. Sensations of recent motion are increased by the fine walls around the central sculptural cavity, which evoke flow like the tail of a comet.

As a whole, the sculptures distil movement akin to a raindrop landing in a puddle, its splash suspended in time. Bright glazes in primary colours signpost the temperament of each piece. Bold yellows impart a zestful energy; reds signal explosiveness or bodily interiority; blues suggest a damp coldness; pinks exude a soft opulence. As we enter into the sculpture an interior emotional landscape is alluded to. Are these sculptures somehow representative of memories? Or might they be fragments of emotion that now 'rain down' on us as a part of our interactions with others? In some works, the emotional landscape is readily accessible; in others, it is enclosed and seemingly unfathomable. Like Szymborska's poem, Regel uses symbols derived from nature to ask us questions about our own interior states, our emotional relationships with others and, of course, to nature.

As Regel's work progressed, exterior space was expanded as interior spaces were contracted. One particular body of work (not formally titled as a series) was inspired by tree trunks and branches, though they eschew a straightforward imitation of nature. Complex glaze surfaces produced from numerous firings afford them an ethereal presence, producing a surreal forest of the uncanny. Trees, of course, are a prescient symbol of landscape and thus have a potency in European folk customs. Christmas trees, for instance, have evolved from the pine tree as a pagan symbol for seasonal renewal and longevity. In Poland, there is a famous folk poem, often cited around New Year celebrations, that links trees to cosmology:

There is a pine tree standing in the middle of the yard	Stoi sosna śród podworca
Your nectar grows on the pine	Na tej sośnie twój pożytek rośnie
And there is a barrel of tar on the bottom	A w spodku becka smoły
And angry bees in the middle,	A w środku jare pscoły,
And four wheels on top	A na wierzchu stery koła
And a falcon on every wheel.	W każdym kole po sokole.[50]

Here, the tree stands for fundamental principles. The tree is divided into three sections representing birth, marriage, and death.[51] The four wheels and birds at the top of the tree represent the four sides of the world.[52] As Brzozowska-Krajka has argued in her study of Polish folklore, 'the tree growing in the centre of the world puts the world into order (*axis mundi*) and combines all its parts. It is an important element of cosmological myths, pointing to the substance of all things'.[53] Although Regel's sculptures could be about cosmological potency – the seemingly burnt trees symbolizing deforestation or the rapaciousness of wildfires – the poem leads me to consider her works as representative of individual bodies. These twig-less branches,

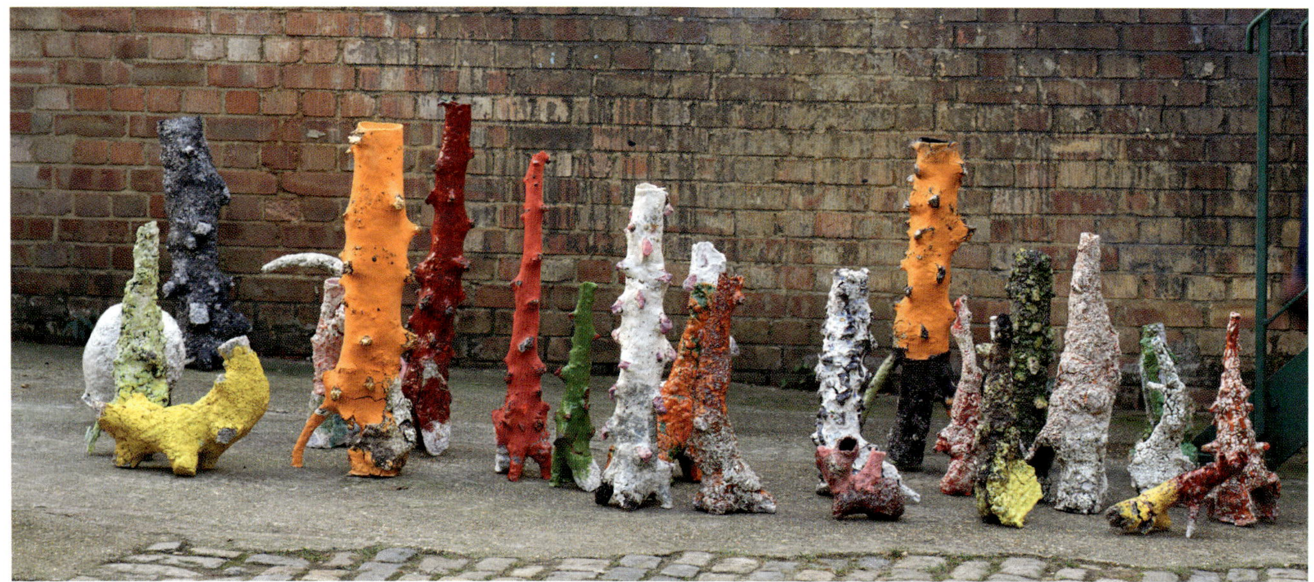

Group of untitled tree-like forms.
(Photograph by Sylvain Deleu)

where each knot seems to reference the trauma of loss, or a change in life direction, could stand as an emotional biography of an unknown individual. Biographies afford the appearance of linearity and logic, but they never really are; all of our lives are the product of choices, the cutting of possibilities, the curtailing of alternatives. The horizontal direction of each sculpture, and the nodules that adorn the surface, capture this parallel sense of growth and curtailment. As before, glaze invites speculation about the nature of each sculpted biography: of joy, triumph over adversity, bitterness or regret.

As when a young olive plant
Among tall trees – lacking twigs
And leaves, being but a tender shoot,
Climbs in her mother's path –
Lopped by a hasty pruner's knife
That clears sharp thorns and rampant growth,
Soon wilts, and shorn of natural strength
Drops to the feet of her beloved dam
So it befell my gentle girl.
Hardly risen above ground
Under their gaze,
Veiled in poisonous fumes
Of dreadful Death, she fell insensible
At her care-full parents' feet [...].

Jako oliwka mała pod wysokim sadem
Idzie z ziemie ku górze macierzyńskim szladem,
Jeszcze ani gałązek, ani listków rodząc,
Sama tylko dopiro szczupłym prątkiem wschodząc;
Tę, jesli ostre ciernie lub rodne pokrzywy
Uprzątając, sadownik podciął ukwapliwy,
Mdleje zaraz, a zbywszy siły przyrodzonej,
Upada przed nogami matki ulubionej.
Takci sie mej namilszej Orszuli dostało:
Przed oczyma rodziców swoich rostąc, mało
Od ziemie sie co wznióswszy, duchem zaraźliwym
Srogiej śmierci otchniona, rodzicom troskliwym
U nóg martwa upadła [...].54

Because trees grow higher and thicker with age, the respective height of each sculpture potentially signifies the length of a human life. Such a reading recalls a lament by the classical Polish poet Jan Kochanowski (1530–84), an extract from which is given on page 84. Seen through the prism of Kochanowski's writing, Regel's work offers a stark, even brutal, depiction of life and its extinction. The smaller sculptures allude to a life cut short, stunted growth, wasted potential. As leafless, ashen-bleached branches, these sculptures confront us with the prospect of death, even as they represent the tree, the symbol of perpetual life.

One line in Kochanowski's poem stands out as particularly appropriate for ceramics: 'veiled in poisonous fumes of dreadful death'. The toxicity of firing – the noxious fumes created by metal and organic glaze materials as they burn – makes ceramics symbolically redolent with death, brittleness and permanence. For most artists, to fire a work is, in effect, to 'kill' it; playful malleability with form is curtailed by the fixity of flame. Yet, any ceramic artist worth their salt can resurrect great life and vitality from this 'funeral pyre'. Indeed, Regel has developed techniques that enable her to alter the actual form of a sculpture across firings. By mixing stones and porcelain together, previously fired pieces can be augmented or fused together in new ways. This enables her to retain a playful approach until she is much surprised by the results. It is at this point, when the unexpected is achieved, that the artist considers the work complete.

The interweaving of life and death locates Regel's work 'in between' states. This 'in betweenness' is most obviously expressed in the *Metamorphosis* series. From the inception of a piece, Regel contemplates how glaze can be deployed so that it transforms in the kiln to become an integral part of the actual form. Certainly, Regel's use of glaze has

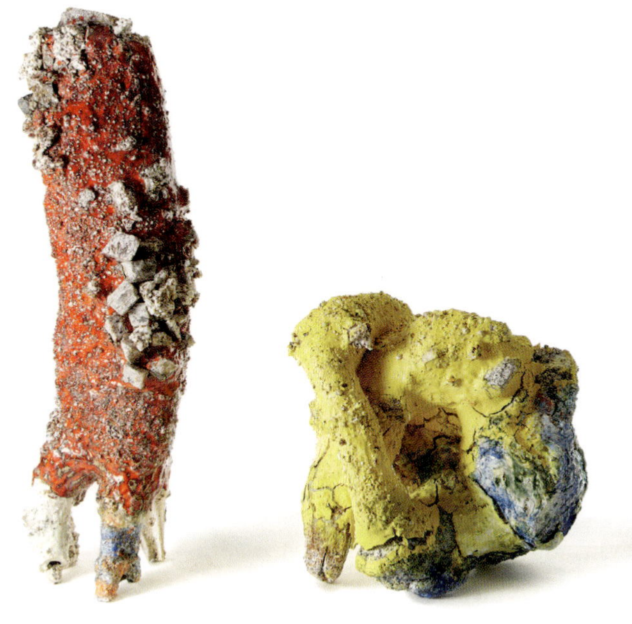

Elka (2018) and *Lonia* (2018).
(Photograph by Matthew Booth)

become more nuanced and painterly. The sculptures work against simplistic distinctions between painting (where oil paint can be applied in thick layers to become textural, even sculptural) and ceramic sculpture (where glazed surfaces can create the same depth of colour as oils). Of all Regel's works, I find the *Metamorphosis* series conveys impenetrability with the greatest force. The rich surfaces express emotion, but as the vessel form has been discarded, the interior is walled off from the viewer. This leads us to question whether the emotional expression presented to the world is in fact genuine or merely a façade. The importance of the interior is further alluded to in the twisted, knot-like pieces, where the form coils in on itself, squeezing itself ever tighter in an apparent state of nervous anxiety.

Regel's preference for abstraction rather than realism in her sculptural investigations of the natural world enable her to transcend 'organic abstraction'.

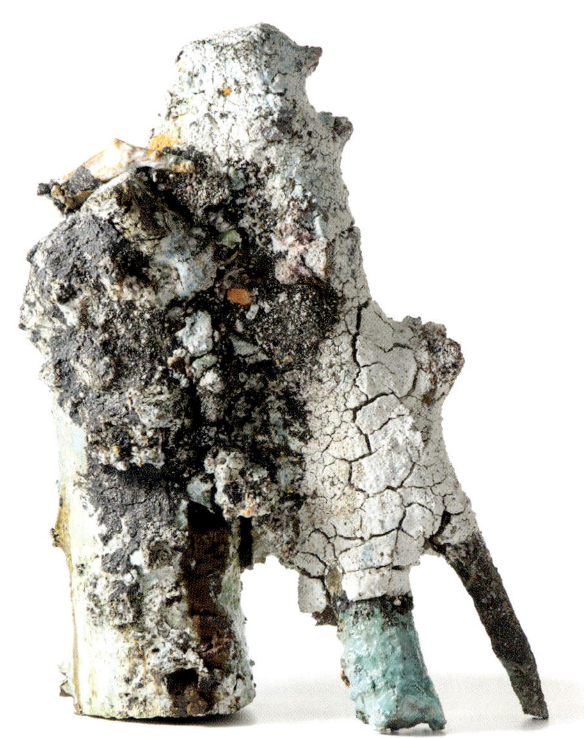

Landscape 5 (2018).
(Photograph by Matthew Booth)

Hers is a definitively emotional terrain. Larger works, or groupings of work, seem to symbolize, if not personify, relationships. When *Volcanic Totem 1* and *Volcanic Totem 2* (both 2019) are placed together, for instance, the orange trunk-like form seeks to engage with the other. Narratives of acceptance, rejection, incompatibility, or the attraction of opposites can be read into these works, but in the same way that their interiors are hidden, so a definite meaning is never confirmed. The centrality of emotion to Regel's work is seemingly captured in *Ba* (2019), its title suggestive of sheep, but for me a work more akin to the shape of a heart, its legs a reminder that hearts can wander.

In one sense, Regel's works are testament to a love of nature, its perpetuity and ethereality. Yet, if Szymborska's poem captures our inability to fully experience nature, this appears to be reflected in Regel's enfolded forms, their apertures hinting at an interior that we will never comprehend. By extension, we might concede that Regel's sculptures express

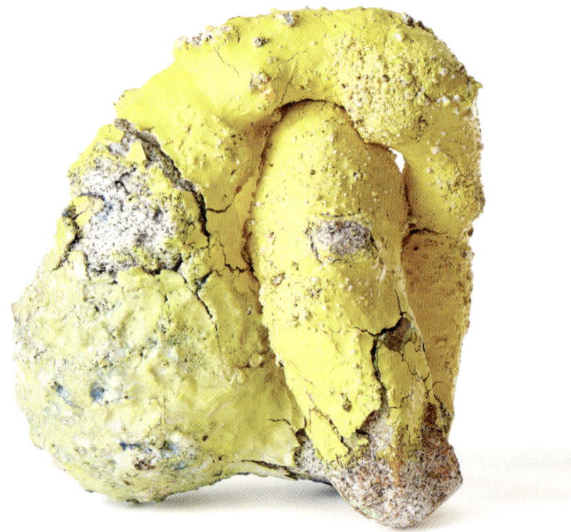
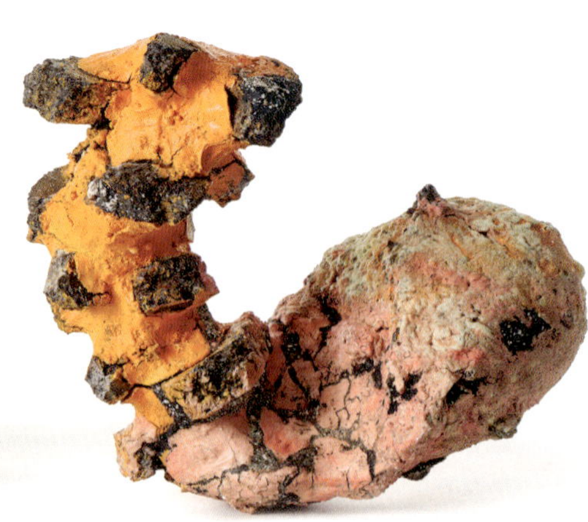

Lonia (2018) and *Untitled* (2018).
(Photograph by Matthew Booth)

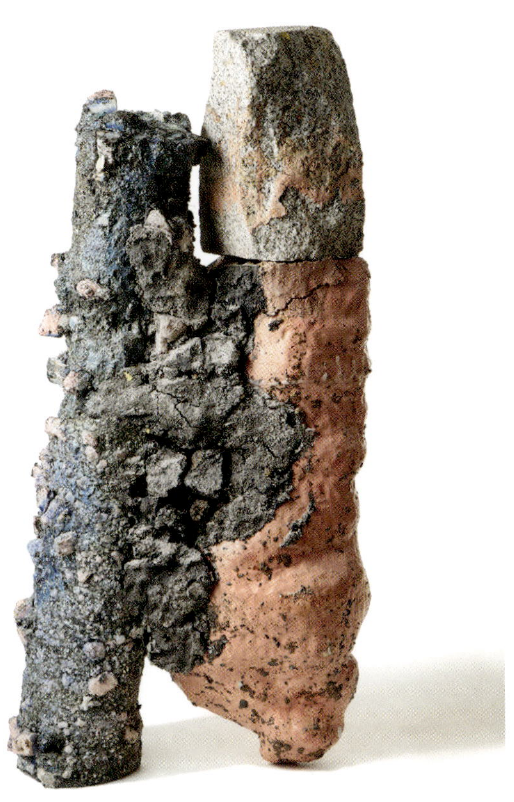

Nomad (2020).
(Photograph by Matthew Booth)

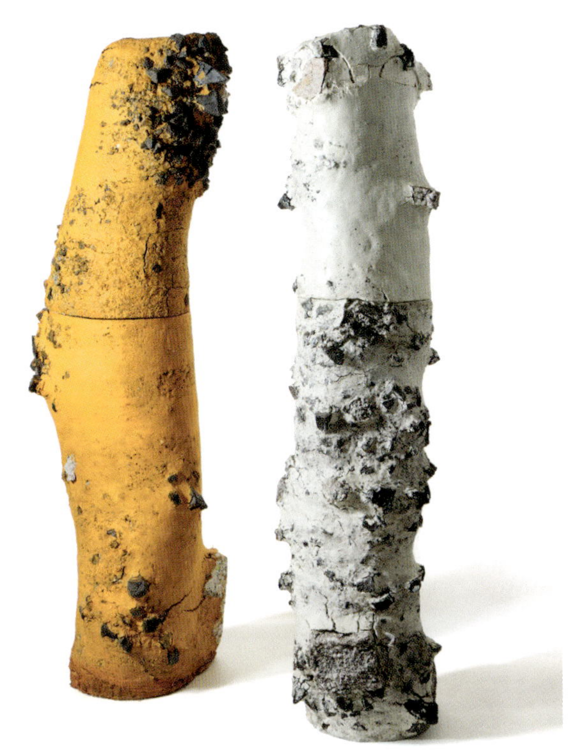

Volcanic Totem 1 and *2* (2019).
(Photograph by Matthew Booth)

our inability to fully grasp the feelings and experiences of others. However, this gloomy reading is at odds with her joyous use of colour and wonderfully tactile surfaces, a language that can be widely understood. Perhaps there is a sense that, despite the existential separation, connections between people remain vital. As with Szymborska's *Conversation with a Stone*, Regel's work proposes that whilst we may never fully experience an/other, through conversation we might at least come to understand.

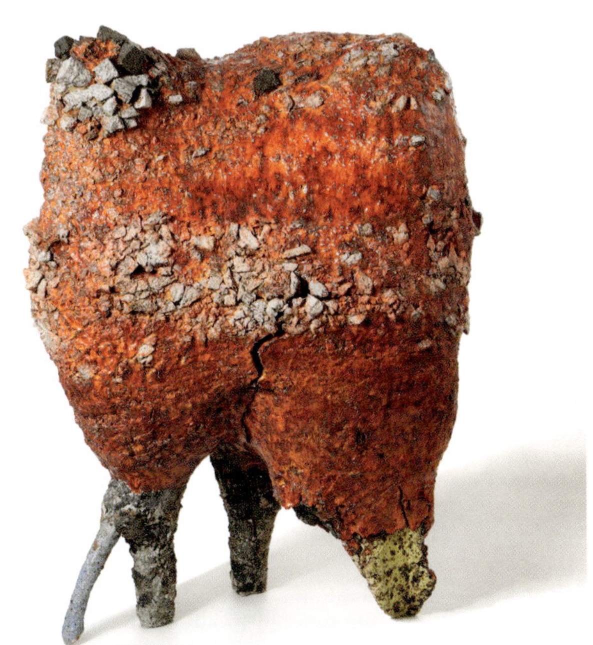

RIGHT: *Ba* (2019).
(Photograph by Matthew Booth)

Nathan Mullis

Between Worlds

> Organic Abstraction was the fictile arts' first aesthetic style. Before the arrival of the more analytical and self-conscious aesthetic of classical form, potters relied upon the natural forms and surfaces that they found within their environment for inspiration. The earliest pots came from mimicing [*sic*] vegetable forms such as gourds (that were probably man's first vessels) or from copying basketry made from grasses, bark and twigs.[55]

In his essay for the 1995 Crafts Council exhibition *Pandora's Box*, Garth Clark observed that organic abstraction 'refers to a loosely defined style characterized by an ongoing exploration of biomorphic or organic form and surface'.[56] As a natural substance, clay is perhaps the ideal material for capturing the elemental. One of the most acclaimed twentieth-century British ceramic sculptors in this style, Ewen Henderson (1934–2000), referenced the landscape in both painting and ceramic practice. He referred to himself as neither a painter nor a sculptor, but as 'an artist in fluxed earth'.[57] Similarly, often indebted to landscape in both form and title, Gordon Baldwin's autobiographical sculptures have been hugely significant to the development of British ceramic sculpture.[58] Clark observed that early pieces by Jill Crowley and Ruth Duckworth, as well some work by Henry Pim and Sara Radstone, exhibited a similar rawness indebted to rugged urban structures in a state of collapse.[59]

The sculptures of Nathan Mullis exhibit facets of Clark's definition of organic abstraction. They

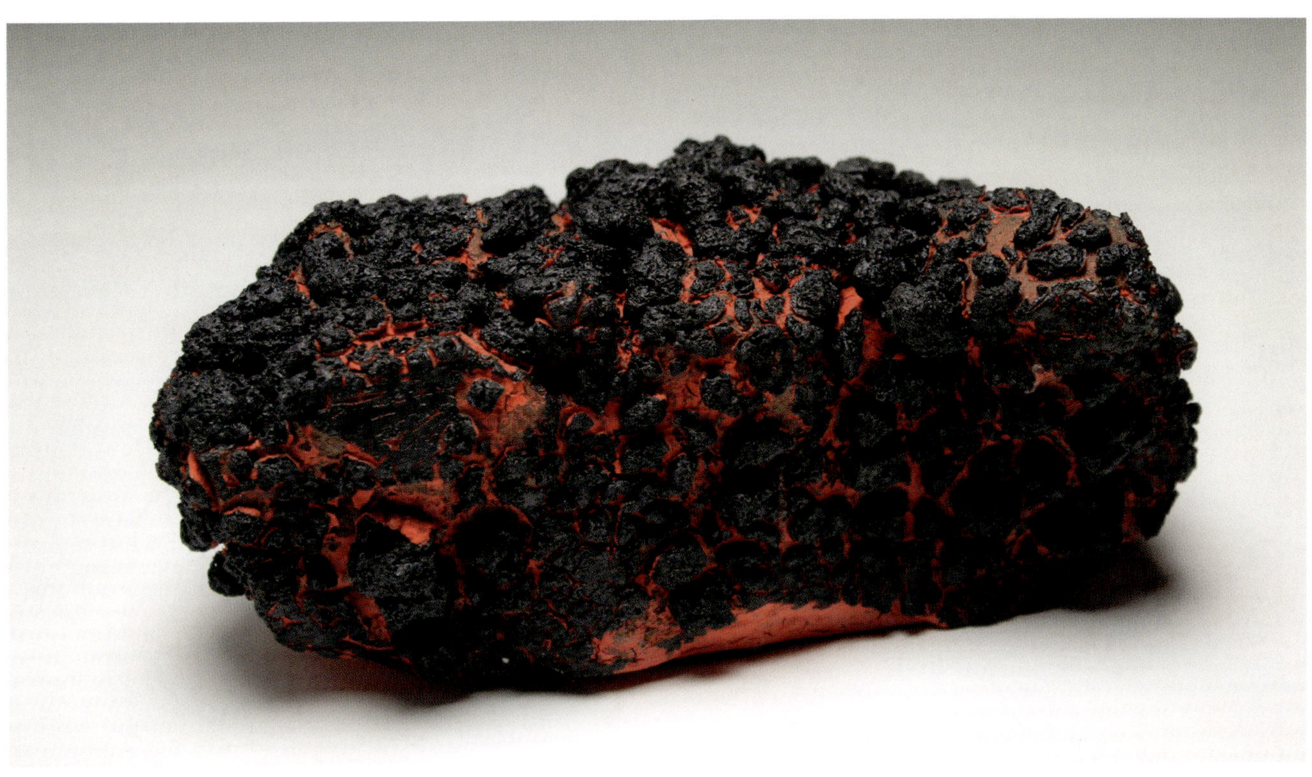

Small Worlds [Red and Black].
(Photograph by Nathan Mullis)

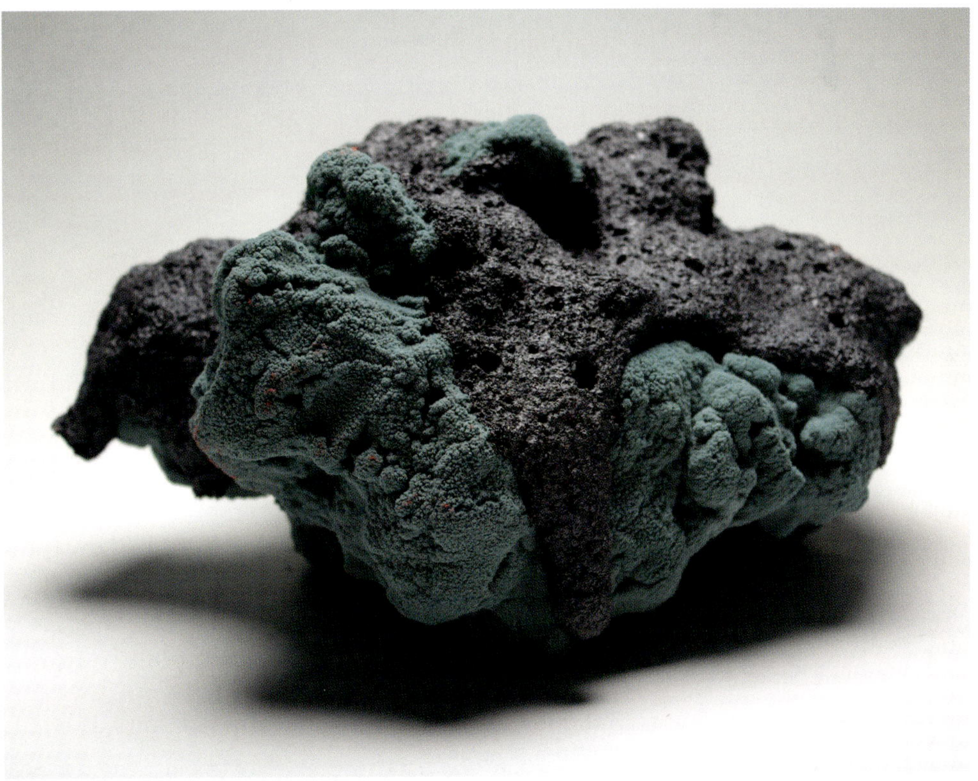

Small Worlds
[Green and Black].
(Photograph by Nathan Mullis)

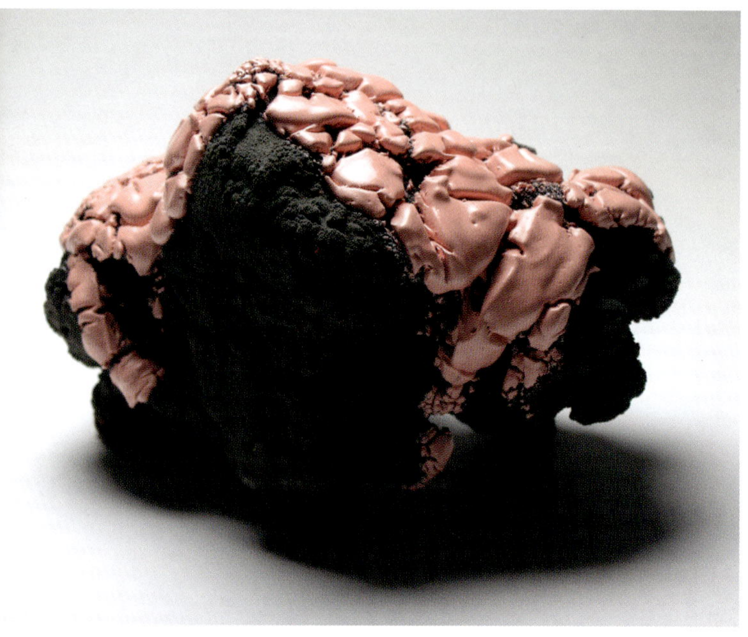

Small Worlds [Dark Brown and Pink].
(Photograph by Nathan Mullis)

reference geology, configurations of rock, volcanoes and eruptions; the surfaces undulate like the Welsh landscape that lies beyond his Cardiff studio. Yet, his sculptures do not seem especially 'natural'. In fact, they appear resolutely man-made. Organic abstraction is a loose term that is not dependent upon representations of the natural, and in any case, all ceramics involve the mark of the artist's hand, their artistic intuition and technical skill.[60] Nevertheless, the works discussed here sit uneasily with the kinds of organic abstraction observed by Clark. This partly arises from Mullis's palette: the brilliant deployment of vibrant blues, shocking pinks and gaudy greens do not look 'natural'. Rather, they seem to have materialized from another world, from the reveries of science fiction

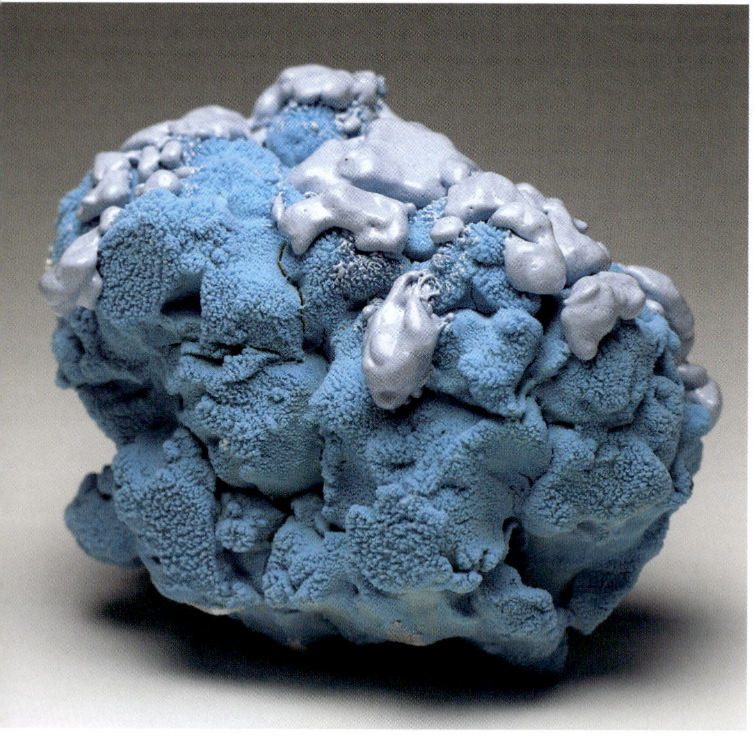

Small Worlds [Two Blues].
(Photograph by Nathan Mullis)

RIGHT: Detail of *Small Worlds* sculpture.
(Photograph by Nathan Mullis)

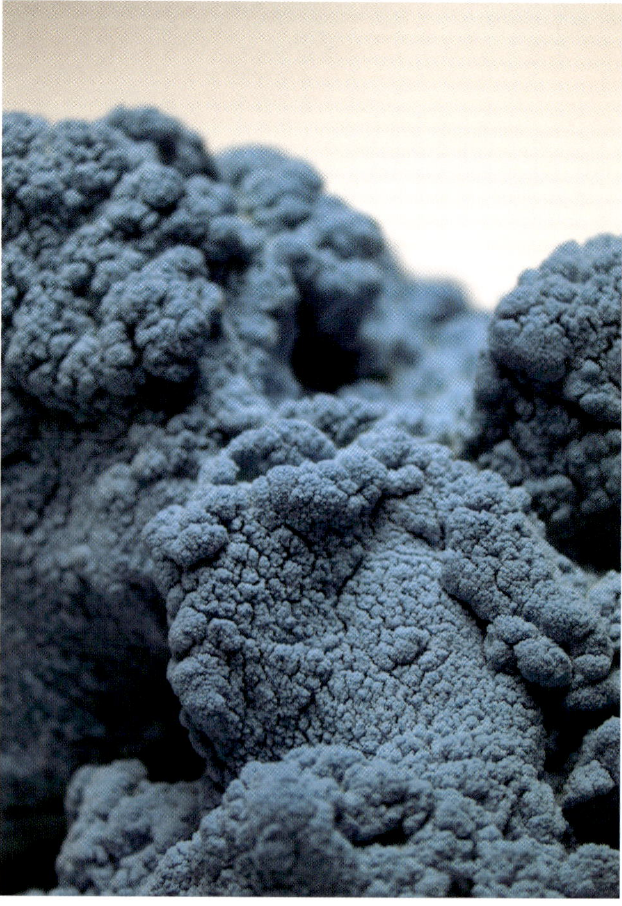

or fantasy. Less like a representation of natural geology, they are more akin to the fleeting interior landscape of the imagination. These are as much 'inorganic' as organic abstractions; figments of dreams made manifest in clay.

The works discussed here, collectively titled *Small Worlds*, were made between 2017 and 2020. 'World' is a word that can refer to organic matter and geology (i.e. planet Earth), but it can also invoke something more transient like an atmosphere, environment or state of being. One can enter a world of make-believe or leave one world behind and arrive into another. As 'small worlds', these sculptures exist in the twilight between the real and the imaginary, the known and the unknown, the organic and the inorganic. This conceptual indeterminacy is embedded into the very structure of the work. A number of the pieces are relatively small in size and yet surprisingly heavy in weight, as if the pressure from two opposing forces has crushed the form and compacted its molecules.

Each piece is complete and self-referential; a miniature landscape comprised of its own distinct ecology. Lacking a specific title, the spectator has a crucial role to play in activating the resonance of each work. When we visit one of the *Small Worlds*, we bring our own experiences and reminiscences of earthly landscapes: images of volcanoes, mountains, canyons, rocks, and fissures, all suggest a recognized geology. Yet, this gives way to feelings of unfamiliarity, difference and alienation. As if landing on an alien planet, there is a sense of surprise and curiosity. Colour becomes more intense, the impact of shadow more significant, and the fissures that create detail on the surface seem more lavish. Feelings of hot and cold, a discovery of mysterious substances and the traces of unknown vapours pervade the horizon.

Mullis has invested much time and effort into researching the effects of materials embedded into

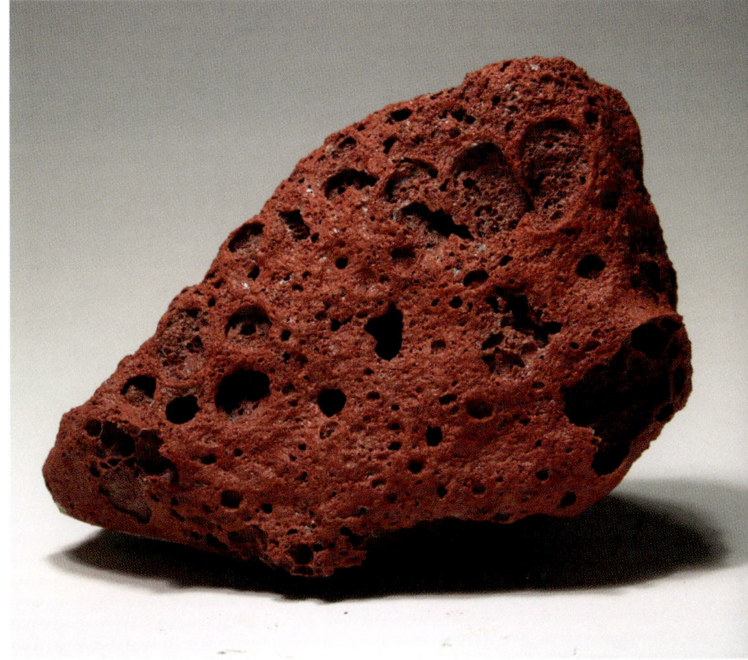

Small Worlds [Red].
(Photograph by Nathan Mullis)

the structure of the clay, as well as the application of glaze to a form. This experimentation has enabled him to create spectacular combinations of colour and texture. The strategic use of volcanic glazes offers a smoother, more viscous counterpoint to the rocky, even granular, textures of the sculptural body. The choice of colours draws attention to the textural differences between these two elements, almost as though a creature or alien substance has landed on a rock and become fused with it. Like asteroids, these works stand as records of past events, the collisions and fusions that constitute a journey – perhaps our journey – through space and time.

Mullis's interest in the interplay between the physical and the perceptual can be traced to Chinese *gongshi*, 'Spirit Stones', sometimes referred to as 'Scholar's Rocks'. Found across China, Korea and Japan, these rocks act as a focal point for meditation, or for the rumination of philosophical

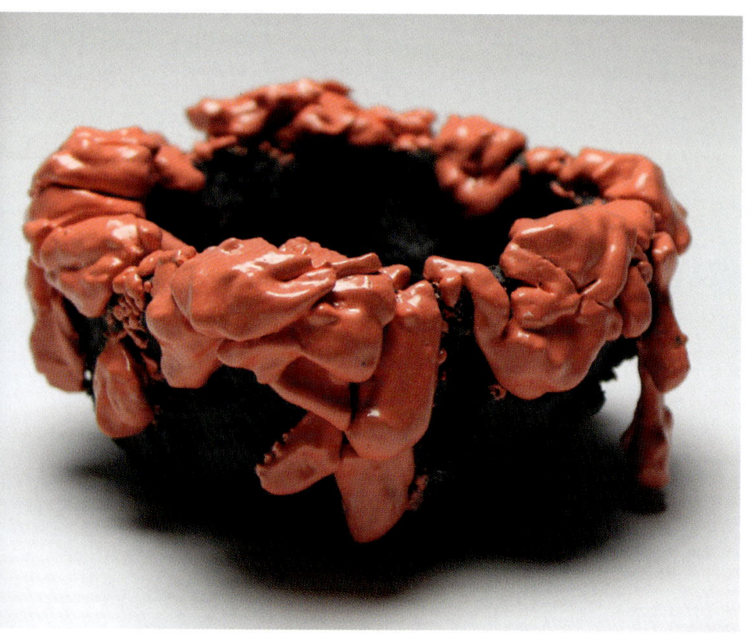

Small Worlds (Vessel) [Black and Red].
(Photograph by Nathan Mullis)

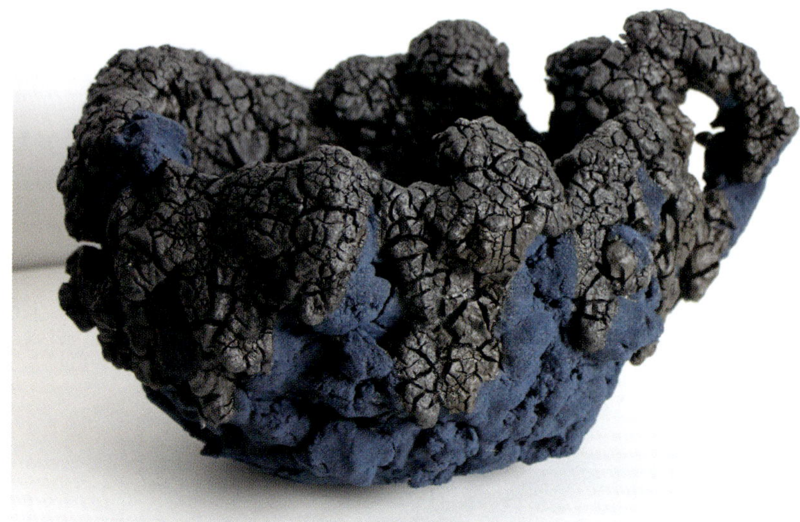

Small Worlds (Vessel) [Black and Blue].
(Photograph by Nathan Mullis)

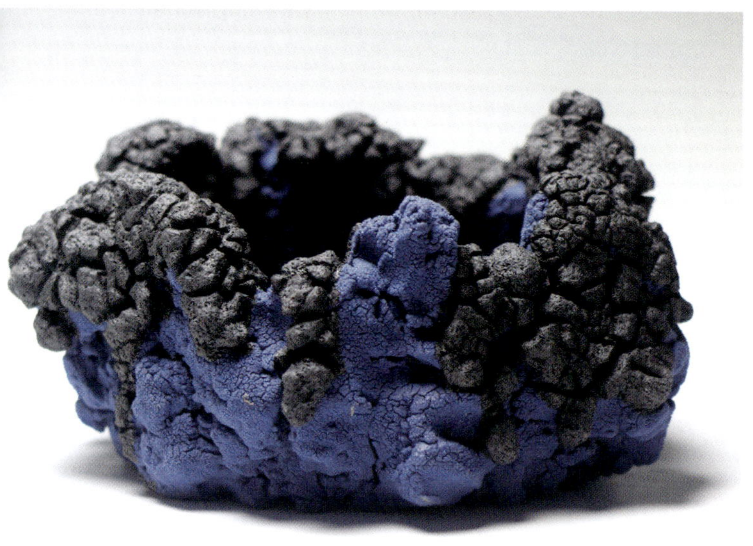

Small Worlds (Pitcher) [Black and Blue].
(Photograph by Nathan Mullis)

questions. They were admired by the literati for their gnarled shapes, formed by erosion from the wind and rain over thousands of years. By the Tang Dynasty (618–907), they became a feature of formal garden design in China, and an important cultural reference point in literature. The best *gongshi* were considered to exhibit the four qualities of elegance, rhythmic shape, exquisite beauty, and openings or holes within the fabric of the stone. Asymmetry in the rock was an integral part of their appeal.

The Chinese poet Bai Juyi (772–846) wrote a poem called *A Pair of Rocks*, in which he reflected upon two natural stones he found on the shore of a lake. His poem records that they were 'strange and ugly; of vulgar use they are unworthy; people of my era abandon them'.[61] Nevertheless, he had them transported to his own garden, where he used them as a focus for contemplation. The second half of his poem muses on the decline of the human body with age, and the discovery of solace and friendship in the permanence of the rocks.[62]

The *Small Worlds* sculptures are ceramic equivalents of the *gongshi*; their asymmetry, texture, and natural appearance reference the exterior world, yet the obviously manufactured nature of their aesthetic speaks to the interior psyche. By unifying the external and internal worlds into the very fabric of their composition, these sculptures become physical loci for the ponderings of the mind.

The melding of the natural and the man-made is intensified in other of the *Small Worlds* sculptures. While many of the works in this series are asteroid-like in form, others are nominally containers. The smaller of these works, simply called *Vessels*, exist somewhere in between the form of a tea bowl or mug and a volcanic crater, the glaze emerging lava-like over the rim. The larger works, *Pitchers*, allow for a greater interplay between interior and exterior. In contemplating them, I am reminded of my father working on building projects at home, of craters of sand on the driveway, the addition of cement and water and their mixing with a shovel. I recall the cement solidifying into clumps as it was mixed which, as a child, seemed to me like some kind of sorcery. It is of no coincidence that Mullis's father was a builder by trade, and that the shape of these sculptures emerges from his own memories of building sites.

As vessel forms, these works contain references to the manipulation of materials to build our habitats, our own 'small worlds'. In this sense they are containers for carrying ideas about alchemy. Indeed, the transformative effects of mixing raw materials is the conceptual impulse behind the work, but also the necessary process through which it is realized.

Mullis's technical investigations are methodical, as evidenced by a series of developmental works (*untitled* [1] and [2], 2020) in which glaze and form are blurred. Glazes run across and between the surfaces of these forms producing a strong sense of movement. It could be argued that these works

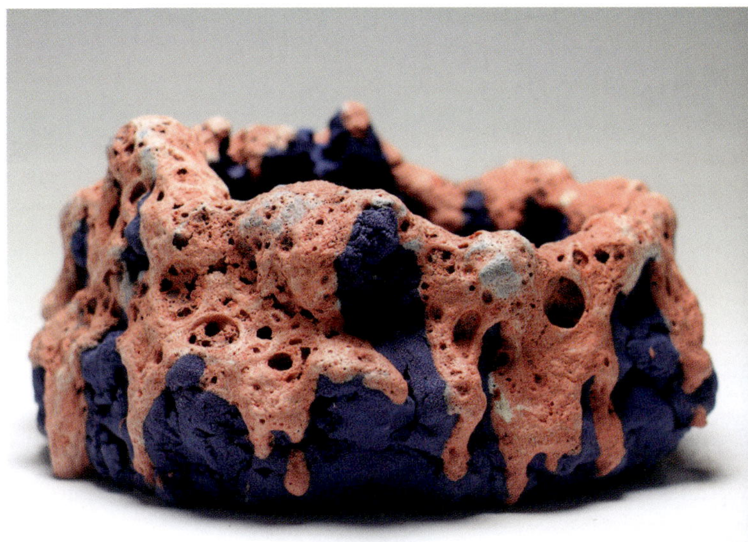

Small Worlds (*Pitcher*) [Pink and Blue].
(Photograph by Nathan Mullis)

are reminiscent of the brightly glazed vessels of the American artist Brian Rochefort, but I do not believe this is the case. For one thing, Mullis's approach to form is more experimental; he uses shape as a skeletal structure upon which glaze will flow in particular ways during firing.

For example, the gaps between the nodes of *untitled* [1] allow the glaze to take on a sculptural quality, blurring the division between body and glaze, form and surface. A recent discovery is the marbled glaze that runs down the sides of *untitled* [2]. These glazes are extremely painterly, reminding me of the mid-eighteenth-century British craze for agateware. Produced by mixing different coloured clays together, the variegated marble swirls of agateware were used across the potteries in Stoke-on-Trent from the 1730s until around the 1780s.[63] Where these explorations will lead Mullis is difficult to predict, but this latest series of work seems to bridge the aesthetic past with the future, fusing the eighteenth to the twenty-first century.

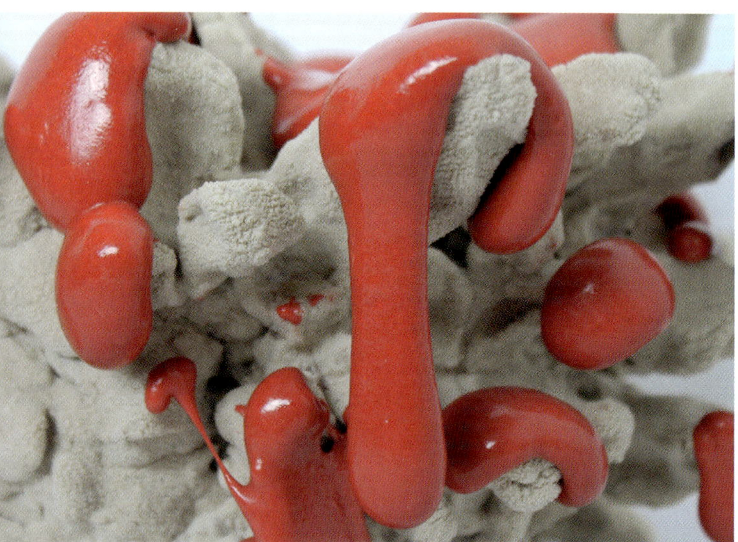

Untitled (2020) [1].
(Photograph by Nathan Mullis)

Some may feel that Mullis's work simply sits at the abstract end of organic abstraction. All art is the product of imagination. The work of Ewen Henderson, Gordon Baldwin – indeed all organic abstractionists however defined – has been predicated upon a utilization of the material and the mind in equal measure. Any shift from the organic to the abstract requires a transformative process tied to human skill and the imagination. Yet I still find Mullis's work to be different. The power of the imagination is more prescient in these sculptures. His forms are as concerned with the interior as much as the exterior world. As works of art, they are tangible manifestations of dream. Thus, his sculptures exist in the aperture between the physical and imaginary worlds.

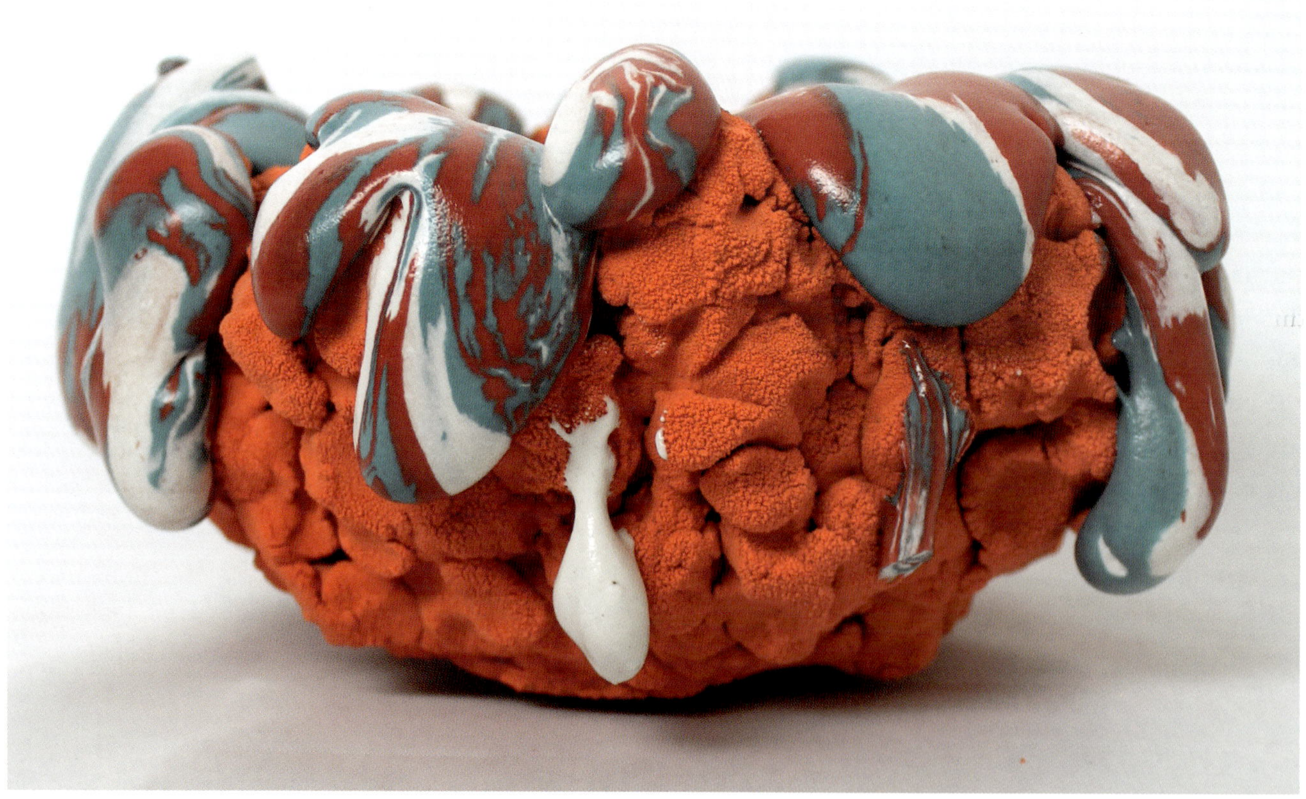

Untitled (2020) [2].
(Photograph by Nathan Mullis)

Mella Shaw

Prayers for the Future

Clay has long been the intermediary between the spiritual, the material and the animate. For Jews, Christians and Muslims, clay is the material from which Adam/ Ādam was made. In China, the goddess Nüwa used clay to mould child-bearing figures. In Hindu mythology, Ganesha was formed from clay, and in Yoruba culture, Obatala used it to make all humanity. It is the material from which our bodies came, and the dust to which it shall return. Perhaps for this reason, clay objects have figured in ritual practices from the earliest times: from tomb figures in ancient China to the *turbah*, often a slab of clay, manifesting the purest soil for use in daily prayer by some Islamic faiths. Indeed, many ceramic artists still fashion a kiln god from clay and place it on top of their kilns to ensure a good firing. As a symbol of humanity's relationship with the Earth, clay is imbued with spirituality. Yet, rarely is this material used to express our contemporary relationship with

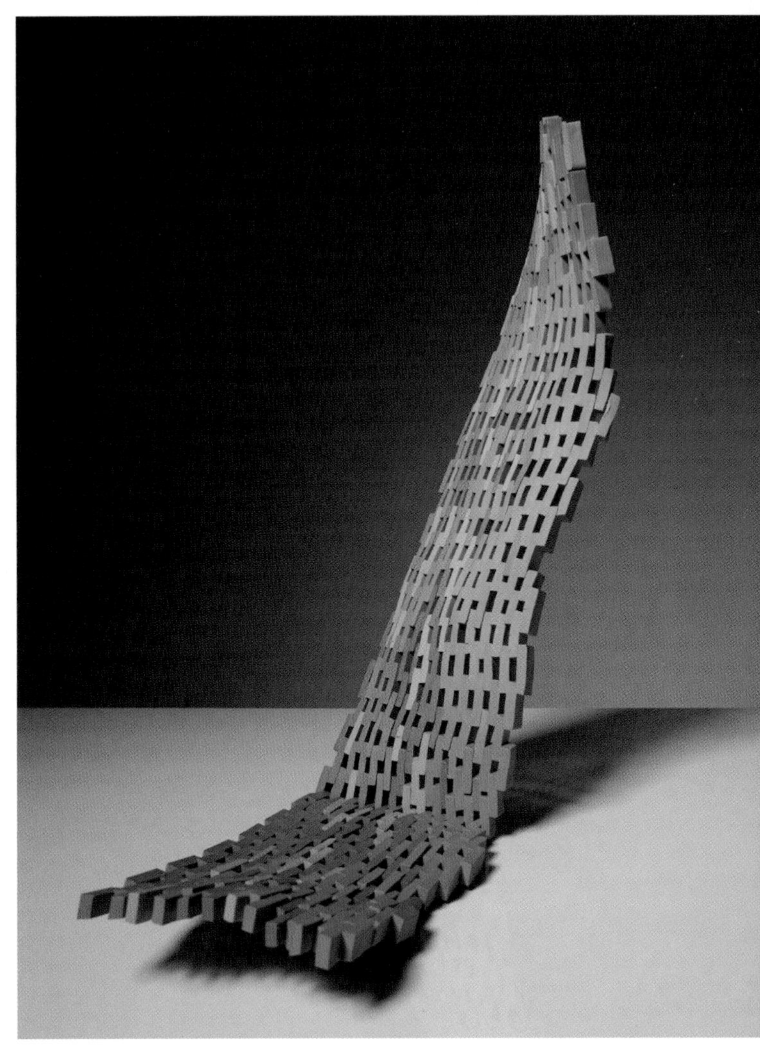

Blue Wave (2013).
(Photograph by Sylvain Deleu)

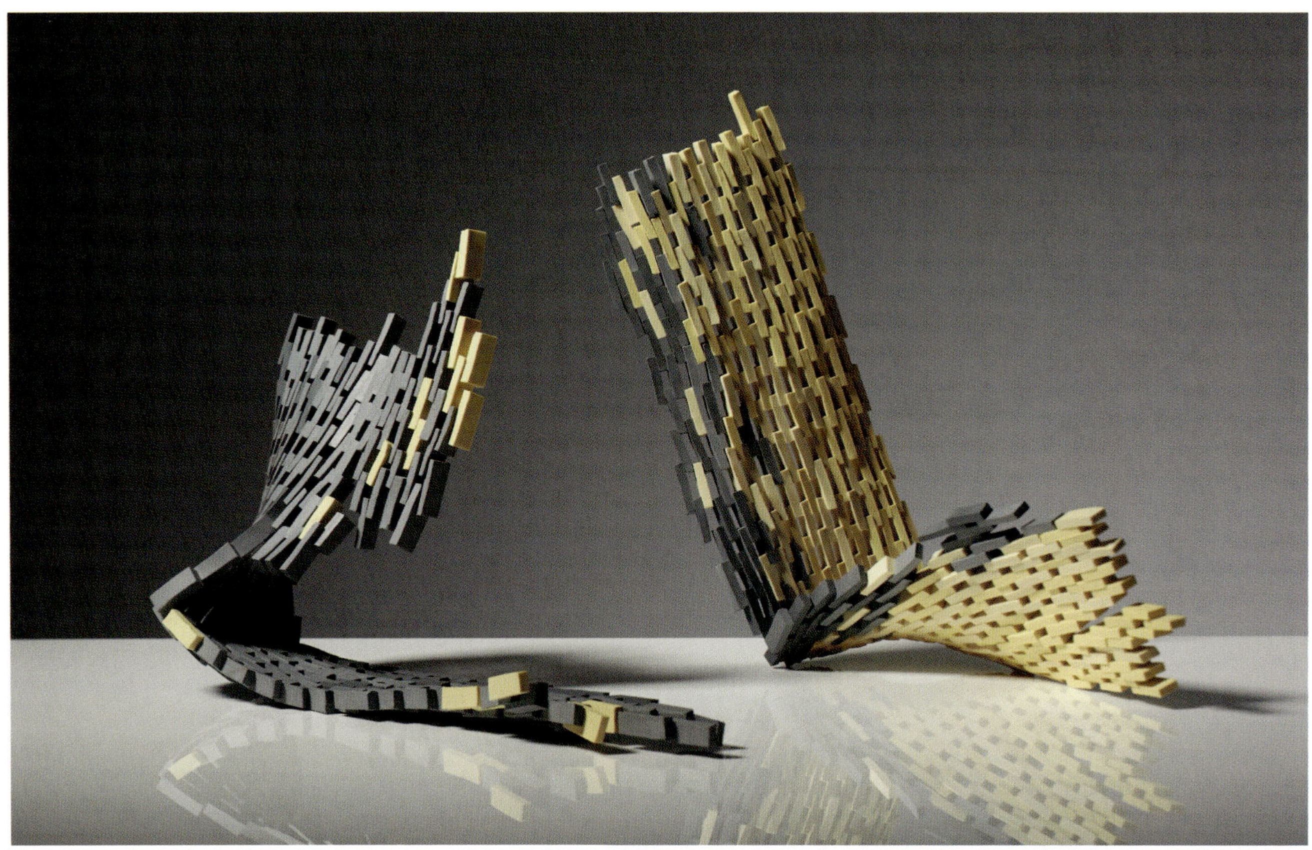

Bridges (2013).
(Photograph by Sylvain Deleu)

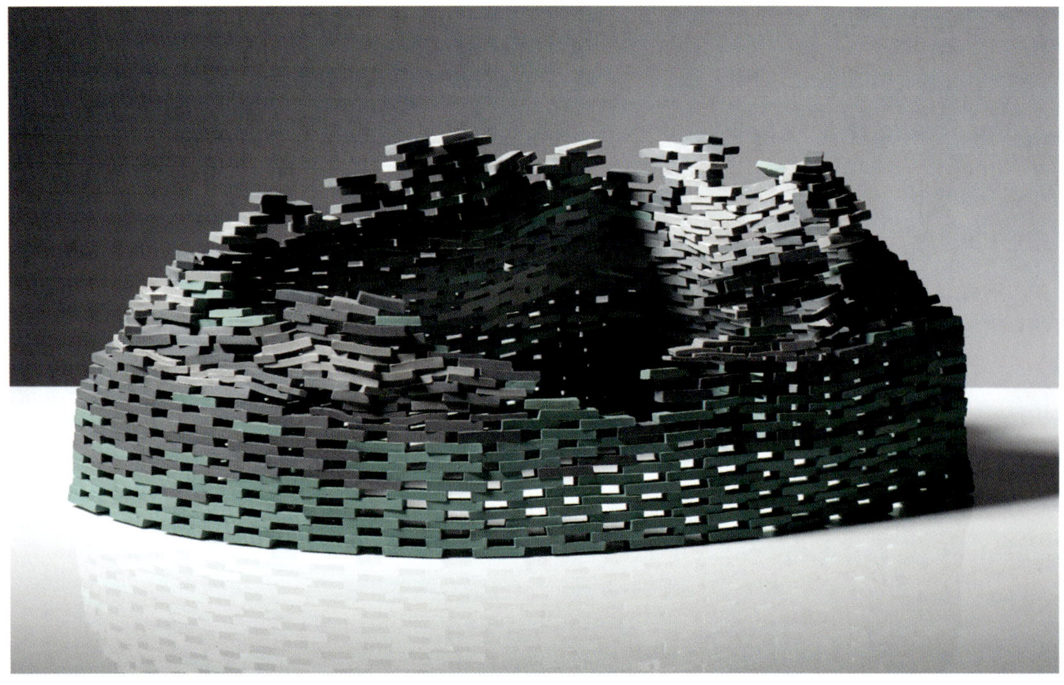

*Saudades –
Tumbling Form*
(2013).
(Photograph by
Sylvain Deleu)

it, our dependence upon it, our desecration of it, and our appreciation of it. The work of Mella Shaw highlights how we interact with our environment in the here and now. She interrogates our choices, the good and the bad, and in synchrony with a gradual shift in comprehending the ecological challenges we face, proposes a more mindful, and hopeful, relationship with our world.

I write this essay in April 2020. I am required by the UK government to stay at home to prevent the spread of the contagious Covid-19 virus, the global pandemic that has so far brought over ninety countries – half of all humanity – into confinement and has taken the lives of hundreds of thousands of people. I try to focus on writing to escape the horror of hearing how, in the last twenty-four hours alone, another 1,000 people have lost their lives to the virus. Earlier in the year, the 'Black Summer' in Australia left forty-six million acres of land destroyed by bush fire, while Antarctica melted under record temperatures of +18.3°C. After centuries of humanity imposing its will on the planet no matter the cost, there is the sudden and very uncomfortable realization that humans are a vulnerable species. Might these terrible events finally provide the shock we need to re-evaluate our relationship with nature? On this question, Shaw's work has much to say.

Thresholds (2013) was a series of sculptures created from small hand-cut porcelain pieces, brick-like in shape, which were assembled into the sculpture and then fired in position. Bricks are, of course, an overt symbol of how we shape environments; they are derived from a natural resource, yet their

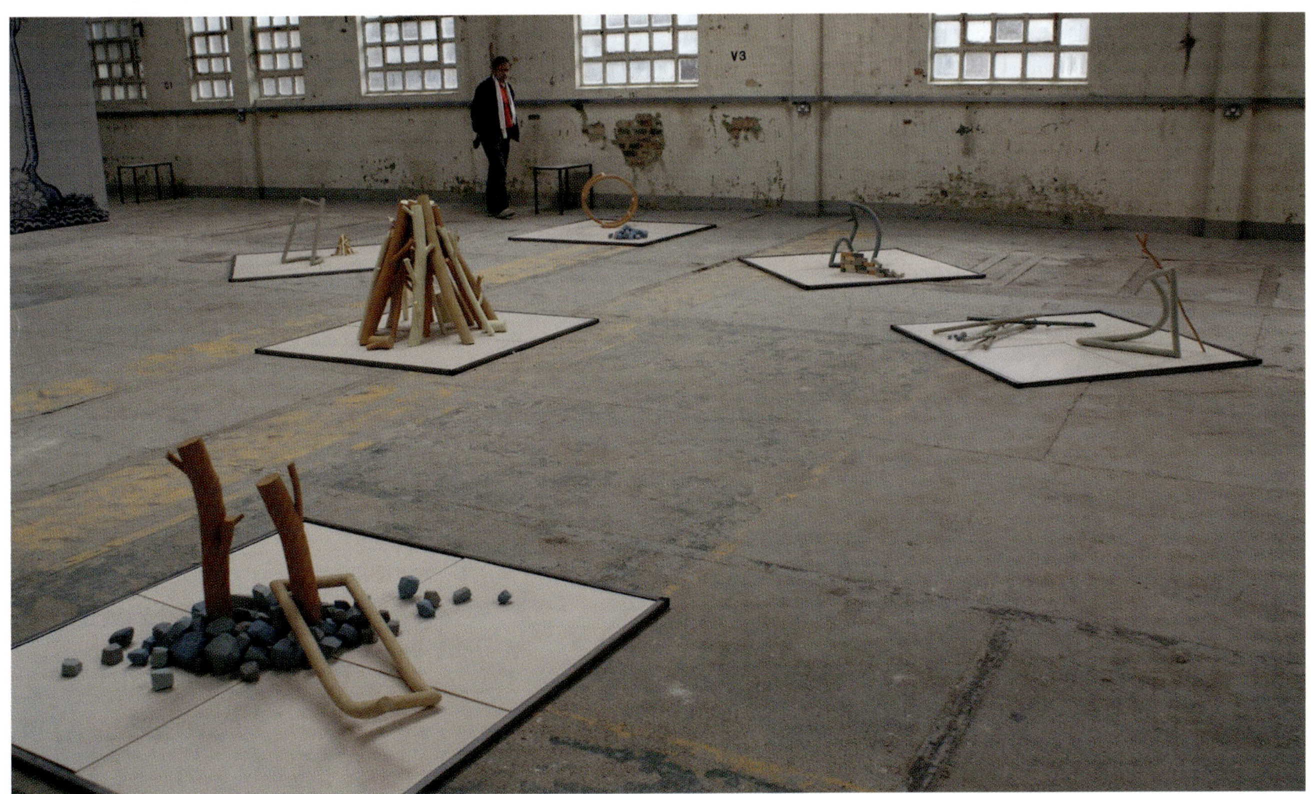

Notes on a City (2015).
(Photograph by Mella Shaw)

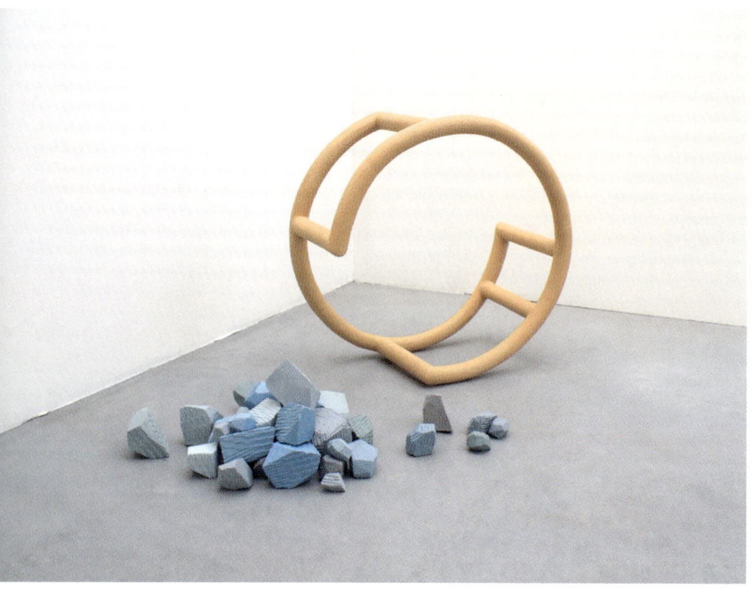

Postcard One (2015).
(Photograph by Mella Shaw)

primary function is to shield us from nature. Bricks are thus inherently antagonistic: they are derived from clay, reminding us of our relationship with the earth, yet, as a manufactured material, they shield us from the very thing the material represents. During the virus pandemic, whole populations were required to stay inside, and so bricks became one of the frontlines in virus protection.

Made from bricks, each of the *Thresholds* sculptures evokes architecture, and by extension, the way in which we construct our civilization. Solid brick walls are often used to divide, but the mesh structure of Shaw's sculptures creates something more liminal, more in between, offering the possibility of both communion and protection. The bricks are placed to form a rhythm that cumulatively expresses strength and stability. Structures like *Blue Wave* and *Bridges* (both 2013) rise from the ground, capturing the Dutch etymology of the word 'clay', '*klei*' which means 'to climb'. However, *klei* can also mean 'to cleave', and at a particular point in each of Shaw's structures, such as in *Saudades – Tumbling Form*,

(2013) the rhythm breaks down and the formation shatters. Evoking both resilience and collapse (on both a personal and social level), these sculptures speak of our complex predicament, of existing on a threshold between chaos and order, death and life, the needs of nature, and sustaining a civilization.

The ambivalent relationship between the urban and the rural was developed further in *Notes on a City*, an installation derived from a residency in Stockholm, and shown at AWARD, part of the 2015 British Ceramics Biennial. The installation consisted of six different stations, or 'postcards'. By placing the works on the floor, spectators viewed them from above, as though looking out at a city from an aircraft window, down onto a map, or even at the structures made by a colony of insects. This distancing invited a critical questioning, even an anthropological speculation, on the relationships between the natural and the man-made. Each postcard consisted of two kinds of object: representations of organic material – porcelain rocks, stoneware twigs and trees, and geometric forms suggesting the architectural world of the man-made.

In some postcards, such as *Postcard One*, the organic and man-made elements were separated, and the rural and the urban appeared at odds with one another, almost like two opponents in a boxing ring. Another postcard suggested a more convivial sense of connection; stoneware branches were grouped together into a *tipi*-like construction which sat proudly, if precariously, like a house of cards. A more caustic postcard consisted of two apparently dead trees surrounded by fallen rocks. One of the trees was bounded by a stoneware geometric shape, as if it had landed around the tree after being thrown in a game of quoits, the violent impact having dislodged the rocks. Taken as a whole, *Notes from a City* highlighted the uneven attitudes to urban engagements with nature. Some urbanites care, others do not; some save, others destroy.

In *HARVEST*, an installation first shown at the 2018 Collect art fair, Shaw depicted the destruction of marine ecosystems caused by the disposal of plastics into the sea. Contemporary research estimates that as much as eight million tonnes of plastic is dumped into the sea each year and, should this continue, by 2050 there will be greater weight of plastic in the ocean than fish. Plastic breaks down into microplastics, which fish mistake for food. The plastic particles remain unprocessed in their bodies and are eaten by other fish, and humans of course, further up the food chain. For her installation, Shaw used press moulds and slip-casting to create a large number of ceramic fish and representations

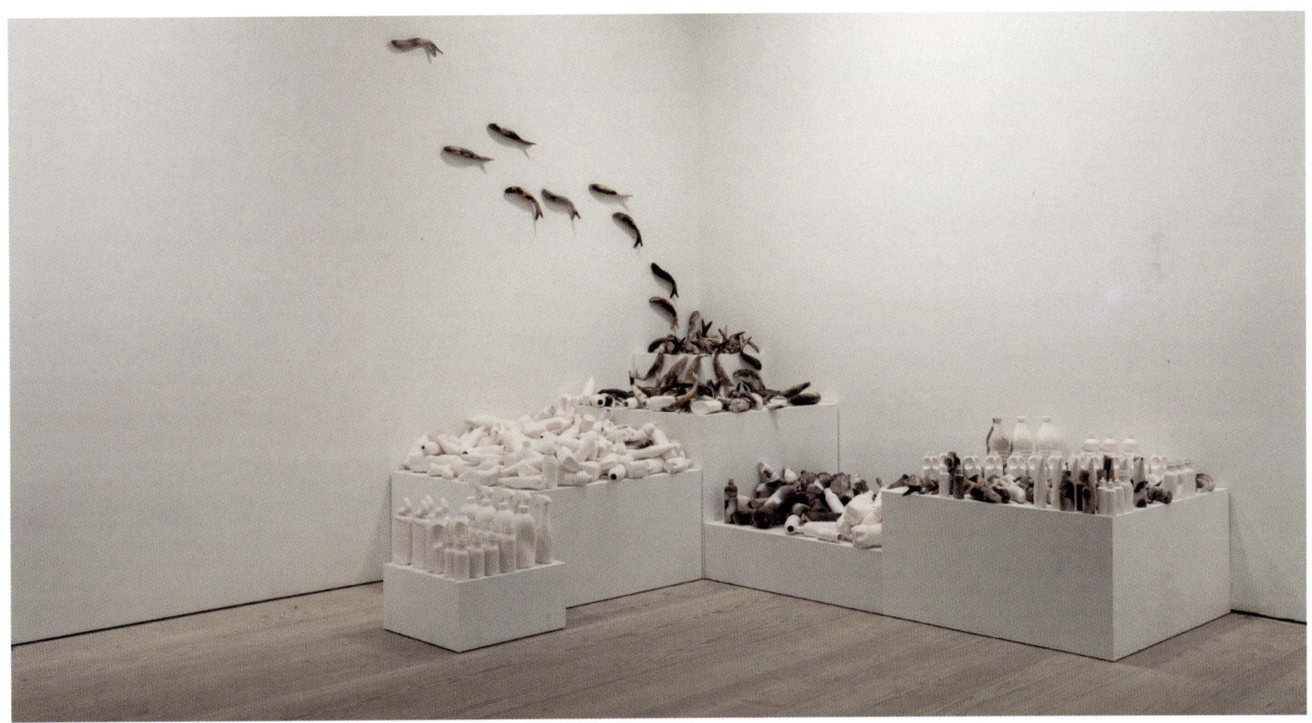

ABOVE: *HARVEST* (2018).
(Photograph by Sophie Mutevelian)

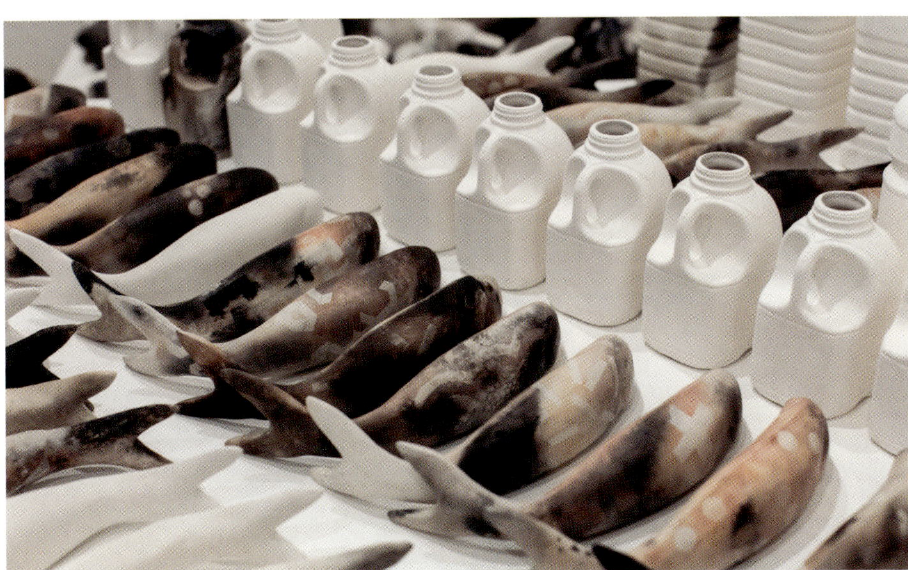

RIGHT: Detail of *HARVEST* (2018).
(Photograph by Sophie Mutevelian)

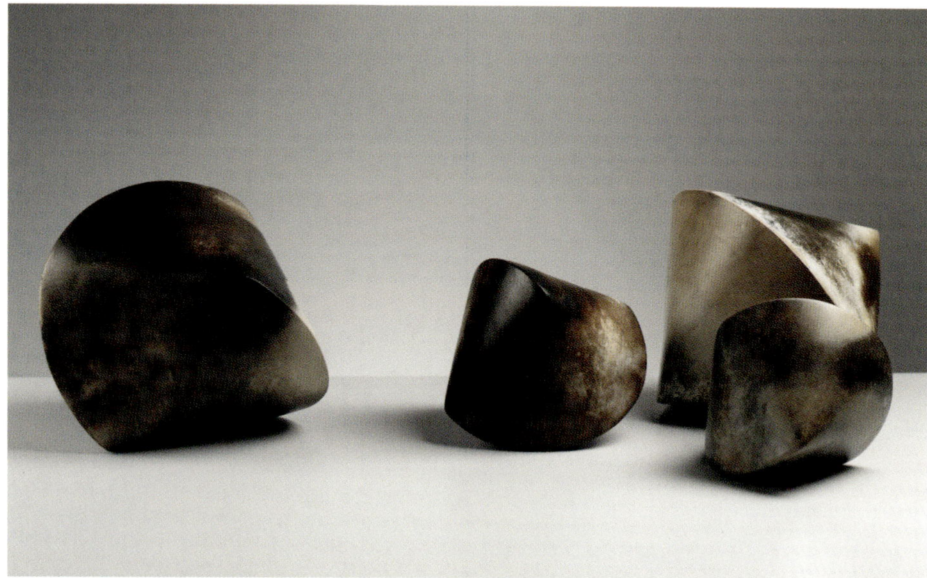

Janus Forms (2019).
(Photograph by Shannon Tofts)

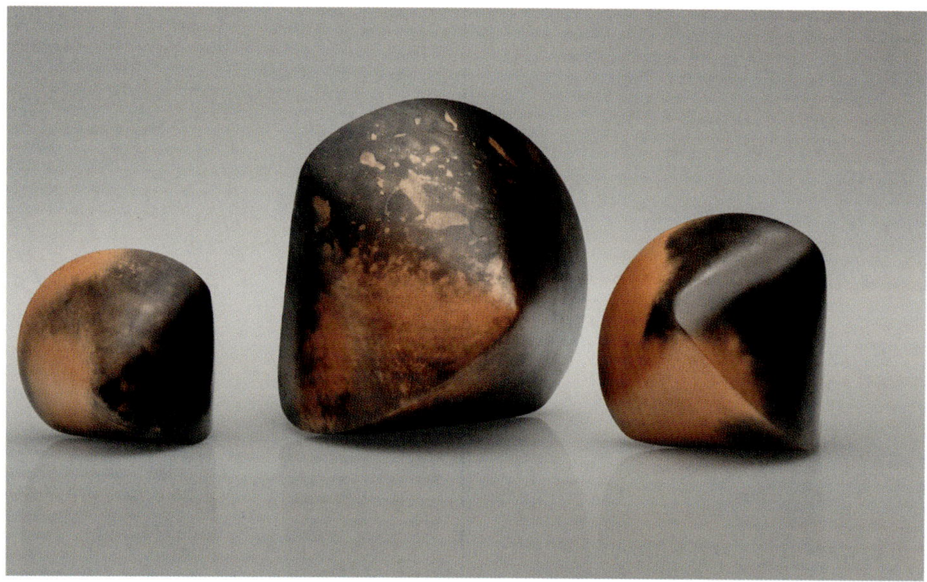

Janus Forms Terracotta (2019).
(Photograph by Toby Long)

of plastic bottles. In one section of the installation, fish appeared to have been dropped onto piles of the bottles, as if sorting through the plastic detritus to find the catch is now a daily activity for fishermen. A few lucky fish swim away up the gallery wall, but given the saturation of plastic in the installation, their future is by no means certain. Another section arranged the fish and bottles into the display lines of a fishmonger's. Shaw thus posed the question: when you buy a fish, how much of it is actually a plastic bottle? The striking use of smoke-firing gave some of the objects a powerfully decayed, dirty appearance. In its unromantic depiction of fishing, *HARVEST* demonstrated that humans reap what they sow.

What hope, then, is there for escape from this dystopia? It is one thing to identify the problems, quite another to proffer solutions. Following *HARVEST*, Shaw developed a series of smaller elliptical forms that cannot be fully grasped by the eye; they must be held in both hands to comprehend the entirety. This arises from Shaw's experience working in museums, where objects are kept behind glass, can usually only be viewed from one direction, and cannot be touched. Because they present as two-faced objects, Shaw named these works *Janus Forms* after Janus, the Roman god of transitions, famed for his two faces that bring together the past and the future. Bonnie Kemske, reflecting on her own physically interactive ceramic sculptures, noted how 'touch gives you a place in the world, it grounds us in our environment'.[64] By grounding us through touch, the *Janus Forms* invite a prayer for a better future (indeed, they can be used in the practice of meditation to encourage mindfulness). They ask us to see with our hands, become aware of new connections with our surroundings, consider where we have been, and where we hope to go.

This attention to surroundings was developed in a further series of works that placed the *Janus Forms* into compositionally dependent relationships with other objects. Evoking the postcards from *Notes on a City*, the sculpture *Beholden* (2019) consists of different ceramic elements carefully resolved into a satisfying composition. As with the postcards, the piece consists of organic rock-like forms and smooth sculptures. There is precariousness in the placement of each form; they sit on an awkward side or teeter on an edge. Any of the forms can be moved and the sculpture is thus open to an infinite number of compositional possibilities. These sculptures thus express the impermanence of structure, of how we arrange our lives as a species, and how we are approaching a tipping point in the relationship with our planet, in the very mutability of the composition.

In another work, *Untold* (2019), a repurposed sculpture from the *Thresholds* series is folded to teeter over an edge. A *Janus Form* functions as a

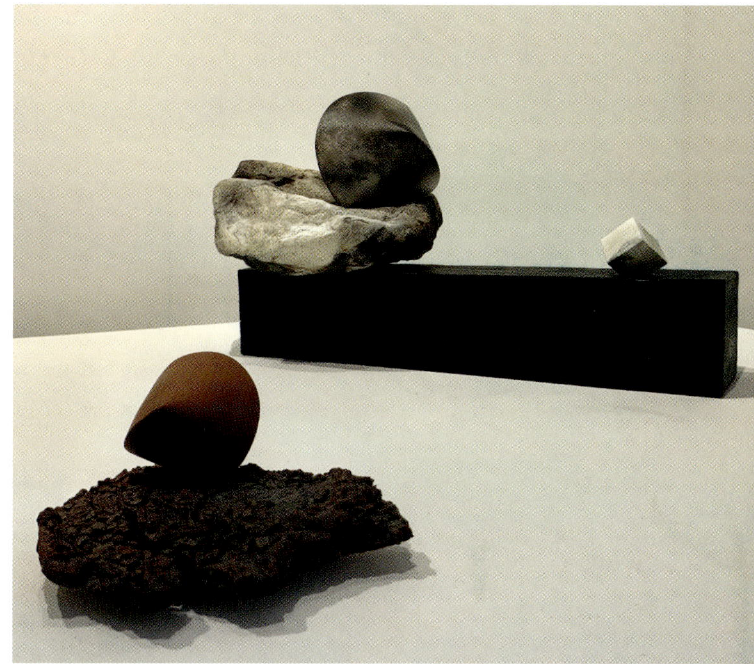

Beholden (2019).
(Photograph by Mella Shaw)

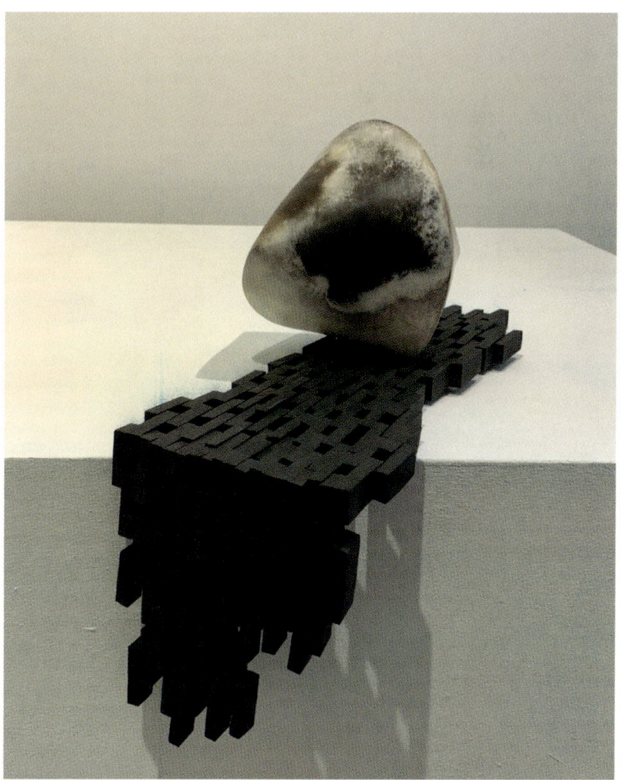

Untold (2019).
(Photograph by Mella Shaw)

compositional counterweight, as if to prevent the structure from tipping off the edge. In the here and now, the symbolism is potent. As I hear the news of yet another 1,000 deaths from Covid–19, I cannot help but think if the year 2020 does not elicit a fundamental change in our relationship with the planet, what hope is there for our species?

In the final series of work discussed here, Shaw highlights the dangers we face, but also the wonders we might yet find if we can make new connections with the natural world. The *Rare Earth* series of sculptures solidly unite the organic and man-made, the textural and the smooth. There is a sense of amazement, joy, and celebration of the elemental in these works, but also a stark warning. The cuboid forms in *Rare Earth 1* (2019) support, and are enmeshed within, the organic rock-like form. Can we find a way to support nature to recover, and to live within the confines of what it can safely provide? *Rare Earth 2* (2020) references the structure of pyrite – 'Fool's Gold' – in the form, and thus expresses the folly of exhausting the planet's resources for short-term financial gain. Our planet can support us, but only if we can support it. Might the terrible events of 2020 bring us to re-evaluate our relationship with nature? Let us follow the lead of Shaw's work and pray that we can approach the future with greater ecological awareness.

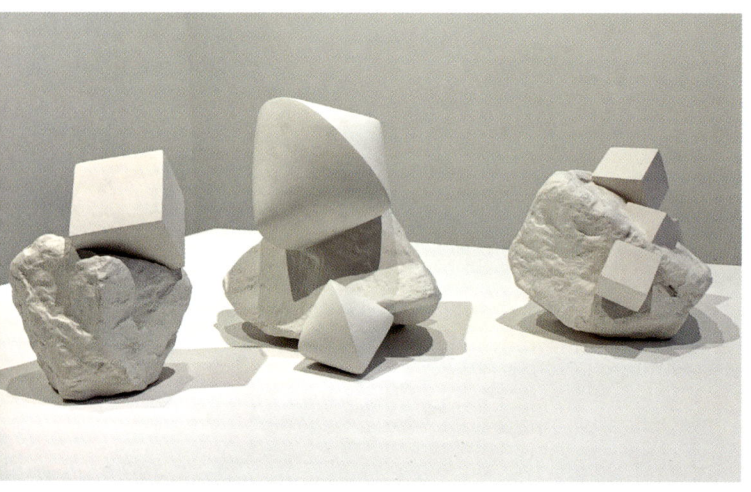

Rare Earth 1, Set (2019).
(Photograph by Mella Shaw)

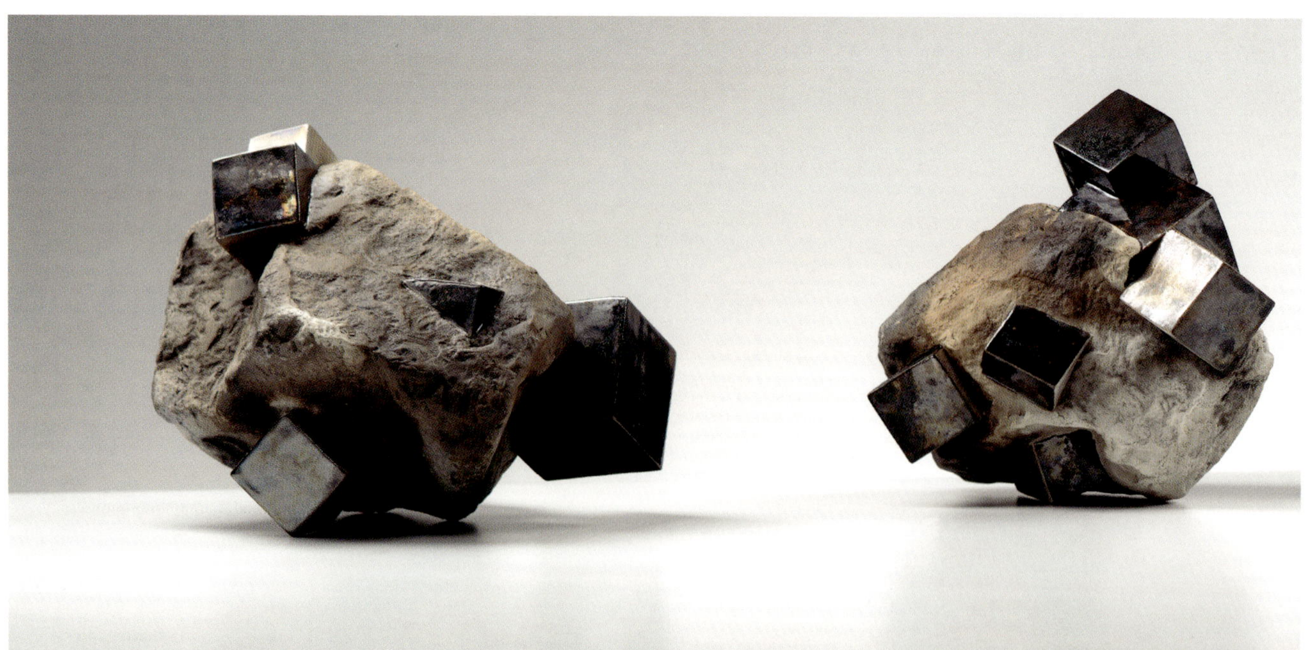

Rare Earth 2, Fool's Gold (2020).
(Photograph by Shannon Tofts)

Tessa Eastman

Bridging the Divide

The concept of centered structure – although it represents coherence itself, the condition of the *epistēmē* as philosophy or science – is contradictorily coherent. And as always, coherence in contradiction expresses the force of desire.[65]

Jacques Derrida

The work of the French philosopher Jacques Derrida has pulled apart the notion of structural certainty. The centre, or nucleus, of a structure is always considered its focal point, where the rules are enforced, and where configuration is fixed. Yet Derrida proposed that the centre is, in fact, totally separate from the rest of a structure because of its inflexibility. The centre is where structure is most inflexibly 'structural', where it sticks to the rules, and its observance of the rules is why it is called the 'centre'. In contrast, all other parts of the structure permit flexibility, can play with the rules, and this is why those parts are *not* the centre. Derrida argued that while the centre *seems* to be part of the wider structure (it appears to regulate it), it is in fact so systemically different, has such distinct genetic make-up, and is so inflexible, that it is its own organism. He thus observed that coherent structures are, in fact, structurally incoherent.[66]

Tessa Eastman uses structure (as it pertains to sculptural expression) to highlight the incoherence of the binary oppositions we use to construct our perceptions. She keenly deconstructs notions that are regarded as incompatible opposites: life and

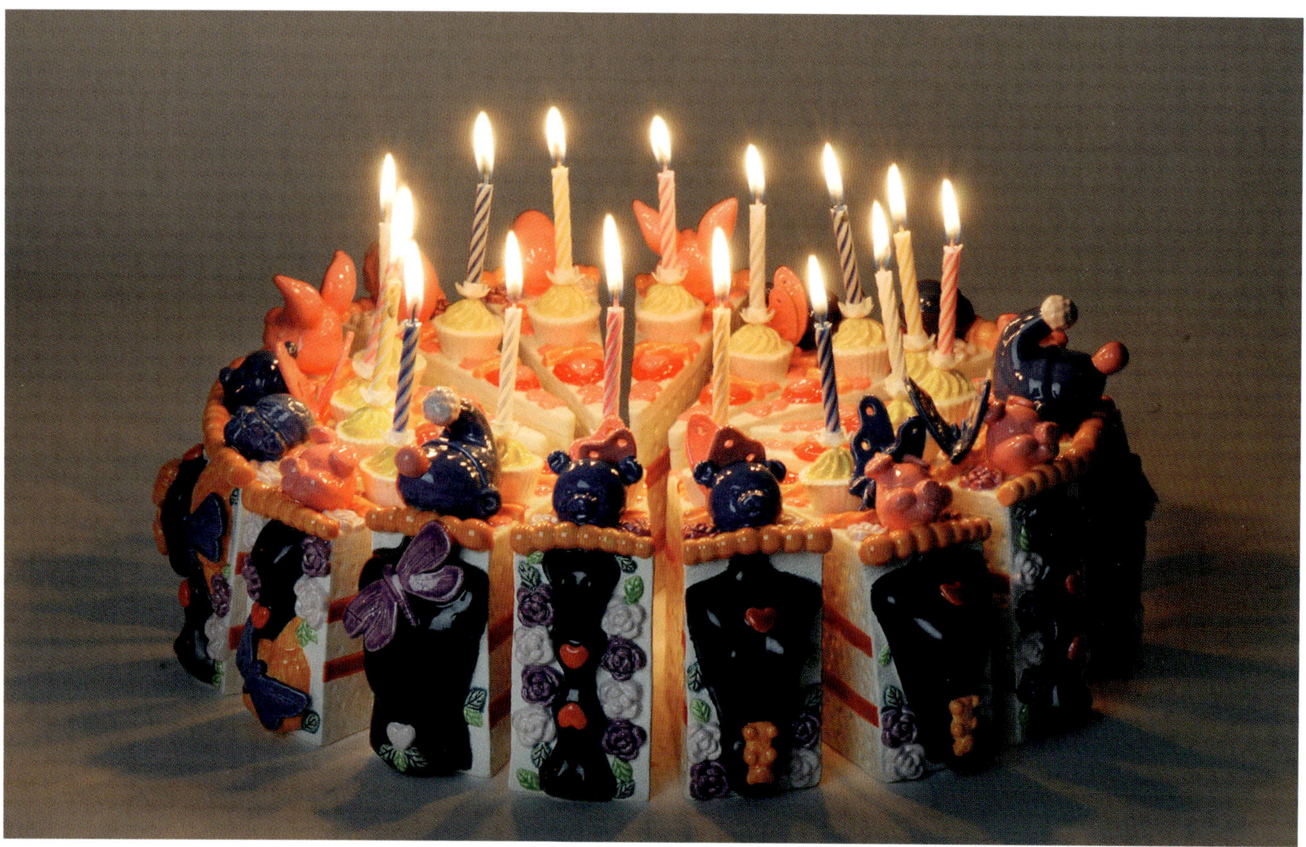

Burning Slices of Death (2012).
(Photograph by Sussie Ahlburg)

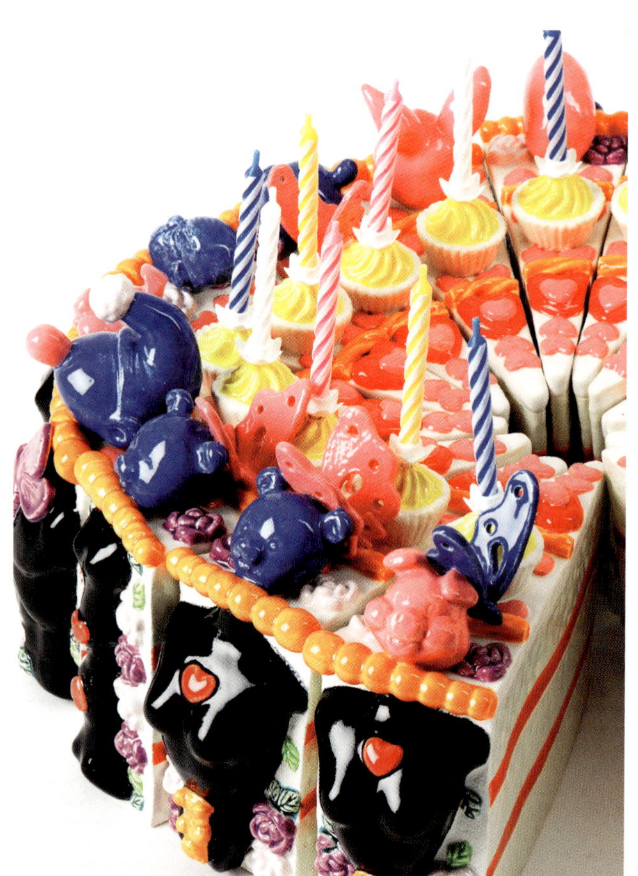

death, the sentimental and the brutal, fantasy and reality. Being a British ceramic sculptor, and from a culture where death and sentimentality are usually kept under wraps, this is not at all usual. By bridging the gap between these oppositions, her work, like Derrida's analysis of linguistics, exposes our attempts to mask the incoherence that lies beneath the veneer of human rationality.

Eastman's deconstructive approach first surfaced in her early works. Almost everywhere these days in our globalized world, birthday cakes are a liminal symbol of change. Either a family member or friend painstakingly bakes them with affection, or perhaps

LEFT: *Burning Slices of Death* (2012).
(Photograph by Sussie Ahlburg)

they are less painstakingly selected from a supermarket shelf or catering catalogue, but cakes are always consumed as part of a series of rites to mark this special day. At first glance, Eastman's slices of cake in *Burning Slices of Death* (2012) seem excessively saccharine. They are overloaded with colourful iced decorations and sweets that risk pushing sugar levels to breaking point. Yet, a closer look reveals how the icing consists of pig heads, animal skulls, carcasses and dead insects. They are a reminder that birthdays are also markers of advancing maturity, of one step further away from the day of birth, and one step closer towards the moment of death. Dualities of life and death, and youthfulness and adulthood, are here synthesized in porcelain. If such analysis seems gloomily morbid, *Burning Slices of Death* retains an anarchic sense of humour. A cake smothered in the imagery of dead animals is hardly the celebratory cake of choice, yet the inclusion of a real candle on each piece draws attention to the brief luminosity of life before its inevitable extinction.

In fact, *Burning Slices of Death* is already dead. It was complete as a sixteen-slice work only when it left the artist's studio. The slices have since been sold individually and have made their way to new homes, almost in the manner of cake remnants given away in a goody bag at the end of a party. Despite the death of the work as a whole, it is nevertheless preserved in its component pieces. As a series of moulded porcelain objects, each individually decorated slice has the potential to outlive both the artist and the buyer, and will either be passed down through generations, or resold on the open market. This work, therefore, exists in between a number of dichotomies: of the lovingly handmade and the capitalist mass-produced moulded product, of emotional investment in artistry and the pragmatic need to make a living, of sentimentality and brutality, and of continuity

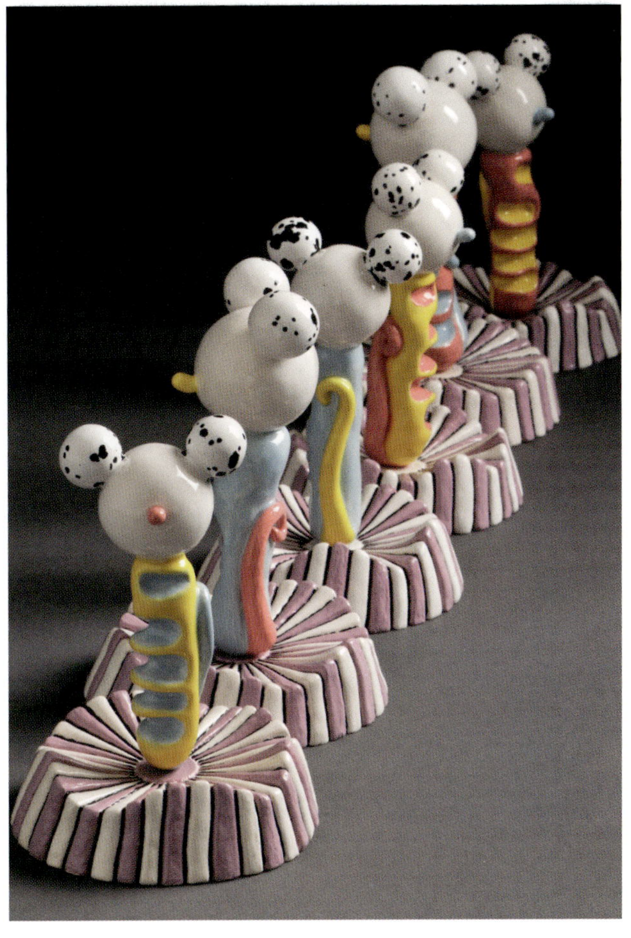

Mama Maraca Mice (2011).
(Photograph by Sussie Ahlburg)

and change. Yet, above all else, the *Burning Slices of Death* are enduring monuments to the fragility and transience of life.

In other early works, toys, objects from which we derive the sincerest forms of pleasure as children, are rendered uncanny. For her *Mother and Child* series, Eastman made a number of rattle-like mouse figures, each impaled on a purple, white and black base. Entitled *Mama Maraca Mice* (2011), the head of each mouse contains handmade ceramic balls, so that the piece can be used as a maraca-like toy rattle. The limbless bodies of each figure are brightly glazed in combinations of blue, pink and yellow, and feature the imprint of four fingers and a thumb, further implying the utilitarian nature of the object. Yet, this toy is definitely not a toy: it is a kind of meta-ornament that has implied utility.

The *Mama Maraca Mice* offer a critique on the glibness of toys; especially those that equate true childhood with perpetual carefree play. The face of each mouse is vacant save for a brightly coloured nose, with ears sparsely decorated with dabs of black glaze on an otherwise shiny white sphere. This is a reference to the psychological design of some toys (such as *Hello Kitty*), which do not have facial features so that children can project the emotions they feel onto the object. Here, the effect is intensified into a kind of Jeff Koons-like abstraction, which dissolves the separation between innocence and worldliness. Whilst the blank face may be receptive to emotional projection, the body speaks of a different psychology: the finger imprints on the body of the mouse hint at the tight grip of parental anxiety. Thus, like a clown at the circus who provokes both laughter and terror, the *Mama Maraca Mice* describe the joy associated with infant toys, but also the exhausting desperation of parents when absolutely nothing, not even white noise from the infant's favourite rattle, will stem the flowing tears.

A desire to experiment, and a period at the Royal College of Art from 2013 to 2015, meant a move away from prepared glazes, and the opportunity to approach work with even greater conceptual clarity and technical mastery. Three subsequent series of works, entitled *Crystal Formations, Crater Explorations* and *New Arrivals* demonstrated a change in aesthetic direction, and a turn towards geological and biological structure, the very architecture of the natural world. This avenue enabled successful experiments that fused shape and surface with greater dexterity and confidence. For instance, the *New Arrivals* series

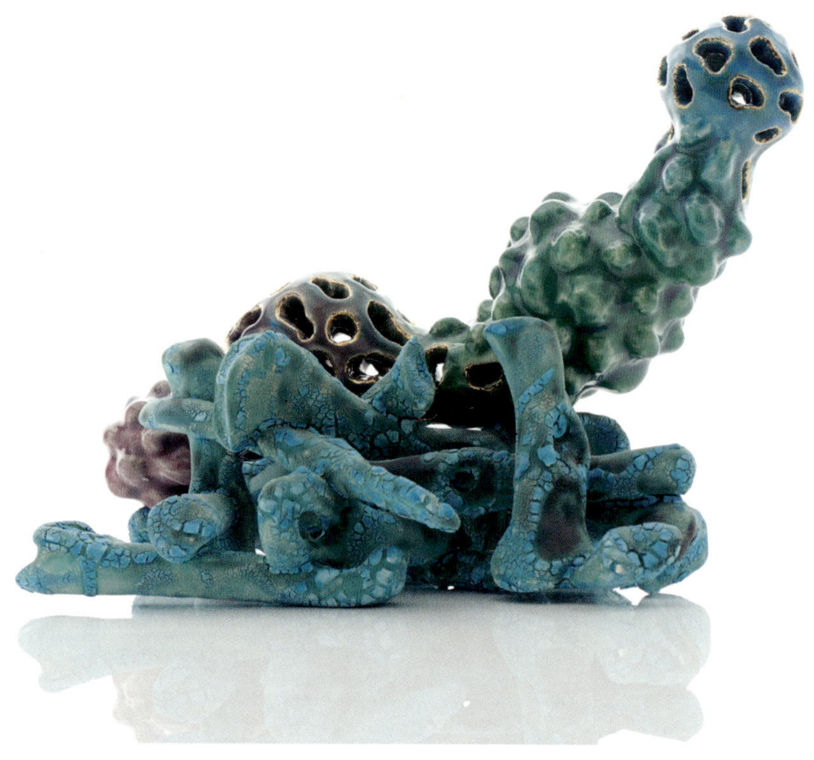

Symbiosis (Creature in Bone Nest) (2015).
(Photograph by Sylvain Deleu)

enabled Eastman to reconcile apparently antithetical forms into a hybridized but carefully balanced piece. The shapes that Eastman used in this series – spherical cell-like objects attached to regular net-like supports – speak to the separation of centre and structure proposed by Derrida, but also evoke something of the beautiful yet ominous microscopic imagery of a virus feeding upon a healthy cell to multiply and increase its infectiousness. Eastman develops a new sculptural language to once again remind us of the complexity of an interpenetrated world, and how the basic principles of life and death are utterly intertwined.

The integration of life with death via natural structures was also significant to *Creatures of the Deep* and *Symbiotic Creatures*. In these two series of work, Eastman explored life on the fringes of the known, creatures that might live in the fissures of volcanic rocks or in the dark recesses of the oceans. Being of the earth, clay is redolent with the symbolism of death, of ashes-to-ashes and dust-to-dust. Yet, decomposition releases nutrients that enrich the soil, and thus death nurtures the ecosystem on which all life depends. In the same way, Eastman gives the dead clay a new structure, surface and purpose, and breathes into it a new life. This transformation is underscored by her choice of glaze. Lively forms, with lighter, shinier glazes, feed upon underlying structures that are tactile and lava-like.

In *Symbiosis (Creature in Bone Nest)* (2015), for instance, the textural surface of the bone-like base suggests decaying coral, yet its vibrant blue-green colour implies a bountiful richness and plentiful food source. The larval creature that sits upon it is of the same colour, alluding to its absorption of the nest as foodstuff. Hollowed out globular joints inspired by tree root formations, which are further highlighted with 22k gold lustre, animate this worm-like creature. Far from being content, however, the creature seems to be rearing away from its nest, as

though straining for the sun, or seeking out new territories. Deprived of its home and food, it faces an uncertain future. Eastman depicts the creature as being trapped in a state of dependency: it recognizes the finite nature of the resource upon which it sits but is incapable of responding to its diminishing situation. As our planet rebels with greater voracity against its human desecrators, this seems an ever more salient point to drive home. Yet, collectively, these works are more than simple *memento mori*; they are a celebration of transience, of recognizing one's place and impact on the world, of understanding the inevitability of death, but ultimately of revelling in the dynamism and vibrancy of life.

In her *Cloud Bundles* series, transience remains a key area of investigation. Clouds are, after all, one of the most transient entities in nature: they are in a constant state of mutation, of coming into being, and of receding into nothingness. As holders of water, clouds sustain life through their central role in the water cycle. Whilst Eastman's clouds nod to this natural phenomenon, they are by no means literal representations. Rather, they are, like the technological repositories of the same name, storage containers of data sets. Eastman's clouds invite us to access a wealth of memories, emotions and associations.

When I was younger, I can recall lying on the grass in my grandmother's garden and looking up at the blue and white sky. In the clouds I would see animals and people: all manner of imagined dramatic scenes playing out between different kinds of characters as the wind shifted the clouds out of sight. I am hardly alone in having this memory. But in prompting this remembrance of childhood, Eastman's work reminds us of how we used to playfully activate our imagination. This activation of memory, of a kind of emotional movement, is expressed in the relationship between the different aspects of each cloud. Clouds are grouped together according

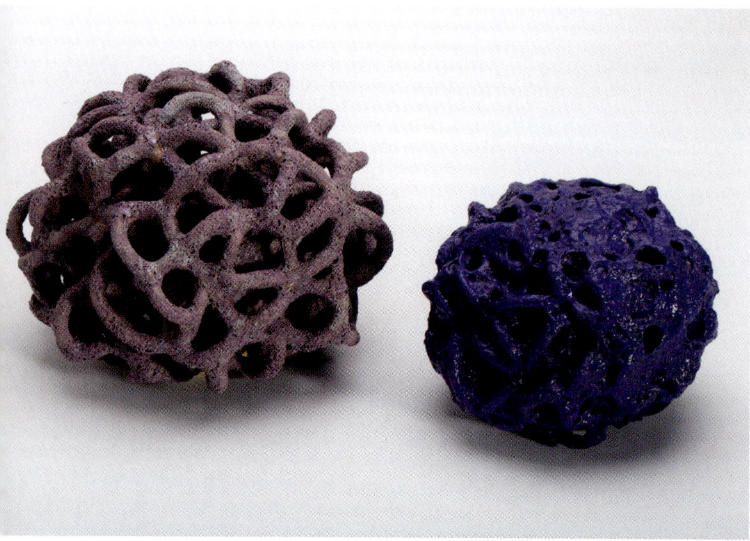

Low Density Matt Purple Cloud (2017) and *High Density Gloss Purple Cloud* (2018).
(Photograph by Juliet Sheath)

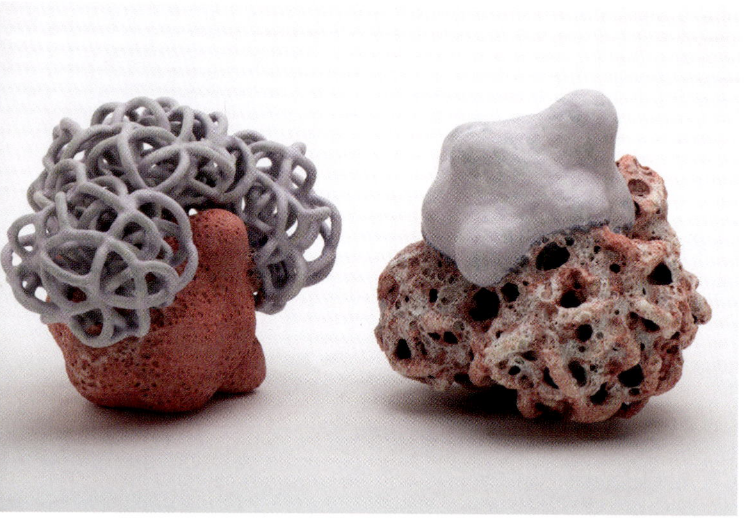

Pink Lavender Baby Cloud Bundle (2018) and *Lavender Pink Baby Cloud Bundle* (2018).
(Photograph by Juliet Sheath)

to whether they 'cocoon', 'erupt', 'burst', 'sprout' or 'conceal'. They are always in motion, just like the processes that enable us to remember, or repress our memories. The *Cloud Bundles* function as sculptural portraits of remembrance, of thinking, and of being. But they are also reminders of mutability and

incoherence. Like a cloud releasing water in a rainstorm, our memories flood before our eyes as partial happenings. But the cloud also reminds us of the transience of these reminiscences, and how we remember things differently, at different stages in our lives, in different places, and with different people.

It is of no surprise therefore that structural individuality is a central concern of these cloud sculptures, where compositional differences provoke divergent phenomenological interpretations. For instance, the loose structure and matt surface of *Matt Purple Cloud* (2017) suggest lightness and openness; air can literally pass through to the core of this piece. In contrast, *Gloss Purple Cloud* (2018) is tighter, evincing sensations of heaviness, compactness and solidity. The deployment of different configurations and surface treatments is intensified in the cloud bundle sculptures. Here, a dialogue is established between two oppositional structures, giving the works a sense of emergence and expansion. In each sculpture one component seems to reluctantly concede to the forces of the other. In *Pink Lavender Baby Cloud Bundle* (2018) and *Lavender Pink Baby Cloud Bundle* (2018) the combination of structure and surface treatment alters perceptions of weight and density. The loose structure comprising the bottom section of *Lavender Pink Baby Cloud Bundle* seems weighed down by the heavier, more solid, lavender cloud above. In contrast, the upper section of *Pink Lavender Baby Cloud Bundle* is looser, and seems to be trying to pull, even raise, the heavier, tighter pink section that resolutely anchors itself to the ground. It is in the interplay of these dynamic forces that the sculptures achieve a sense of movement and vitality, harnessing structural disjointedness to conjure emotionality. Yet, the precise associations they stir ultimately lies in the eye of the beholder. For work so concerned with structure, they invite responses that are startlingly amorphous.

As Eastman's confidence has grown, so the size of her sculptures has increased. Works such as *Standing Cloud Pinky White* (2019) and *Erupting Purple Midnight Cloud Cluster* (2019) are expansive pieces that offer a greater surface area for the deployment of glaze. The rich mottling of colours in these glazes demonstrates her technical growth and maturity in approach. Their size – each is at least forty centimetres in diameter – gives them an enhanced sense of drama, as if the viewer were looking down on a raging storm from the safety of an aeroplane window. Colour intensifies their dramatic effect but also clues us in to their temperament.

Standing Cloud Pinky White has a benign sense, as if two cloud shafts are embracing in a state of mutual support, perhaps even sorrow. In contrast, *Erupting Purple Midnight Cloud Cluster* is more explosive, its horizontal composition and colour suggestive of the rumbling expansion of a volatile thunderstorm. These two works utilize the same sculptural language to express opposite emotions – compassion and malignancy – demonstrating Eastman's ability to harness clay as an instrument for personal expression. A thirst for experimentation and development has led to the incorporation of lustre glazes. In *Glam Punk Crystalline Cloud* (2020), magenta shards erupt from the cloud surface like a mountain range. The rich bluey-red of the cloud surface emanates energy, suggestive of the compressed forces that produce crystalline structures. These are imaginative and distinctive works by an artist who is carving a unique path in British ceramics.

Some audiences for ceramic art remain challenged, if not outright perplexed, by works that do not take the literal shape of the vessel. Yet there have been a number of British ceramicists whose work has addressed questions of containment

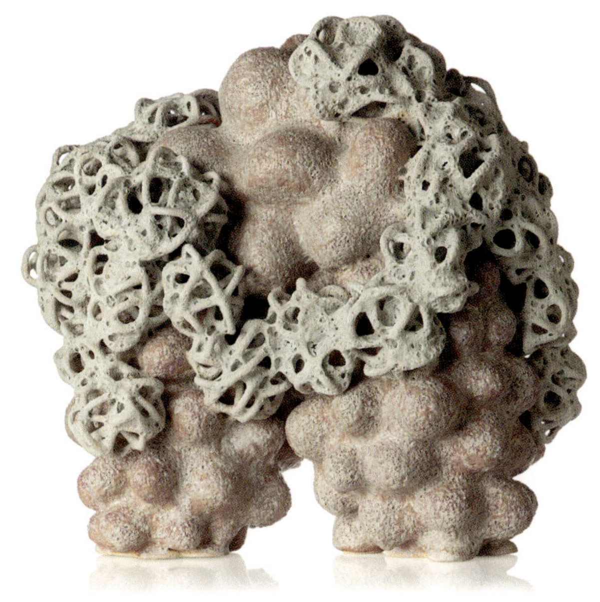

Standing Cloud Pinky White (2019).
(Photograph by Juliet Sheath)

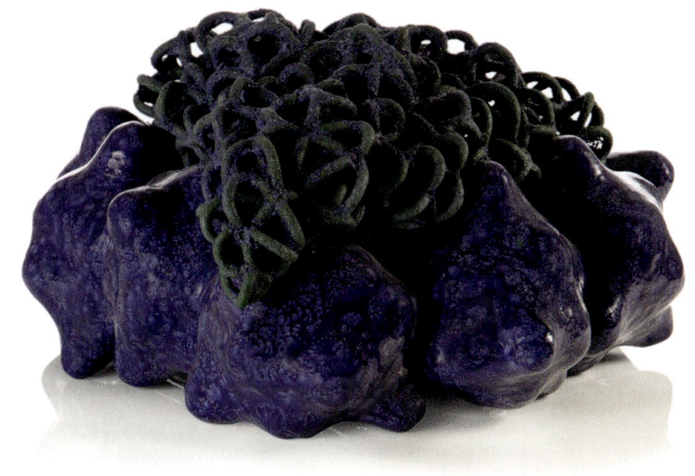

Erupting Purple Midnight Cloud Cluster (2019).
(Photograph by Juliet Sheath)

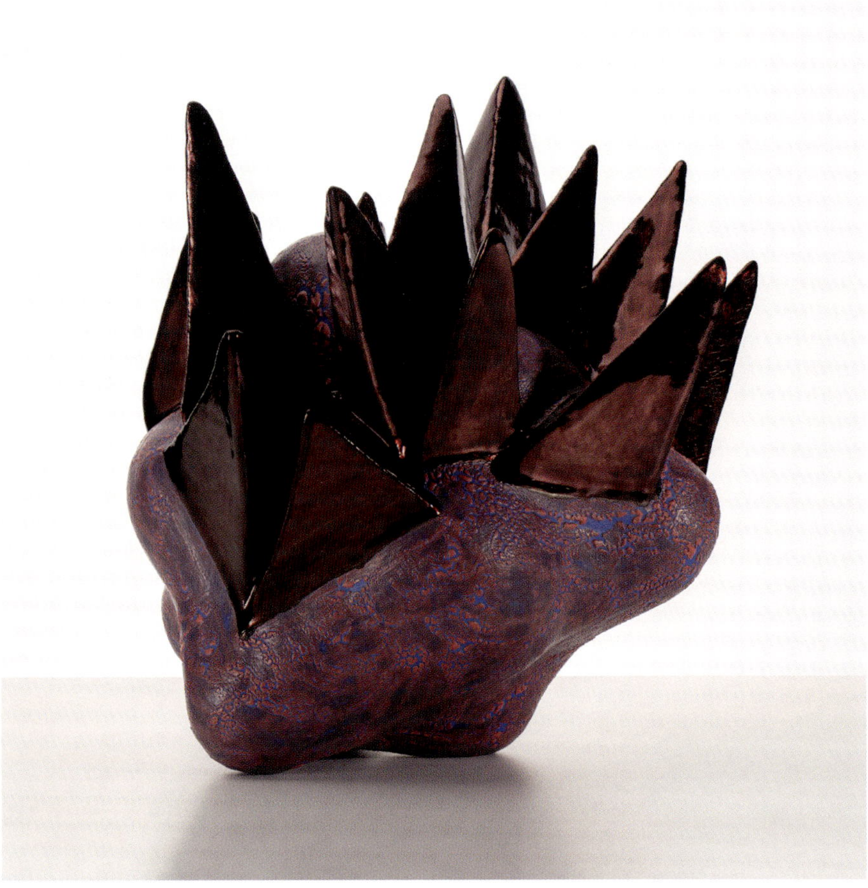

Glam Punk Crystalline Cloud (2020).
(Photograph by Juliet Sheath)

without resorting to the vessel. The late Mo Jupp, for instance, explored containment of the head through his series of clay helmet sculptures, whilst Sara Radstone's practice has explored caskets as vessels in the sense of a ship or canoe, and sculptures inspired by the notion of books as containers of knowledge. The organic anatomical sculptures created by Jacqueline Poncelet in the mid-1980s investigated questions of containment through enclosure and interior space, whilst Barnaby Barford's *Tower of Babel* (2015) playfully repurposed the notion of the vessel by producing thousands of ceramic shops (containers of goods) as a means to critique capitalism.

Alongside the more sculptural output of Richard Slee, the last two artists in particular offer a genealogical line of introduction to Eastman's work, signalling her own contribution to a tradition that approaches the idea of the vessel as a conceptual question, rather than as a formal device. Steeped in an understanding of the vocabulary of ceramic traditions, and yet existing happily in between the art/craft divide that still seems to generate so much discursive heat, Eastman has broken new ground formally and conceptually to become an individual voice in contemporary ceramics. As the opening quotation by the philosopher Jacques Derrida highlighted, 'coherence in contradiction expresses the force of desire'. Eastman's work is coherently incoherent, and all the more emotively powerful because of it. It teeters on the edge of the vessel, but also of unlocking an exciting future direction for ceramic sculpture.

Annie Turner

Deep Structures

Annie Turner's ceramic nets, traps, boxes, ladders, and mussel shell dishes are products of place. Her forms are abstracted responses to the Suffolk landscape in which she lives and works: the terrain of meadows, woodlands, Martello towers, North Sea shores and tidal surges. Of particular interest to Turner is the detritus caught on the sandbanks of the River Deben, a river that rises near the mid-Suffolk village of Debenham. Recorded in the Domesday Book as 'Depbenham', it is thought that the village took its name from the River Deben which, in old English, might have been called 'Dēope', meaning 'the deep one'.[67] The word 'dēope' or 'dīope' appears as the adverb 'deeply' in extant Anglo-Saxon poetry, such as *The Wanderer:*

Se þonne þisne wealsteal wise geþōhte
/ Ond þis deorce līf dēope geondþenceð,
[...] he who has brooded over these noble ruins,
/ and who deeply ponders this dark life,

frōd in ferþðe, feor oft gemon / wælsleahtaworn [...].
wise in his mind, often remembers / the many
slaughters of the past [...].[68]

A deep pondering over the ruins and slaughters of the past seems especially apt for the River Deben. On its journey from Debenham to the Deben Estuary and the North Sea, the river snakes its way past the world-famous Anglo-Saxon burial site of Sutton Hoo on the outskirts of Woodbridge.

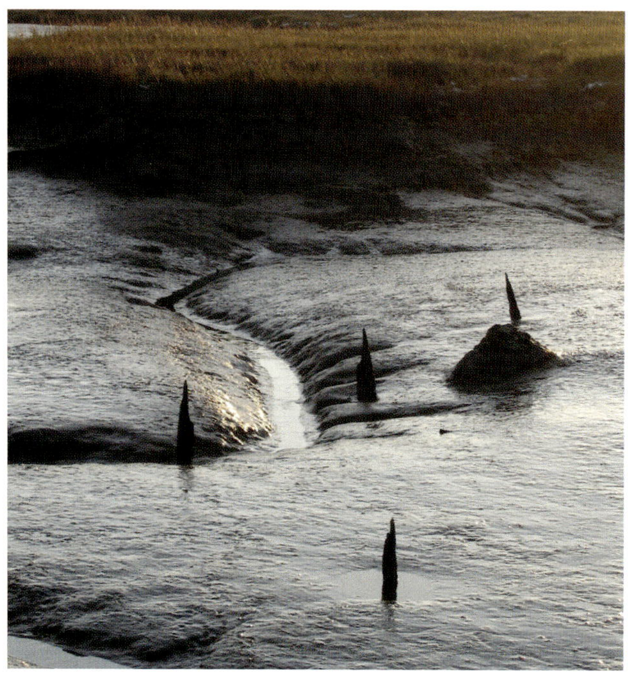

Witheys, River Deben.
(Photograph by Annie Turner)

stoneware exterior in the *Mussel Bed* pieces – gives them a jewel-like preciousness that places them beyond commonplace utility. In particular, the fusing together of porcelain and stoneware in the *Mussel Bed* forms is a complex process because each material behaves differently in the kiln. The river landscape that inspired the *Mussel Bed* forms is expressed in the marks of feathers and shells that have been impressed into the porcelain surface. These works may be small in size, but they are the products of focused attention and technical capability. This care in production accords them a special status, and the imagination is left to wonder whether they were made for an archaic religious ceremony.

Similarly, Turner's *River Ladders* could be the skeletons of boats; the tapered shapes are reminiscent of the wooden Anglo-Saxon ship unearthed at Sutton Hoo. Made to hang vertically on the wall,

At first, some of Turner's forms look like ritual objects excavated from a burial site. Theoretically, as contemporary studio ceramics, her *Claw* or *Mussel Bed* pieces could be used as functional ware in a kitchen. Yet, the technical accomplishment in their making – the thin clay wall that forms each *Claw*, or the combination of a porcelain interior with a

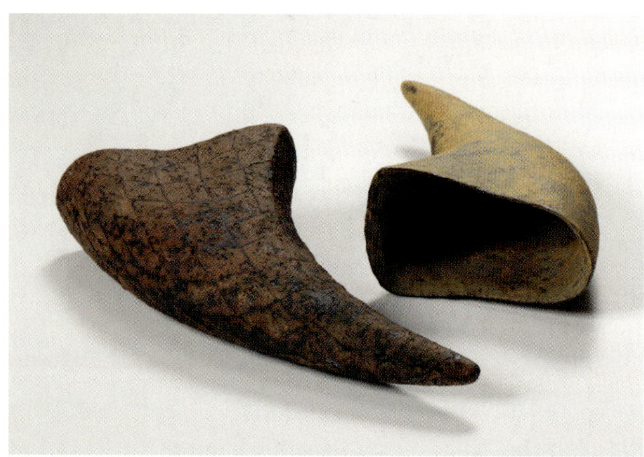

Claws.
(Photograph by Michael Harvey)

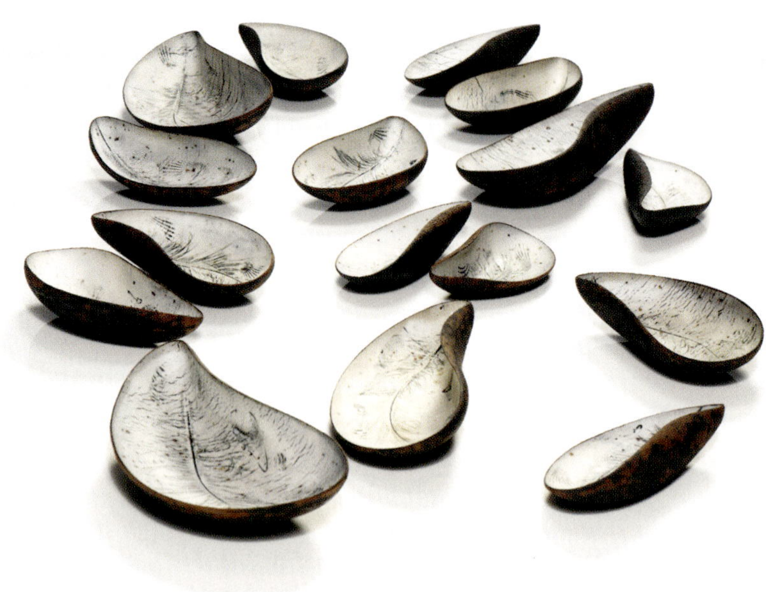

Mussel Bed.
(Photograph by Michael Harvey)

they more precisely recall the ladders used by boatmen to climb down to their boats at low tide. Such ladders, abstracted by Turner into smaller ceramic forms (typically around 25cm long), emphasize sensations of rhythm and tone. Indeed, while they can be displayed as individual works, the structure of each ladder is intensified when placed in series as a group. Awareness of the repetition of form enables the eye to perceive the interplay of light and shadow on the wall; the areas between and around the struts of each ladder become integral to the composition of the work as a whole. The rusty colours capture the erosion of metal in saltwater, but they also suggest sand, clay and mud. As ladders they are symbols of industry, but as ceramic sculptures made from clay they are representative of the natural world. This uncanny 'in betweenness' is, as with the *Claw* and *Mussel* forms, an important aspect of their visual appeal.

The *River Ladders* draw attention to the importance of structure as a focus for Turner's formal explorations. In thinking about the significance of structure, and of the fact that the River Deben might originally have meant 'deep', I am reminded of the concept of 'Deep Structure' proposed by the French anthropologist Claude Lévi-Strauss (1908–2009). Lévi-Strauss sought to understand the deepest meanings of ancient cultures, and to find a methodology for comparing the primal motivations behind different kinds of practices. Wedding rituals, for instance, are expressed in different ways in different cultures – a Chinese wedding is different from a Hindu wedding is different from a Christian wedding and so on. Yet, at the most basic level, all of them mark the change in status from individuals into a new coupled unit. How and why? Lévi-Strauss sought to schematize the processes behind different cultural acts to discover commonality:

It will be necessary to develop the analysis of the different features of social life, either for a given society or for a complex of societies, so that a deep enough level can be reached to cross from one to the other; or to express the specific structure of each in terms of a sort of general language, valid for each system separately and for all of them taken together.[69]

Lévi-Strauss sought to compare cultures by looking beyond what he perceived to be surface differences. Instead, he focused on the deep structures that had the potential to connect all of humanity, and

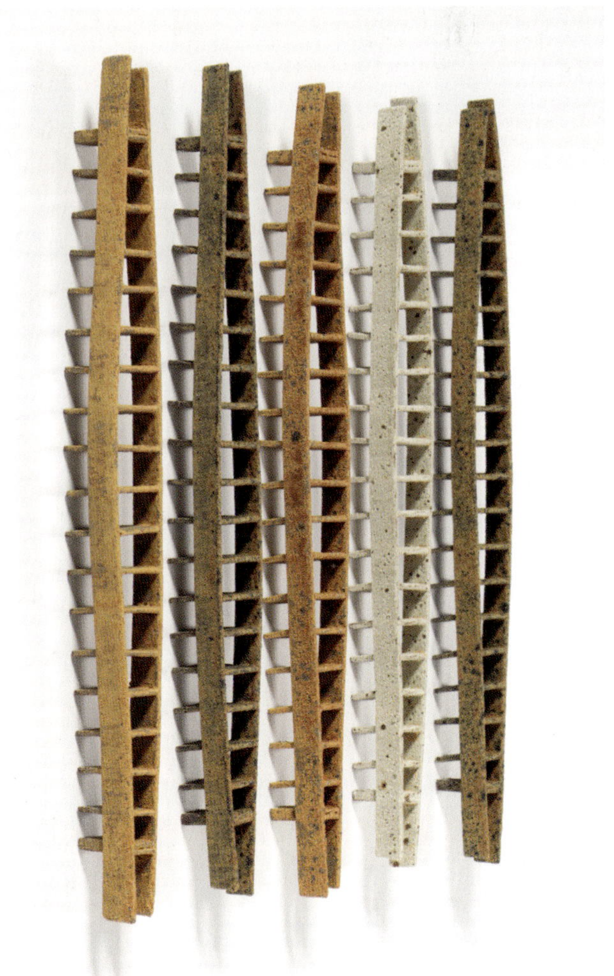

River Ladders.
(Photograph by Michael Harvey)

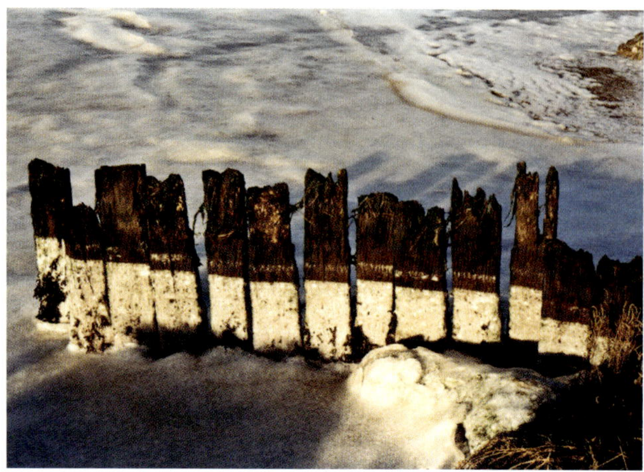

Frozen Tide Line, River Deben.
(Photograph by Annie Turner)

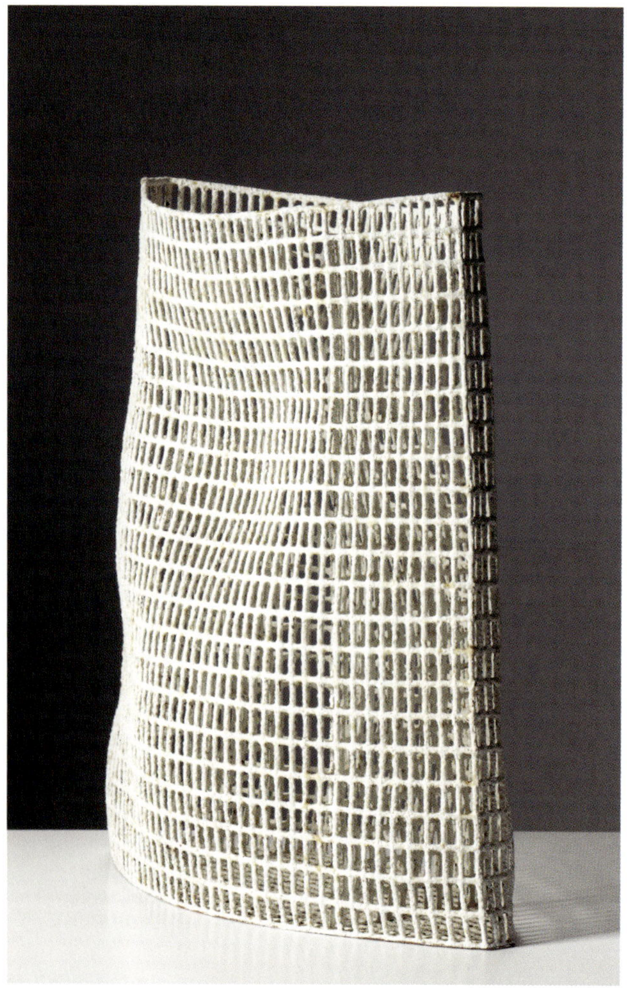

Drift Net.
(Photograph by Michael Harvey)

therefore offer a deeper understanding of why different cultures need to mark fundamentally similar things (like marriage).

I find that the concept of deep structure resonates with aspects of Turner's work. As has been established, her forms are a response to a very specific landscape, and yet they hold power because they have a wider resonance. At its most basic level, her work explores how humans interact with their environment, placing emphasis on ancient structures that have a genuinely global importance. Net structures have become the most sought-after examples of Turner's output. Fishing nets existed across the ancient world: for instance, in Ancient Egypt, pre-European Maori cultures, and amongst Native American tribes. Nets are functional hunting equipment, but they are representative of the human struggle for survival. Without the ability to effectively catch food, we cannot hope to survive. Turner's net pieces thus evoke methods of fishing that have existed across different cultures and time periods for millennia. Some of Turner's net forms, such as *Net* and *Sinker*, have a structural resilience that seems to have successfully weathered the onslaught of the tide. Others, such as *Drift Net*, express malleability and collapse, a yielding to the demands of the currents. The colours of each work allude to different degrees of exposure to the elements. The beige and brown pieces suggest silt and sand, of the coagulation of material around an imagined metal interior. In contrast, the white pieces present as resolutely man-made objects, suggesting that nets can never fully integrate with the natural landscape.

These structures also express different emotional states: of proud and enduring resistance against pressure, or of suppleness and responsiveness to the surrounding environment. Turner's work is expressive without being judgemental; her work seems to assert that there is no right or wrong way to respond to the events that life throws at us, but that we nevertheless

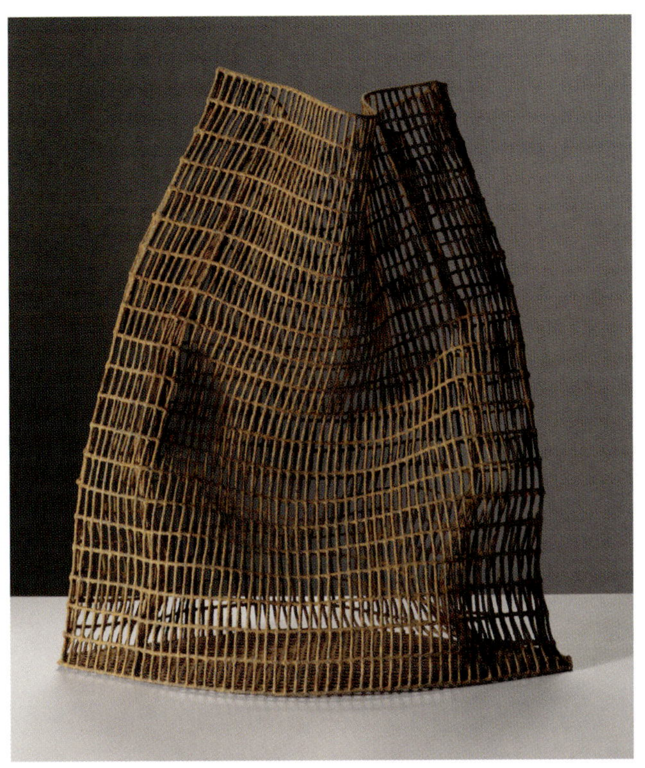

Net.
(Photograph by Michael Harvey)

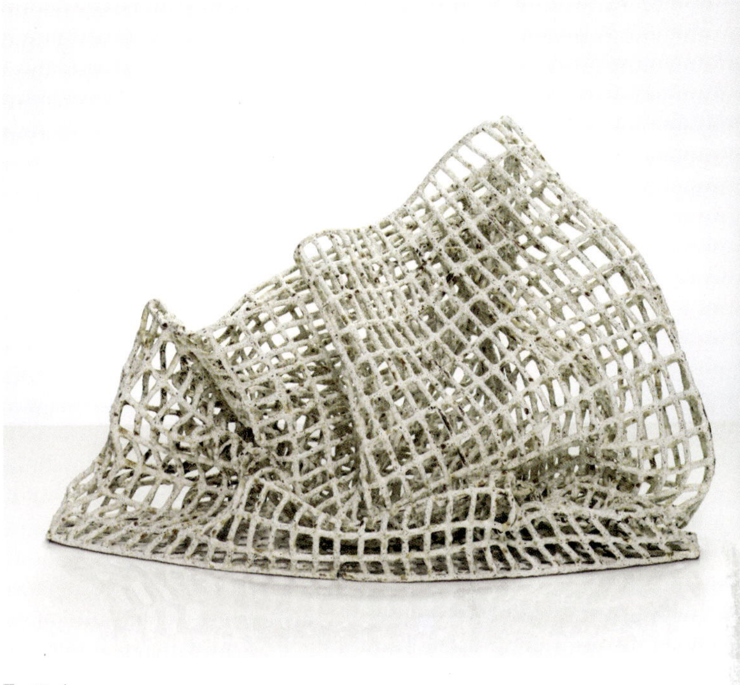

Sinker.
(Photograph by Michael Harvey)

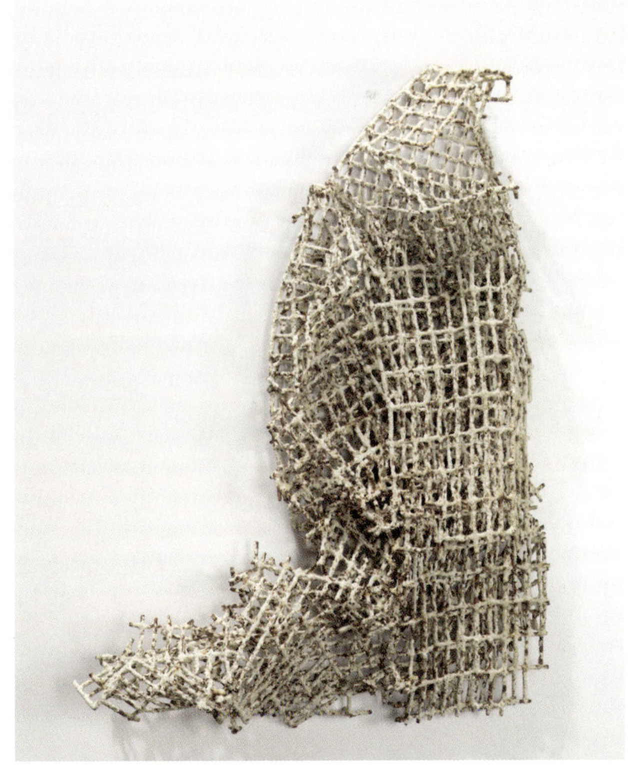

Flotsam.
(Photograph by Michael Harvey)

must accept our vulnerability to exterior forces. This sense of powerlessness is captured in *Flotsam*, a net piece in a state of collapse. As the title suggests, this structure has been abandoned, left to rot; it floats according to the mercy of the current. Once placed on the wall, it is a remarkable portrait of loss, grief and desolation. Collectively, these works powerfully connect the contemporary with the ancient, and our internal emotional landscapes with the exterior contours of geography.

Although much smaller in scale than her net pieces, the *Mussel Box* forms have a similar emotional impact. Some of these works consist of two cage-like boxes; a taller and more intricate form is placed inside a shorter and more open one. The fact that the interior box is finer gives it a sense of vulnerability. In contrast, the more robust exterior box seems protective against the outside world. Or is it

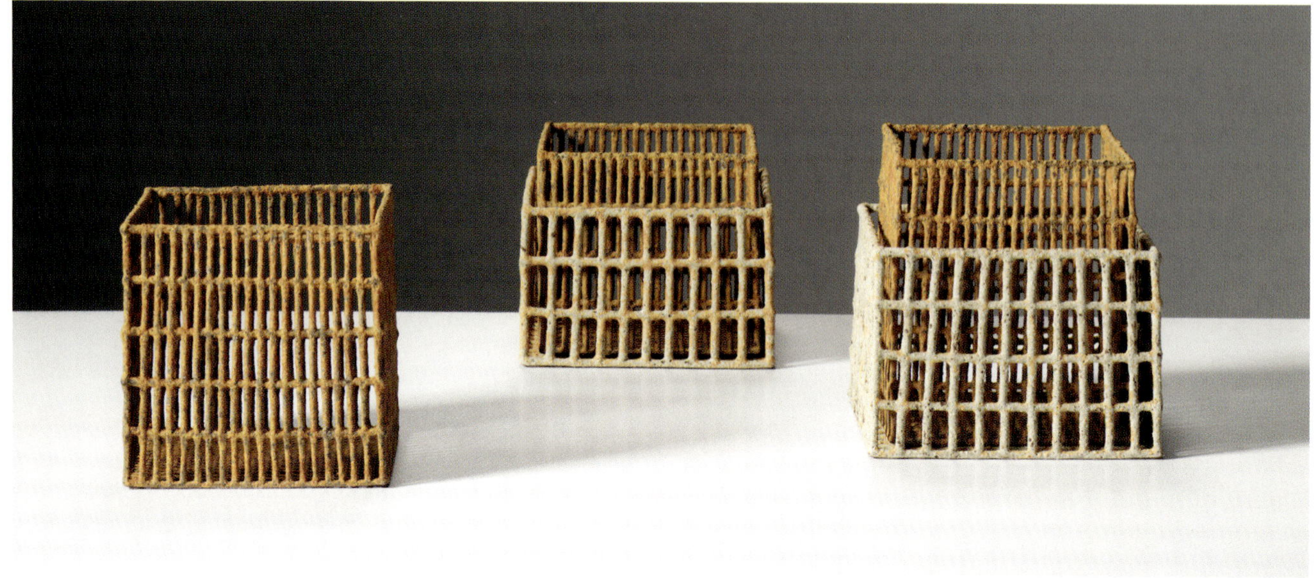

Mussel Boxes.
(Photograph by Michael Harvey)

the opposite, that the interior box is in fact imprisoned by the exterior one? Or is this a reference to the domestic, of a place in which something needs to be protected, or even trapped? In some of these works, Turner places loosely bundled remnants of fishing nets, intensifying the sense of the domestic by rendering the work into a kind of nest. The fluency and virtuosity of these pieces reminds me of the quasi-ritual objects explored at the start of this

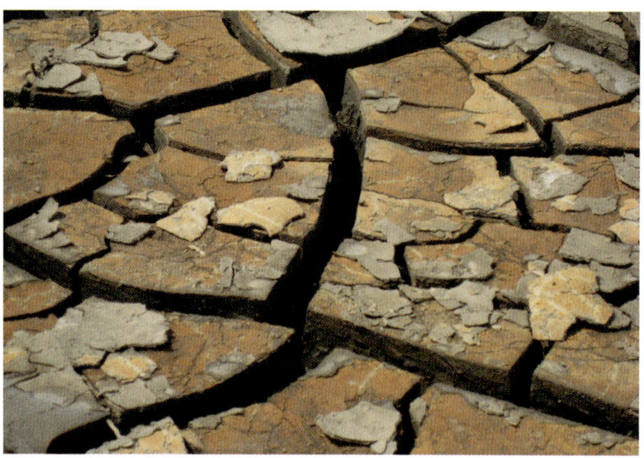

Creek in Drought, River Deben.
(Photograph by Annie Turner)

chapter. The strength and power of Turner's work lies in its ability to evoke a diverse range of emotions and narratives from the placement of geometrically simple but technically accomplished forms.

Definitions of the word 'deep', selected from the Chambers dictionary, offer a pertinent summation of Turner's sculptures:

Deep: far down from the top or surface; in a specified number of rows or layers (*lined up four deep*); said of emotions.

As quasi-archaeological remnants of a pre-industrial river culture, Turner's work could have been excavated from deep in the earth. Yet, as contemporary works of art, they have a deep emotional resonance as abstract portraits of feelings. Inspired by the Suffolk landscape, these sculptures reveal something fundamental about the primal dependency humans have upon the natural world. Inspired by the tides of the River Deben – 'the deep one' – they are, in every sense, deep structures.

Henry Pim

Structures of Feeling

Ceramic art, like all art, is connected to the wider social, economic, and political concerns of a culture at a given time in history. This approach to cultural analysis was advocated by the Marxist literary critic Raymond Williams (1921–88) in his essay entitled *Structures of Feeling*. For Williams, art was not an isolated thing; it was enmeshed into an ever-evolving cultural landscape. He considered that the meanings of art were always enriched by, and offered insight into, the wider culture in which they existed. As a consequence, the critic must become a kind of detective who looks for clues and seeks out patterns of correspondence that can demonstrate how and why an artwork has value. These patterns are what Williams meant by 'structure': patterns build up until they reveal a fundamental structure that highlights the values of a cultural moment in time.

However, it is impossible to conclusively prove that one person's interpretation of art is absolutely 'correct'; analysis of this kind is always subjective. It is necessary, therefore, to piece together the available evidence, speculate on any gaps, and make a case before a jury – you, the reader – to see if they are convinced. Williams signified the subjective nature of this interpretation in the term 'feeling'. Thus, 'structures of feeling' represents a mode of analysis that searches for pattern and presents an argument on the meaning of art as it is subjectively 'felt'. The implication of Williams's argument is to recognize that the meaning of an artwork does not remain static. Rather, it shifts as it travels through time to mean different things in different historical moments.

It is, for example, no longer possible to look at Vermeer's *Girl with a Pearl Earring* in the same way as seventeenth-century audiences did. Today, the

Girl with a Pearl Earring is everywhere. Most visitors go to the Mauritshuis in The Hague to see the painting only because they have seen it already; they know it from books, the internet, postcards, key rings, or even as images of parody. The *Girl with a Pearl Earring* still reveals something of the concerns of the seventeenth century, but any historical reading of it will also be informed by the iconic status it achieved during the twentieth century. Its cultural meaning, and significance, has changed.

I begin my reflections on the work of Henry Pim in this way for three reasons. The first is that 'structures of feeling' represents the methodology I deploy in this essay (in fact, across the entire volume). The second is that Pim's sculptures present themselves to me as a product of history viewed through the lens of the contemporary. His structures seem to emerge out of the British industrial landscape of nineteenth-century gas holders, Victorian seaside pier struts, and mid-twentieth-century Trellick-like tower blocks. They appear as a contemporary recontextualization of a particular kind of engineering that has been woven into the fabric of the British psyche. Yet, Pim's work consists of much more than an architectural model. Each sculpture has an emotional vibrancy. Thus, thirdly, Pim's work provokes feelings. In a statement that could easily describe one of Pim's sculptures, Williams explained 'structure of feeling' as:

> talking about characteristic elements of impulse, restraint, and tone; specifically affective elements of consciousness and relationships: not feeling against thought, but thought as felt and feeling as thought: practical consciousness of a present kind, in a living and interrelating continuity. We are then defining these elements as a structure: as a set, with specific internal relations, at once interlocking and in tension.[70]

For me, this sense of impulse and restraint, tone, interlocking tension within structure, and unification of thought and feeling, describe Pim's work at both an ideological and technical level.

Pim's sculptures are impressive in their own right as abstracted and totemic considerations of how and why we build. As constructed engineering, the sculptures express the human need for stability and protection. Yet any sense of rootedness to a specific location is diminished by the fact that these structures – as works of art – can be moved around, or positioned on any side, at will. In this sense, they are both permanent and temporary constructions that can be arranged into an endless series of ever-shifting skylines. Although the structures are strong enough to endure, being made of ceramic, they are also vulnerable to collapse from the shock of impact. Ultimately, then, Pim's work captures the contradiction of conservation and renewal, perhaps even the reality of the modification to which our urban landscapes are constantly subjected.

If, however, we consider Pim's work in relation to the broader context of the British cultural sense of self, especially the legacy of the Industrial Revolution, it is possible to find deeper resonance in his choice of form. His work strikes me as particularly British: references to the legacy of industry, living environment, community, and seaside leisure can be detected. This is not referent of any particular kind of politicized nationalism, more the product of curiosity arising from an aesthetic exploration of British architectural and industrial history. For instance, the gas holder – a large storage tank surrounded by scaffold-like supports – became a feature of most British towns and cities by the mid-nineteenth century. A gas holder overshadowing rows of terraced houses is indelible on the British cultural memory as a stereotype of urban working-class neighbourhoods. Yet, despite their industrial associations, many gas holders

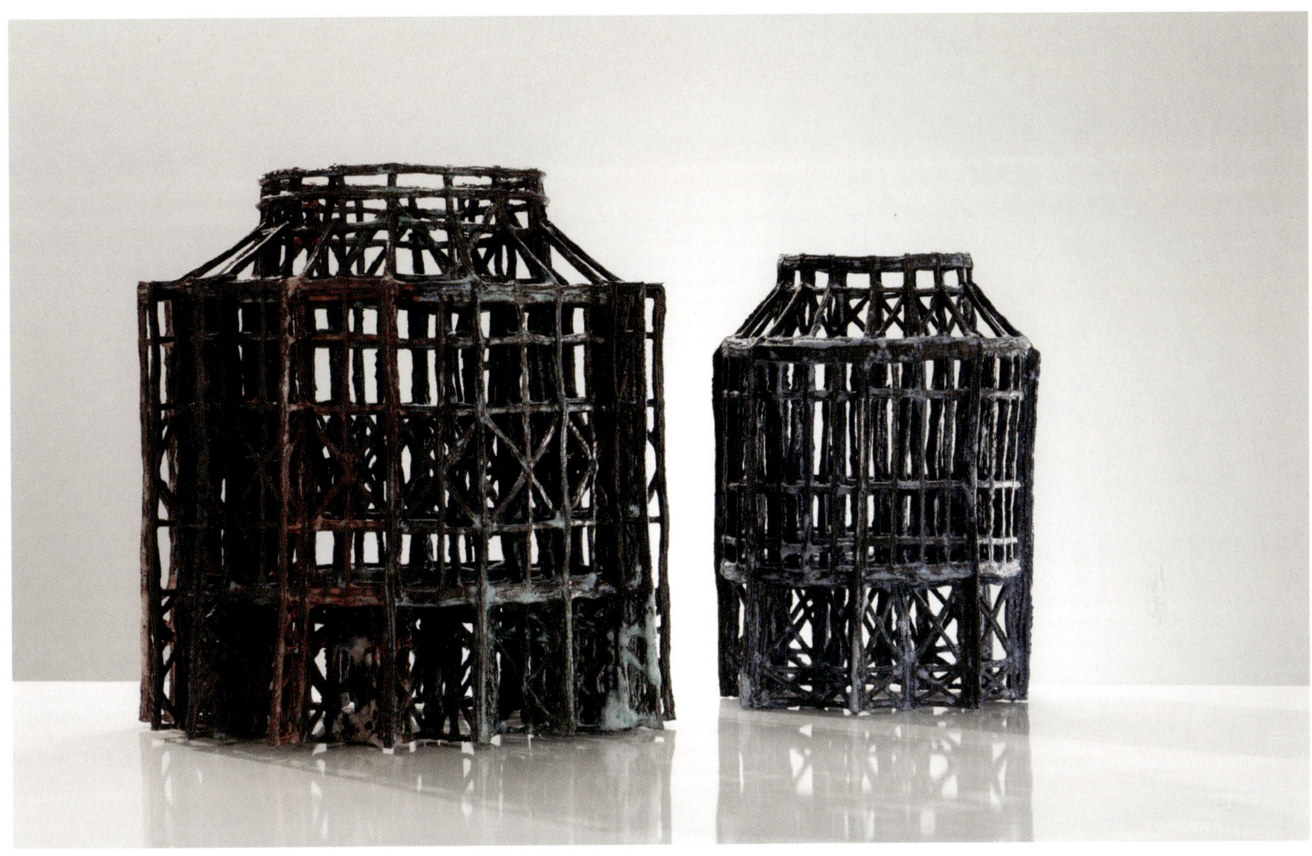

Monster Pleat and *Large Pleat* (2018).
(Photograph by Michael Harvey)

are protected with listed status, even as they have become sites for re-development (in Kings Cross, London, a development of luxury flats was built inside a repurposed gas holder structure in 2018). Gas holders occupy a peculiar place in the British architectural imagination. Pim's structures ask us to look at this industrial aesthetic differently, with disinterest in its practical and industrial use.

Works such as *Monster Pleat,* (2018), *Large Pleat* (2018) and *Red Cone* (2019) develop the complexity of the gas holder structure to create a rhythmic journey that travels along lines and through spaces. Pleasure is derived from simultaneously looking at and looking through each sculpture. Lines are powerful not only in relation to each other, but in relation to the

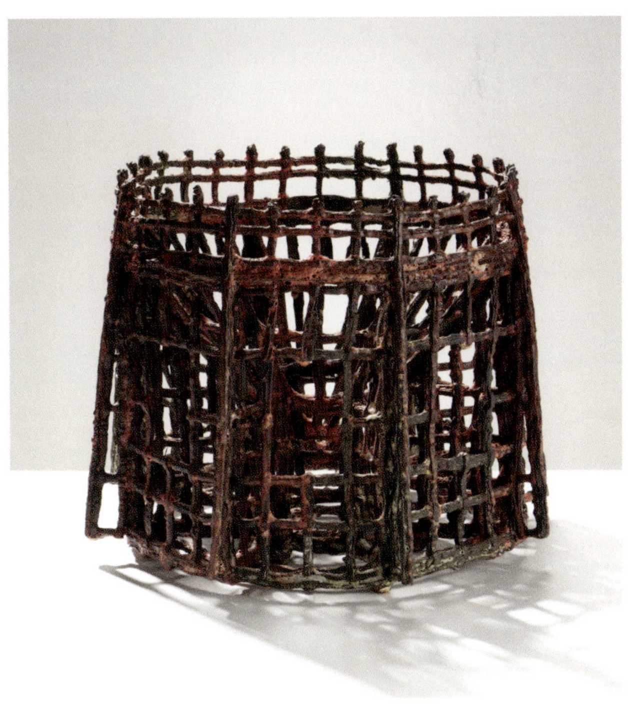

Red Cone (2019).
(Photograph by Michael Harvey)

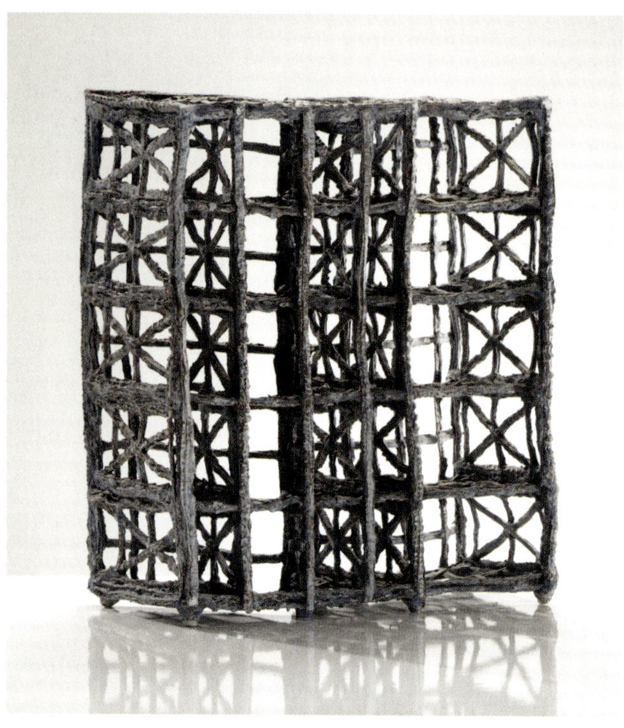

Blue Wall (2018).
(Photograph by Michael Harvey)

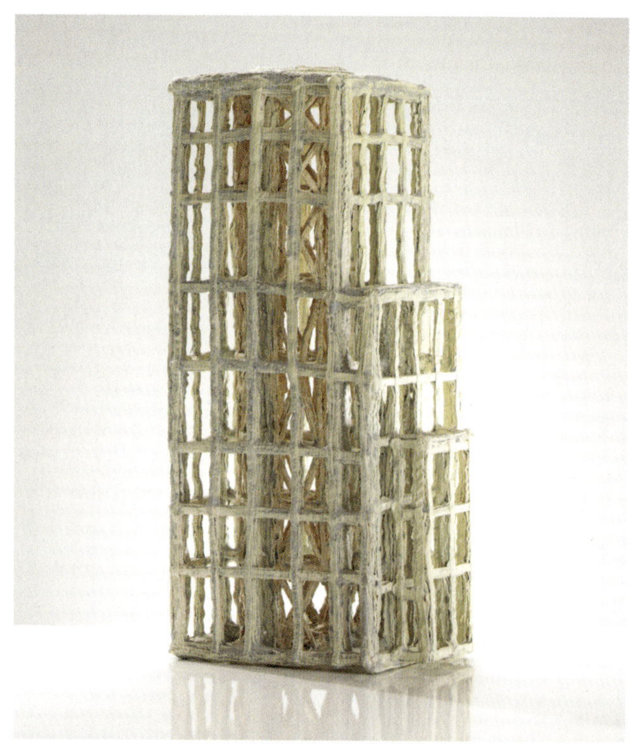

Yellow Structure (2016).
(Photograph by Michael Harvey)

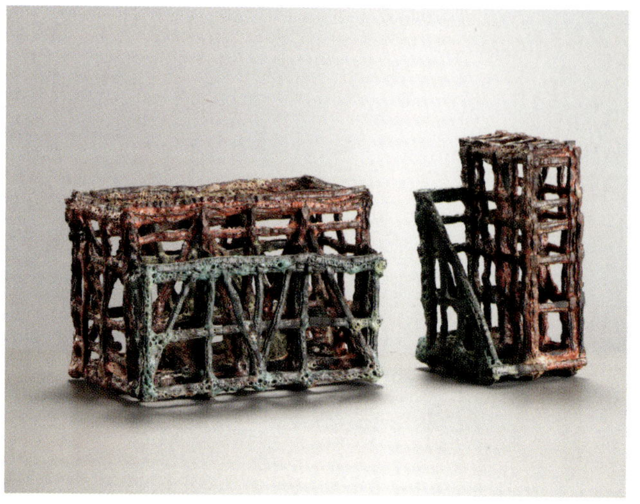

Box Forms (2017).
(Photograph by Michael Harvey)

space they enfold. Where there are more lines, there is tighter rhythm, greater drama, and a stronger sense of three-dimensions; where there are fewer lines, the sculpture relaxes, extends a greater awareness of space, and the lines organize into two-dimensional windows framing a void. The multicoloured, yet darkly metallic colours of the sculptures enhance the silhouette of the shape, affording it a greater spatial presence. These works are sculptures, of course, but they might equally be regarded as three-dimensional line drawings that survey the expressive potential of presence and absence.

Other sculptures, such as *Yellow Structure* (2016) and the small series of *Box Forms* (2017), evoke abstracted tower blocks. As a relatively modern design, tower blocks have become cost-effective construction projects in both industrial and domestic settings. The emphasis on the rectangle in these sculptures is suggestive of both windows and rooms. In many modern flat developments, the interior is segmented in such a way that people co-exist but are not provided with the tools of meaningful communal interaction. This sense of fragmented community, of togetherness without interaction, or a kind of collective individualism, is alluded to in these sculptures. The transparent interior of works like *Yellow Structure* suggest to me an absence of meaningful interior connection. The 'community in the sky' ideology that modernist architects dreamed of has, in reality, produced a modular experience that facilitates community only in ambivalent, sometimes even dystopic, ways.

The Industrial Revolution produced industrial architecture, but it also produced leisure. Factory production was no longer reliant on the seasons but could be managed as a year-round activity. To maintain a productive workforce a religious 'day of rest' (Sunday) was firmly established by the middle of the nineteenth century. From 1871, workers were entitled to an additional four days of paid leave per year to be taken as holiday. As railway transportation increased, families might afford a day trip to the seaside, where the pleasure pier grew to become an important attraction. Like gas holders, piers now have listed status and are considered iconic markers in the British cultural landscape.

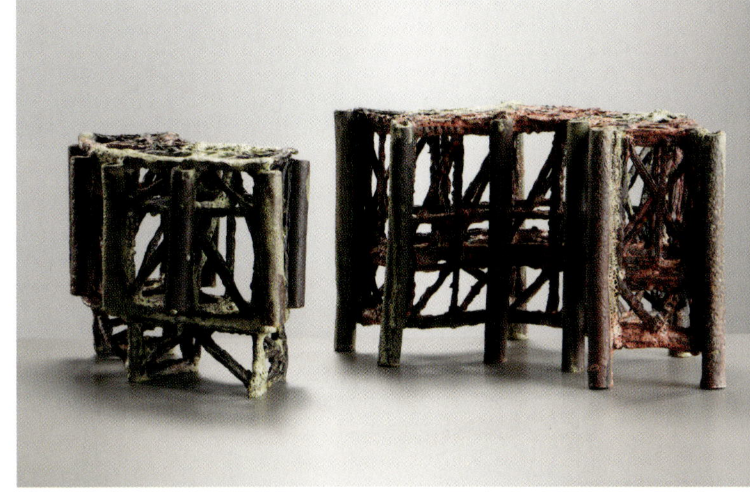

Piece on Stilts (Pair) (2018).
(Photograph by Michael Harvey)

Pim's works do not obviously reference the pleasure pier. Yet, for me, sculptures such as *Piece on Stilts* (2018) are evocative of them, particularly the iron girders that anchor the pier to the seabed. Perhaps this association arises from the colour and texture of the sculptures: the yellows and reds of rust, the greens of seaweed, and the volcanic glaze textures evincing molluscs and barnacles. The sensation

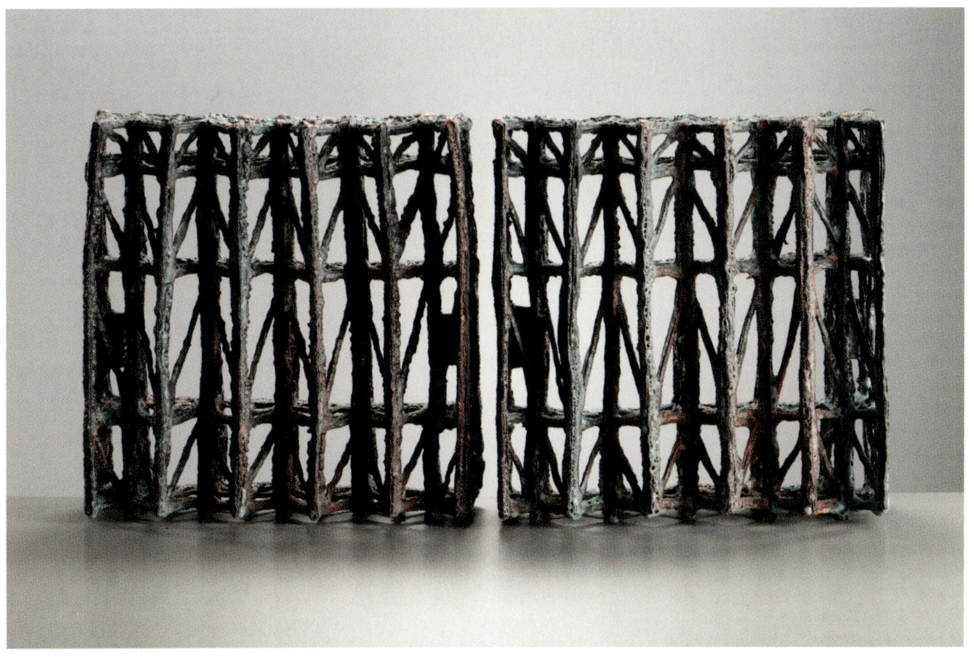

Pleated (2019).
(Photograph by Michael Harvey)

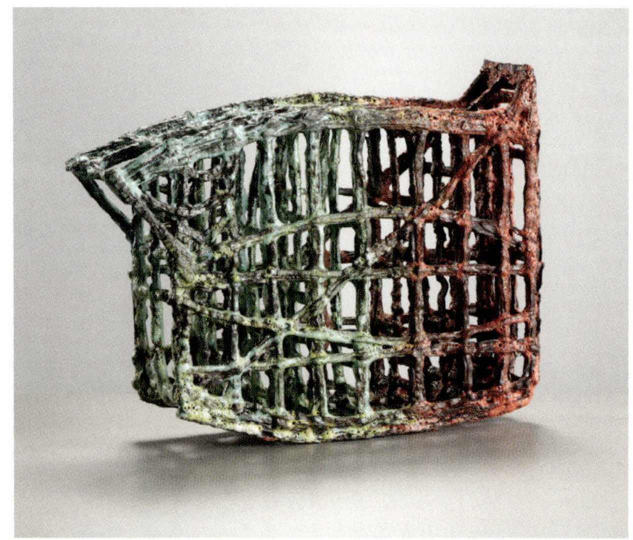

Red Rocker (2019).
(Photograph by Michael Harvey)

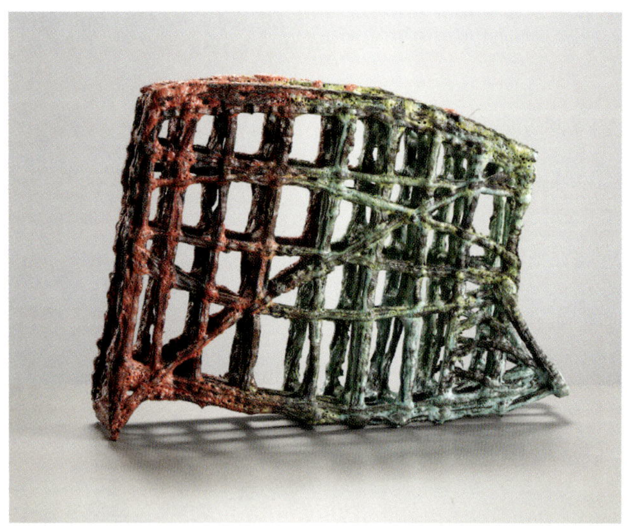

Red Rocker (2019).
(Photograph by Michael Harvey)

of waves undulating around the iron engineering beneath the pleasure pier can sometimes feel unnerving, the structure vibrating as each successive wave strikes. How can such seemingly flimsy metal posts withstand the daily onslaught of the tide, let alone the power of the winter storm? Of course, sometimes they do not; many piers have been lost to the energy of the sea. Yet, it is this precarious sense of structural tolerance and fragility that is captured in Pim's work. His sculptures portray both the strengths and weaknesses of structure. Like the pier, his pieces have sturdiness as free-standing constructions, yet the impact of an exterior force threatens structural integrity.

Pim's work is made from conjoined sections of paper clay. Following a biscuit firing, each piece is fired a number of times in order to achieve the desired surface effect. There is, as a consequence, a tension between design and discovery in the production of each piece. Although planning must be significant to enable construction to become possible, there is also the presence of a strong intuitive sense learnt from experience that can only be deployed in the act of making. This enables planned elements of structure to combine in new and surprising ways. *Red Rocker* (2019) encapsulates the contradictions I find so arresting in Pim's work. There is a sense of movement and stasis here: as a structure it is resilient, but it is also designed to rock on one of its curved planes. For me, the shape of the work nominally evokes a Victorian rocking horse, and thus demonstrates Pim's ability to abstract and rearticulate historical engineering into a new artistic language. Rearticulation is in fact key since the work can be placed on any side so that it occupies space in different ways.

As a moveable, and moving, structure, *Red Rocker* expresses something of the constant movement of culture identified by Williams. What was considered functionally industrial in one historical period has become source material for aesthetic investigation in another. As archives of cultural nostalgia, familiarity, modernity and the possibilities of cultural change, Pim's sculptures are affecting; in this sense they are unquestionably 'structures of feeling'.

Martin Smith

Un/Divided Lines

> Every touching of architecture is multi-sensory;
> qualities of space, matter and scale are measured
> equally by the eye, ear, nose, skin, tongue, skeleton
> and muscle. Architecture strengthens the existential
> experience, one's sense of being in the world, and
> this is essentially a strengthened experience of self.[71]
>
> *Juhani Pallasmaa*

In his analysis of architecture, Juhani Pallasmaa argues that we do not encounter space as a purely visual phenomenon; rather, it engages all of our senses. The movement of air, the smell of a room, reverberations of sound, and the sensations of our own body moving across space, are integral to our daily experiences of architecture, and by extension, our sense of place in the world. Pallasmaa's argument rests upon an acknowledgement of architecture as a viscerally expressive form and, as a consequence, a plastic art that has equivalence to painting and sculpture.[72] Much earlier, Piet Mondrian (1872–1944) had considered this too, but from the perspective of painting. Mondrian implicitly recognized that if his 'new plastic' abstract art was to become truly transcendental, pure and universal, it needed to have applicability beyond the realm of fine art – the canvas – and into daily life. Mondrian hypothesized that if architectural questions of volume, plane and linear space could be framed in terms of fine art painting, specifically the use of lines to create dynamic space, architecture could also become abstract art.[73]

The work of Martin Smith is further proof that the divide between architecture and art is porous.

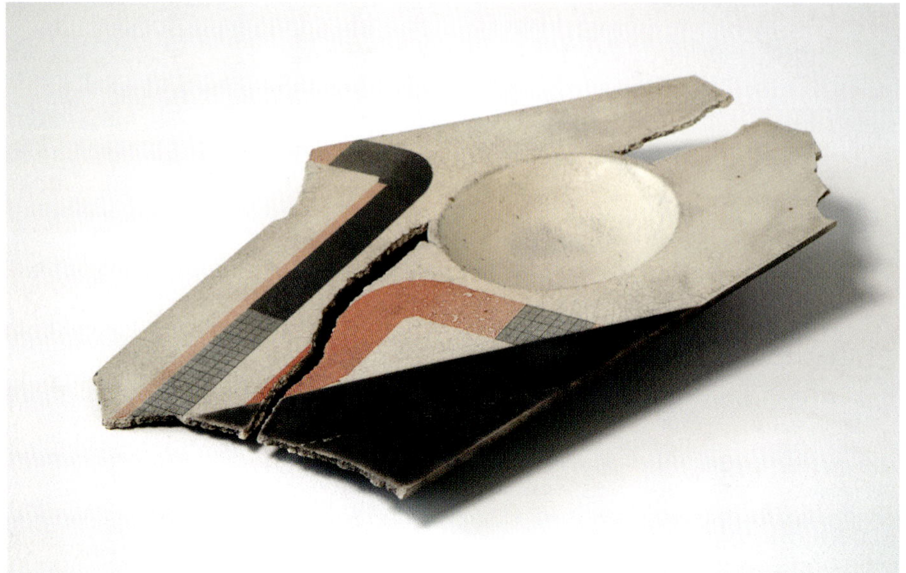

Bowl (1977).
(Photograph by Martin Smith)

His approach is indebted to an understanding of architecture as both a practice and a discourse. Yet, he has also drawn upon a range of disciplines, including most obviously ceramics as a technical process and its association with domesticity, but also sculpture, painting and even music. Smith situates himself in between disciplines; disciplinary lines are broken only for individual elements to be reconfigured and merged into his own distinctive sculptural vocabulary. If, following Pallasmaa, architecture strengthens the sense of self in the world, Smith's work exudes his own concentrated mindfulness and attention to each moment, an ethos developed through the interplay of imagination and its physical realization. Each piece is testament to his skill and ingenuity, but above all his playfulness. We are invited to sense the dynamism of each work, the cutting of lines through space in arresting combinations of rhythm and tone, the manipulation of our perceptions of mass and volume, and the variance between our visual perception of a surface and its tactile reality. As a consequence, to look at one of his pieces is not so much to see it but to experience it as a series of visceral sensations, to feel 'one's sense of being in the world'.

I visited Smith in the summer of 2020, in the midst of a mini retrospective of his work shown across two sites in London – the Marsden Woo Showroom and his own studio. To see so many works from across his career is a rare occurrence in Britain. A regular exhibitor at Marsden Woo, and participant in group exhibitions worldwide, his most significant public shows have taken place abroad. In 1996, for example, Smith had a major retrospective at the Museum Boijmans Van Beuningen in Rotterdam, exhibiting eighty works made between 1976 and 1996.[74] There have only been two significant public shows of Smith's work in Britain across his more than forty-year career: a touring exhibition, *Forms Around A Vessel: Ceramics by Martin Smith*, which began at the Leeds City Art Gallery in 1981, and an installation called *Wavelength* at Tate St Ives and Ruthin Craft Centre in 2001.[75]

Perhaps this stems from a bias against ceramics as a serious material for sculpture. Had Smith worked in bronze, things might have been different. Or maybe it derives from the fact that some 'complain that Smith's vessels are too cold, calculating and intellectual'.[76] This strikes me as a rather puzzling criticism. All artists plan out their work to some extent before they embark upon production, and Smith makes playful alterations to each piece as it develops, as do most artists. Only a fascistic fetishism with clay as a necessarily hand-touched and messy material could produce objection to his finely crafted lines and use of moulds. Ceramic is a material not a doctrine; leave each to their own.

In any case, mould-making in ceramics has existed for centuries. Smith is simply working within and across established modes of making. Yet, what I find remarkable is how Smith holds disciplinary lines in suspension even as they are merged. Out of this highly selective interdisciplinary weaving a distinct body of sculptural work has emerged. As a response to the retrospective, I have framed this essay around a discussion of works from across a forty-five-year period. It is not an exhaustive discussion by any means, but through the limited number of works I have chosen, I seek to demonstrate how self-imposed constraints and the unwavering pursuit of particular conceptual questions – here, pertaining to the circle – have compelled Smith into ever more complex terrain.

Smith's early work in raku, produced in the late 1970s, is perhaps most associated with an imposing range of bowl forms, their exterior decorated with dynamic black-and-white geometric patterns. While these works demonstrated his early interest in the possibilities of shape and pattern to create rhythms around curved planes, these forms were ultimately abandoned in 1978. Of more enduring interest to Smith were the possibilities opened up by the handful of sculptural raku pieces produced for his graduate show at the Royal College of Art in 1977. I regard these works as a significant pivot in the development of his practice; they deconstructed the vessel into an opened-out sculptural form that facilitated the investigation of horizontal, even tilting, planes, in addition to the vertical and the spherical.

Works such as *Bowl* (1977) and *Dish* (1977) represent an initial response to the conceptual questions that Smith would pursue across the next forty years. The significance of a circular recess, suggestive of the vessel, is retained, but emphasis is instead placed upon its sculptural and geometric value in generating composition. It becomes a spatial anchor point to capture

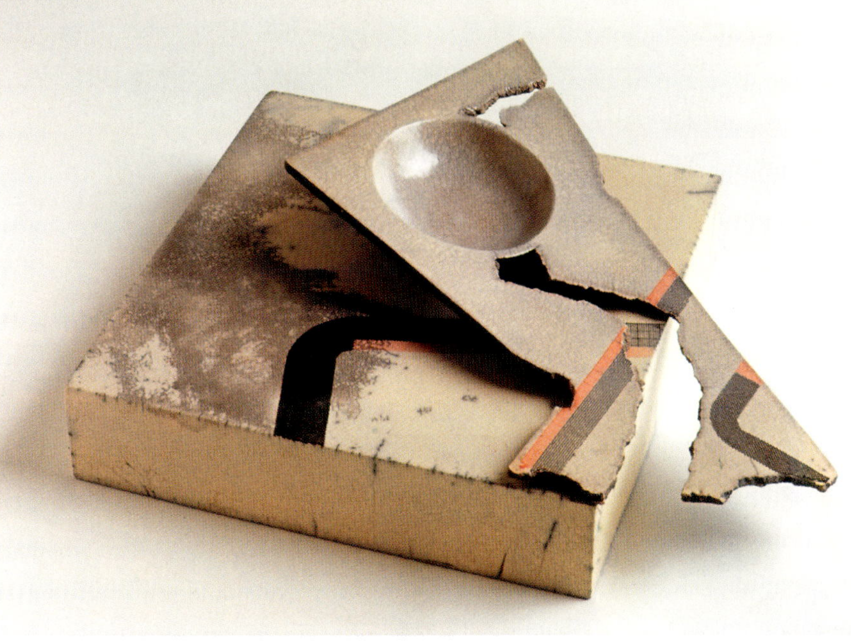

Dish (1977).
(Photograph by Martin Smith)

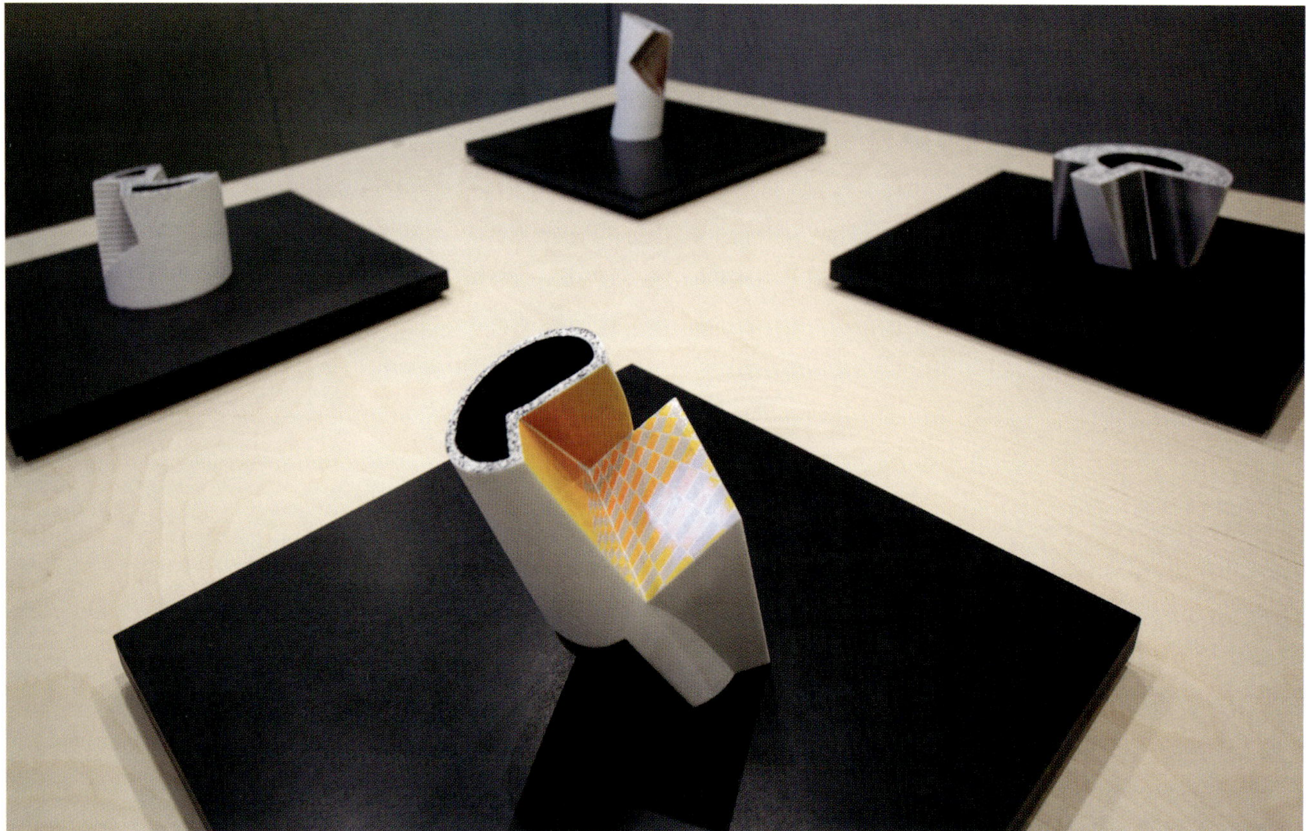

Spaces & Places installation at Marsden Woo Gallery London 2017.
(Photograph by Phil Sayer)

and reflect light, provide a focus for the centre of the form, and offer a playful riff on the possibility of function. The significance of geometric lines and curves, also found on the early raku bowls, is redeployed on these works as enamel transfers. These transfers create relationships between the two- and three-dimensional aspects of the form, drawing attention to angular contours that create presence.

In *Bowl*, for instance, there is a complex interplay between shape, surface and transfer markings. The triangular stripe of black towards the bottom right of the work echoes and supports the rim running across the opposite edge of the form. This draws the eye across the work in a way that drags against its actual edges. The eye tries to process this spatial disjuncture, expressed as simultaneous recognition of

a parallelogram and a rectangle. This produces a generative friction upon which the presence of the work is dependent. The enamel transfers also direct attention to the impressed 'bowl' shape. This functions as both a sculptural circle (evoking the modernist reliefs of Ben Nicholson, or the geometry of Constructivism) but also gives the audience a nod towards the implied utility of the work. *Bowl* is not really a bowl; it is the amalgamation of abstract painting, the bowl as a conceptual form associated with containment, an exploration of material, and fine art sculpture.

The crackled fault lines that ripple across the surface are perhaps the least Smith-like elements of these works. Nevertheless, they allude to his interest in texture, so important to his practice, and yet so disguised by his reputation for clean formal lines.

In *Dish*, the shadow formed by the fissure across the top form echoes the curve of the enamel transfer to the centre of the base section. Such compositions demonstrate Smith's playfulness and control as an integral aspect of presence, making the relationship between components particularly significant. The tilting of the top section of *Dish* is placed in such a way that it has compositional balance with the base. The way the top section teeters on the edge of the base perhaps evokes a different sense of balance, but the intrusion of the work into exterior space is noteworthy. The black enamel transfer line at the very tip of the protruding wing directs the eye to the edge of the work and out into the exterior space of the everyday. In this sense, *Dish* reminds us of our own presence, and of our changing perspectives as we explore the work from different directions. Like architecture, it reminds us that we inhabit the world from particular points of view.

I now fast-forward forty years to 2017 and the *Spaces & Places* exhibition shown at Marsden Woo. This series of work revealed a different, more confident, and greatly refined aesthetic. These works were purer in colour and tone (the raku process had long since been discarded), investigating relationships between the horizontal and vertical plane with greater dexterity. There was a strong sense of development, of course, but these works nevertheless extended the fundamental questions that first arose in 1977. As before, geometric shapes are utilized as elements in sculptural composition even as they allude to the functional history of ceramics via reference to the vessel. Geometric transfers again direct the eye around the work, but here Smith deployed them to manipulate perspectives of space and surface. Transfers instigate visual sensations that draw attention to space, which recedes more in the eye than in actuality. The black interiors are not smooth but highly textured, recalling the rough terrain of

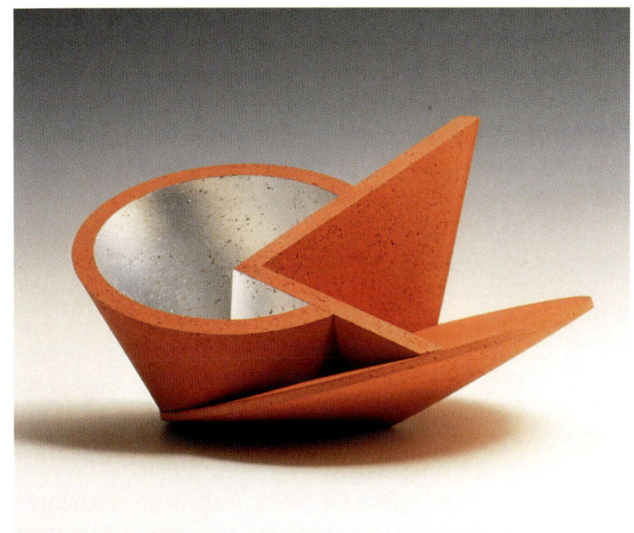

Vessel (1990).
(Photograph by Martin Smith)

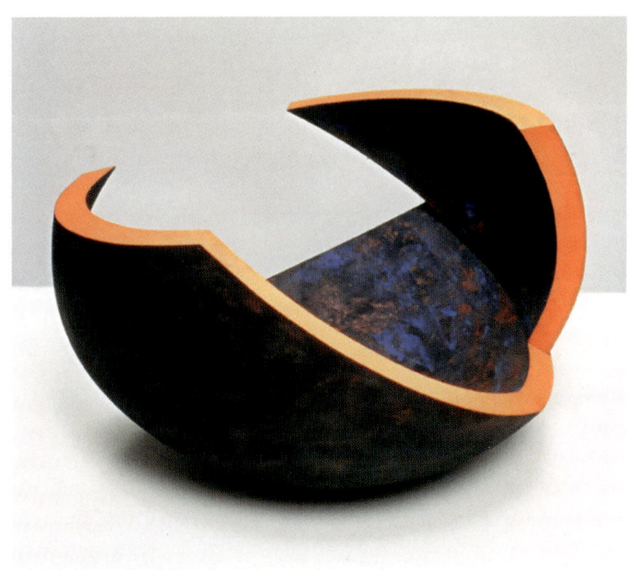

Bowl (1985).
(Photograph by Martin Smith)

the fissures in the earlier raku pieces. Indeed, as in *Dish* (1977), the use of a base to ground each piece provides it with its own relational space. These latter pieces are a genuine tour-de-force: dynamic, surprising, seductive, powerful and fun. They are also the product of formal explorations tirelessly honed.

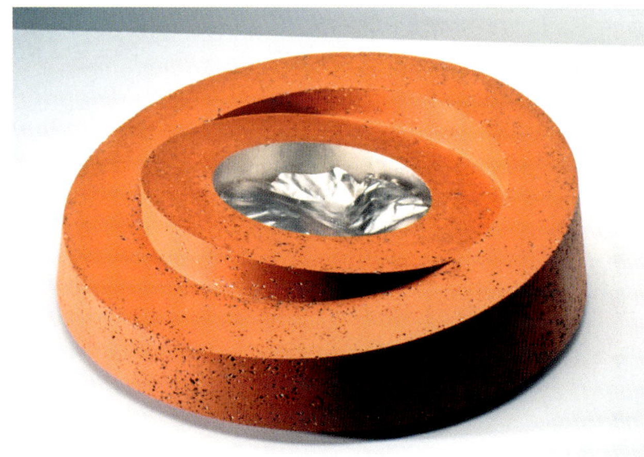

Shift & Rotate No. 2 (1996).
(Photograph by Studio Tom Haartsen)

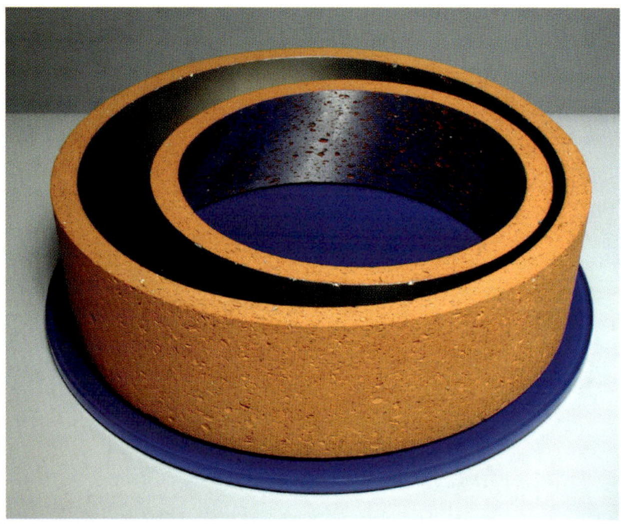

Sound & Silence No. 6 (2005).
(Photograph by Martin Smith)

A small selection from the many works produced in the intervening period shows how conceptual questions have been explored with focus and resolve. What is the sculptural possibility of line and curve? How can angular lines and tilting angles affect the rhythm and presence of a work? How can colour produce tone through the interplay of light and shadow? *Vessel* (1990) is a masterful response to such compositional questions. Lines slot together to produce an arresting form full of angular corners. The terracotta clay, evocative of bricks, links the work with architecture. The application of silver leaf to the interior brings vibrancy to the work, highlighting the significance of interior space as the substance of our living environments. Once again, balance is key. This piece could not be achieved without careful planning, refining and moulding. Recalling the stylish architecture of modernism and the sculptures of Naum Gabo, it stands as a celebration of the possibility of clay as a sculptural material. The earlier *Bowl* (1985) echoes *Vessel*, but whereas the latter depends on presence, *Bowl* is redolent with absence. Absence does not, however, mean expressionless. Rather, the voids between the different petal-like fronds of *Bowl* are resonant with energy. These energized spaces are brought to the viewer's attention by the terracotta outlines that pulse through the darkened blue-black interior and exterior walls.

Constraints of material or approach require ever-greater ingenuity. *Shift & Rotate No. 2* (1996) re-examines the circle as a key expressive element (as documented in the 1977 works), but develops subsequent pieces, such as *Vessel* (1990), with even greater dexterity. How can an angular tilt add presence to concentric circles? The response to this question produced a piece with great poise, the calmness of suspended circles offering a counterpoint to the undulations of the viscous-like silver interior. The piece has a great sense of emergence and movement. In comparison, as the name suggests, *Sound & Silence No. 6* (2005) is a much quieter work. Here, two circles are not tilted but placed on a level surface to create compression and expansion within the interior space. The base is made from glass that has been coloured blue, developing the significance of the base as a compositional element as first explored in 1977. The blue colour of the base determines the possibilities for the silver interior to reflect or absorb light – to make 'sound' or be 'silent'. As such, this work in particular demonstrates Smith's mastery of architectural thinking: the construction of space as an environment that can provoke a visceral response in the viewer.

The suspension of straight and angular lines within and across circles was explored further in works such as *Static Shift No. 1* (2013). Here, two concentric sgraffito circles – one placed off centre – were incised into a thrown black form. The result produced a kind of optical effect: the eye is confused as it cannot mark the centre, making the piece appear to whirl in space. A sense of spinning, if reconfigured for a different form, exists in *Static Double Tilt No. 3* (2013). Here, the concentric lines placed at different angles rise up the body of the work giving it a sense of emergence, almost as if the work were being thrown before our very eyes. Smith is an accomplished thrower, having worked with Robin Welch (1936–2019) on production ware at his studio in Stradbrooke, Suffolk. Indeed, the form of *Static Double Tilt No. 3* is evocative of some of Welch's production ware, particularly the goblets and cylindrical vases, even as the beautiful curve of the base gives the work a distinctive presence in silhouette that is the trademark of Smith's approach.

The slightly earlier work *Two Corners* (2012) deploys the concentric circle across a series of nineteen dinner plates displayed in a white box. Lines ripple from designated origins – one in the bottom left corner, the other in the top right corner. The circles lose energy and become straighter as they move away from their starting points, creating faster and slower rhythms as lines intersect at different speeds. Each plate has a compositional centre, even though it is clearly part of a series. The plates are also positioned in two layers, making the edges between the individual plates tremor as opposing patterns collide. The eye has to choose between registering the distortion of the pattern at the edge of an individual plate or looking across the work in totality to find

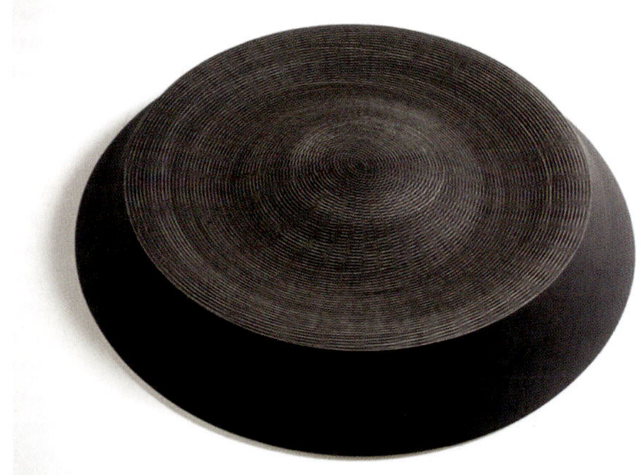

Static Shift No. 1 (2013).
(Photograph by Phil Sayer)

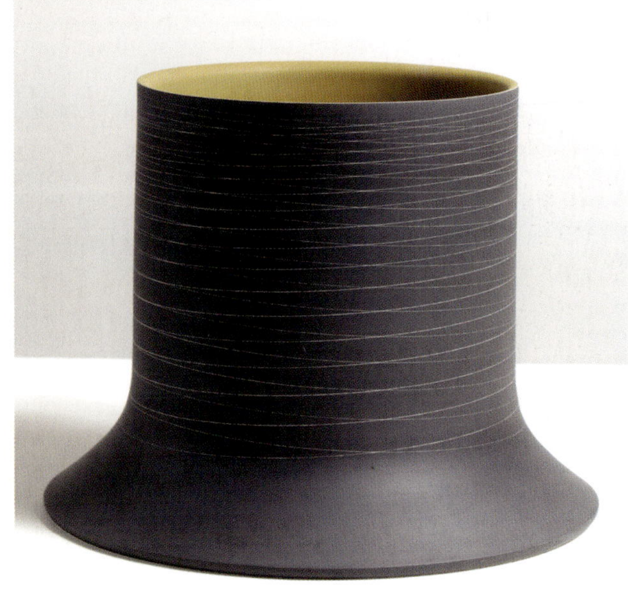

Static Double Tilt No. 3 (2013).
(Photograph by Phil Sayer)

resolution. It is hard to process both at the same time. Such explorations of the expressive possibilities of lines and curves evoke the 1970s paintings of Bridget Riley, but Smith has arrived here as a consequence of his own investigations. Indeed, the

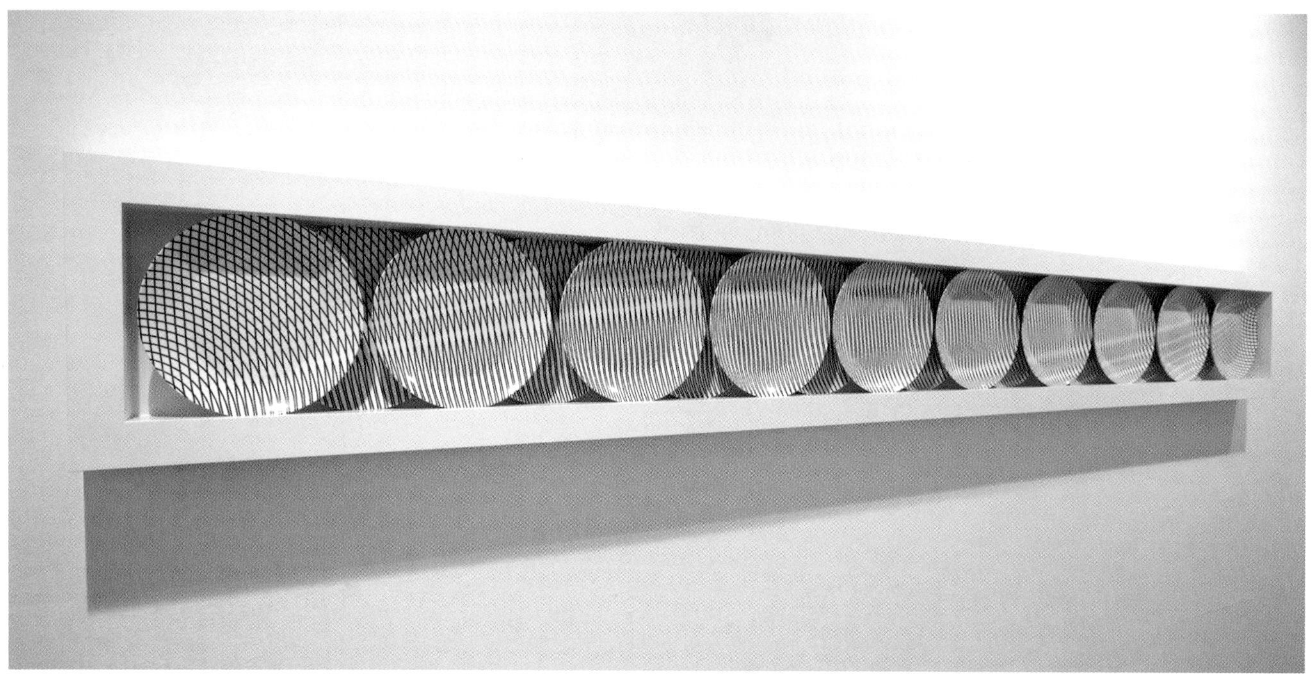

Two Corners (2012).
(Photograph by Phil Sayer)

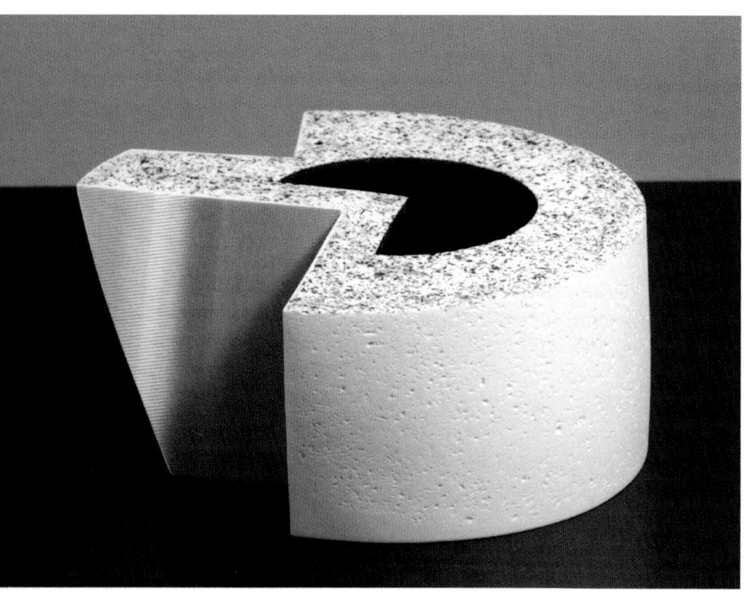

Space & Place No. 12 (2017).
(Photograph by Phil Sayer)

plates are exhibited as though on a dresser, a reference to the role of the plate in domestic kitchen displays. The retinal games of *Two Corners* mirror Smith's own blurring of disciplinary lines, but they also capture something of his playfulness and desire to provoke visual sensations.

The above analysis of a small selection of Smith's output leads me back to work from 2017, and the consideration of it as an advanced response to the conceptual questions first encountered at the beginning of Smith's career. To focus on a specific work, for example *Space & Place No. 12* (2017), is to recognize how Smith grapples with compositional questions of geometry, angularity, line, curve, plane, tone, the deployment of texture and use of transfers, space, interior, the relationship between interior and exterior conceptualized as a kind of möbius strip, balance, and, above all, playfulness. Smith's tendency to use '&' in the titles of many works demonstrates a desire to fuse interdisciplinary elements into one statement,

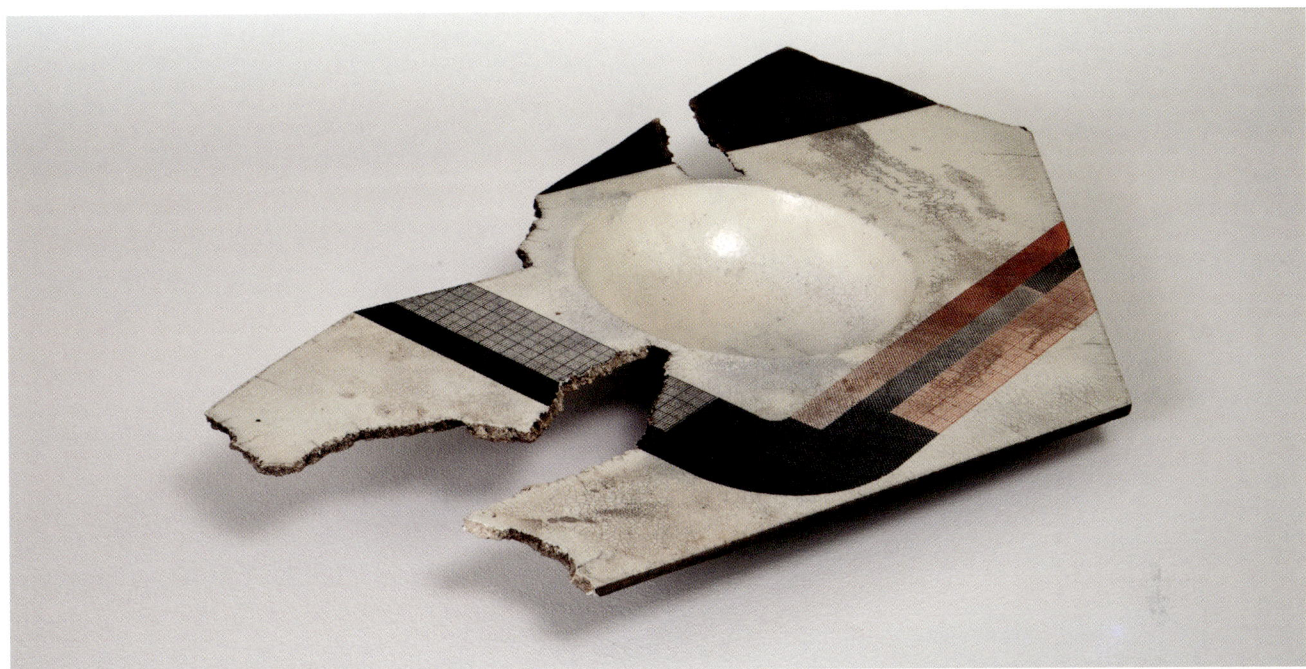

Bowl (1977).
(Photograph by Martin Smith)

even as they remain discernible as disciplinary-specific reference points. Lines are un/divided.

This suspension is also explored in *Bowl* (1977), another piece from the opposite end of Smith's career timeline. The forty-year gap between these two pieces evidences how a self-imposed focus on particular questions demands constant reinvention. This includes a technical growth fuelled by the possibilities of using different materials and the analysis of his own processes, and it is perhaps for this reason that Smith works in series. Yet, the more constrained the conceptual questions are, the more imaginative the responses must be in order to avoid repetition. Indeed, mindfulness is crucial to Smith's practice; if he is not fully occupied with the problem at hand then it cannot have been worthy of investigation. Conceptual complexity must be all-encompassing, integrating all facets of Smith's creativity and skill. This, for me, is what aligns his work so closely with architecture. As Pallasmaa has argued:

An architectural work is not experienced as a series of isolated retinal pictures, but in its fully integrated material, embodied and spiritual essence. It offers pleasurable shapes and surfaces moulded for the touch of the eye and other senses, but it also incorporates and integrates physical and mental structures, giving our existential experience a strengthened coherence and significance.[77]

Smith's architectural works pulsate as three-dimensional rhythmic structures through space. They exist to provoke a response in the viewer: the pleasure of sight, the excitement of discovery, the change of surface contours and texture, the surprise of touch, the play of light. No wonder I feel excitement when I encounter a work by Smith and look admiringly at its resolved composition. These sculptures move beyond the eyes and penetrate the body through the skin.

Aphra O'Connor

Planes, Frames and Spatial Games

In order to create, we need lines, forms, colors. These can be taken from our surroundings: from nature or from whatever has been created for use, utility, necessity. Or from imagination; but the latter can go beyond visible forms only by distorting them. Nothing really comes directly from us, nothing is truly new.[78]

This quotation from the modernist painter Piet Mondrian (1872–1944), written in 1938, was found in a folder of his handwritten notes and musings. It was, as the note goes on to make clear, intended as a critique of the desire to document reality, which Mondrian viewed as the scourge of most art practice. He considered this need too naturalistic, too subjective, too specific, too concerned with verisimilitude, and thus ill-placed to imagine a new future. Mondrian instead espoused the need for abstraction, which he labelled as the 'new plastic'. Developed from the Dutch word *beelding*, 'new plastic' conveys the meaning of structure, image-formation, and of plasticity of material (i.e. the plasticity of paint – or clay – in its innate ability to be physically manipulated by an artist).[79] For Mondrian, painting had to correspond to the universal, to be understood by all humanity, and across all time. This universality demanded only the most abstract of shapes – the flat line – and primary colours. This, Mondrian believed, expressed the universality of his 'new plasticity' because it was the purest form of artistic expression.[80]

Aphra O'Connor freely admits to being inspired by Mondrian's use of line and colour. I do not propose that she closely adheres to Mondrian's rigorous agenda for 'new plasticity'; one might turn to the work of the Danish artist Bodil Manz for that, whose smooth porcelain forms use lines of applied colour to segment space. However, I do consider that Mondrian's ideas offer a helpful framework for exploring O'Connor's practice. Indeed, it seems significant that she has moved away from the documentary towards the abstract. Her first exhibitions in 2016 and 2017 consisted of pieces made in response to materials discarded from a decommissioned steelworks in Redcar, as well as a boatyard near her hometown of Whitby (such as *Scrapped*, 2016, and *Traces Of*, 2017). The resulting works – sculptures, two-dimensional prints and fabric designs – offered a document of presence and absence; of industrial material reworked to become present as an artwork in an exhibition accessible to new audiences, but also testament to the shrinking fortunes of Yorkshire labour industries. Such an approach speaks to the innovative site-specific documentary ceramic practices explored by other British artists, such as Neil Brownsword. Although highly abstracted, these works by O'Connor were nevertheless rooted to the kind of naturalism that Mondrian criticized.

In 2017, O'Connor's work moved away from the documentary towards industrial design as the basis for abstraction. The pioneering Victorian designer Christopher Dresser (1834–1904) became the starting point for an exploration of how form, specifically lines and curves, can produce compositional dynamism. Dresser began his life as an industrial designer, and his understanding of engineering enabled him to produce designs that appeared more in keeping with the twentieth rather than the nineteenth century, even if they were resolutely tied to a Victorian aesthetic.[81] O'Connor's series of *Supported*

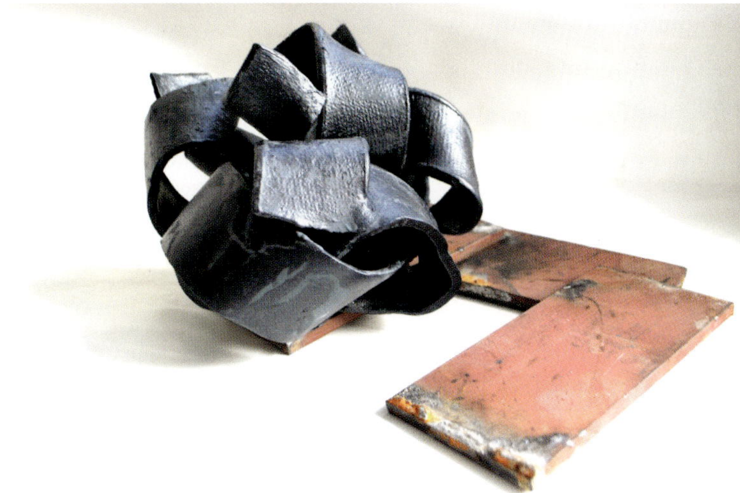

Scrapped (2016).
(Photograph by Aphra O'Connor)

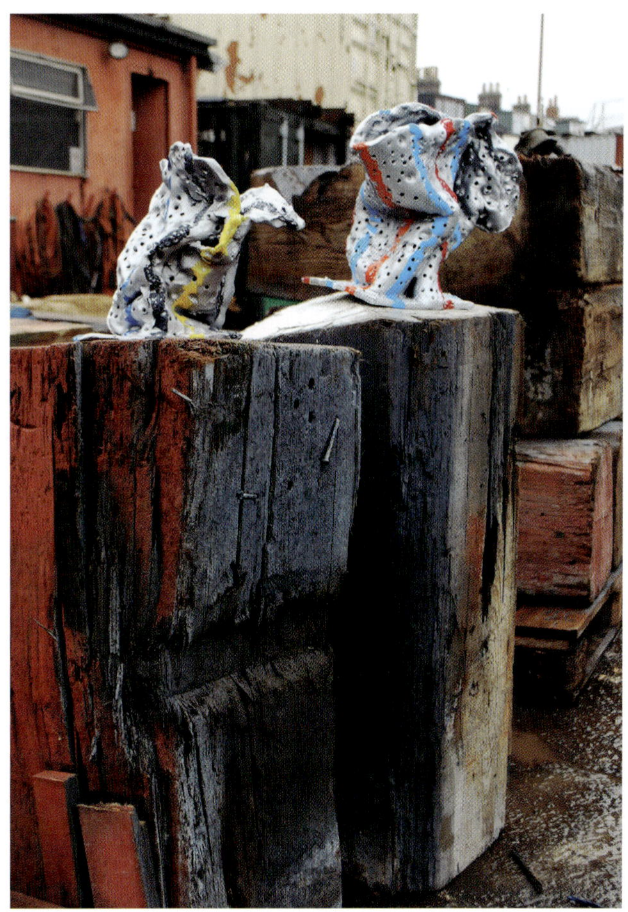

Traces Of (2017).
(Photograph by Aphra O'Connor)

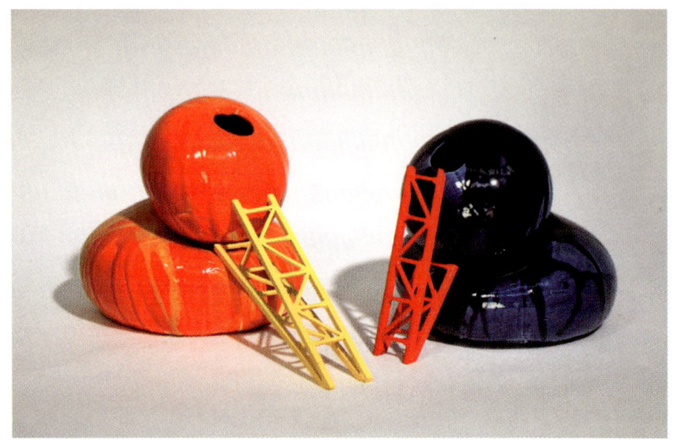

Supported Gourds (2017).
(Photograph by Aphra O'Connor)

Gourds (2017) respond to Dresser's 'Goat's Head' vases (vases that were vaguely hourglass in shape and composed of two spherical sections seemingly attached by four goat heads to the exterior). O'Connor collapsed the vertical axis of the Dresser vase to connect the two spheres and place them at an angle. The spheres are supported by two brightly coloured steel ladder-like structures, their colour chosen to stand out against the central body.

These works draw attention to the ambivalent relationship of Dresser's designs with twentieth-century modern design. The lean of the Dresser-inspired spheres against the supportive, but tonally separate, industrial structure suggests that he was a design radical, but not necessarily a direct pre-cursor to Modernism as some have claimed.[82] On a symbolic level, the *Supported Gourds* also capture something of the relationship between nature and industry, where the more organic spherical forms contrast with the sharp lines of the steel ladder-like structures. Perhaps these sculptures serve as a reminder that industry and nature need to be mutually situated to be sustainable.

Seeking a new direction, O'Connor opted to study at the Royal College of Art (RCA) from 2017 to 2019. Her practice developed substantially during this time, gaining greater confidence in her handling of abstract form. Her graduate work still utilized found objects as the basis for moulds (for example, buckets and jelly moulds), but the shapes became abstracted into ceramic collages featuring bright, often primary, colours. These decisions were a product of the artist's own analysis of Mondrian's aesthetic.

Of course, Mondrian was first and foremost a painter, and his ideas relate to abstract art as a two-dimensional practice. He did, however, consider the applicability of his ideas to architecture, and to a lesser extent, sculpture. In a sketch for an essay, unpublished in his lifetime, Mondrian suggested that:

> Generally architecture and sculpture are seen as a construction of volumes. Volumes have a three-dimensional aspect. [...] Seen as a construction of planes, sculpture and architecture can take a new path and become abstract art.[83]

Mondrian's 'new plastic' ideas on painting were concerned with dividing the canvas into straight lines, which he called 'planes' of space. Spatial problems, such as those arising from buildings and sculptures, needed to explore similar ideas of linear spatial composition. Thus, he suggested that spatial disciplines needed to be explored through the

> erection of lines or by the application of planes. As in reality, form must be expressed in equivalent relationship with the determined space. In reality they do not always have that appearance. However, the great technical problem is that neither lines nor planes speak for themselves but become resolved within the whole.[84]

Just as Mondrian sought compositional balance in his use of line and colour on a canvas, he suggested that the participation of architecture and sculpture

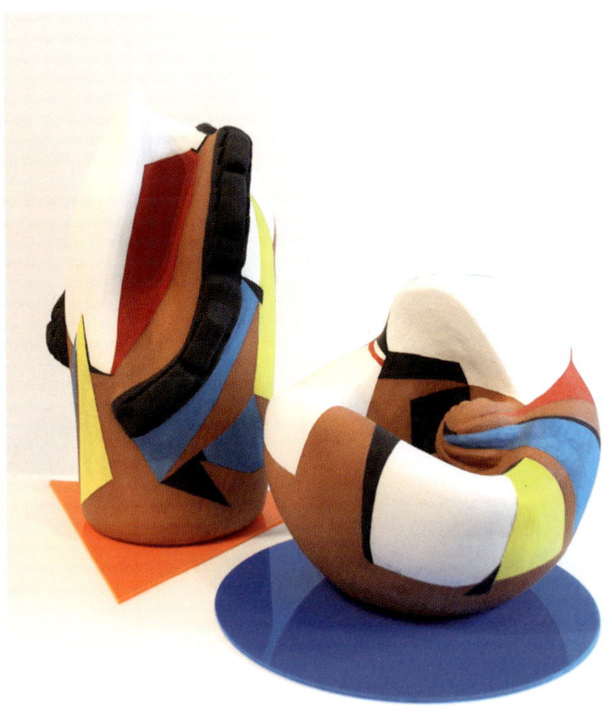

Flexure Shift and Torsion Intersection.
(Photograph by Aphra O'Connor)

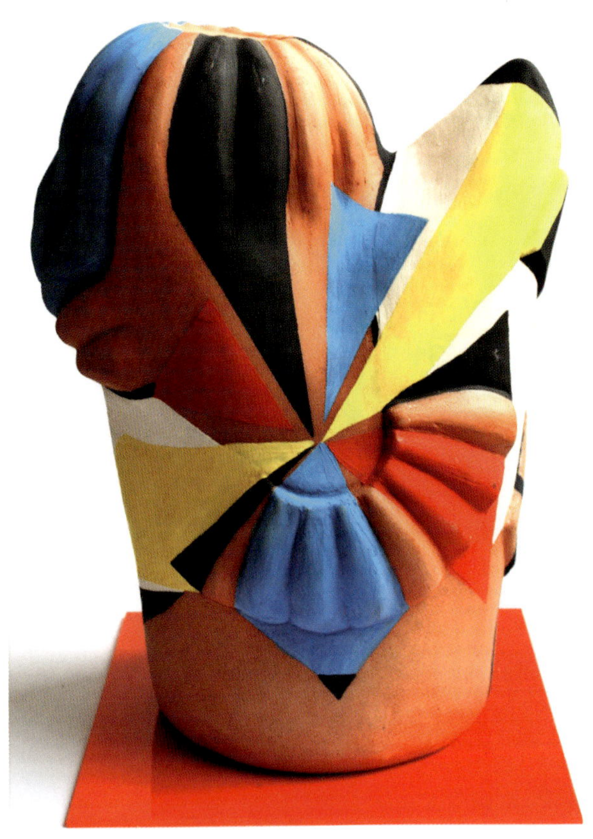

Imbricate Drape.
(Photograph by Aphra O'Connor)

in the 'new plastic' rested on a similar resolution of space. Lines needed to shape the overall space (what he called the 'macro-space'), but also create smaller spaces (what he called the 'micro-space'), and to then ensure that these spaces were in harmony with each other. By achieving balance between the 'macro' and 'micro' space, he argued, 'statutes and pictures are worlds in themselves that reality as a whole reflects'.[85]

O'Connor's post-RCA work echoes this 'new plasticity', for her collaging process is reliant on abstracting the found objects that form the moulded skeleton of each work. What might be regarded as a mechanical process of ceramic reproduction is circumvented through distinct compositional approaches to each work that render it unique. Thus, pieces become part of a series with a shared language but persist as individual ideas with their own sensibilities. The process of collaging these moulded pieces together enables O'Connor to investigate relationships between the 'macro' and 'micro' spaces described by Mondrian. Of course, the relationship between the overall space a sculpture might occupy, and its own interior compositional space, is fundamental to any sculptural enterprise. Yet, in her decision to demarcate her work with areas of colour, a tension is produced between the sculptural 'macro' spaces of the work and the interior 'micro' spaces of flattened colour. It is in the flattening effect of planes of colour that O'Connor's work expresses a sculptural response to Mondrian's 'new plasticity'.

In her terracotta *Dynamic Equilibrium* series (2018–19), O'Connor developed an understanding of how

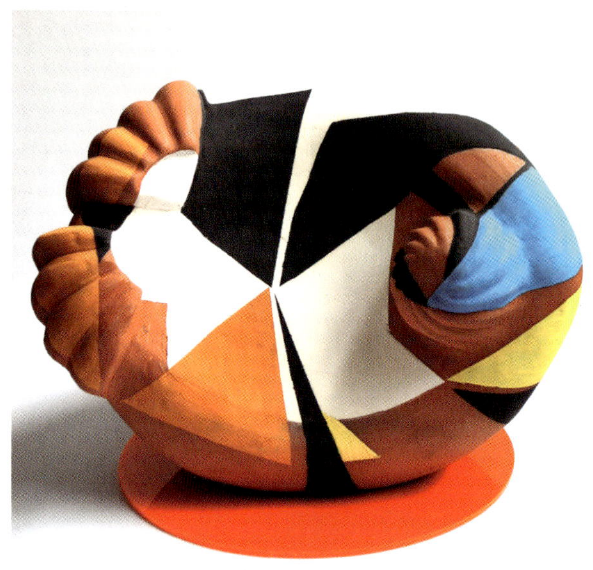

Rigid Fissure.
(Photograph by Aphra O'Connor)

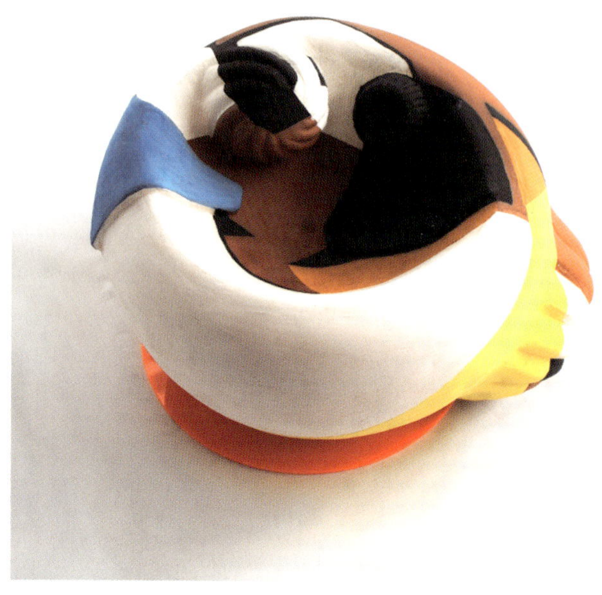

Deep Plastic Lean.
(Photograph by Aphra O'Connor)

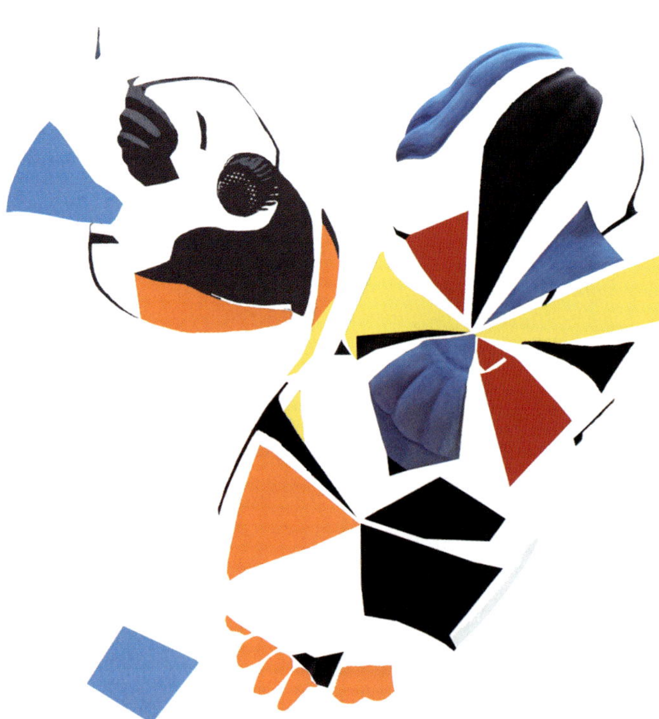

Dynamic Flux I.
(Photograph by Aphra O'Connor)

colour behaves when applied to different compositional and plastic forms. Vibrant yellows, reds or blues might flatten a sculptural recess (e.g. the red line across the upper recess in *Flexure Shift*) but might also draw attention to a protrusion (e.g. the blue line that highlights the central node in *Torsion Intersection*). Colour compositions with a focal point might serve to unify the elements of a sculpture (*Imbricate Drape; Rigid Fissure*), but might also refute a compositional centre, thereby giving the sculpture a sense of expansion (*Flexure Shift*). Black and white might flatten and become subservient to other colours (*Flexure Shift* and *Imbricate Drape*), but they might also dominate and thus animate a composition, highlighting planes as dynamically significant (*Torsion Intersection* and *Deep Plastic Lean*). The unglazed terracotta functions as an important element in the decoration, but these sections are also naked reminders of the material of the sculpture itself.

O'Connor utilizes terracotta as both sculptural and tonal material. Although leaving unglazed areas exposed is a commonplace technique in ceramics, it does have the effect of drawing renewed attention to the underglaze colours in O'Connor's work. Colour appears as a kind of visual shock, a bolt of energy, that shoots across the sculpture and trembles in suspension, purposely working with and against the three dimensions of the surface. Finally, each sculpture is placed on a plastic plinth, determining a local space for the work, mediating between the 'micro' space of the work and the 'macro' space of its environment. Thus, there is a delicate compositional and spatial relationship in the *Dynamic Equilibrium* series, which, as Mondrian demanded of sculpture, uses tension and balance sensitively to achieve resolution across the whole.

Mondrian argued that 'because of its corporeality, a volume can have the same degree of abstract expression as a picture only when it is non-perspectively seen'.[86] Whilst I argue that some of the planes in O'Connor's *Dynamic Equilibrium* series do work non-perspectively (i.e. they flatten the contours of the sculpture), some of the sculptures have become the basis for work in print. The print *Dynamic Flux I* (one of three prints developed from the *Dynamic Equilibrium* series) was drawn from the sculptures *Imbricate Drape*, *Deep Plastic Lean* and *Rigid Fissure*. The print was made by photographing the three-dimensional works, and then using computer software to flatten and manipulate the images to form a collage. Interestingly, the white paper, like the terracotta clay in the sculptures, remains a significant spatial and compositional device, and is self-referent of its own medium (the paper is both the medium and the message).

These flattened images are abstractions of abstract sculptures; or collages of collages. They highlight O'Connor's adept ability to work across the plastic possibilities of art: of planning through drawing and design, into three-dimensional

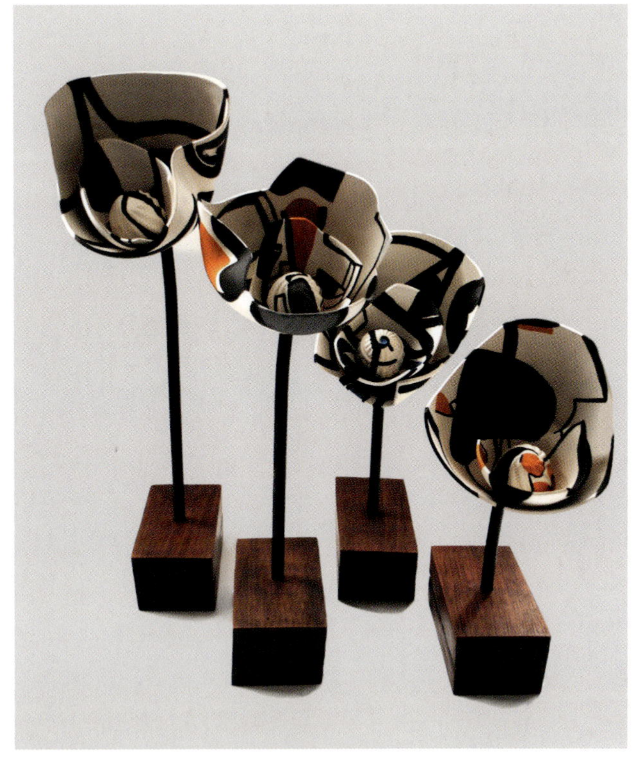

Ubiquity Construction series (2019).
(Photograph by Aphra O'Connor)

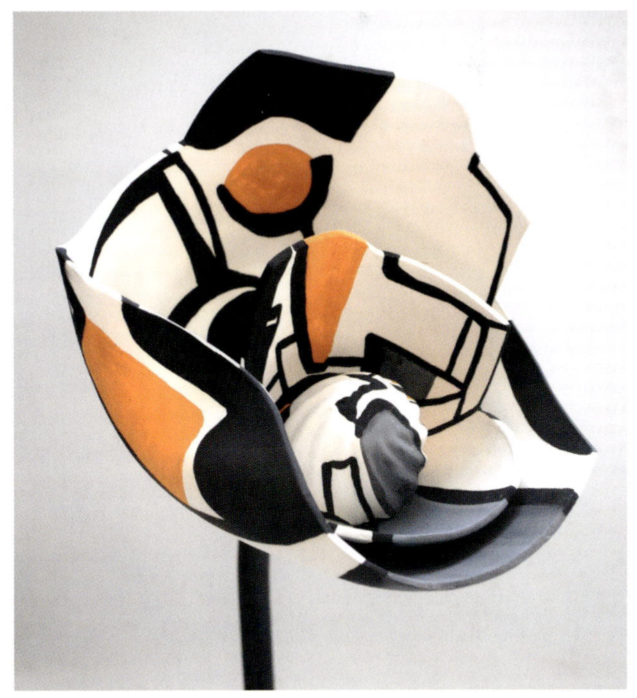

Ubiquity Sculpture 2 (2019).
(Photograph by Aphra O'Connor)

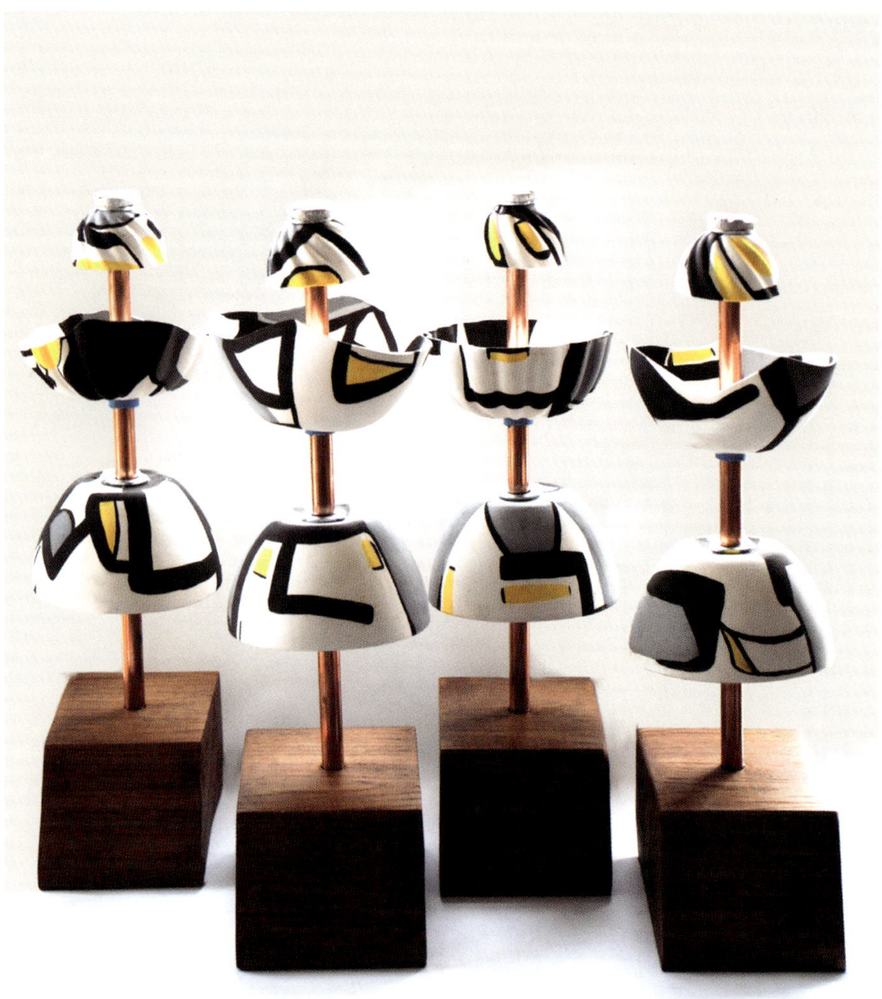

Ascending Construction (2020).
(Photograph by Aphra O'Connor)

sculpture through clay, through explorations of colour as contour, and back into colour as flattened space in a two-dimensional setting. Some of these prints have, in turn, become the basis for fabric designs. Indeed, fabric – which can be flattened or contoured as required – seems an appropriate Janus-faced medium for O'Connor's spatial games.

Subsequent work has explored further this interplay between the three-dimensional and two-dimensional. The *Ubiquity Construction* series (2019) placed earthenware sculptures onto steel supports.

These flower-like sculptures highlight the significance of the viewer's perspective in reading the work. Held at a particular angle, there is a process of discovery, of hidden elements revealed, as the viewer approaches the sculpture. Whereas the lines flow around the *Dynamic Equilibrium* series, in works such as *Ubiquity Sculpture 2* (2019) the lines fragment the sculpture, leaping between petals. Yet they also weave around and across the edges of each frond. Discovery of these correspondences enables appreciation of compositional balance, unifying 'macro' and 'micro' space. The ultimate anchor is the support, for the black steel rod that holds the structure up is both functionally and compositionally instrumental. The subsequent series, *Ascending Construction* (2020), developed these ideas further with the disintegration of the sculpture into three distinct phases mounted onto a copper support. Here, the 'macro' space is extended so that the viewer must jump between sections of the sculpture to read connections between the 'micro' spaces. The eye jumps around the sculpture to pursue its compositional flow.

As O'Connor's confidence has grown so shape and space have been controlled with greater dexterity. *Agglutinate Curlicue* (2020) integrates form and mark with a new compositional tautness. The moulded protrusions are sculptural curves that also recall handles, making the work referent of domestic utility. Yet, as with the pots of Alison Britton or Elizabeth Fritsch, the sculpture stands beyond use; its primary function is to utilize lines and curves to facilitate visual impact. The black and yellow triangles guide the eye towards compositional centres that work with and against the sculpted body. The division of the work with a yellow Perspex plate once again asks the eye to vault between sections, but the plate also connects and harmonizes the overall composition.

O'Connor's painterly sculptures pay homage to European Modernism: arcs, spheres and lines are the basic compositional elements of all aspects of her work. Yet it does not follow that O'Connor is a modernist subscribing to the ideology of abstraction as universalism. She seems to me to be more of a 'Postmodern Modernist': an artist in the Postmodern tradition who samples and quotes from Modernism to find her own artistic language. However, the possibilities she explores are related to modernist questions of line, structure and form, and her work does express something of the abstract qualities that Mondrian sought in sculpture.

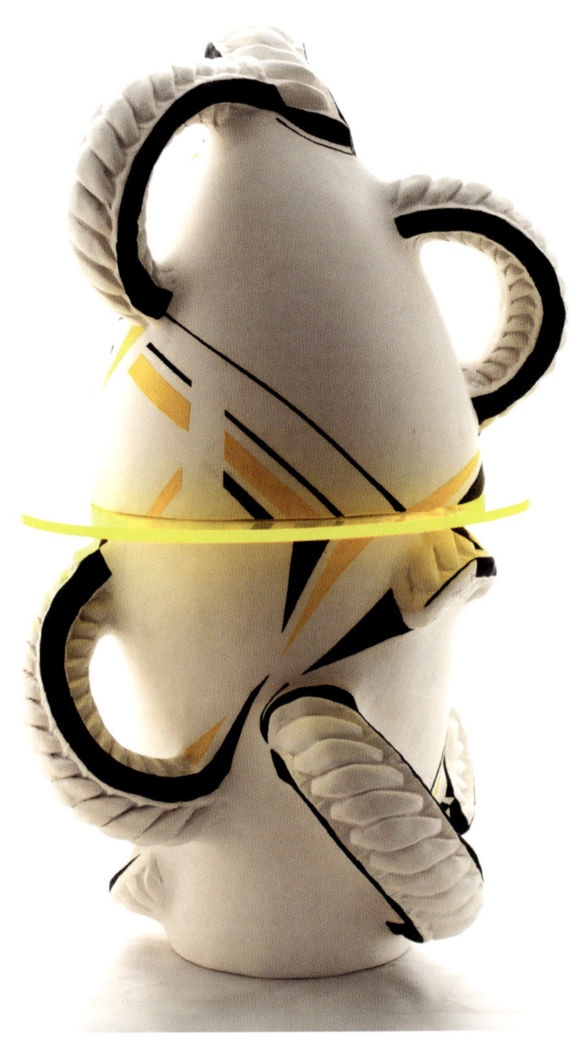

Agglutinate Curlicue (2020).
(Photograph by Aphra O'Connor)

Her method of working, through a process of moulding and hand-building, planned and spontaneous design, is both intellectual and intuitive. In this respect, she resonates with the implications of Mondrian's ideas: 'In plastic art the laws of reality are established by the force of intuition,' he said. 'Therefore art is the true mirror of reality.'[87]

Patricia Volk

Compositions in Sympathy

The common ground between music and painting seems to lie in the organization of their abstract qualities. In music it's very clear, such things as the accumulation of sound, the dispersal of sound, the ebb and flow, the rise and fall, the contrasts and harmonies are arranged according to certain principles. In picture-making the masses, the open and the closed spaces, the lines, tones and colours can be organized in a parallel way. It's as though these relationships are built up in all their complexity in order to provide a vehicle for those things which cannot be objectively identified but which can nevertheless be expressed in this way. Music articulates this indefinable content and it seems to me that this also applies to abstract painting [...].[88]

Bridget Riley

The harnessing of sound as an abstract entity into the expressive form of music is an oft-used analogy for the plastic arts. Of course, Bridget Riley speaks of spatial construction within the confines of a two-dimensional canvas, the manipulation of foreground and background to evince new sensations of depth. It is not, however, a great leap to apply such arguments to sculpture. As Barbara Hepworth observed: 'I am convinced that a sculptor must search with passionate intensity for the underlying principle of the organization of mass and tension – the meaning of gesture and the structure of rhythm.'[89]

Does this analogy also apply to ceramics? In 1978, Elizabeth Fritsch opened a touring exhibition at Leeds Art Gallery entitled *Pots about Music*. Like Bridget Riley,[90] Fritsch observed a musicality in the frescoes of the Italian painter Piero della Francesca (c.1415–92), noting how he used 'colour in a most musical, rhythmic, atmospheric way'.[91] Fritsch proceeded to observe of her own practice how 'a pot is like a tune; both are rooted in having been ancient folk objects; both use minimal resources (hands and craft); both are recognizable and accessible; both are in fact kinds of archetype on and through which new and changing structures may be built'.[92] For a trained musician like Fritsch, there was an inevitable correspondence between music and ceramics; between space and silence, where 'the forms and the painting tend towards the minimal'; and between space and time, where she considered the 'grouping of rhythmic figures and pots in Space as corresponding with the grouping and rhythms of tunes in Time, both involving counterpoint and modulation'.[93]

Volk's work is not directly inspired by music, but her work has a musicality that, in the same vein as above, bonds the abstract with the expressive and the spatial with the lyrical. Riley, Hepworth and Fritsch are representative artists of disciplines to which Volk's work speaks, but within which she herself does not easily sit. Volk is not only a painter, a sculptor or a ceramicist: she is a fusion of all three. Many ceramic artists might feel that they also occupy such territory.

Yet Volk still seems different. For a start, Volk really *does* paint: her sculptures are finished with acrylic paint rather than glaze. Some might raise an eyebrow at this approach, but as Edmund de Waal has noted, such 'defensiveness, a feeling that it is inappropriate for potters who by definition work with clay to "play", or to allow others to take such liberties, has had excessive significance'.[94] Indeed, Volk does not sit easily within the wider tradition of British ceramics. Fritsch, for instance, may make

sculptural work exploring mass, line, form, colour and tone developed from an understanding of fine art practice, but it is always rooted to the form of the vessel. Riley sometimes uses acrylic but has rarely ventured into three dimensions, and when she has, the preoccupation with expansive canvas-like surfaces has been retained.[95] Barbara Hepworth is most associated with works in patinated metal, wood and plaster, but some of her sculptures were painted, especially after 1939, and a handful in very bright colours.[96] Though their work is different, each of these artists share parallel investigations into line, tone, rhythm and mass, and thus have something to offer an analysis of Volk's own distinctive and innovative output.

During the course of her thirty-year career, Volk's sculpture has been extremely varied. She usually works in series exploring a particular line of enquiry. Once an investigation has run its course, she substitutes it for a new set of conceptual problems. For this reason, Volk's output has taken the form of sculpted heads, spherical and ovoid-shaped sculpture, wall reliefs, towers, and slabs. Yet, these shifts in practice are nothing more than a new iteration of a fundamental question: what is the expressive potential of line, tone, colour, mass and rhythm? In order to examine how this question is answered in Volk's work, this essay takes a non-chronological approach. It begins with sculptures that exist in series, as more obviously rhythmic constructions, before moving towards the singular. It also begins with Volk's expansive use of three dimensions and moves towards a horizontal compression of space. To curate her work in this way is to seek to highlight her inventiveness as a sculptor, but also to argue why clay is a pertinent, if not the only, material in which she could work.

Individuals (2013) is Volk's largest ceramic installation to date. Three-and-a-half metres in length, it consists of seven ceramic sculptures painted in acrylic and placed on black supports. The works are individual in the sense that they exhibit distinct spatial and tonal qualities, yet they are forced together in an arrangement that is carefully composed, and so they are part of a group. Differences between the sculptures are heightened by placing them in series;

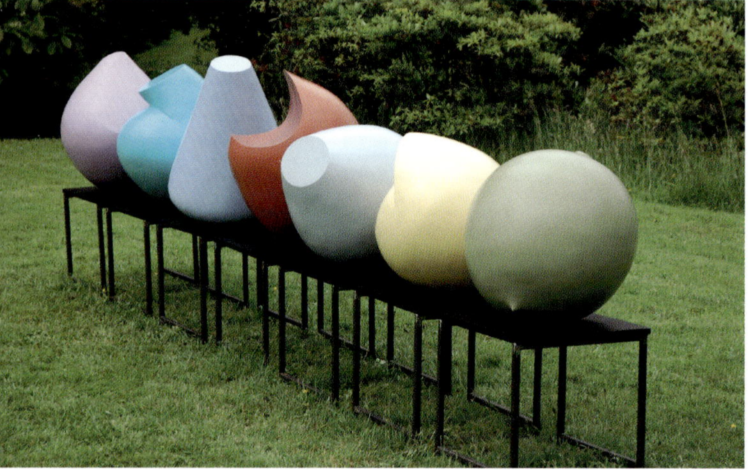

Individuals (2013).
(Photograph by Patricia Volk)

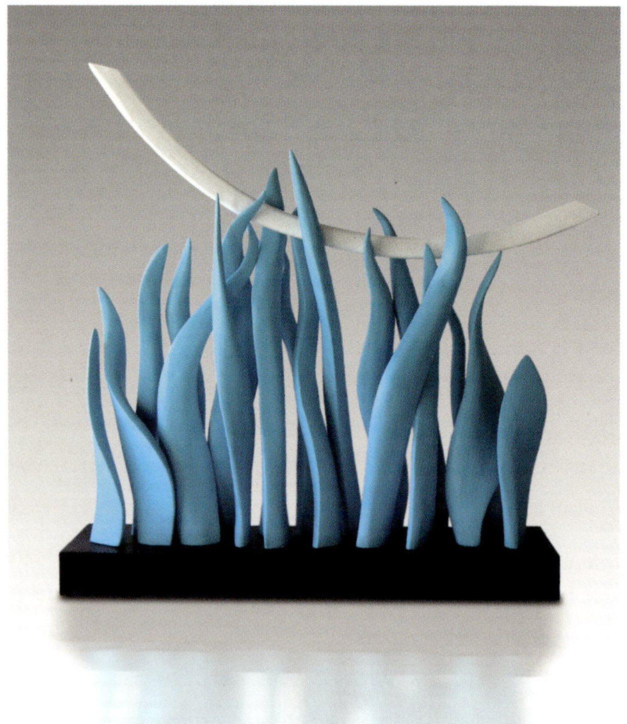

Crowd (2010).
(Photograph by Patricia Volk)

the eye becomes attuned to rhythmic, spatial and tonal relationships, between curve and line, and axis and balance, as it moves through the sequence of work. The positioning of the darkest tone in the centre of the arrangement anchors the others, and colour is modified towards the yellow spectrum at one end, and towards the blue-green spectrum at the other. The monochrome acrylic painting on these forms enables light to play an active and dynamic part in the rendering of three dimensions through tone, yet it also flattens other surfaces, foreshortening them to appear almost two-dimensional.

This installation is an investigation of line, tone, colour, mass and tension, but it is also a personified one. What might these sculptures represent? Do they stand for humans as social beings? Do they yearn for isolation or integration? Such emotions might also be read into *Crowd* (2010), where the spatial rhythms seem even more evocative. The white arc supported by the light blue waves evokes all kinds of relationships – of a group supporting an individual, of currents pushing through the sea, or even of wind rushing through the grass. Do the blue waves refute or support the implied movement of the white arc? By addressing herself to formal sculptural questions, like any good sculptor, Volk evinces a complex spatial narrative that poses questions rather than reveals answers.

Some of Volk's output is a kind of assemblage of shapes. At first sight, these assemblages seem very distinct from *Individuals* and *Crowd*, but they explore the same personified territory. The form of *Dervish* (2016) does indeed evoke spinning: the way the large bulbous tear-shaped section teeters on the base suggests poise and movement, like a pirouetting ballet dancer. The elements placed above function as counterpoint, keeping the form poised in space, and thus echoing the use of arms for balance in the spiralling turns of the Dervish. *Paternal* (2019)

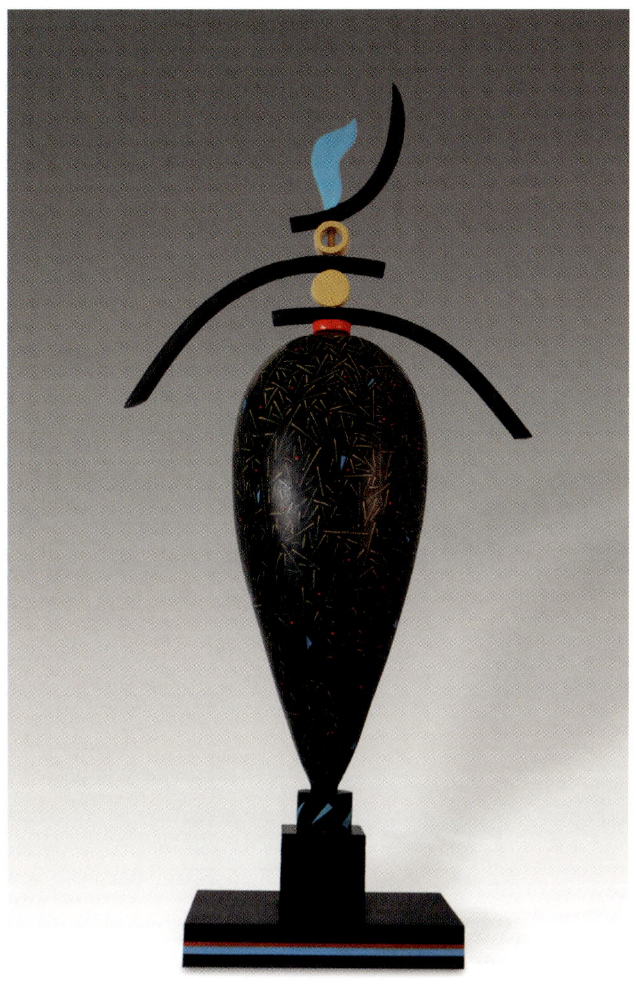

Dervish (2016).
(Photograph by Patricia Volk)

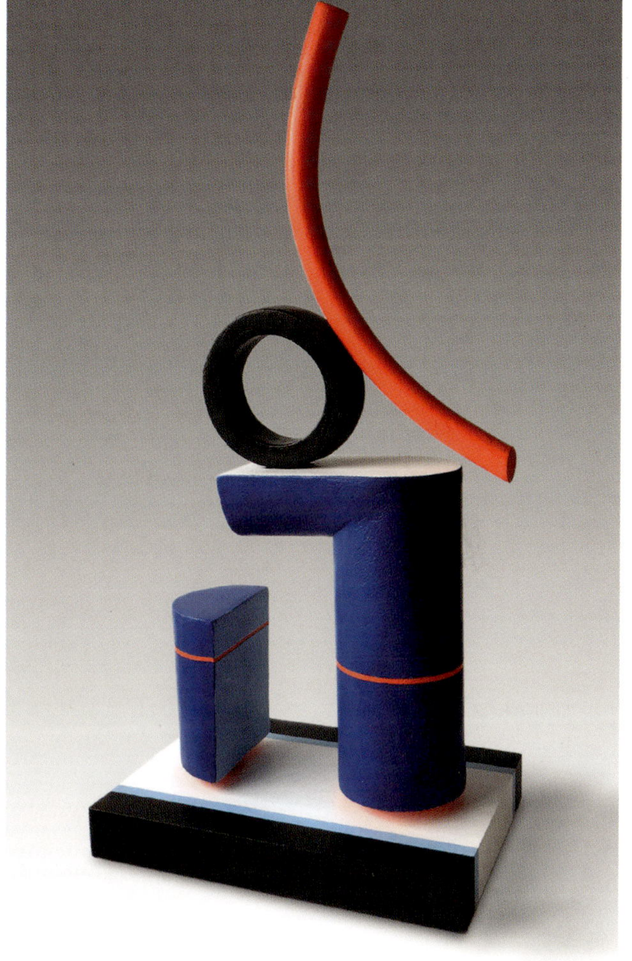

Paternal (2019).
(Photograph by Patricia Volk)

seems equally personified; the larger blue sculpture carries the red arc and the black circle, protecting the smaller (child) figure which shelters beneath.

These four sculptures move from an expansive use of three dimensions to smaller enclosed spaces. Others, such as *Bond* (2018), *Attract* (2010) and *Lift* (2008), close space down even more, existing almost like spatial reliefs or three-dimensional paintings. This might be interpreted by some, I suppose, as a sculptural weakness, but criticism of a perceived retreat from three dimensions is hardly new. Indeed, Elizabeth Fritsch sought to develop an 'interplay between two and three dimensions both in the forms and the painting, e.g. the paradoxical effects of curved space, flatness, etc'.[97] Through repeated investigation, Fritsch developed a kind of trademark vessel that manipulated its own sense of volume, either by seeming flatter or more rounded than it actually was. Such approaches drew their critics, not least Philip Rawson who, in 1985, without referring to Fritsch by name, argued that 'so chillingly often we are nowadays given pots that retreat, flattening themselves and huddling back into diagrams'.[98]

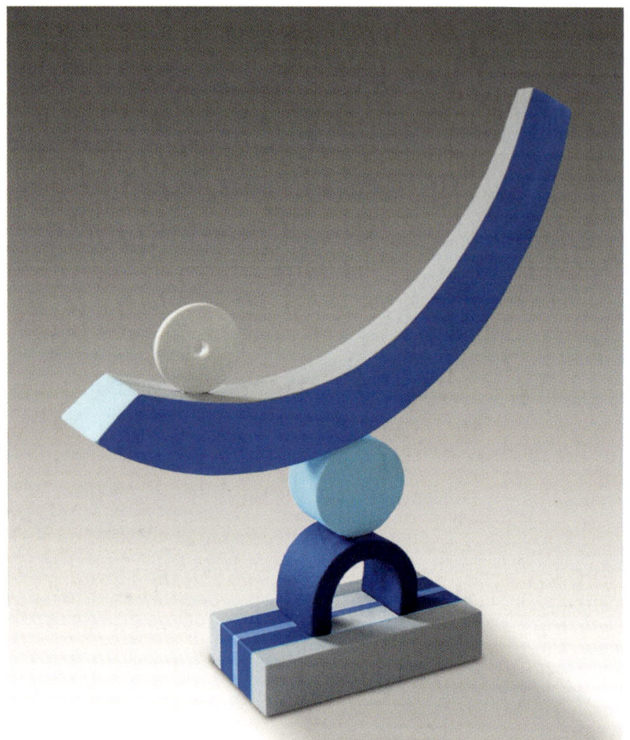

Sweep (2016).
(Photograph by Patricia Volk)

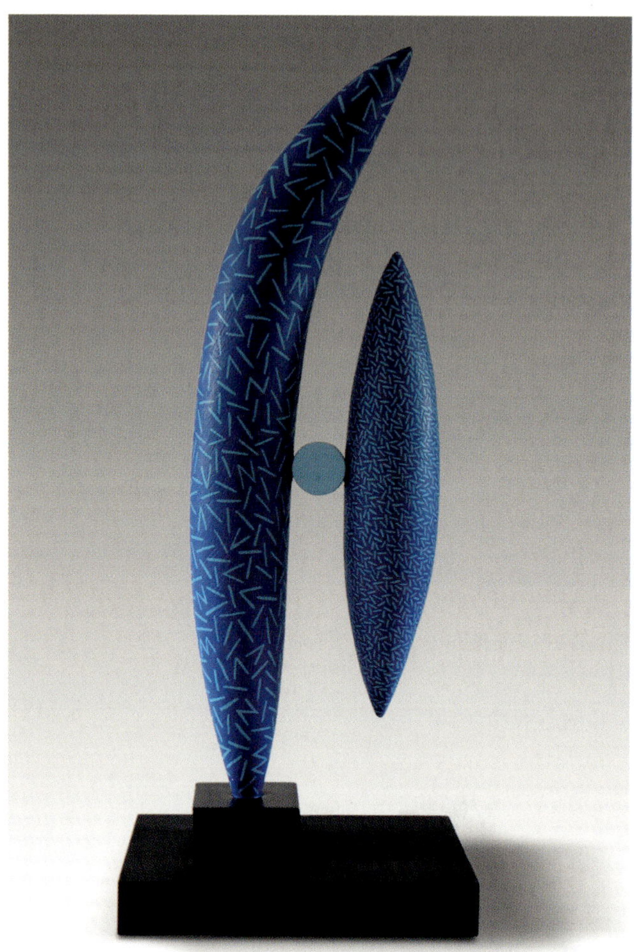

Bond (2018).
(Photograph by Patricia Volk)

Volk is not interested in the same dimensional tricks as Fritsch, but her work does move along a continuum between three and two dimensions to exist in a state of two-and-a-half dimensions; as fully rounded forms nevertheless working across a vertical rather than, or as well as, a horizontal plane. This, it seems to me, is a perfectly legitimate mode of sculptural enquiry.

If we view Volk's work as a commentary on human relationships, the vertical plane seems entirely appropriate. Indeed, much of Barbara Hepworth's personification (such as *Family of Man*, 1970) was placed on the vertical axis. Sculptures such as *Bond* and *Attract* further evidence Volk's ability to fuse form with the expression of emotional states. In *Bond*, the light blue dots separate the two figures. The 'child' is detached from its 'parent', but there is a bond that can never be fully broken. In contrast, the placing of oppositional forms in *Attract* suggests ambivalence.

Is the left-hand form cosying up to, or moving away from, the right-hand form? Do opposites really attract? Volk's careful application of marks offers additional narrative to each piece. The brilliant blue across the vertical forms in *Bond* connect them, as does the painstaking application of light blue dashes, which, although beautifully applied, evoke the battle scars of experience. In *Attract*, the light blue dots and stripes communicate both a bond of togetherness and an irresolvable separation. Volk uses acrylic marks to complicate the narratives of her shapes, imbuing in them expressions of acceptance, dependence, tension or resignation.

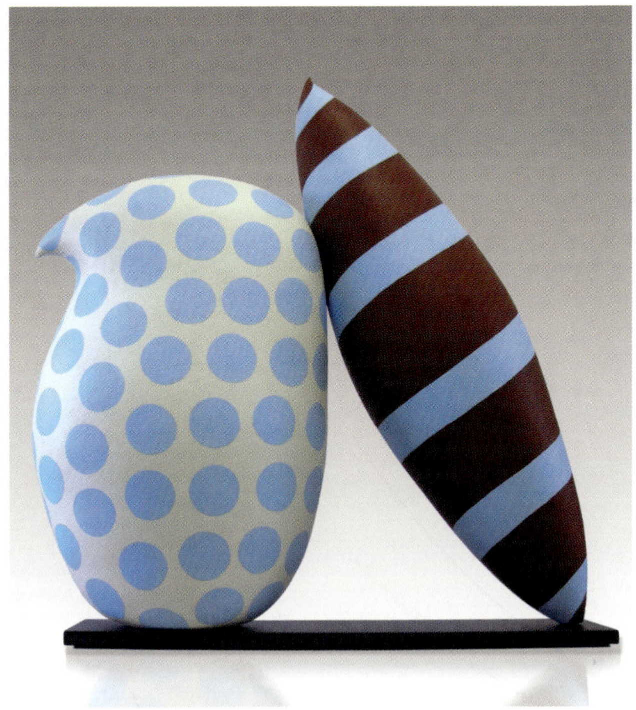

Attract (2010).
(Photograph by Patricia Volk)

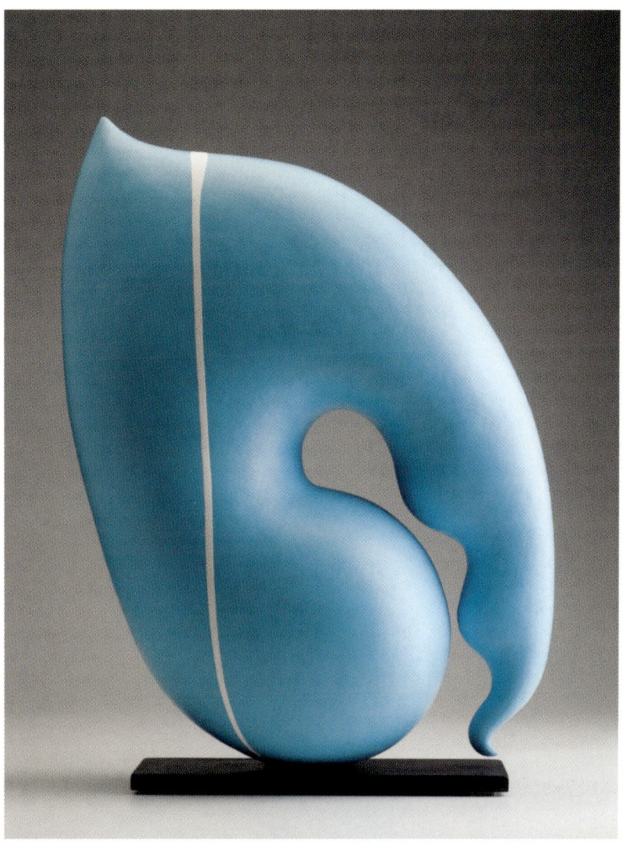

Lift (2008).
(Photograph courtesy of Patricia Volk)

Not all of Volk's work is hominoid in ambition, however. Some works, not unlike that of Bridget Riley's paintings, simply invite us to consider the expression of movement as a pleasure in its own right. *Sweep* (2016), as a representative example, consists of an arc which rushes through the space like an active brushstroke. The white disc that sits on the left-hand end of the arc implies stasis, a kind of sculptural full-stop. As a consequence of these opposing energies, the sculpture becomes expressively tense. Such sculptures are simply about, as Paul Klee once said, 'taking a line for a walk', leading the eye on a pleasurable journey around form.

One of the more pared down sculptures that Volk has made is *Lift*. Here there is a singular shape, in one colour, with one line. Compositionally, the bulbous lower section seems to support the upper section, which cannot raise itself from the ground. The application of a white line separates the sculpture into two tensional sections. The line does not follow the curvature of the left-hand edge of the sculpture but follows a more-or-less vertical axis. This gives the impression of the left-hand section raising away, as though it seeks separation from its heavier self. The right-hand part of the sculpture, unable to lift itself, is left sapped of energy. *Lift* is a quiet and intensely moving statement of the complexity of emotion, perhaps even of being an artist, of success building from failure, of elation into despair, and the possibility of hope.

Finally, *Embrace* (2019) and *Cog* (2019) bring together the different elements of Volk's practice. They consist of individual sculptural 'arms' locked in a state of intense imbrication. Not obviously personified in form, they nevertheless convey togetherness, if also an inability to separate without

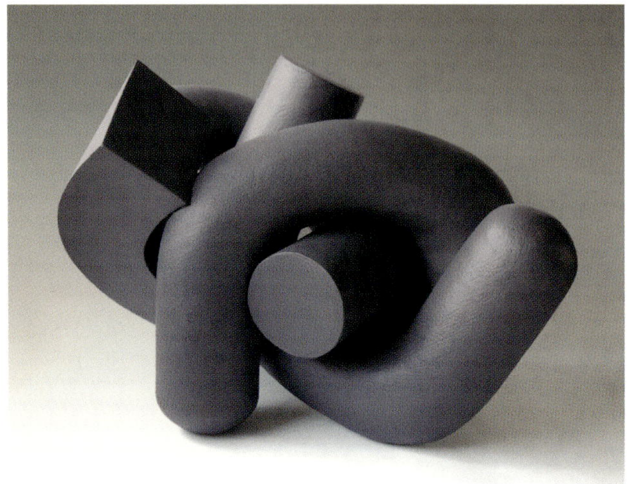

Embrace (Dark Grey) (2019).
(Photograph by Patricia Volk)

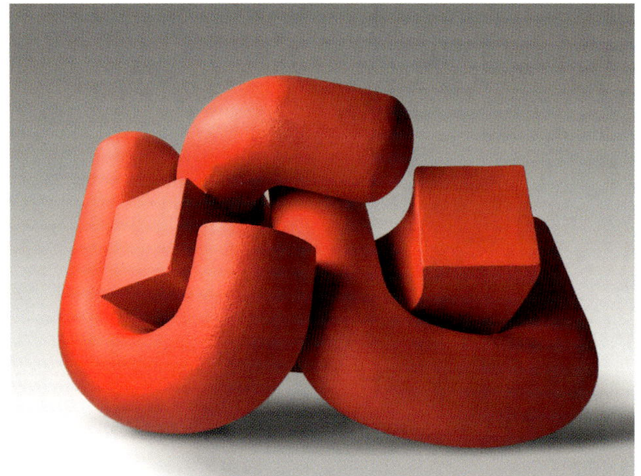

Embrace (Red) (2019).
(Photograph by Patricia Volk)

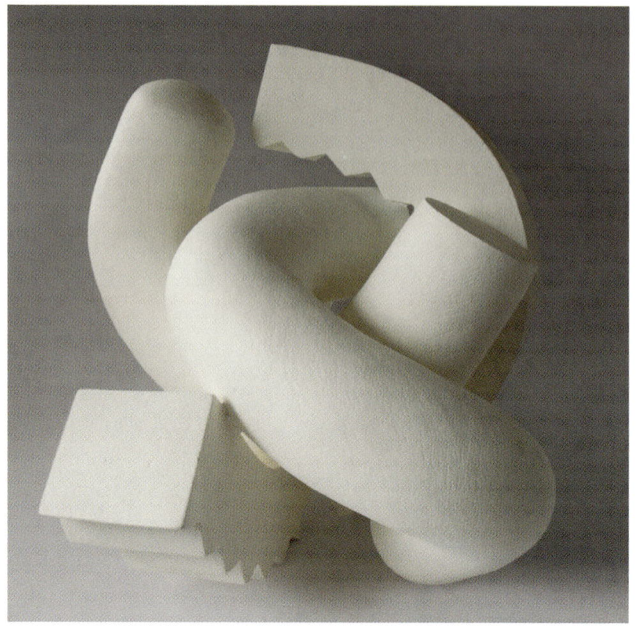

Cog (Shell) (2019).
(Photograph by Patricia Volk)

destruction. Whether each *Embrace* is supportive, or suffocating, is very much in the eye of the beholder and dependent on how colour is interpreted. For me, perhaps *Embrace (Dark Grey)* is a more benign composition than the capricious *Embrace (Red)*. In *Cog*, the teeth in two sections disrupt the smoothness of the other 'arms', yet any linear disparity is harmonized by colour. Here, the elements might be caught in a forceful struggle or a gleeful dogfight. Perhaps

the lack of clarity offers greater poignancy. In these times of fracture and isolation, and in the aftermath of a global virus pandemic that demanded social isolation, Volk's sculptures remind us that as communal creatures we need to embrace.

Volk's work would be difficult, if not impossible, and certainly prohibitively expensive, to produce in any medium other than clay. To cast these sculptures in bronze (and Volk has cast a handful of sculptures) would complicate her intuitive compositional process, not only in form, but of modifying form in relation to colour and tone. Volk works instinctually through trial and error, seeking emergent correspondence between different shapes that might form an engaging composition. Success is, therefore, hard won, and work is not so much what she does but who she is. In each piece, there is a profound sympathy for the complex predicaments of life. It may not be directly inspired by music but, for me, her work sings.

Ken Eastman

Phenomena

As you read this text, you are in fact moving between two interconnected kinds of 'looking'. One is focused on the individual words as they unfurl in each sentence. Your eyes move along each line from left to right analysing the role each word plays in creating meaning. Yet the other kind, paradoxically, involves *not* looking. You are aware through your peripheral vision that each word is part of a wider structure; that words are arranged into a sentence, and these sentences are part of paragraphs laid out in spatial rhythms down the page (you are, in fact, registering the white space around the paragraphs in your peripheral vision right now). But you cannot give equal focus to the individual word, the sentence, the paragraph and the entire page all at the same time. If you could, you would be able to scan a page instantly like a photocopier. An extensive volume would be absorbed in minutes. Thus, to read is to actively look, but also to actively *not* look, at the same time.

This process of looking / not looking was interrogated by Maurice Merleau-Ponty (1908–61), a French philosopher who sought to understand how we perceive and actively engage with the world around us. In a passage that expands the point made above, Merleau-Ponty suggested that:

> To see an object is either to have it in the margins of the visual field and to be able to focus on it, or actually to respond to this solicitation by focusing on it. When I focus on it, I anchor myself in it, but this 'pausing' of the gaze is but a modality of its movement: I continue within one object the same exploration that, just a moment ago, surveyed all of them. With a single movement, I close off the landscape and open up the object.[99]

Thus, Merleau-Ponty suggested, in order to see an object we have to move from the general to the particular. He considered it critical to 'suspend the surroundings in order to see the object better, and to lose in the background what is gained in the figure, because to see the object is to plunge into it and because objects form a system in which one object cannot appear without concealing another'.[100]

Systematic concealing is important for Merleau-Ponty because it explains how we perceive three-dimensional objects. For instance, how can you grasp the full dimensions of a cup when you can, at best, only see fifty per cent of it? To see a cup is also not to see it, to have to focus on one part because its full dimensions are hidden from view. Indeed, Merleau-Ponty suggested that we can only perceive the three-dimensions of an object through indirect attribution. By this he means that we consider the object in perspective (its relationship to other objects), and further imagine the object from directions other than our own line of sight:

> Each object, then, is the mirror of all the others. When I see the lamp on my table, I attribute it not merely the qualities that are visible from my location, but also those that the fireplace, the walls, and the table can 'see'. The back of my lamp is merely the face that it 'shows' to the fireplace. Thus, I can see one object insofar as objects form a system of a world, and insofar as each of them arranges the others around itself like spectators of its hidden aspects and as the guarantee of their permanence.[101]

Therefore, to see a three-dimensional object is to perceive it through its relationship to other objects. Our brain processes visual evidence, such as perspective, to realize the three-dimensional object in our minds, even when we cannot see all of it with our eyes. Interestingly, modernist artists have sought to disrupt this attribution by distorting our perception, using our imagination of vessels as three-dimensional objects against us (see, for example, the works by Ben Nicholson and William Scott reproduced in the chapter on Alison Britton, page 30). In such works, we are forced to realize that we can never fully *see* a vessel. Our visual reading of a cup is, in fact, more two-dimensional than our three-dimensional perception of it. Similar territory has been explored in British ceramics by Elizabeth Fritsch and Linda Gunn-Russell.

I begin this discussion of Ken Eastman's work with a rather lengthy discussion of Merleau-Ponty because, for me, his sculptures depend upon this interplay between looking and not looking. To close in on the form of one of his pieces is to comprehend the beauty of a sculpted line, its local characteristics of tone, rhythm, light, shadow and colour. Yet, by discovering the compositional interplay between marks across the work as a whole, the complex rhythms that give each of Eastman's sculptures vigour and presence are opened up. His work asks us to look and not look, to modulate between focus and survey, and shift from the part to the whole and back again. More importantly, Eastman's sculptures capture the fragmentation and distortion of perception that Merleau-Ponty describes, articulating how our attribution of one side of a form to all sides is fictive. With a cup, for instance, we are certain of its three-dimensional presence because we use the elements of the cup we can see as the basis for our multi-directional imaginings. Eastman's sculptures distort this imagining; whilst we can discern that the object is three-dimensional (specifically through its perspectival relationship with a surface), we are unable to perceive the exact nature of its dimensions. As with much sculpture, our perception is disrupted for the purposes of an aesthetic experience; we are invited to discover surprising contours as they undulate in compositionally resolved flows.

Stuff she does (2019) is a bold and dynamic work that is comprised of horizontal and vertical undulating curves. Photographs of this work from four

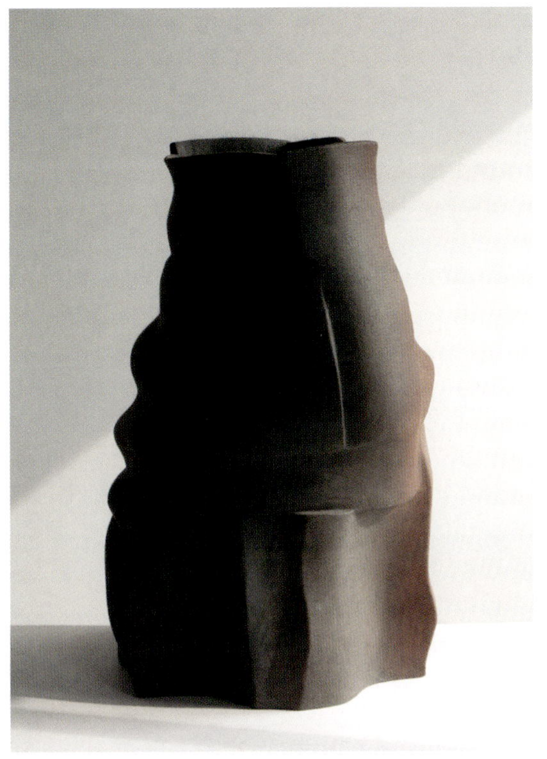
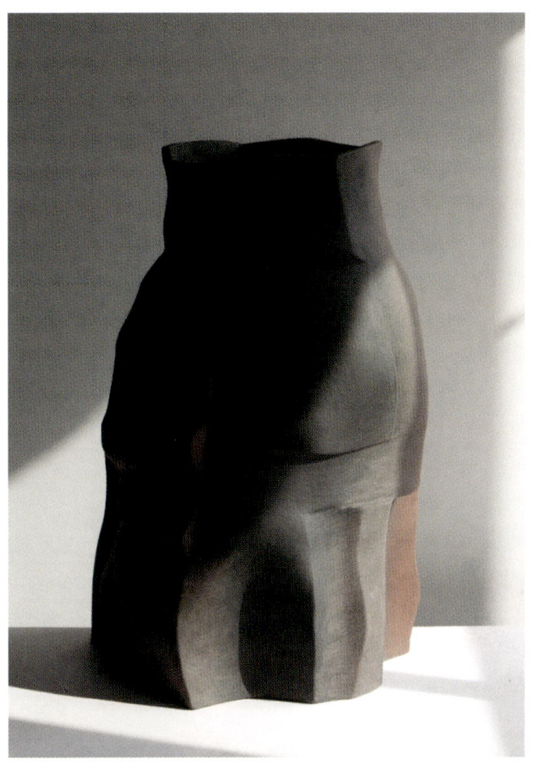
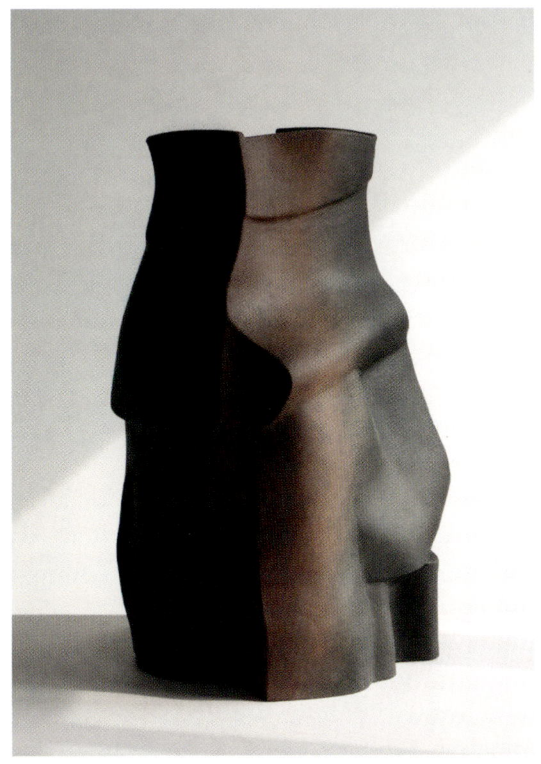
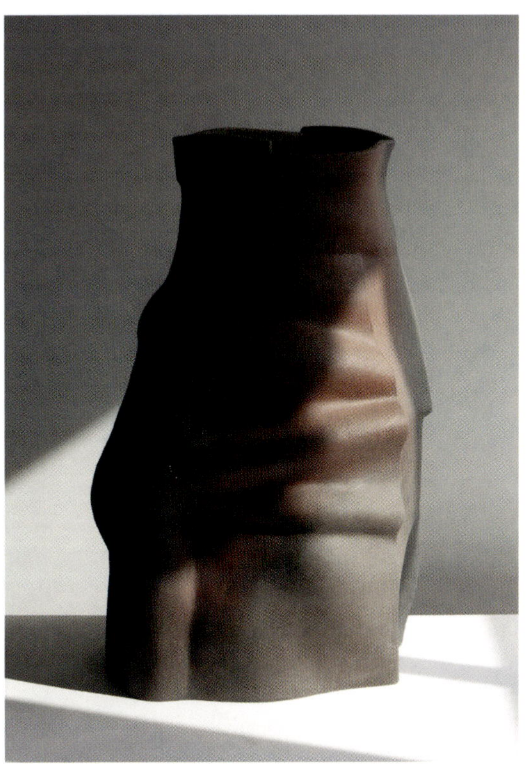

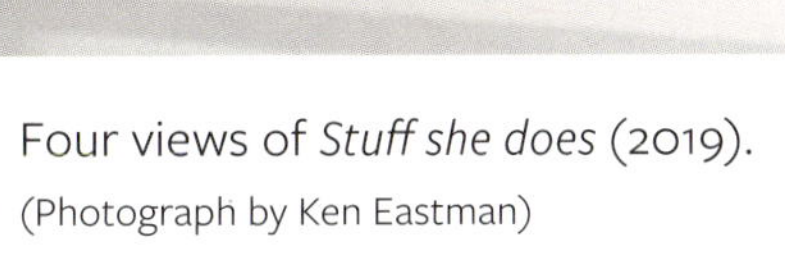
Four views of *Stuff she does* (2019).
(Photograph by Ken Eastman)

directions demonstrate how it is impossible to imagine the other sides when confronted with only one. Unfortunately, photography is a limited means of documenting three-dimensional forms, and this is especially true of Eastman's work. Even from these four photographs of the same piece, it is a challenge to perceive the relationships between each side. In truth, his sculptures can only be fully experienced in person, where the eye is free to move between looking and not looking, around and across all of its dimensions. It then becomes possible to perceive how lines ebb and flow like music; the eye is taken on a rhythmic journey that increases and decreases with speed according to the length of line and size of shape. Shadows oscillate around elevated curvatures, tricking the eye into

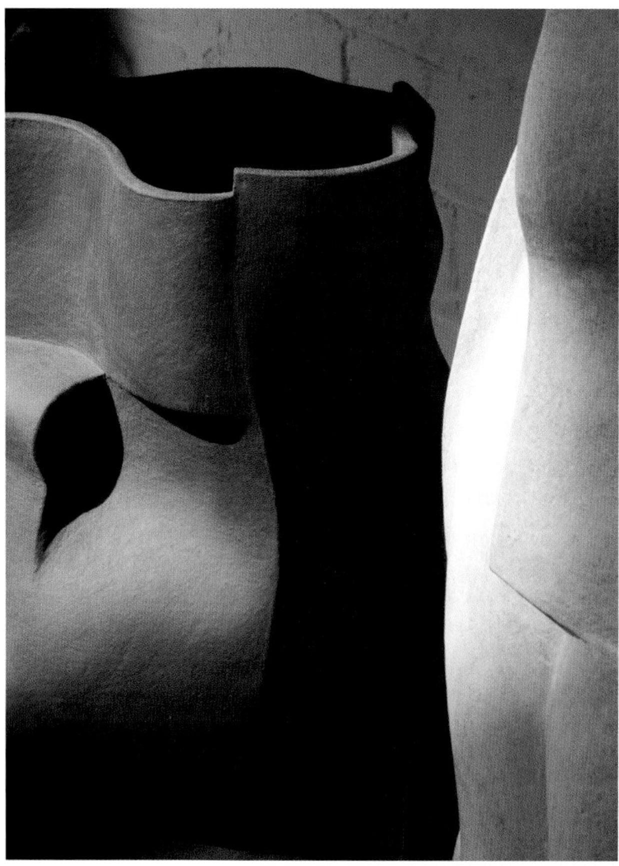

Detail from *Let me tell you* (2019) (left) and *About time* (2019) (right).
(Photograph by Ken Eastman)

finding greater depth to the surface than is actually present. Eastman's compositions afford a constant sense of discovery, producing a rich array of perceptive and emotive phenomena, a musicality, a lyricism, and a painterly depth.

Sensations of movement are a strong feature of Eastman's works. Such sensations are intensified by the prominence of interior space. Eastman often (though not always) works in a form rooted to the vessel, enabling interior space to feature in the composition. In one sense, internal space symbolizes emptiness – an interior of air, a vessel without any contents. Ironically, the sides of the vessel delineate space and thus 'emptiness' becomes contained; the 'nothing' becomes 'something'. Of course, these interior spaces are far from empty. The width of the 'rim' of each form controls a discharge of energy. In a relatively closed form, such as *Hilly's song* (2020), there is a sense of compression, of force building within the work that seems to push against the external vessel walls. In others, such as *Sea change* (2019), the wide mouth suggests force having escaped, of pressure released from confinement.

This sense of movement is strengthened or lessened by the strategic deployment of tone and colour. Eastman is, quite rightly, highly regarded for the astonishing depth of colour on his surfaces, often achieved through multiple firings. Eastman applies colour with a brush, giving the fired surface a painterly quality that resembles some Abstract Expressionist painting, particularly Barnett Newman (1905–70) and Mark Rothko (1903–70). Colour, however, becomes more meaningful on the surface planes in relation to light and shadow. Light brings out a deliberately placed nuance of shading, enabling one relatively small section of sculpture to modulate from a rusty brown, to black, to grey, to light muddy brown (as exemplified by *Let me tell you*, 2019). Eastman places much emphasis on the

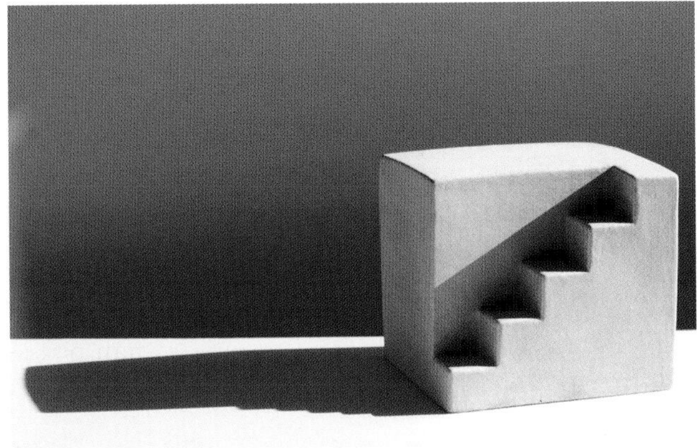

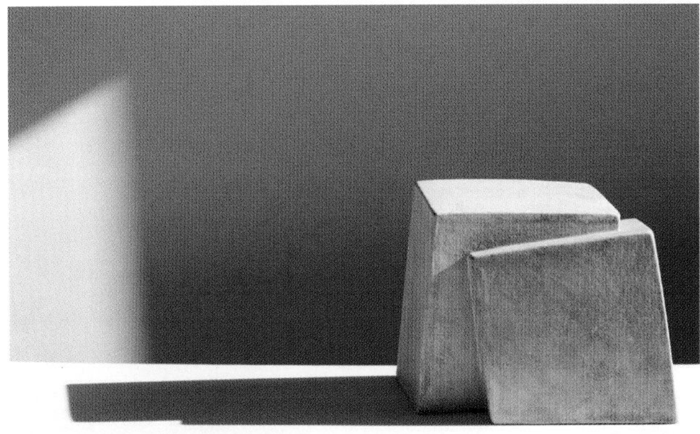

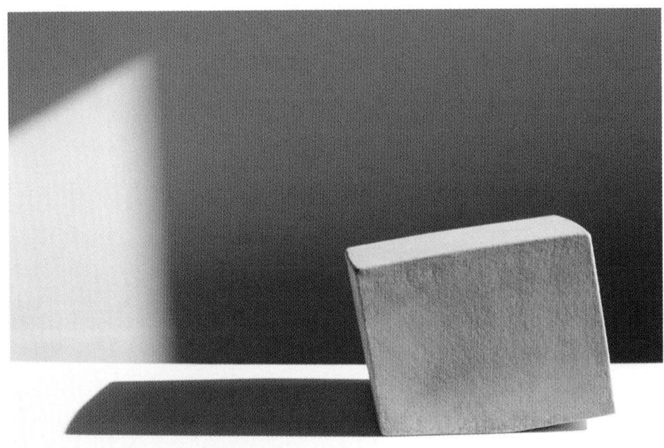

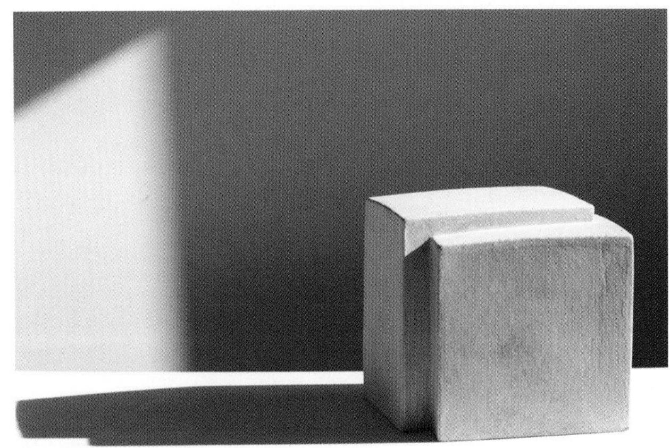

Familiar places series I II III IV (2016).
(Photograph by Ken Eastman)

way in which the curvature of surface reflects or absorbs light, and how shadow can accentuate concave shapes. His control – the precision of lines, and his understanding of how compositional decisions will augment or depart from previous ones – is quite remarkable. Honed over many decades, Eastman's technique evinces an elegant spontaneity that flows through each form with apparent ease.

Works that are not developed from the vessel form nevertheless evoke similar sensations of movement. In the *Familiar places series* (2016), recognizable architectural shapes are rendered unfamiliar by surprising shifts in perspective. The cube is a shape redolent with domesticity; homes are often depicted as cubes by children, with equally square windows and sometimes equally square doors. The incorporation of a staircase up the side of *Familiar places series I,* itself a symbol of movement between the floors of a house, re-enforces such symbolism. Yet here, shapes sit at oblique angles, transforming these into uncanny testaments of place. *Familiar places series III* leans at an awkward angle, implying unsteadiness, even imminent movement. *Familiar places series II* suggests two forces suspended in embrace-like equilibrium, perhaps extending the symbol of domesticity to family relations. In *Familiar places series IV,* conjoined forms look set to detach themselves in a process of extension and separation, like the enlargement of a house as a family grows, or a sense of collapse as family members leave. Although

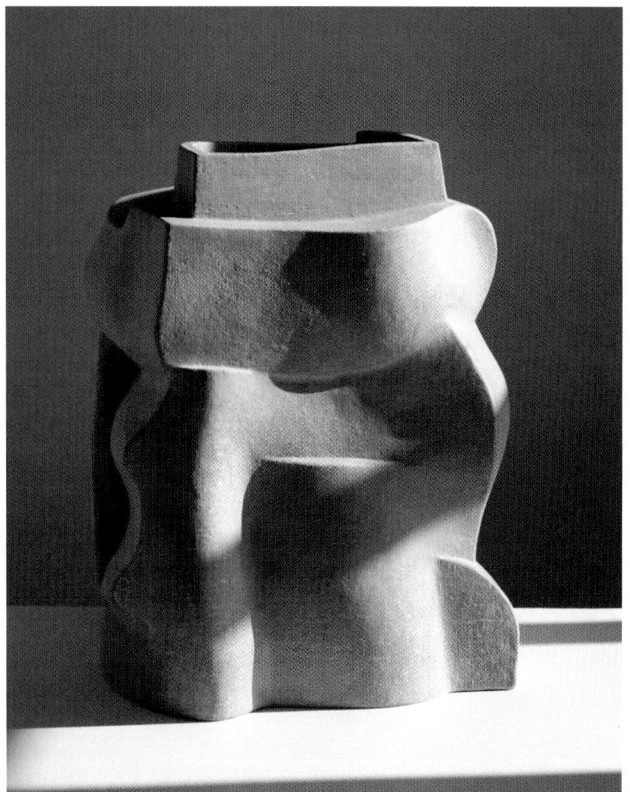

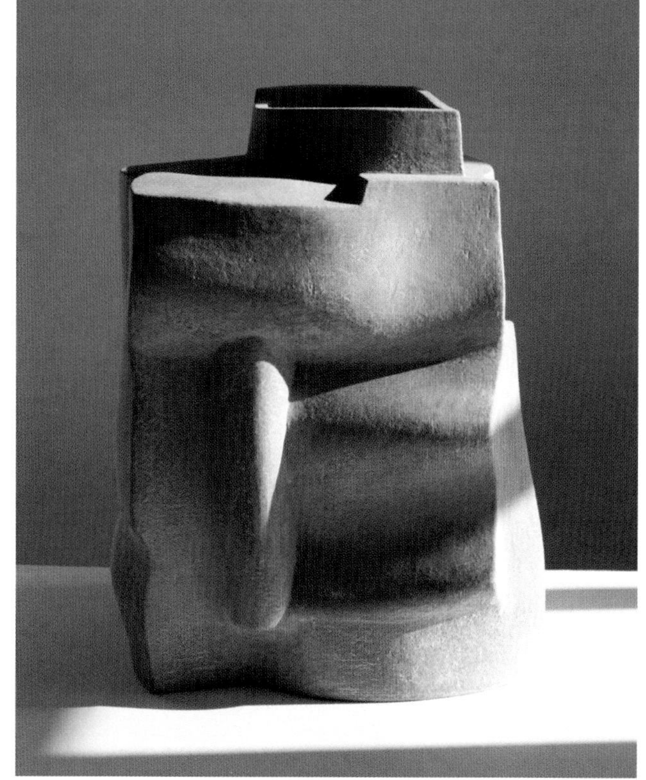

Hilly's song (2020).
(Photograph by Ken Eastman)

interior space is concealed, these works are dependent upon a sense of force enacted from within the walls of the form that expands the exterior.

For me, Eastman's works seem less like 'ceramic sculptures' or 'sculptural vessels'; more like 'paintings on a three-dimensional clay canvas'. Such emphasis draws attention to how his work sits comfortably across different categories of art practice. For instance, *Hilly's song* reminds me of the paintings of Georges Braque (1882–1963), whose Cubist approaches rendered still life objects and landscapes as abstract geometric compositions. For Braque (and Picasso) gradations of tone within a shape suggested three-dimensions, even as the non-perspectival composition rendered the overall image as two-dimensional.

Similar effects can be discerned in *Hilly's song*, except, of course, this work is three-dimensional.

This does not mean, however, that Eastman's work is indebted to Cubist sculpture. While sculptors such as Jacques Lipchitz (1891–1973) created abstracted, geometric forms, they were usually based upon figuration or the depiction of nature. Although Eastman's work can be said to be similarly concerned with shape, this is not for the purposes of disguising figurative compositions. Rather, his work is a painterly and sculptural celebration of what shape can convey as a language in its own right; the emotions it can elicit, the meanings it can evoke. In his sculptures, shapes function like musical chords, lines become key signatures, and tonal gradations facilitate modulation between major and minor scales. *Hilly's song* is indeed musical; it conveys a sense of joy, love, exhilaration in sharing a moment with someone else, even if its white/grey colour suggests a fading memory, a regret that something has passed. Whether this is really the impulse behind the work is beside the point; Eastman has a remarkable capacity for loading vessels with meaning, to make them speak to us, even if they only reveal us to ourselves.

As 'paintings on a three-dimensional clay canvas', colour is singularly important. Eastman's more vibrantly coloured pieces draw attention to the challenge that underpins all of his practice: how to resolve form, colour and tone so that there is dynamic balance between coherence and dissonance. The abrasive interplay between these compositional energies gives each piece a particular kind of tonal and emotional presence. In *Sea change*, for instance, the juxtaposition between coloured sections suggests indecision, or perhaps the changing of someone's mind about something or someone. The relationship between form and colour in *Sailwave* (2015) does indeed suggest a wave breaking, the surge echoed in the circularity of the vessel (another sea-related word). Yet, *Sailwave* is not, or not only, an abstracted response to natural phenomenon. Feelings also come in waves: elation, sadness, loneliness, closeness. *Sailwave* suggests the transience of emotion via reference to the shifting sea. Similarly, the colours of *Inland green* (2019) evoke feelings of sitting beneath a tree, the grey stripe suggestive of shade. Yet, this piece also seems to stand for the activation of memory, of remembering the feelings associated with a specific time. After all, memories are, like Eastman's works, the collaging together of the different recollections of the senses.

Eastman's sculptures are assemblages of different facets. They draw attention to how we perceive the three-dimensionality of objects from all sides. While Merleau-Ponty considered three-dimensional objects as phenomena that are both physically and imaginatively conceived, it is also possible to

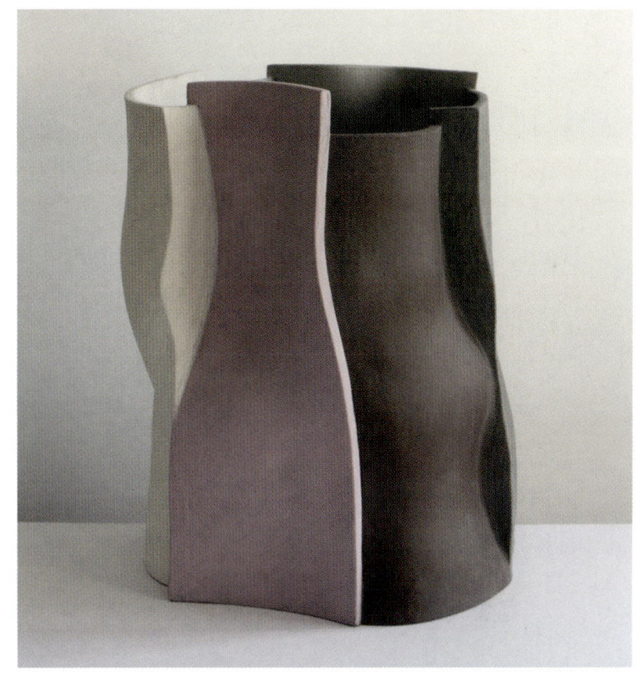

Sea change (2019).
(Photograph by Ken Eastman)

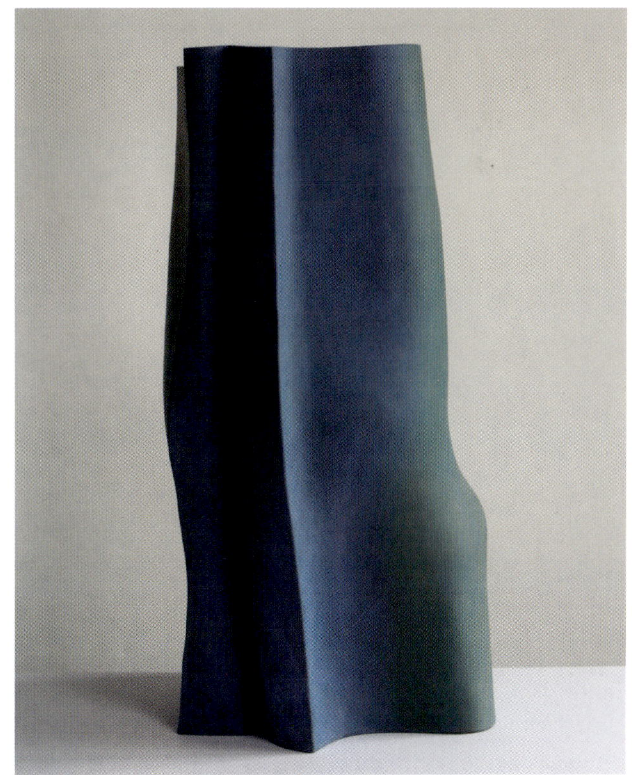

Sailwave (2015).
(Photograph by Ken Eastman)

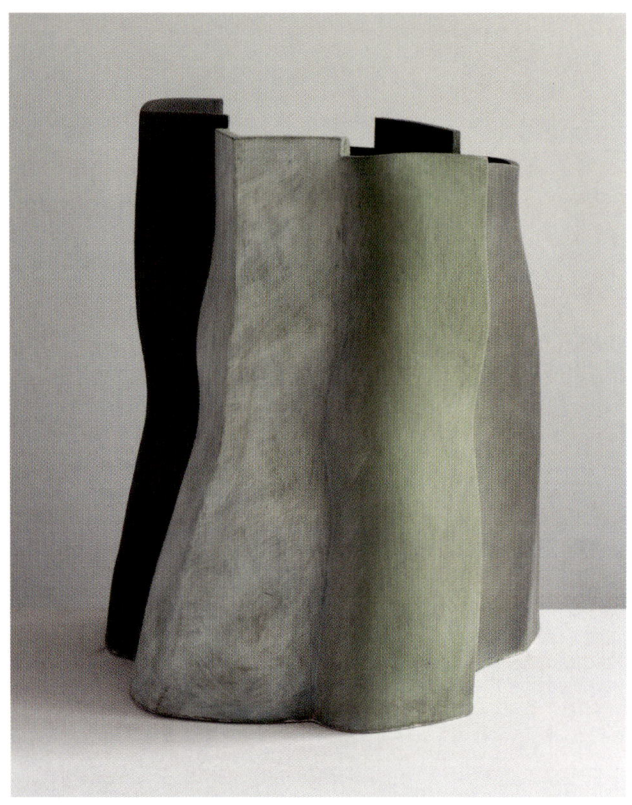

Inland green (2019).
(Photograph by Ken Eastman)

consider 'sides' as psychological phenomena, as expressive of traits of ourselves. Indeed, *Object with memory* (2016) seems to highlight the significance of emotional attachment, here expressed literally, that we have to objects. Nevertheless, if there is an intentional impulse behind each work –– the title of each work certainly provides clues –– I am left feeling that to append one meaning to it is to diminish the possibility of play, something that is, in actual fact, an important facet of Eastman's creative process. Interpretation is what it is: facets of perception. Eastman's work is about phenomena, how we perceive the world from different perspectives, and how open-ended works have the potential to become emotionally meaningful in different ways to different people. After all, when considering emotion, to be 'open' is also to be 'exposed', 'vulnerable', 'honest', even 'frank'. For me, this emotional depth establishes Eastman as one of the most compelling artists of his generation.

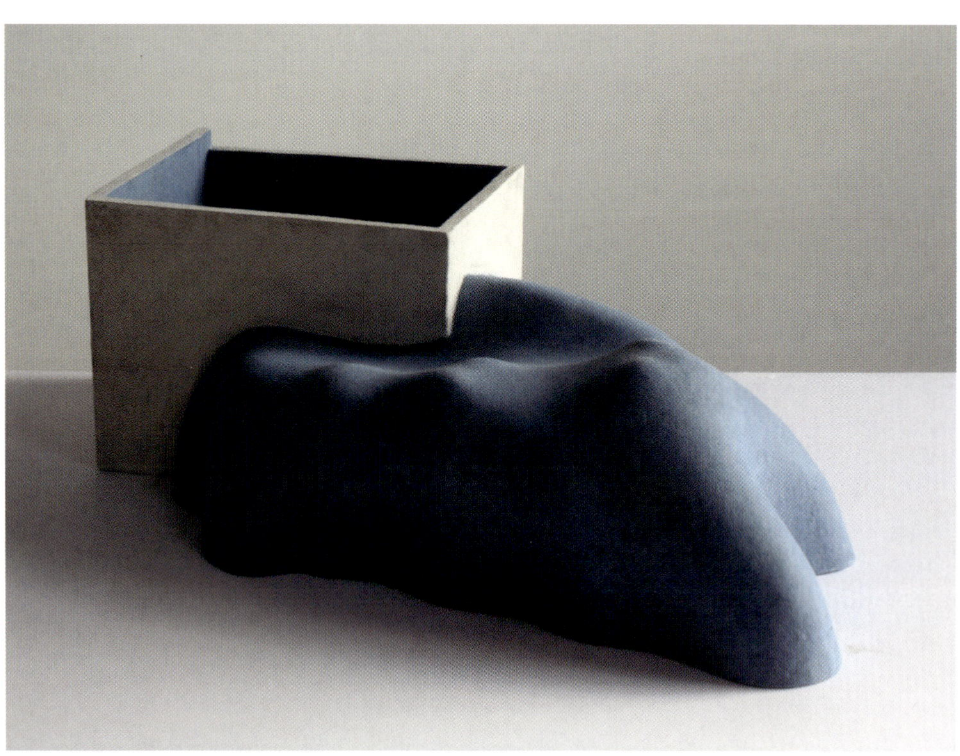

Object with memory (2016).
(Photograph by Ken Eastman)

Nao Matsunaga
Placed Spaces

One of my favourite works by Nao Matsunaga is a sculpture entitled *Onetime Fountain* (2016). It has a fluency that I find consistently arresting; the twists and turns of the modelled clay create dynamic and engaging spaces. In fact, I find these spatial absences to be the most vibrant elements in the composition. Two circular spaces hover above the base towards the outer edges, out of which a central space emerges. This space takes the eye up an invisible body that forms the 'backbone' of the sculpture. Lines interweave into a resolved rectangle at the top. I am also drawn to how the glaze (which was added prior to a second firing, the sculpture placed horizontally in the kiln so that the glaze could run in a different direction to the vertical plane of the skeleton) affords colour a sculptural as well as decorative function. I am left feeling that this piece could not really have been planned; it has the energy of chance discovery. Intuition seems to have played a key part in generating a balanced and satisfying composition. Is this an abstracted

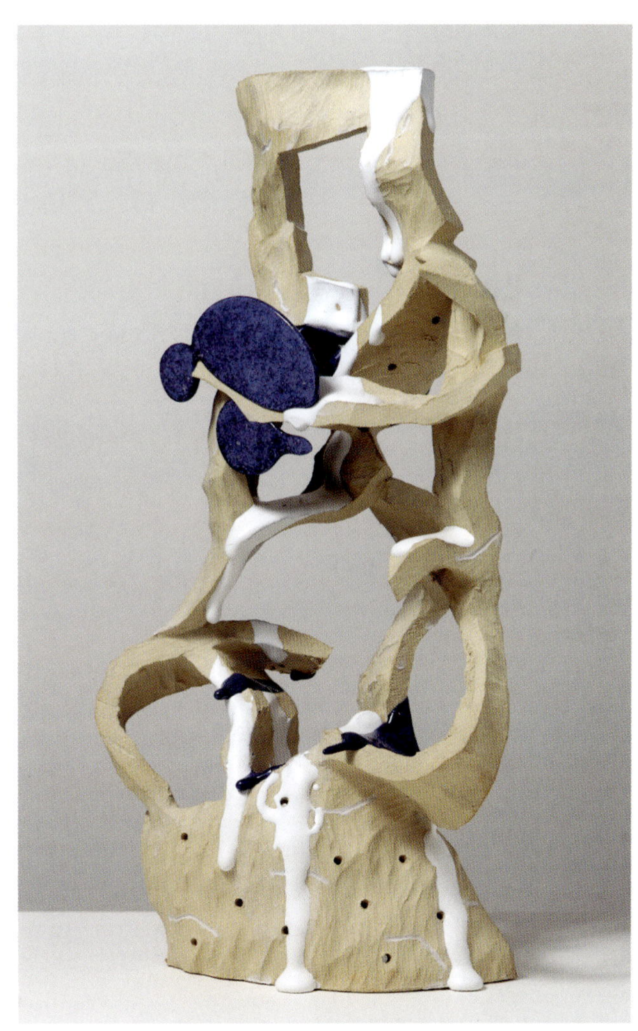

Onetime Fountain (2016).
(Photograph by Phil Sayer)

figure holding a child? Or is it a volcanic explosion of rock? Is it a totem from an obscure religious cult? Or a kind of scholar's rock, a gorged stone that was so important to classical Chinese garden design?

The spatial relationships that I find so engaging in *Onetime Fountain* offer a point of departure for a wider investigation of Matsunaga's work. Inspired by the above analysis, this essay focuses on the concept of relational space – spaces that are dependent upon other spaces to exist – as an aesthetic idea, but also as a way of considering the politics of identity. Matsunaga was born in Osaka and spent his formative years in Japan. He came to the UK when he was twelve, and has resided here ever since, even though his parents remain in Japan. Is this important to understanding his work? Not necessarily. It would be reductive to propose that his work is a straightforward document of his multicultural identities. Nevertheless, I propose that in some of his work, identity and aesthetics seem to coalesce, and this offers potentially illuminating threads for wider considerations of his practice.

The famous Japanese designer Uchida Shigeru (1943–2016) once described what he considered to be fundamental differences between Japanese and Western approaches to design. Uchida believed that there were:

> two directions for design themes. They are the way to grasp a 'thing' or 'object' as a subject and the way to consider a 'relationship' as a subject. Supposing we call the former 'object as precedent', the latter can be called 'relationship as precedent'. Japanese culture is that in which everything is 'relationship as precedent'.[102]

While I am not entirely convinced that such clear-cut and neat divisions inexorably separate all Japanese and Western approaches to design, I nevertheless find Uchida's point interesting in relation to Matsunaga's work. If we return to *Onetime Fountain*, there is a sense of 'relationship as precedent' in the determination of space according to its compositional relationship with other spaces. These spaces are, of course, themselves reliant on the twisted lines of clay, the outlines that delineate and animate spaces with energy, thereby giving vibrancy to the sculpture as a whole. In this sense, Uchida might have concluded that Matsunaga's work speaks to a very 'Japanese' design aesthetic. Yet, if Western design emphasizes 'object as precedent', then *Onetime Fountain* might also be considered very 'Western'. It is an object in its own right; it does not depend on other sculptures for its presence, nor for the creation of meanings. It is self-referent of presence; the work is 'present' as a material object, but it also explores how line, texture and colour can activate presence in otherwise empty spaces. If we follow Uchida's observations, *Onetime Fountain* is *both* Japanese and Western.

How might this aesthetic fusion map on to multicultural identities? This seems particularly salient given that cultural space might also be considered as relational. For instance, a white sculptor working in Britain is, simply, a sculptor. A Japanese sculptor working in Britain is almost always racially marked – and overtly so – as a *Japanese* sculptor, or a *British Japanese* sculptor. Identity is formed in relation to the dominant ideological and cultural space within which people find themselves. For an artist working and exhibiting in both Britain and Japan, this identity politic might even become a series of choices. Is the artist a Japanese sculptor when exhibiting in Britain, but a British sculptor when exhibiting in Japan? This might seem like semantic game-playing, but it alludes to the significance of relations of cultural space to identity, and in turn, to the classification of an artist and their work.

The postcolonial theorist Homi Bhabha recognized how the fusion of differing relational spaces – here invoked as cultural, national and ethnic tropes – can combine to create identities that are unique. To be Japanese is to be in one set of relational spaces; to be British is to be in another. To operate across both is to bring them together in new ways, what Bhabha describes in the rather dense passage that follows, as 'hybridity':

> All forms of culture are continually in a process of hybridity. But for me the importance of hybridity is not to be able to trace the two original moments from which the third emerges, rather hybridity to me is the 'third space' which enables other positions to emerge. [...] I try to talk about hybridity through psychoanalytic analogy, so that identification is a process of identifying with and through another object, an object of otherness, at which point the agency of identification – the subject – is itself ambivalent, because of the intervention of that otherness. But the importance of hybridity is that it bears the traces of those feelings and practices that inform it, just like a translation, so that hybridity puts together the traces of certain other meanings or discourses. It does not give them the authority of being prior in the sense of being original: they are prior only in the sense of being anterior. The process of cultural hybridity gives rise to something different, something new and unrecognizable, a new area of negotiation of meaning and representation.[103]

Hybridity can thus be understood as the bringing together of a range of relational spaces, of finding an ambivalence through an identification with otherness. Following Bhabha's ideas, it could be argued that Matsunaga's formative years in Japan do not necessarily make him 'originally Japanese'; rather,

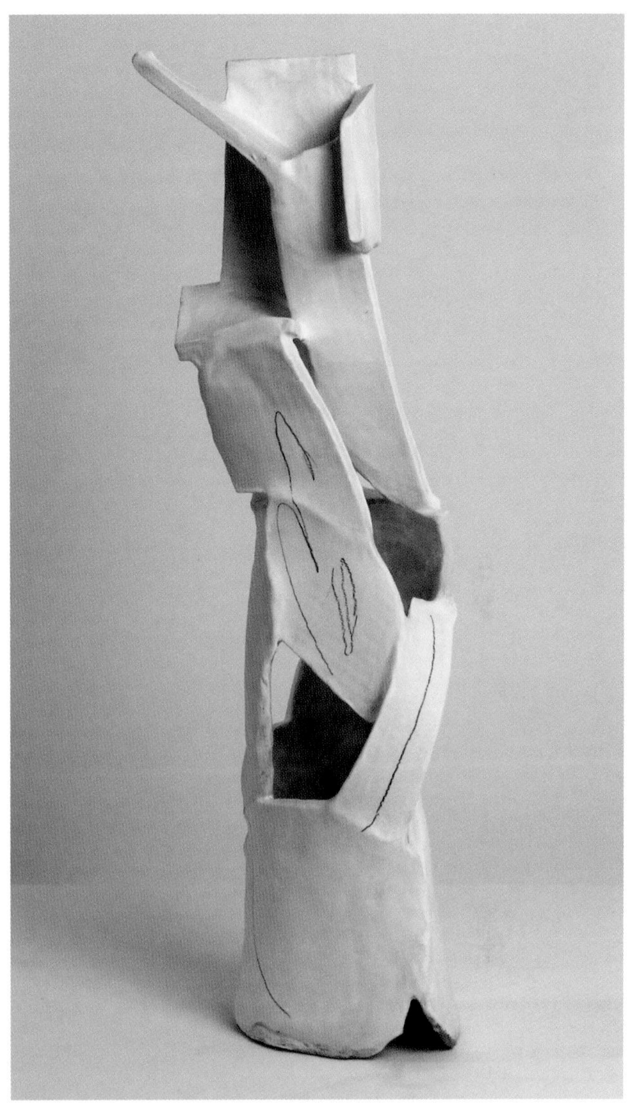

Now, Aligned (2019).
(Photograph by Nao Matsunaga)

he is neither wholly Japanese, nor wholly British, but a unique blending of both that coalesce in a particular way, and take on a particular relevance depending on where he chooses to live. If his identity rests in a position of 'otherness' from both contexts, Matsunaga works in what Bhabha defines as a 'third space'. It does not automatically follow that a third space provokes a sense of alienation or exile (though it might); rather the third space opens up a distinctive vantage point from which to create highly

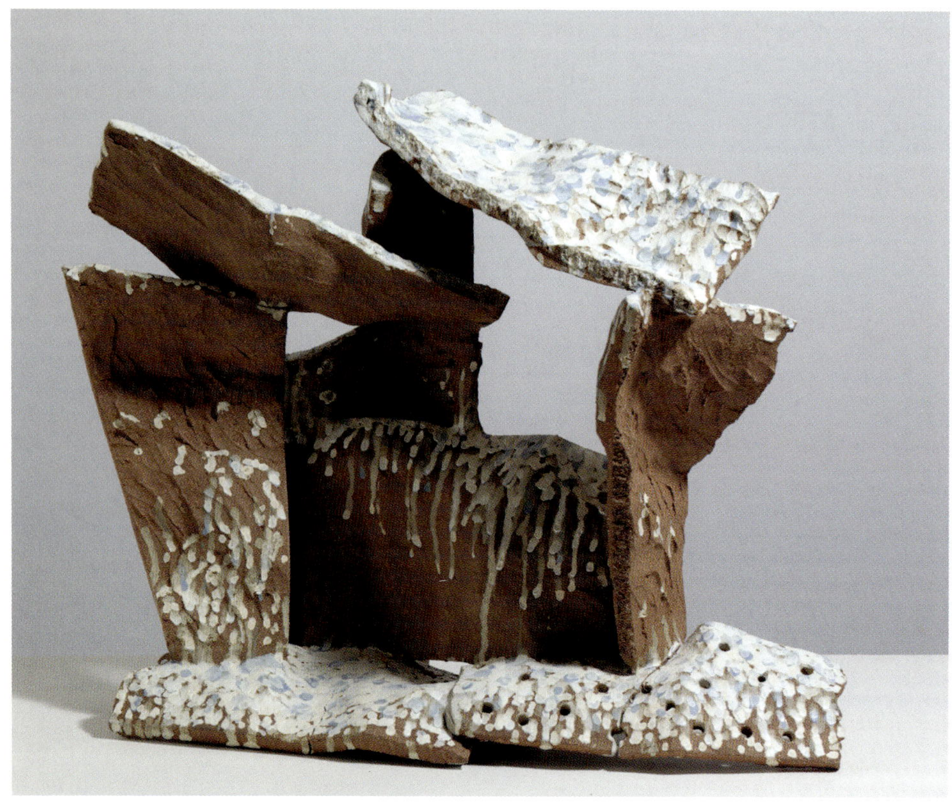

PSURB Glaze (2016).
(Photograph by Phil Sayer)

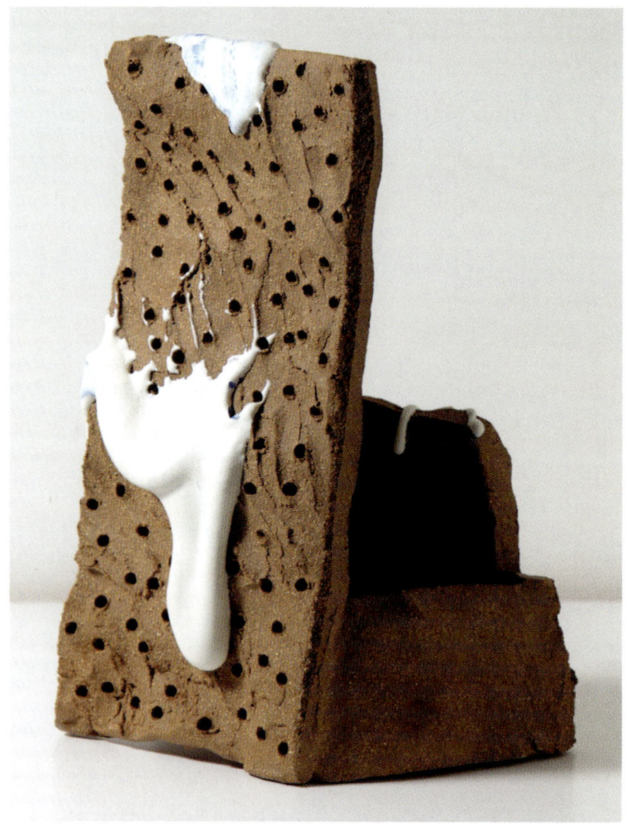

Mattress Studies 2 (2016).
(Photograph by Phil Sayer)

individualized work. If Matsunaga's aesthetic challenges some of Uchida's observations about opposing approaches to Japanese and Western design, perhaps this arises from the fact that Matsunaga responds to both cultural contexts. His work explores space as a relational aesthetic, but this might also be tied to his own hybridized and relational combinations of culture, identity and national belonging.

Of course, the organization of spatial relationships is a basic component of all aesthetic composition. All sculpture, ceramics, painting and drawing involves the resolution of questions of space. In Matsunaga's work, however, questions of relational space have a particular emphasis; for me, this rests in the activation of spatial cavities to make them dynamically resonant. *PSURB Glaze* (2016), for instance, highlights how spaces between the clay slabs are integral to the composition. Jagged triangles and rectangles are created by the slab-built sections themselves as well as the gaps between them. The interplay between these elements takes the eye on a rhythmic journey across, around and through the work. I am always intrigued by the fact that these rhythms have been discovered by intuition. As the title of another work, *Now, Aligned* (2019), implies, the composition has been found rather than schematically planned; the directional flow that takes the eye up the body of this sculpture has been arrived at through playful exploration. At first glance, other works have less relational space within the sculptures themselves. In *Mattress Studies 2* (2016), for example, the blocks form a rigid series of rectangles that give the sculpture a sense of solidity and heaviness. However, the holes in the front section are themselves a series of spaces, each intuitively placed in relation to the others.

While many of Matsunaga's sculptural forms are found in the process of making, *The Illusion of Reflection 2* (2016) perhaps stands slightly apart from his other work. This piece is an interpretation of a Korean moon jar, the thirteenth-century perfectly spherical jar, normally thrown in two sections and merged with a seamless join. Matsunaga's approach to having a pre-determined form was to deconstruct it. *The Illusion of Reflection 2* (one in a series of works exploring the moon jar form) is a coherent composition, but one that is nevertheless severed into two relational sections. The upper section, nominally evoking something of the moon jar by creating a contained space, features a series of cracks and fissures that are reflected in the fragmented lower section. The lower section also features legs that support the 'jar', giving the sense that this work could move around the gallery or the studio. As a consequence of these 'legs', I cannot help but read *The Illusion of Reflection*

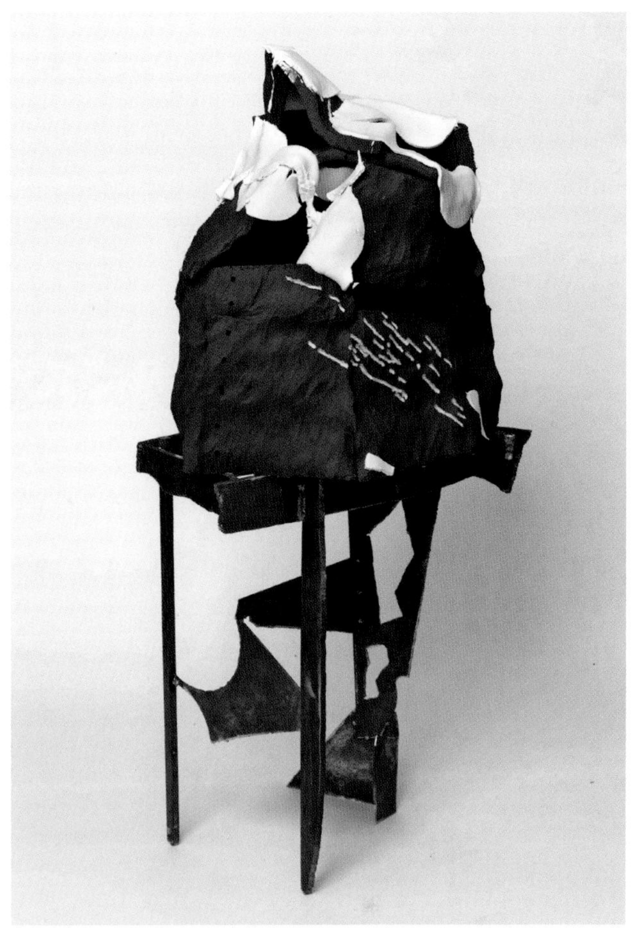

The Illusion of Refection 2 (2016).
(Photograph by Jon Stokes)

2 as anything other than a response to the globalized journey of the moon jar, shifting as it has from a thirteenth-century Korean vessel to a stock part of the vocabulary of contemporary British ceramics (as exemplified in the work of artists such as Adam Buick and Akiko Hirai). The sense of global travel and 'in betweenness' in *The Illusion of Reflection 2* captures something of the hybridity of being both East Asian and British. It is a quiet statement, but one that is nevertheless present as the work grapples with different cultural reference points.

Such questions of identity surface more readily in works such as *I Wish I Knew How Good It Would Feel To Be A Tree* (2017), a riff on the 1967 Nina Simone is indelibly implanted into the surface of the clay. The face itself has a slightly confused look, exuding a rather quizzical sense of yearning. The terracotta colour of the clay stands apart from the black wooden body and metal legs, as though the face has been transplanted onto it. The disassociation between the ceramic face and the rest of the sculpture gives the sense of a projected image, a dream or a ponderance, the projection of the artist's own persona into a different body. In this sense, *I Wish I Knew How Good It Would Feel To Be A Tree* opens up a relational space to question identity and belonging. What would it be like to feel securely rooted to one place?

The shaping of wood to explore questions of identity can be found in a slightly earlier series of painted carved wooden masks, collectively titled *Masking*, which were made in 2016. Masks are an instrument for disguise, an object designed to replace one face with another to obscure the expression of emotion. Yet, Matsunaga's masks are not realistic acts of pretence; they are almost caricatures of anger, shock and bewilderment, painted with colourful lines and bold colours. Masks have been an important part of Japanese culture, especially in the performing arts, for many centuries. Beautifully carved examples of painted masks can be found in museum collections around the world. Yet, Matsunaga's masks do not follow a particularly traditional Japanese aesthetic. Perhaps in creating masks as art (rather than as performance props) they speak to a Western preoccupation with the mask as art object; a thing to be admired rather than used. For me, this places his masks in intercultural territory. Matsunaga prises open the gap between a mask as a performative object of identity and as a decorative work of art. These masks have the potential to be both, and thus quiver between conceptual categories.

The *Masking* series also highlights the importance of drawing and painting to Matsunaga's practice. Drawing also returns us to the idea of

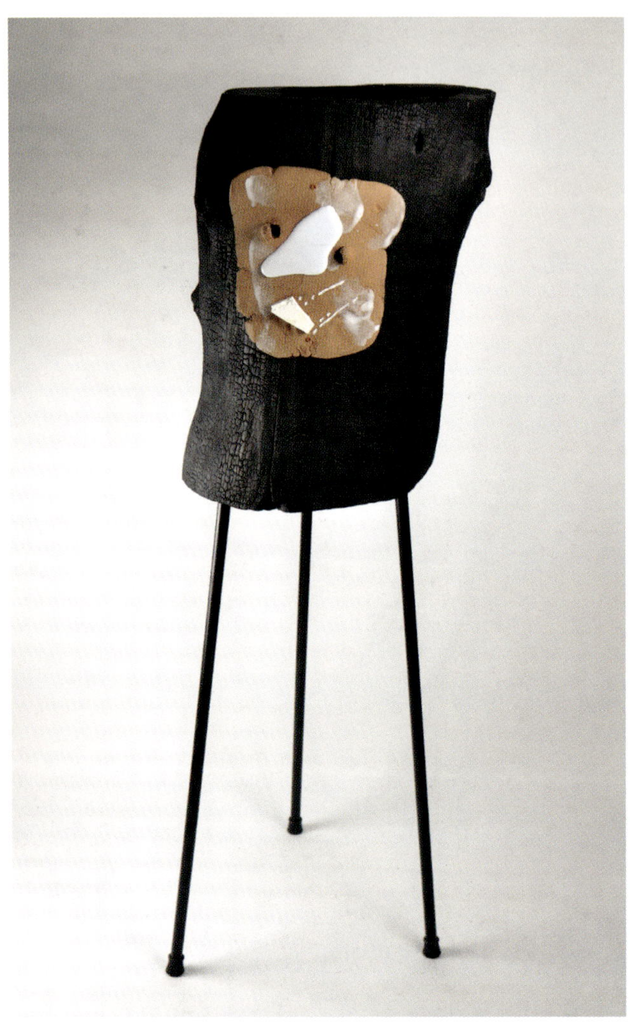

I Wish I Knew How Good It Would Feel To Be A Tree (2017).
(Photograph by Nao Matsunaga)

standard *I Wish I Knew How It Would Feel To Be Free*. Trees are grounded; they have roots, a strong sense of belonging to the landscape in which they sit – a sense of belonging achieved through years of growth and maturity. The body of *I Wish I Knew How Good It Would Feel To Be A Tree* is constructed from a beautiful piece of wood, which is supported on a metal tripod, with a ceramic face-like sculpture hung onto the body. The use of ceramic to make the face seems to me to be psychoanalytically important. Perhaps making ceramics is more readily imbued with the identity of the maker; the fingerprint of the artist

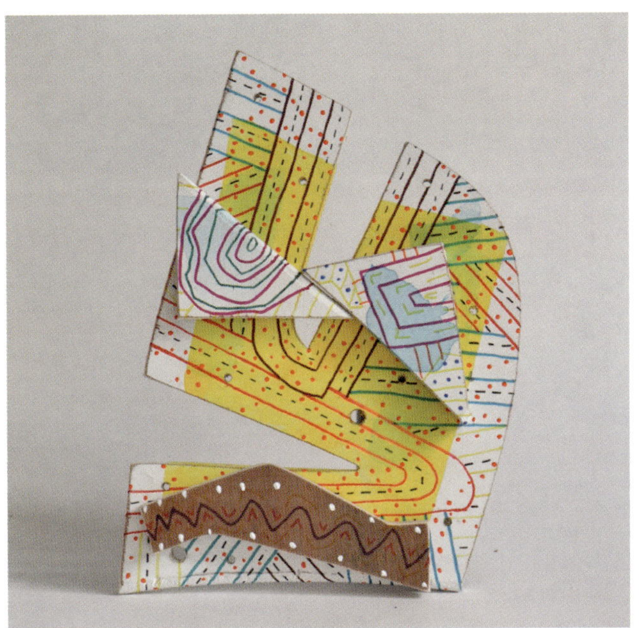

Masking (2016) [1].
(Photograph by Nao Matsunaga)

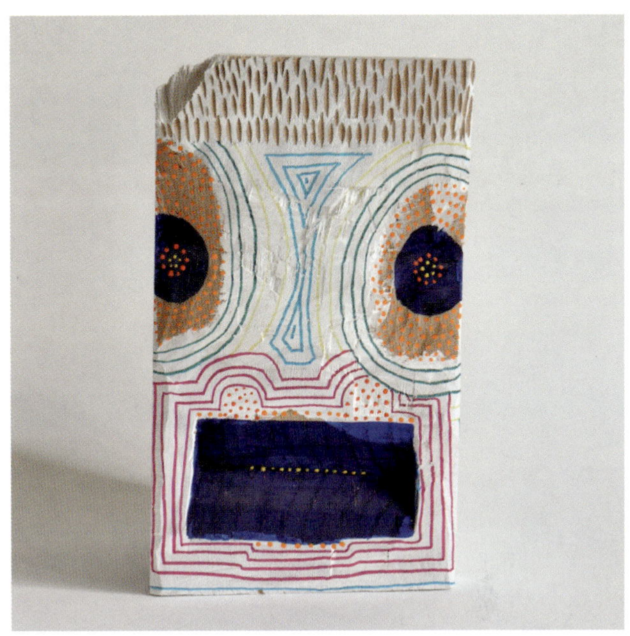

Masking (2016) [2].
(Photograph by Nao Matsunaga)

relational space as an aesthetic principle. In his works on paper, relations between blocks and lines are a recurring motif. Space is demarcated in quite distinctive ways: by silhouette (as in the two untitled works from 2018), or by areas of flat colour (*Untitled* (2015) and the two untitled works from 2018). Line is an important compositional element, taking the eye on a journey across different terrains of the drawing – as in *Untitled* (2018) [1] and *Untitled* (2015) – or by forming a plane or barrier through which the viewer must look to comprehend a second spatial composition – as can be discerned in *Untitled* (2019). In all cases, spaces are contingent upon others for compositional balance. In this sense, Matsunaga's lines are both descriptive and sculptural; they carve the paper into sections of space to create vibrancy, but they also take the eye across the composition from one point to another. Lines invite our eyes to travel around the drawing. Space becomes marked as a compositional point of departure, of return, or of transient passing.

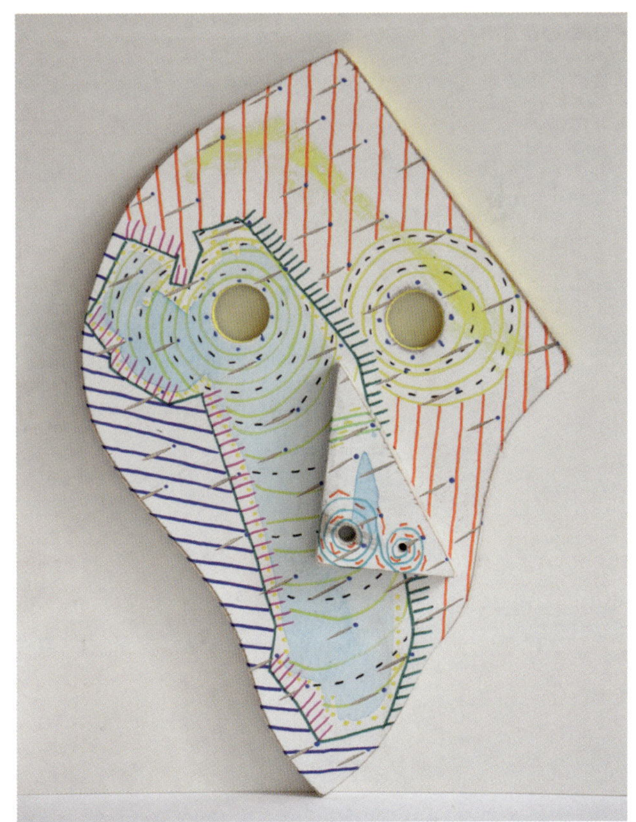

Masking (2016) [3].
(Photograph by Nao Matsunaga)

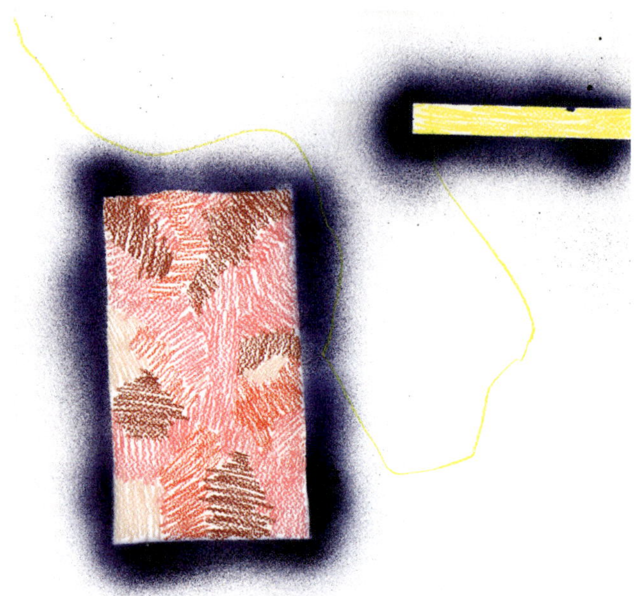

Untitled (2018) [1].
(Photograph by Nao Matsunaga)

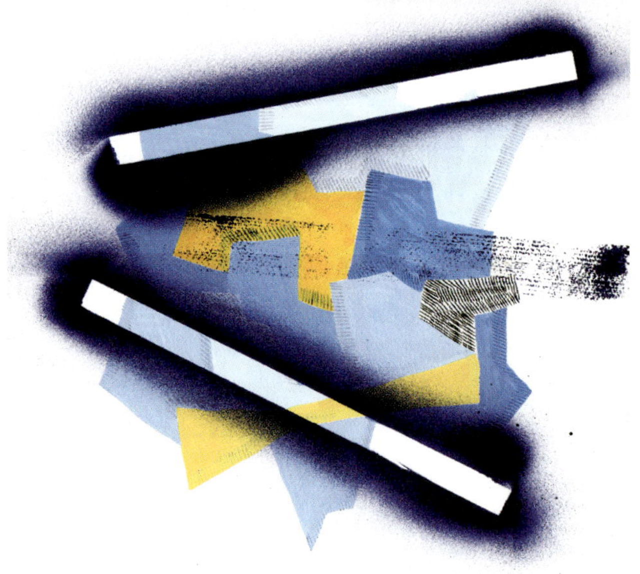

Untitled (2018) [2].
(Photograph by Nao Matsunaga)

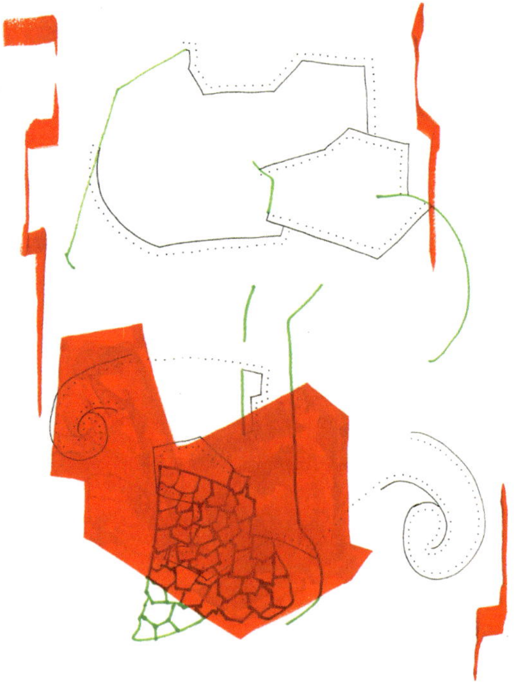

Untitled (2015).
(Photograph by Nao Matsunaga)

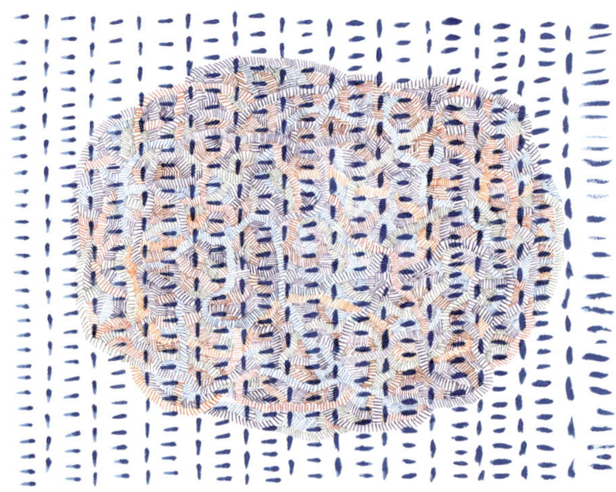

Untitled (2019).
(Photograph by Nao Matsunaga)

In returning to Matsunaga's ceramic sculptures, it becomes clear that two and three dimensions are closely intertwined. As noted earlier in relation to *Onetime Fountain*, glaze is used as both a sculptural and decorative element, a feature of his drawn lines (indeed, I find the composition of *Untitled* (2015) and *Onetime Fountain* to share fundamental strategies). The application of drawn marks with glaze or ceramic pencil almost turns some sculptures into three-dimensional drawings. In *Smile!! If U Wanna* (2017), for example, applied marks work with and across incised sculptural lines in the clay surface. A smiling face seems to appear in the uppermost section, fuelling similar playful questions of identity that can be discerned in *I Wish I Knew How Good It Would Feel To Be A Tree*. Blue and white is a reference to East Asian ceramics, but Matsunaga redeploys the palette, taking 'blue and white' out of antiquity and into the sphere of contemporary sculpture. The form reminds me of a cloud, and therefore a kind of fantasy, a nod to the pervasive influence of the willow-patterned plate, an English design that constructed Asian ceramics according to European aesthetic tastes and expectations.

If Matsunaga's work explores identity, it does so obliquely. His work is not a documentation of what it is like to be British Japanese in multicultural Britain. Rather, his work is a thoughtful analysis of what it means to bridge cultures. In this sense, Matsunaga utilizes relational space as an aesthetic principle in order to interrogate his own relational space as a British Japanese artist. In each work, space becomes an opportunity to create place, a contextual vantage point from which to analyse processes of deconstruction and reassembly. From a position of hybridity, Matsunaga is able to connect ideas and impulses across an artistic terrain that is uniquely his own. His work thus becomes the articulation of a process of arrival: at an idea, a composition, a state of being, perhaps even a resolved identity. Such a reading of his work finds expression in the sculpture *Here We Are Fam (Borgund)* (2015). The sculpture evokes the shape of the famous Borgund Stave Church in Norway, but the title also alludes to the arrival of a family, as a family, at a preordained destination. In Matsunaga's work, relational spaces become powerfully resolved into physical, inhabitable places.

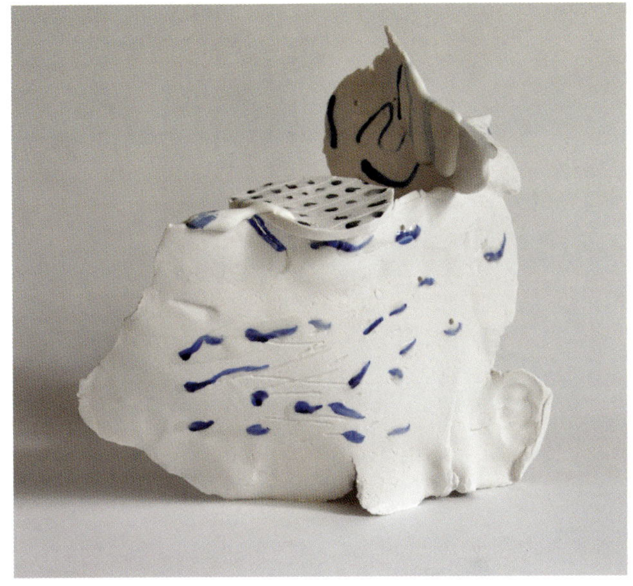

Smile!! If U Wanna (2017).
(Photograph by Nao Matsunaga)

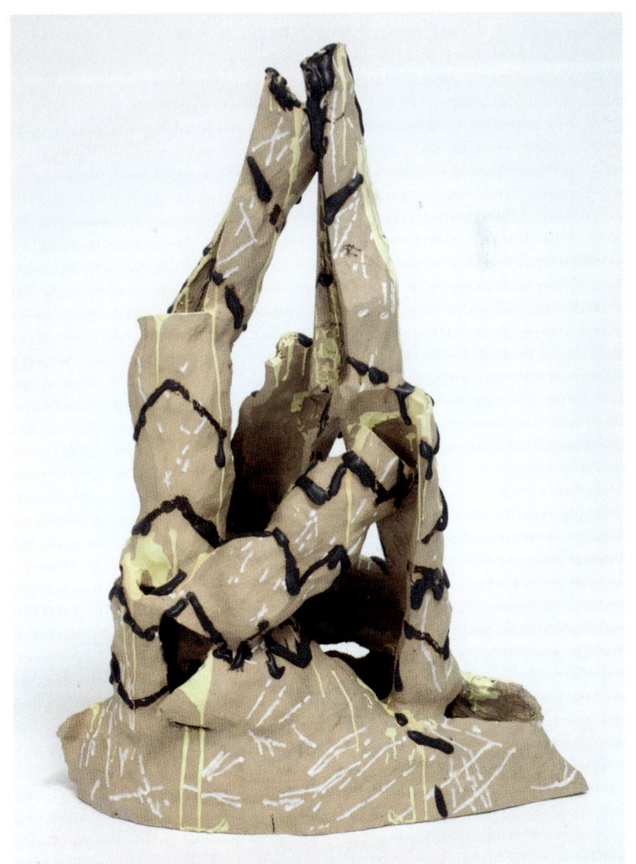

Here We Are Fam (Borgund) (2015).
(Photograph by Nao Matsunaga)

Sam Lucas

Unexplained MsStories

> She comes in, comes-in-between herself me and you, between the other me where one is always infinitely more than one and more than me, without the fear of ever reaching a limit; she thrills in our becoming. And we'll keep on becoming! She cuts through defensive loves, motherages, and devourations: beyond selfish narcissism, in the moving, open, transitional space, she runs her risks.[104]
>
> *Hélène Cixous*

In *The Laugh of the Medusa* (1976), the French feminist Hélène Cixous issued a call to arms for women to write themselves into existence, to spin a web of literature that resists the norms of oppression, and in particular the patriarchal categorization of women according to their phallic lack. She appealed to women to explore the plurality of their experiences through a new non-gendered language (French is 'gendered' with definite articles – the masculine 'le', feminine 'la'). Interestingly, Cixous regarded writing as much a physical act of resistance as a mental one. Objectified for the desire and pleasure of men, 'women are body', she declared, and the more objectified women are, the 'more body, hence more writing. For a long time it has been in body that women have responded to persecution, to the familial-conjugal enterprise of domestication, to the repeated attempts at castrating them'.[105] Women, therefore, need to create themselves in and through 'bodies'.

Upon first encountering the sculptures of Sam Lucas, I am struck by their physicality, a bold hive of strange organic bodies. There is inventiveness, playfulness, and an engaging use of colour and texture, but there is also something unnerving about them. It looks as if these creatures, when disturbed, might pounce upon us, threatening to 'come in' and 'cut through', 'without the fear of ever reaching a limit'. What is it about the creeping legs and exterior sacs that I find so disconcerting? Perhaps they remind me of spiders, of which I am disproportionately terrified.

Of course, a fear of spiders reveals more about the human psyche than the realities of the natural world, and the appearance of spiders in dreams has been the subject of much psychoanalytic study. In 1922, Karl Abraham (1877–1925) observed that 'the spider represents in the first place the wicked mother who is formed like a man, and in the second place the male genital attributed to her. In this the spider's web represents the pubic hair and the single thread the male genital'.[106] Ten years later, Sigmund Freud (1856–1939) similarly suggested that 'a spider in dreams is a symbol of the mother, but of the phallic mother, of whom we are afraid; so that the fear of spiders expresses dread of mother-incest and horror of the female genitals'.[107] Who knew?! Of course, the 'we' that is 'afraid' in Freud's writing is implicitly gendered. It is men who fear the 'phallic mother': the spider's fangs and legs symbolic of an aggressive matriarchy that assumes control of the phallus to conquer and devour men.

These projections are challenged by *Maman* (1999), perhaps the most famous sculpture by the celebrated French American artist Louise Bourgeois (1911–2010). *Maman* is a thirty-foot bronze and steel spider, housing eggs in a steel cage suspended from the midst of its abdomen. Its size evokes Abraham's analysis of the spider's symbolic threat to masculinity, since 'the female spider is far superior in size and power to the male, and during copulation the latter runs a very real risk of being killed and devoured by her'.[108] Yet, *Maman* is a rather beautiful and gracious form, teetering on its extended legs like a pirouetting

ballerina. It exhibits a duality that is both threatening and benign, aggressive and protective. It captures Abraham's wider observation that spiders can be regarded as both positive and negative, a contradiction that 'produces a feeling of "uncanniness" in people'.[109] As a familiar body made strange, *Maman* appears to revel in its threat to patriarchy by virtue of size and apparent determination to weave itself into the narrative thread of equality. Yet, despite appearances, *Maman* does not reduce the threat of the spider to a Freudian hijacking of the phallus; it simply expresses the existence of women on their own terms, and as independent from men. *Maman* stands proudly on its own eight legs.

Sam Lucas does not directly explore the spider as a symbol, but like *Maman*, and as unpredictable and self-governing organisms, her sculptures crawl across the table and along the floor towards independence. Paralleling Cixous in her essay *The Laugh of the Medusa*, Lucas enters the ancient Greek labyrinth to stare directly at the phallic-headed gorgon that turns men into stone. I propose that she combs the classical world to explore, question and critique the construction of women as 'lacking' by psychologists such as Freud, which she then makes relevant to the contemporary through her own original approach to anthropomorphic sculpture. Her uncanny works, which are both humorous and unsettling, appear rooted to the concept of the physical body, but they are also abstracted into the world of fantasy. They exist, therefore, in a psychological twilight between the real and the imaginary. As symbolic sculptures they invite psychoanalysis, and in what follows I tentatively offer an interpretation of dreams.

The *Strange Stranger* series (2018) was a group of table-top freestanding sculptures. Despite being very individualized, they all share one element in common: they stand on three legs. The symbol of the triskelion – three legs intertwined – has a long history, existing in both Paganism and in the classical Greek and Roman worlds. In neo-paganism, the triskelion represents the land, sea and sky, or symbolizes the triple goddess of the moon, earth and childbirth. The symbol was sometimes used to refer to Hecate, the ancient Greek goddess of witchcraft, the night, the moon and ghosts, but who was more often depicted as three conjoined figures encircling a column. Hecate was also imbued with power over heaven, earth and the sea, and associated with three phases of the moon: new, waxing and full. She was worshipped as a protective goddess and provider of prosperity, but in her three-figured form was also regarded as a liminal goddess of entrances and crossroads and placed at such positions in temples.

In the *Homeric Hymn to Demeter*, Hecate was the only god to hear the screams of Demeter's daughter, Persephone, as she was snatched by Hades and dragged to the Underworld to be his bride. Hecate accompanied Demeter on the search for her daughter, and further consoled her when she could return from the Underworld.[110] In this hymn, women are positioned as victims, as objects of the schemes and desires of men. As Virginia Gan Shi White has argued, Demeter's story highlights how 'once past childbearing age a wife stands to lose a significant amount of her societal value'.[111] Yet Demeter retains a degree of agency in the narrative; crops fail while the earth goddess Demeter focuses on the search for her abducted daughter. Once the ensuing famine threatens all mortal life, Zeus is forced into conceding a resolution. As a consequence, the psychoanalyst Carl Jung (1875–1961) suggested that 'man's role in the Demeter myth is really only that of seducer or conqueror', and that the 'psychology of the Demeter cult bears all the features of a matriarchal order of society, where the man is an indispensable but on the whole disturbing factor'.[112] In these myths, three-legged forms exhibit an uncanniness; their emotions are recognisably human, yet as ethereal participants in the world of gods, they cannot be fully comprehended.

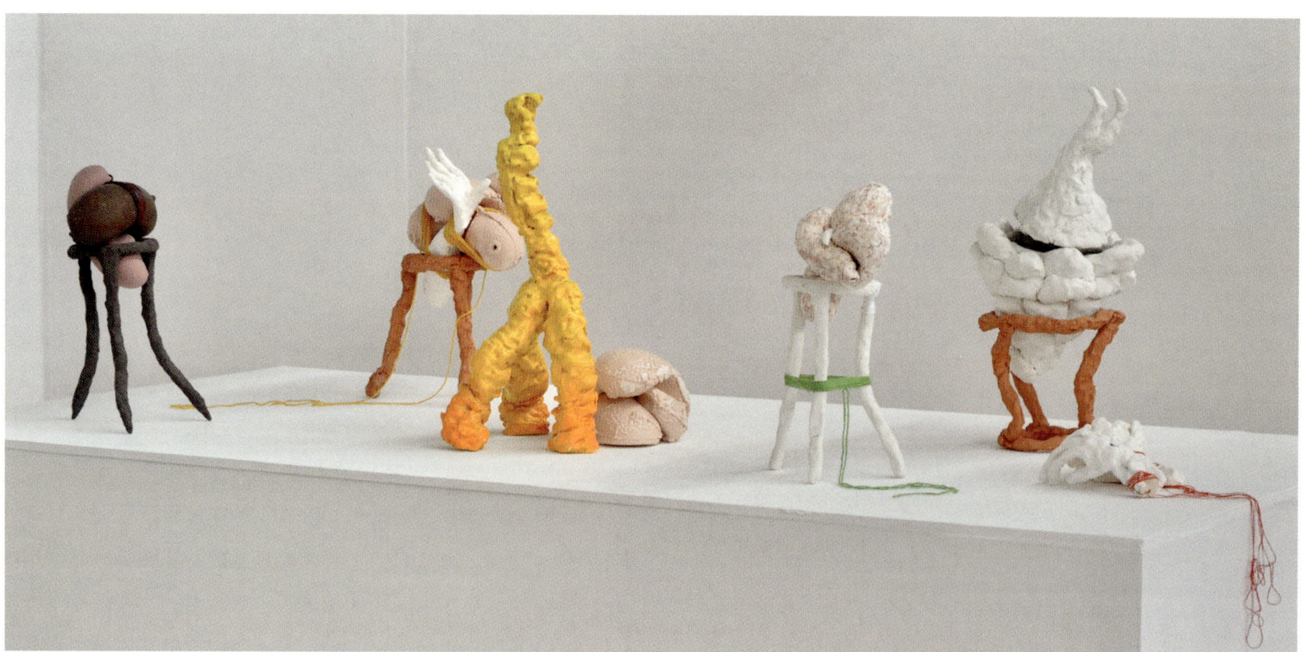

Strange Stranger series (2018).
(Photograph by Sam Lucas)

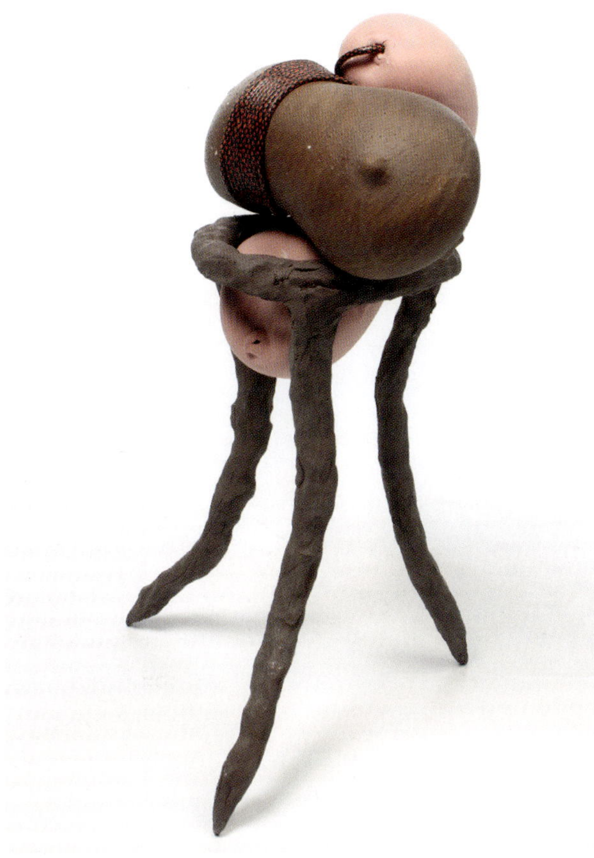

Stiletto (2018).
(Photograph by Sam Lucas)

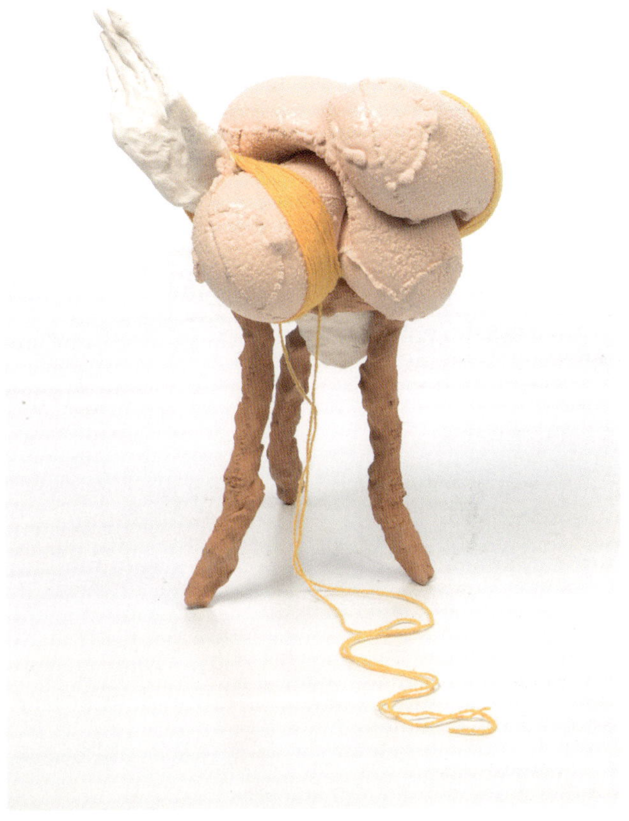

Grasping arm and goose bump' (2018).
(Photograph by Sam Lucas)

The *Strange Stranger* series of sculptures evoke the uncanniness of these ancient deities. Their abstracted form realizes an otherworldliness, yet the familiarity of limbs – legs, arms and internal organs – renders them familiar, recognizable and relatable. The legs of *Stiletto* (2018) teeter uncomfortably on raised ankles, a testament to the discomfort of yielding to meet male ideals of feminine beauty. Yet, there is no sense that this sculpture will fall over; in fact, it carries its load confidently, even fearlessly. It thus expresses a tension between repression and emancipation, of resolution to carry on despite the imposed agony. Similar ambivalence can be found in *Grasping arm and goose bump'* (2018), where the protruding arm rises ambiguously

from the body. Is the arm held out for embrace, or about to snatch at the viewer? Such uncertainty makes sense if we focus in on the mythical significance of geese, as alluded to in the 'goose bump' of the title. In a famous passage from *The Odyssey*, Penelope dreams of twenty geese killed by an eagle. She relates the dream to a beggar (actually her husband Odysseus in disguise), who interprets it as representing the death of her many suitors and the safe return of her husband in the near future. If we read the 'goose' in *Grasping arm and goose bump'* through this story, the sculpture seems to express ambivalence about the nature of relationships and, by extension, the implications of choice on the path a life will proceed to follow.

Carl Jung considered myths as expressions of the unconscious; they are pathways for projection that enable the expression of neuroses onto exterior abstract symbols (e.g. the spider projects the threat of the phallic

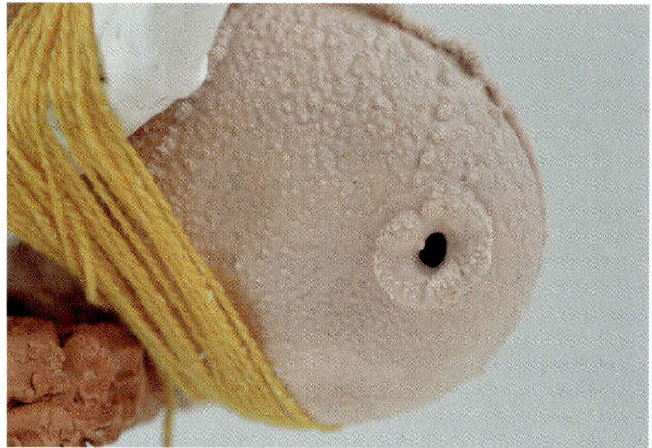

Detail of *Grasping arm and goose bump'* (2018).
(Photograph by Sam Lucas)

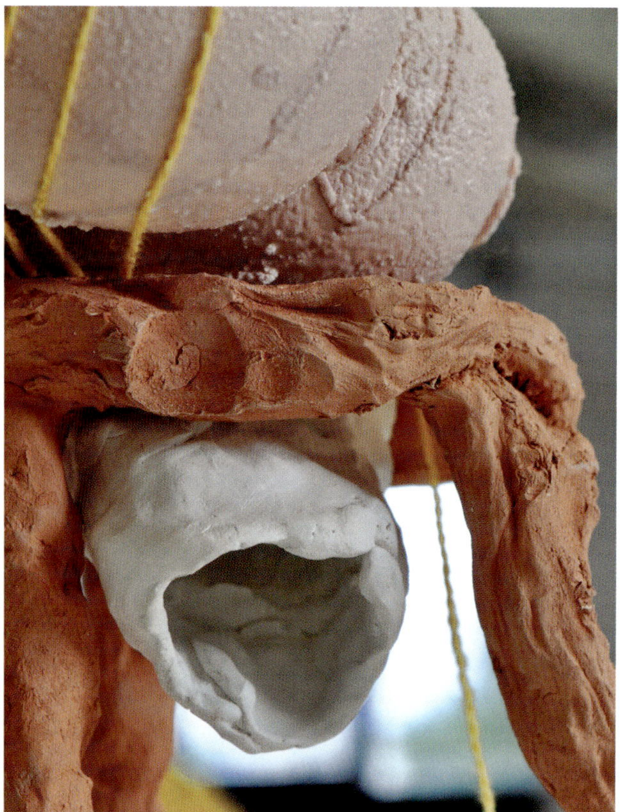

Detail of *Grasping arm and goose bump'* (2018).
(Photograph by Sam Lucas)

mother).[113] In many ways, Lucas' sculptures present themselves as psychological abstractions and projections, but whether they are the personal projections of Lucas herself is anyone's guess. Only she knows. In any case, what is more important is that the work is able to reflect our own projections back at us: we see elements of ourselves in these sculptures. For me, these creatures suggest power, strength, the ability to carry loads, and to do so with control. All of them consist of, and carry, mass: a weight suggestive of both physical and psychological baggage. It is difficult, however, to resist a Freudian reading of the openings within the body structure as references to anything other than female anatomy. This is particularly the case when the kidney-like forms that constitute the body of the sculptures are covered in fleshy glazes. For me, at least, these decisions anchor the sculptures to a discourse about women, their bodies, how their bodies are positioned by patriarchy, and what they might hope to do about it. These are tripods of female empowerment, a riposte to the 'phallic lack' of the eight-legged spider perceived by Abraham and Freud.

Having said this, many of the sculptures in the *Strange Stranger* series incorporate thread into their composition. In some works, thread is tied around the legs as if to curtail movement (*Flesh*, 2018); in others, the colonic or kidney-shaped body sections are bound together (*Tippytoe*, 2019). Oftentimes, thread trails from the sculpture along the floor, like Ariadne's thread guiding Theseus out of the Minotaur's labyrinth. Thread is a gendered material, of course, associated with the feminine and the domestic. Yet, it is also a symbol of production, creativity and labour (as silk is with the spider). In ancient Greek mythology the goddess Clotho, one of the Three Fates, spins the thread of human life. In her control of it, she decides who is to be born and who is to die. To control thread is thus to control the fate of all humanity. I find that the careful placement of thread in Lucas' sculptures evokes all of the above. It stands for the patriarchal ties that bind, domesticity, production, creativity, labour, navigation and memory. However, as the thread of fate, it also positions women as being in charge of their own destinies. In this sense, the sculptures exist in a state of narrative 'in betweenness': the thread trailing behind them as they leave one place but have yet to arrive at another. Sculptures like *Tippytoe* express this sense of movement into the unknown, of coming into being, traversing through the 'moving, transitional space' identified by Cixous.[114]

While the examples of Lucas' sculptures discussed so far could rest on a table, others are significantly larger. At the 2019 British Ceramics Biennial, Lucas exhibited a body of works entitled *Same same but different*. The increase in size facilitated a parallel increase in uncanniness; creatures such as *Stilted* (2019) could

have walked off the set of a science fiction movie like *War of the Worlds*. The fact that they can look you in the eye directly, or even tower over you, means that they elicit the same sensations of wonder and fear as Bourgeois' *Maman*. *Legs Akimbo* (2019) stands out from other sculptures by virtue of its emphasis on the horizontal rather than vertical plane. At first, the work looks like a dismembered body, legs and arms pulled away from the rest of its disfigured bleeding corpse. Yet, upon closer inspection, the legs at the base of the sculpture are intertwined in a sexualized embrace, sending pleasure through nerve-like fabric up to the central body. Sex and death are, of course, antithetical, but they typify the two primary psychological impulses. Freud believed that instincts fell into one of two kinds: the Pleasure Principle (the desire for pleasure and avoidance of pain) or Death Drives

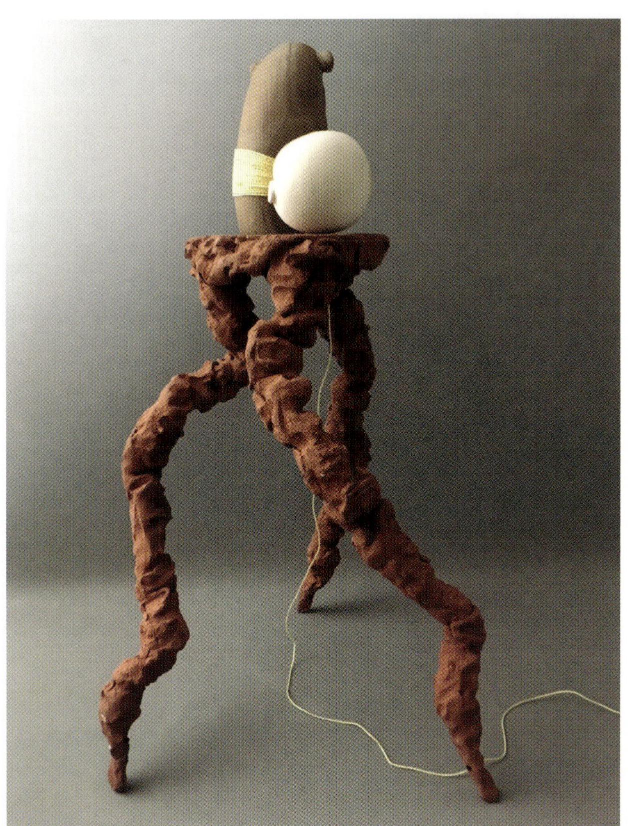

Flesh (2018).
(Photograph by Sam Lucas)

Tippytoe (2019).
(Photograph by Sam Lucas)

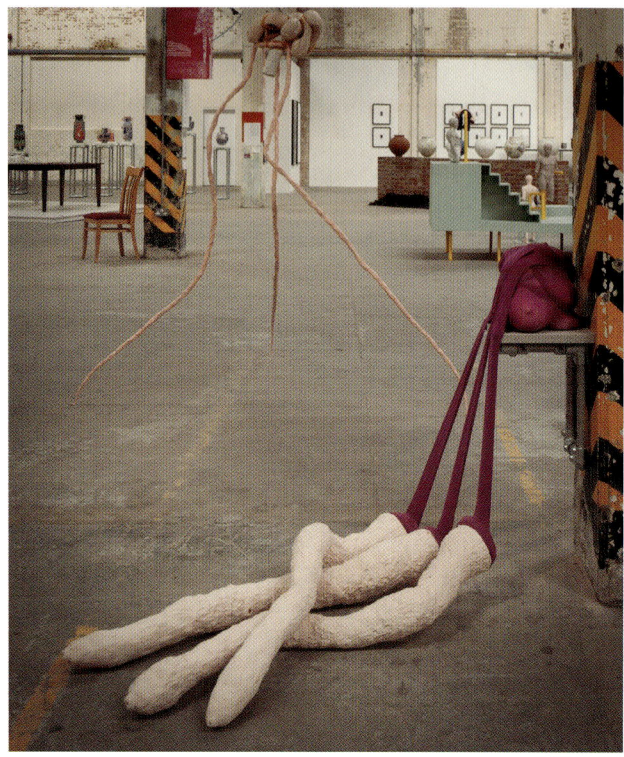

Stilted (2019) and *Legs Akimbo* (2019) shown as part of AWARD at the 2019 British Ceramics Biennial.
(Photograph by Dewi Tannant Lloyd Photography)

(the desire for pain and aggression; the re-enactment of trauma).[115] In its loving embrace and dismembered construction, *Legs Akimbo* expresses the psychological totality of life and death.

Head in the Bin (2019), also exhibited at the British Ceramics Biennial, is nominally related to the shape of the Athenian column-krater vase, so named because of its column-like handles. These classical vases consist of particular formal aspects – foot, fillet, body, neck, handle, mouth – all of which resonate with the image of the human body. *Head in the Bin* replaces the column handles with prone legs, the mouth invoked by the red thread lassoed around them. The body of the figure correlates with the body of the classical vase, and the terracotta bin evokes the pot's foot. There is humour in this piece: one wonders if this is a figure who has had too much alcohol on a night out and

is paying the price with assistance from the nearest receptacle. Equally, there is despair: this figure might compulsively regurgitate from bulimic compulsion. In her fascination for the abstracted female figure in different psychological states, Lucas' work speaks to the narrative tradition of black and red figure pottery, the most prized examples of ancient Greek ceramics. Yet, precisely because of its abstraction, a plurality of narratives can be explored, and reductive or trite commentary is avoided. Lucas trades in mysterious 'MsStories': uncanny open-ended narratives that shape the world from a female perspective.

'She comes in,' said Cixous, 'comes-in-between herself me and you, between the other me where one is always infinitely more than one and more than me.'[116] Lucas' sculptures are certainly more than her; they are capsules that unite contemporary concerns with thousands of years of women's history. Lucas thus becomes a kind of shamanic intermediary between herself and the plurality of women's experiences; like Hecate she is able to use magic to conjure the ghosts of past women into the present. While women's magic has long been demonized, it is, as Dayna Kalleres has argued, also a means to explore 'the fragility of health, the insecurity of human relationships, and occasional resistance to gender stereotyping in struggles over power, authority, and identity'.[117] Lucas materializes iconography from the ancient world, but through her engagement with the uncanny, makes the remote world of the ancient goddesses relevant to the contemporary. Freed from the clichéd imitation of ancient pottery, processes of abstraction empower her to occupy the psychologically symbolic, and to challenge patriarchal norms at the level of the psyche. Like Bourgeois' *Maman* spider, Lucas uses the body – her own body, in fact, as it touches the clay – to write herself into existence on her own terms as a female artist. 'Beyond selfish narcissism, in the moving, open, transitional space, she runs her risks.'[118]

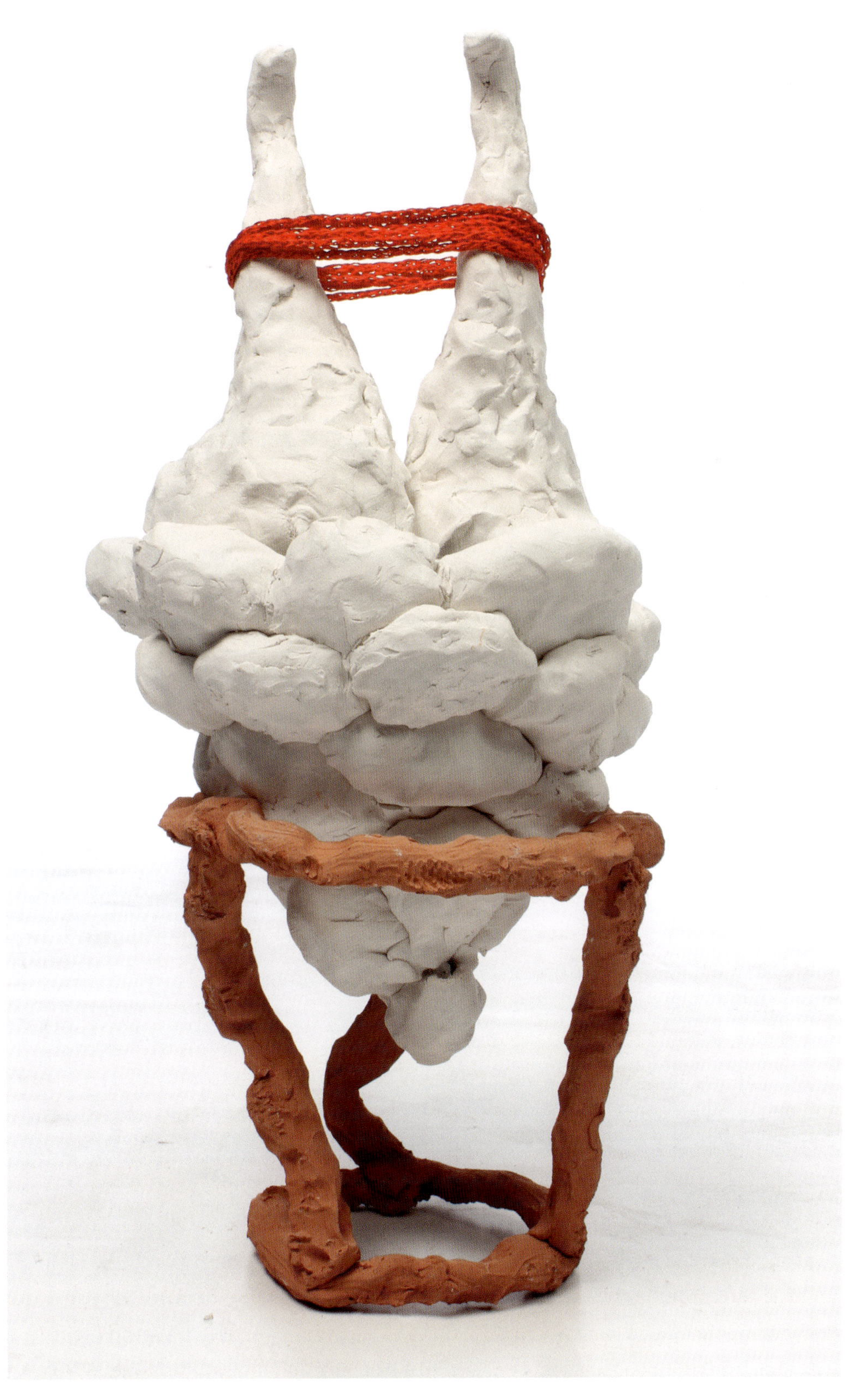

Head in the Bin (2019).
(Photograph by Sam Lucas)

Elena Gileva

Context Dependents

Four letters:

T R E E

From the above, an image has already formed in your mind: you see a large plant, its mid-section a trunk, from which branches bearing leaves rise high from the ground. Why is it that these four letters 't-r-e-e' evoke this large plant? There is nothing natural or logical about calling a tree a 'tree'. Why choose this word? One could, of course, undertake an etymological study to find out how the word 'tree' came into the English language, but this misses the point. I am more concerned with convention; our collective investment in making language happen and meaning possible. There is no natural or causal relationship between object and word. Rather, words obtain meaning through convention, rules (grammar) that we subscribe to when we learn a language. We know language is conventional because not everyone calls a tree 'a tree'. In French a tree is 'un arbre', in German 'ein Baum', in Russian 'дерево', in Arabic 'شجرة' and in Chinese '一棵树'. Different languages express different cultural viewpoints, reference ideology in distinct ways, and offer particular nuances, even as they respond to the same stimulus. Language, therefore, is universal (all humans use it), but expression is specific.

The universality of language and the specificity of its local utterance are central to the sculpture of Elena Gileva. As a Russian artist who has resided in London for several years, but who has also lived in Paris and Vancouver, and had artistic residencies in China and Japan, she is an artist with a truly international background. Since graduating from the Royal College of Art in 2016, Gileva has exhibited in the UK, France, Belgium, Italy, Japan and Korea. Broadly speaking, her work responds to questions of gender, religion and histories of cultural production, especially in her native Russia. Such references,

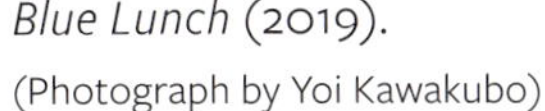

Blue Lunch (2019).
(Photograph by Yoi Kawakubo)

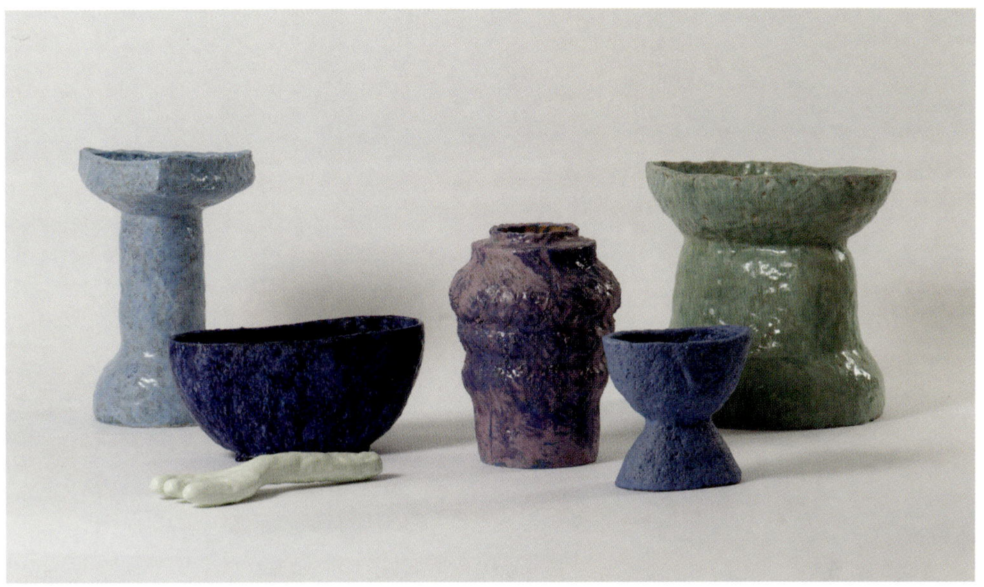

oblique as they are, might be hard to fully discern unless you are familiar with these contexts. Does a lack of familiarity with the impulse behind the creation of each piece matter? For Gileva, no. In fact, it is the point. Her sculptures are singular references that communicate globally, even as they activate culturally specific modes of spectatorship and analysis.

Some of Gileva's work explores the form of the vessel and notions of containment. Although they present as fully made forms, upon close examination we find that many of her vessels have no base. Denied of their utilitarian purpose, the possibility of containment becomes symbolic rather than literal; the vessels are walled-off spaces, architectural and sculptural statements that utilize the vessel as a point of departure for symbolic exploration.

In *Blue Lunch* (2019), for instance, Gileva produced a series of chalices, a bowl, and a fork. They are much larger in size than would be expected (the fork itself is roughly the size of a forearm), which intensifies their symbolic significance. Given her upbringing in Russia, one might link the chalice to Orthodox Christian services of communion, where the foot of the chalice is often kissed as a part of the blessing ceremony. If this

line of enquiry is pursued, a range of interpretations become possible, each of which is dependent on the personal beliefs of the spectator. For believers, the significance of space and size to these bottomless vessels might communicate how immaterial divinity can only be refracted in the materiality of objects. The iconography of the chalice (as used by Christ in the Last Supper) elevates the domestic to the ritualistic; the vessel signifies both the mundane nature of daily life as well as the eternal immaterial spirit of God, thereby uniting heaven and earth. For atheists, these baseless vessels might capture the hollowness of religious promise, even the betrayal of those whom the church ought to have protected. Indeed, the impractical vessel might be read as a symbol of the inability of religion to offer practical solutions to the problems of modernity. The narrative power of *Blue Lunch* stems from its ability to evince such contrasting narratives. It expresses something of the ambivalence that characterizes our age.

Some of the vessels hint at personification. *Blue Pumice Chalice* (2019), placed towards the front of *Blue Lunch*, evokes the stereotype of the hour-glass feminine waist. Following on from the above analysis, perhaps this is a nod to the significance of Orthodox

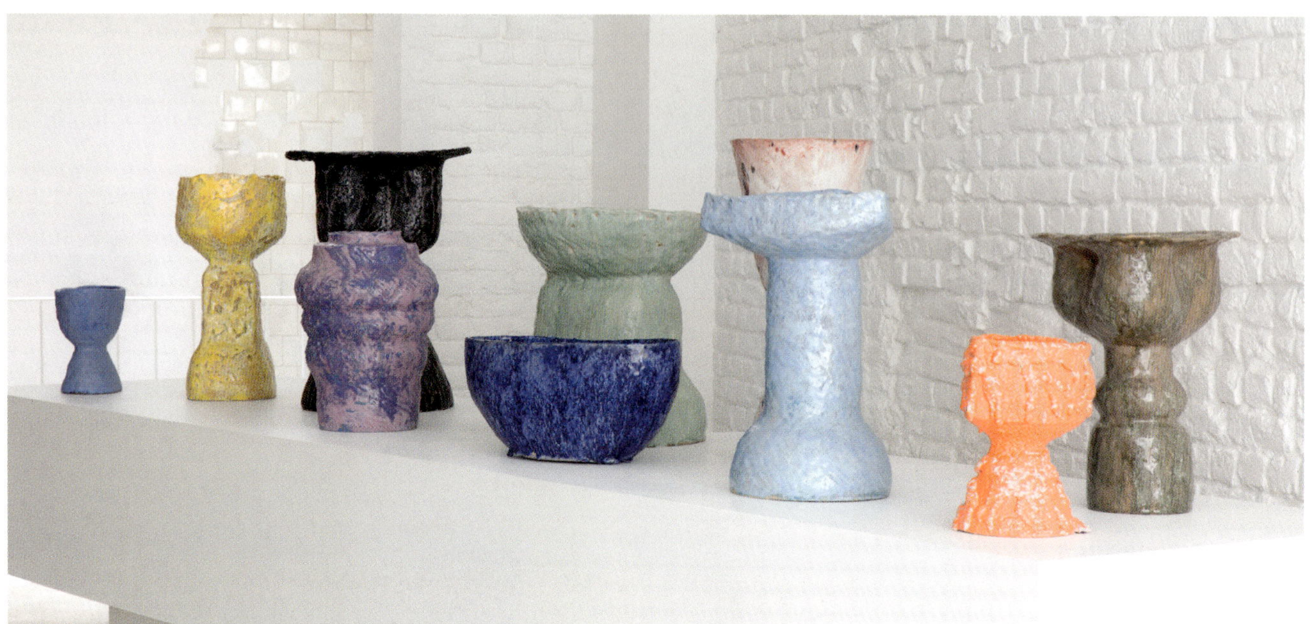

Chalice series (2019). Installation view at the Fracas Gallery, Brussels.
(Photograph by Bea Urhart)

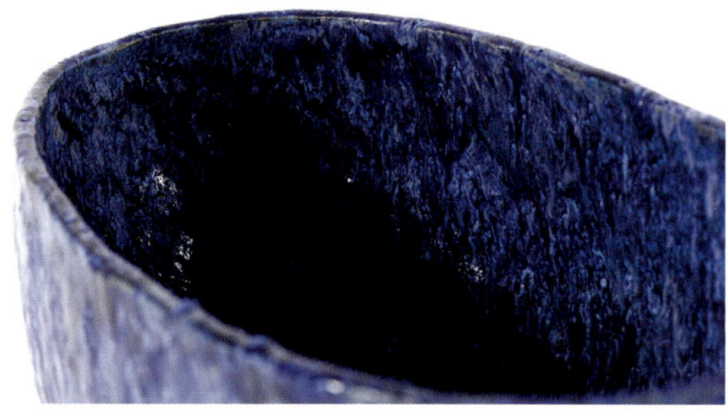

Detail from *Azure Overfow* (2019).
(Photograph by Yoi Kawakubo)

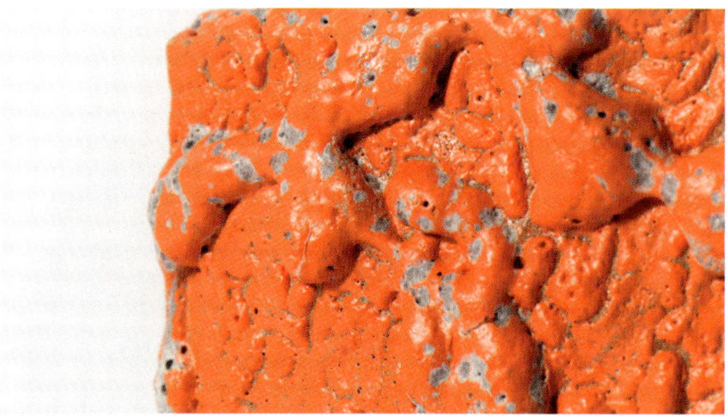

Detail of *Persimmon Chalice* (2019).
(Photograph by Yoi Kawakubo)

Christianity to the daily lives of many Russian women, as well as an expression of the ambivalence that the Russian Orthodox church has towards gender equality.[119] Yet, in communion the wine-filled chalice symbolizes the divinity of blood, reminding believers that all humanity – both men and women – carry blood forged in the image of Christ. Equally, the baseless chalice might be a social critique of the patriarchal treatment of women as surface over substance, as revered objects of beauty with empty interiors. Gileva's work never provides answers; it simply asks questions.

Gileva often redeploys work in new combinations to create different installations. The re-articulation of works in different series alters the lens through which they might be interpreted. The removal of the fork, for instance, denies implied utility. Instead, there is a stronger sense of the chalice as ornament, as was apparent when the *Chalice* forms were displayed at the Fracas Gallery in Brussels in 2019. They became objects to be admired rather than used, perhaps not even destined to be touched. The sense of personification is also increased. The works appear as figures in a delineated space, an uneasy grouping of individuals who share a common purpose even as they seek to differentiate themselves in terms of shape, colour, size and surface. The strong glaze colours serve to carve the work into space, creating a strong sculptural presence to each form, as well as making them attractive to look at. The wonderfully painterly glaze of *Azure Overflow* (2019) has an astonishing depth of colour. Its surface appears akin to an oil painting, evoking but surpassing the painterly coffee sets produced by the ceramic sculptor Andrew Lord in the late 1970s. The waxy sheen is a quite remarkable achievement, especially given its production in a single firing. The glossy surface of *Azure Overflow* contrasts with the craggy textures of works such as *Persimmon Chalice* (2019). Placed in series, these vessels speak of diversity, individuality, differences of belief, ideology, and the significance of personal experience.

The chalice form also appeared in an earlier series of works entitled *Sin Eaters* (2015). In comparison to the later works, these vessels appear heavier, as if weighed down by their contents. The concept of the sin-eater – someone who consumes a meal as part of a ritual to absorb the sins of the recently deceased – is common in religion and folkloric practice. In Christianity, of course, Jesus died on the cross to cleanse humanity of sin. As late as the nineteenth century, it was also associated with ritual practices in parts of Wales and its neighbouring borders in England, where it is said that the

sin-eater cut himself off from all social intercourse with his fellow creatures by reason of the life he had chosen; he lived as a rule in a remote place by himself, and those who chanced to meet him avoided him as they would a leper. This unfortunate was held to be the associate of evil spirits, and given to witchcraft, incantations and unholy practices; only when a death took place did they seek him out, and when his purpose was accomplished they burned the wooden bowl and platter from which he had eaten the food handed across, or placed on the corpse for his consumption.[120]

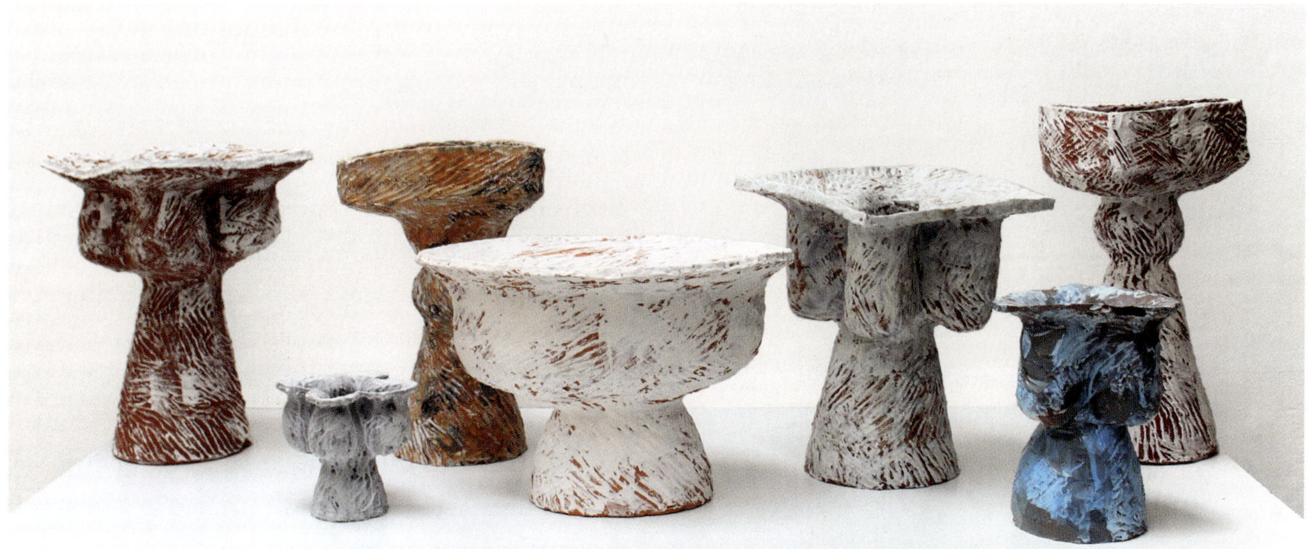

Sin Eaters (2015).
(Photograph by Elena Gileva)

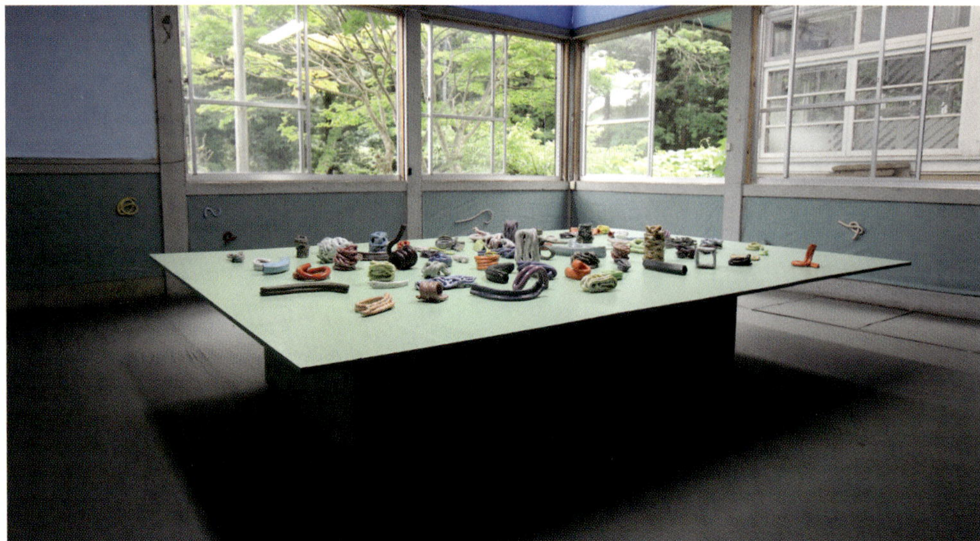

Current Landscape of Uncertainty (2019). (Photograph by Elena Gileva)

Sin-eaters – here typified as male – were prepared to sacrifice themselves for the greater good, either because of their own sense of piousness, or simply because their lack of trade and low social status denied them any other means of employment. Sin-eaters are thus symbolic of the ostracized, exiled and diminished. However, they are also symbolically vital in cleansing sin, thereby ensuring safe passage for the soul into heaven. Gileva's *Sin Eaters* reference the symbolism of the chalice in Christian iconography, specifically the sacrifice of Jesus to absolve humanity of its sin, and the collection of his blood into the Holy Grail – often depicted as a kind of chalice – as he was crucified. Yet, I also find these chalices suggestive of the female form. If the chalice becomes gendered, the vessel as 'sin-eater' becomes a powerful comment on the subjugation of women, of female exclusion and demonization, but also of women as powerful and vital agents in deep healing.

Much of Gileva's output utilizes forms beyond the vessel. *Current Landscape of Uncertainty* is an on-going installation that was first shown in Japan at the Nakanojo Biennial in 2019. It consists of a series of hand-sized tube-like sculptures exhibited on a raised platform. The sculptures are redolent of an industrial aesthetic, referent of the technology behind the production of contemporary ceramic sculpture. Indeed, they could almost be formed from the heating elements of an electric kiln, or the mains wires that supply it. More tellingly, perhaps, they are also suggestive of fragmentation, of elements broken away from the contexts that produced them. Such a reading is intensified by the fact that each individual piece is available for sale. Each time a piece is bought, Gileva will make something completely new to replace it. As a consequence,

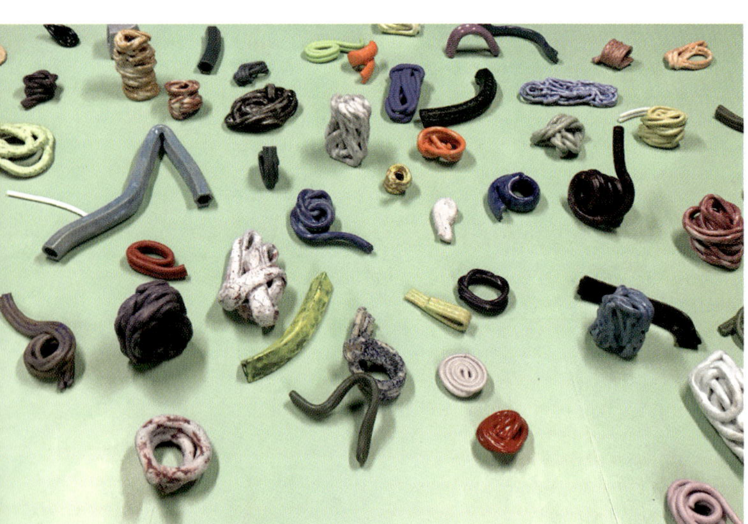

Current Landscape of Uncertainty (2019). (Photograph by Elena Gileva)

the work is in a constant state of mutation; its nature is wedded to the purchase power and shifting tastes of individuals. Thus, *Current Landscape of Uncertainty* represents a celebration of consumer choice that globalization facilitates, specifically the ability to create, produce and access art that has the potential to communicate across cultural boundaries. It is also, however, a comment on the loss of cultural specificity: the de-contextualization of culture into fragments, available for purchase only by those who can afford it.

Another work, *Ulfberht* (2019) is based upon a kind of sword found in Europe between the ninth and eleventh centuries. Gileva's use of different glazes, here realized through multiple firings, suggests an object that has accrued new surface layers over time. There is a sense of the effect of chemical processes, whereby water has oxidized with metal to create new patinas and textures. For me, this work exemplifies Gileva's art. The layers of accumulated glaze on *Ulfberht* highlight how history is always interpreted and reinterpreted from the perspective of the present. The past is always shifting, accruing new meaning and resonances via the politics of our time. Indeed, a medieval sword might symbolize feelings of national pride, defence, military honour, justice, murder, war, crime or national humiliation, depending on the politics and beliefs of the spectator. Such feelings are also embedded into our collective consciousness, our national histories. Our responses to such questions separate us out from a singular national consciousness. Indeed, all of Gileva's work destabilizes fixed meanings, highlighting them as products of conventions with individualized, localized expressions. In this sense, once her work leaves the studio it is free to develop its own meanings. Her works are context dependents: freed from the impulse of their making, they await activation in new times, and in new cultural frameworks, to create ever-evolving meanings.

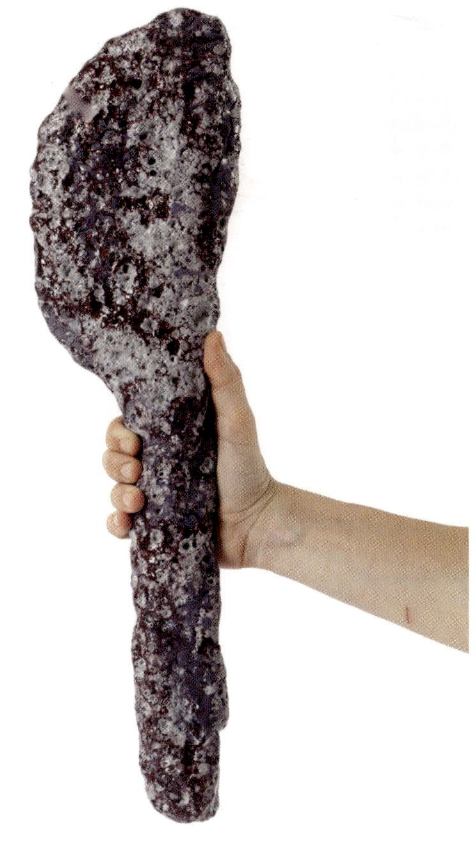

Ulfberht (2019).
(Photograph by Yoi Kawakubo)

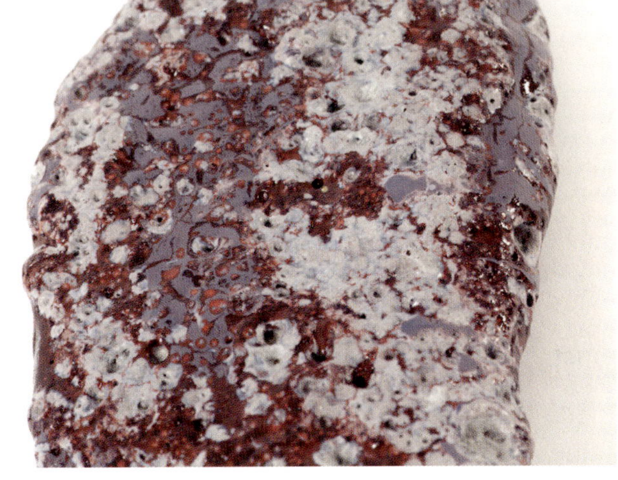

Detail of *Ulfberht* (2019).
(Photograph by Yoi Kawakubo)

Connor Coulston

Portraits of Daily Life

Upon seeing the self-portrait *Aix-en-Provence* by Rembrandt, the painter Francis Bacon remarked:

I think that the mystery of fact is conveyed by an image being made out of non-rational marks... in this Rembrandt self-portrait... there is a coagulation of non-representational marks which have led to making up this very great image. Well, of course, only part of this is accidental. Behind all that is Rembrandt's profound sensibility, which was able to hold onto one irrational mark after another. And abstract expressionism has all been done in Rembrandt's marks. But in Rembrandt it has been done with the added thing that it was an attempt to record a fact and to me therefore must be much more exciting and profound.[121]

Bacon repeatedly expressed admiration for Rembrandt's masterful ability to resolve a series of seemingly disconnected and abstracted marks into one image. Out of brevity and incongruity, Rembrandt's marks coalesced to evoke a subject and, more importantly, powerfully comment upon it. Bacon, himself seeking a balance between the figurative and the abstract in his own painting, found such work inspirational.[122]

To frame Connor Coulston's work through the prism of Rembrandt might seem like gross hyperbole. Yet, I propose that the above quotation offers a fruitful starting point for a consideration of his output, especially in highlighting his capacity for recording social observations through a series of seemingly oblique and non-rational marks. Some of his pieces might even be regarded as examples of ceramic self-portraiture. For example, *Skint Bitch* (2019) seems to respond to the form of the Staffordshire figurine, specifically the dainty ladies of the nineteenth-century aristocracy, who partook in refined leisure pursuits befitting their social status. The class politics of these figures is subverted by Coulston to explore the day-to-day drudgery of the Victorian working-class. Gone are the carefully decorated frilly dresses of the delicate Staffordshire porcelain ladies. Rather, off-white slip evokes the dress of the figure, which, as the meatier terracotta clay is revealed, seems to disintegrate as it nears the floor. The figure carries a chunky basket, but also a bag presumably so laden with supplies that it has to be dragged along the floor. This is a far cry from the quaint scenes of Staffordshire porcelain.

The face of the *Skint Bitch* figure, however, is the artist himself, a photo applied to the figure as a transfer. The feminization of the artist's body could be interpreted in a number of different ways: as queer culture, drag, cross-dressing, transgender, even the crossing of stereotypical gender personality traits (the unification of male and female). Certainly, this is no pantomime dame: despite the terracotta tears, this figure looks set to crush anything and anyone that stands in their way.

The graffiti-like writing that appears across the base of the sculpture highlights the importance of interpreting the work in relation to its title, *Skint Bitch*, but also as a comment on *contemporary* class politics rather than those of history. Is this a portrait of the working classes and the effects of years of austerity in early twenty-first century Britain? Is it an expression of the artist resisting the market demands of figurative sculpture (epitomised by the Staffordshire figure) and the implications on the artist's own financial

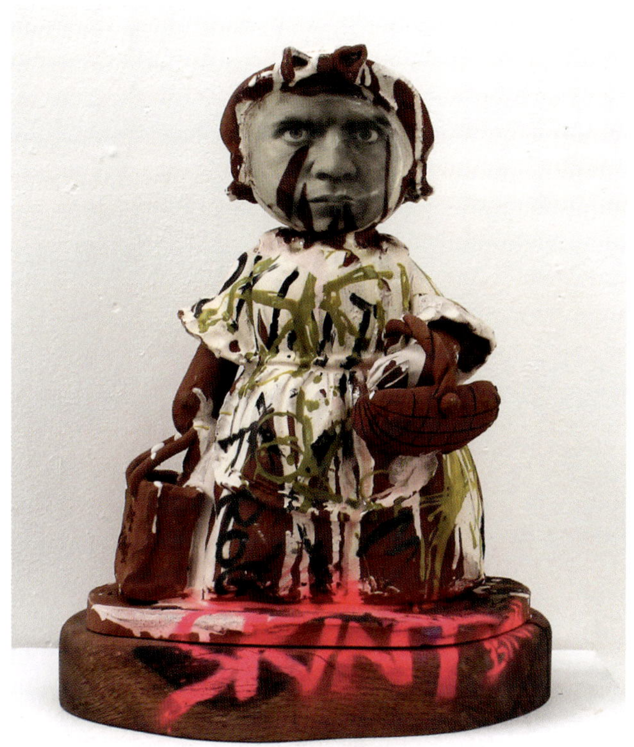

Skint Bitch (2019).
(Photograph by Connor Coulston)

circumstances? Or is it a tongue-in-cheek self-parody of a ceramics tutor moving through the social classes to work at Eton College, a boy's school at the heart of the British establishment? Is it an expression of sassy queer identities? It could be any of these things, and this is what makes Coulston's work so rich. What might first appear as incongruities cohere to accurately describe a number of plausible realities.

This is equally true of *England Till I Die* (2019), which works in a different form of classical portraiture: the bust. Here, the head is not formed by the detailed modelling of an individual's face. Rather, it is an extended middle finger. This act of protest and defiance speaks to the nationalist politics of Britain in the second decade of the twenty-first century,

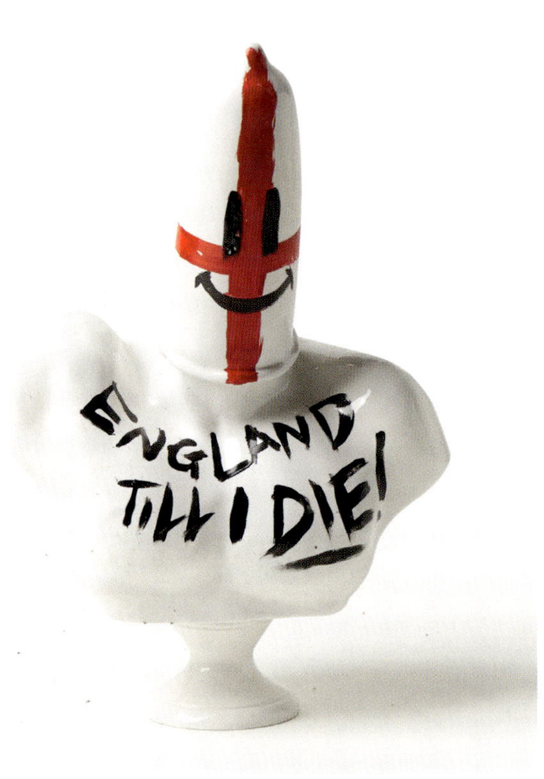

England Till I Die (2019).
(Photograph by Tania Dolvers)

where the concomitant desire to shock the existing political establishment and to 'take back control' led to Britain leaving the European Union. Yet, wearing a condom, this finger is also a penis, a 'dick', and thus British slang for idiocy, as well as a comment on the machismo that stereotypically accompanies fervent nationalism. Wearing its sheath, the identity of the person depicted in the bust is difficult to discern. A painted smiling face on the condom gives away no more psychology than an emoji. Perhaps this concealment is a comment on the British repression of emotion, 'the stiff upper lip'; for even the most passionate debate must be expressed with prudish dignity. It certainly makes the figure more sinister. What could easily be a narrow judgement on British nationalism of the period is opened out to allow the audience a multiplicity of viewpoints. *England Till*

I Die is triumphant, rebellious, welcoming, proud, defiant, ludicrous and obscene. As such, it powerfully captures the complexities of Brexit Britain.

Rembrandt purportedly stated that 'I have painted nothing but portraits'. Of course, this was not the case, but it highlights Rembrandt's opinion that there was little material difference between the specifics of painting a person in portraiture, a domestic scene or a still life. Considering other examples of Coulston's output in a similar vein, that is, as ceramic portraiture rather than as sculpture, enables recognition of how social or cultural critique is centrally important to his work. These commentaries are layered into the work through oblique symbolic references, which cohere to invite a number of viable interpretations.

This is particularly apparent in *Youth of Today* (2019). Four birds are grouped around a tureen: two sit slightly apart from the scene engaged in a private conversation, while another descends to attack a bird nestling on the lid. At first, the work evokes the commonplace scene of birds flitting around an urban park. Yet the birds are blue, like the logo of Twitter. Suddenly the work can be interpreted as a commentary on the nature of digital relationships; the birds are the 'youth' in *Youth of Today*, but they are identified to each other only through their tweets. The work highlights how Twitter might help us communicate with friends, but also offers a covert means of attacking strangers from the comfort of our own home. Indeed, the domestic is referred to in the choice of vessel that forms the central part of the work. The tureen is a homely symbol of the family used for the sharing of food at the dinner table. Historically, it is no stranger to animal decoration, with lids commonly modelled to resemble hens, rabbits, pigs, ducks or whatever other kind of meaty foodstuff might lurk within. In *Youth of Today*, the tureen is graffitied, abandoned and seemingly unloved. Digital communication seems to have

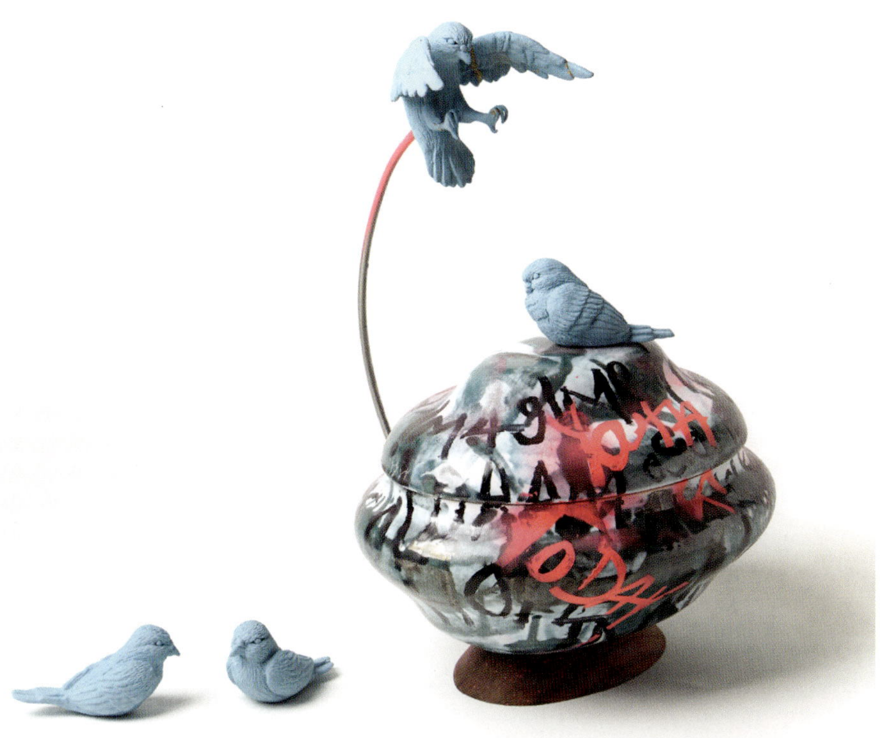

eschewed face-to-face contact, and the time when families came together over the dinner table to talk in person has long since passed.

A concern for the degradation of daily life under the pressure of globalized commercialism can be found in other examples of Coulston's work. In *Salvation Under The Arches* (2019), the logo of the McDonald's restaurant chain sits on top of a pile of rubbish, which is also the foodstuff of a large insect happily gorging on the filth. A shop sign advertising a special offer on beverages (presumably alcoholic) lies discarded in the heap. Despite the evident decay, flowers reach out to bloom from the wreckage. They lay covered in what could almost be putrefied rubbish, but they blossom nevertheless. Is it the alcohol and fast food that are feeding the blossoming flowers? Or are these things responsible for the decay? As in life, there is no straightforward answer in Coulston's art. The work is housed under a glass dome,

inviting spectators to imagine they are looking at a microcosm detached from the everyday. Yet, the recognition of branding logos confirms recognition that we are imbricated into the scene.

In another work, *Sometimes It Feels Like I'm Waiting To Die* (2019), a gravy boat is so deflated that its belly threatens to fold in over its own foot. Once again, ceramic symbols of the domestic are knowingly re-purposed to express the struggle for survival against the daily grind: the stultifying job, the unfulfilling relationship, the draining sense of responsibility. Depression, rarely tackled in ceramic art, is here given strong and powerful expression.

Taken as a group, these works may seem morbid, but I consider them to interrogate fundamental aspects of life. There is decay, depression and aggression, but there is also beauty, friendship and love. Indeed, a number of the pieces discussed above were included in an installation in 2019, entitled *Me, My*

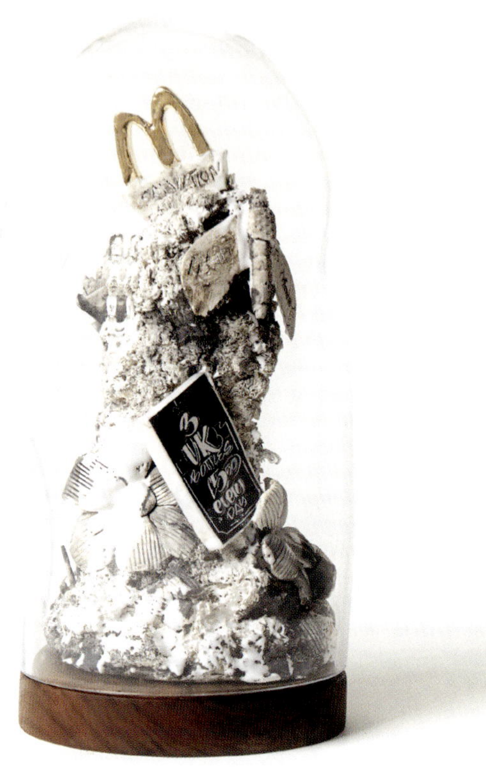

Salvation Under The Arches (2019).
(Photograph by Tania Dolvers)

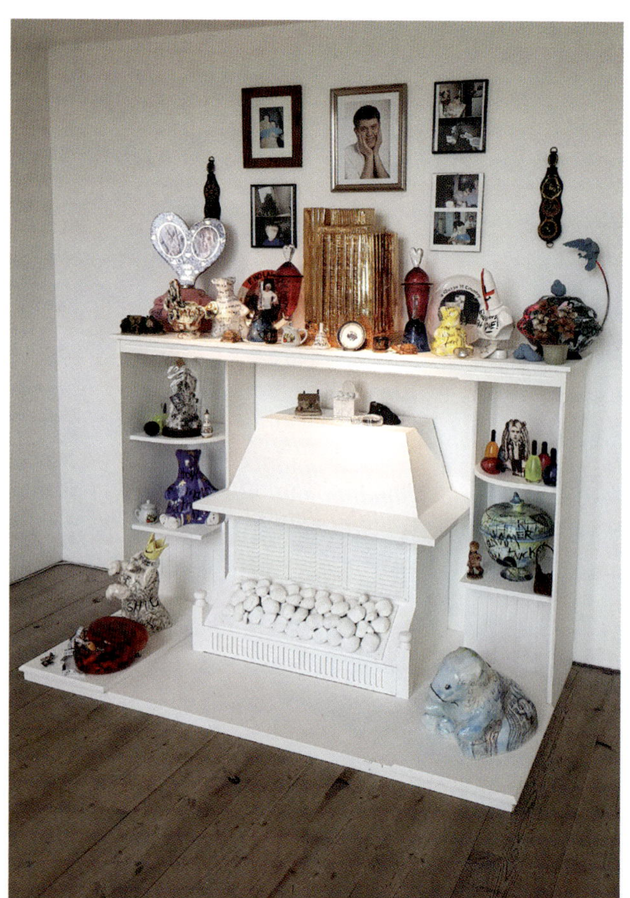

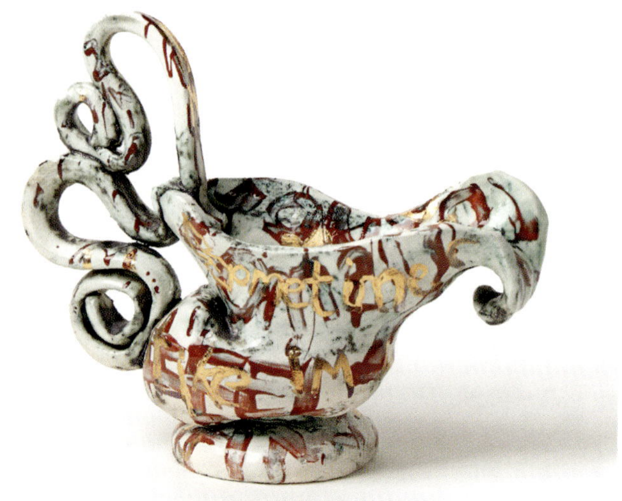

Sometimes It Feels Like I'm Waiting To Die (2019).
(Photograph by Tania Dolvers)

Nan, and Oldham, at the Baltic Centre for Contemporary Art, Newcastle. The works were placed around a fireplace, the focal point of the living room, and resting place for the most-prized family ornaments. The installation highlights Coulston's masterful engagement with the symbolic resonance of the ceramics we use in our daily lives, and how he is able to layer into them our feelings, hopes, frustrations and dreams.

It is perhaps inevitable that Coulston's approach will invite comparisons with the work of Grayson Perry. Yet, I consider such comparisons rather shallow. Coulston's output is in some senses autobiographical, but it is not a candid diary of experience, like some of Perry's earlier work. Coulston harnesses an advanced technical command of the medium to investigate the symbolic and emotional resonance of ceramic form. He has created a series of portraits depicting daily life in Britain in the twenty-first century, 'an image … made out of non-rational marks'.

LEFT: *Me, My Nan, and Oldham* (2019).
(Photograph by Connor Coulston)

Neil Brownsword

Performance Process

> **Performance:** the performing of a play, part, dance, piece of music, etc. before an audience; a dramatic or artistic presentation or entertainment; the act or process of performing a task, etc.; a level of achievement, success, or in commerce, profitability; manner or efficiency of functioning.
>
> *Chambers Dictionary*

'Performance' is a surprisingly expansive word. It relates to the putting on of artistic endeavours – the presentation of a theatricalized experience – but also to business – the performance of a company in terms of profit and efficiency. It can be applied to machinery – how well a car 'performs' on the road. It also exists in our everyday lives; the way we behave in our workplaces when accomplishing a set task is a very different kind of 'performance' to the way we interact with our families at home. Performance is, therefore, a term that can connect artistry with business and behaviour.

Performance is also ephemeral; it is an 'in the moment' activity. In theatre, once a production has ended, it cannot be precisely recreated. Video might document events – what happens on stage – but it never replicates the immediate power of an audience to shape a performance through their response. And what if no video was taken? Exploration of a theatre production from the past, even the recent past, is reliant upon the bringing together of different material objects – props, costumes, photographs, programmes, whatever relics are available – to collage a sense of what happened and why it was significant.

Ceramic production can also be considered as a type of performance. To make ceramics is to perform a task. It speaks to the definition of performance by invoking achievement, profitability and efficiency. As a series of practices, production is a wholly 'in the moment' activity; ceramic objects are simply the relics of the performance behaviours of manufacture. In this sense, theatre production and ceramic production are equally ephemeral. Exploration into the history of ceramic production is equally contingent upon material objects.

The work of Neil Brownsword sits across this expansive definition of performance. He draws upon ephemera and performance-based installations to explore the history of mass-produced ceramics in Stoke-on-Trent. The significance of Stoke to British ceramics cannot be exaggerated. The local availability of materials made the area an important centre for ceramics even by the seventeenth century. By the middle of the nineteenth century, Stoke had grown to become the British capital of industrially produced ceramics, exporting new innovations (such as bone china and transfer printed wares) around the world. After World War II, ceramic production went into sharp decline as production moved to Asia, leaving the city littered with derelict remnants of its industrial heyday. Brownsword began his career in ceramics at the Wedgwood factory in Stoke (his family had worked in the area as production potters for generations). This formative experience gave him a distinct perspective from which to explore British ceramics. Foregrounding production processes, his work inverts the hierarchy that covets the ceramic object, instead drawing attention to the skills of the workforce upon which manufacture depended.

In 2008, Brownsword exhibited a body of work entitled *Poet of Residue* at Galerie Besson, London.[123] The exhibition was comprised of nineteen works made from materials salvaged from derelict ceramic factories in Stoke. Brownsword re-purposed these discarded remnants to create seemingly abstract sculptures. The titles of works, such as *Waster* (2007) and *Crank* (2007), invite contemplation of composition in terms of emotion. For instance, the central

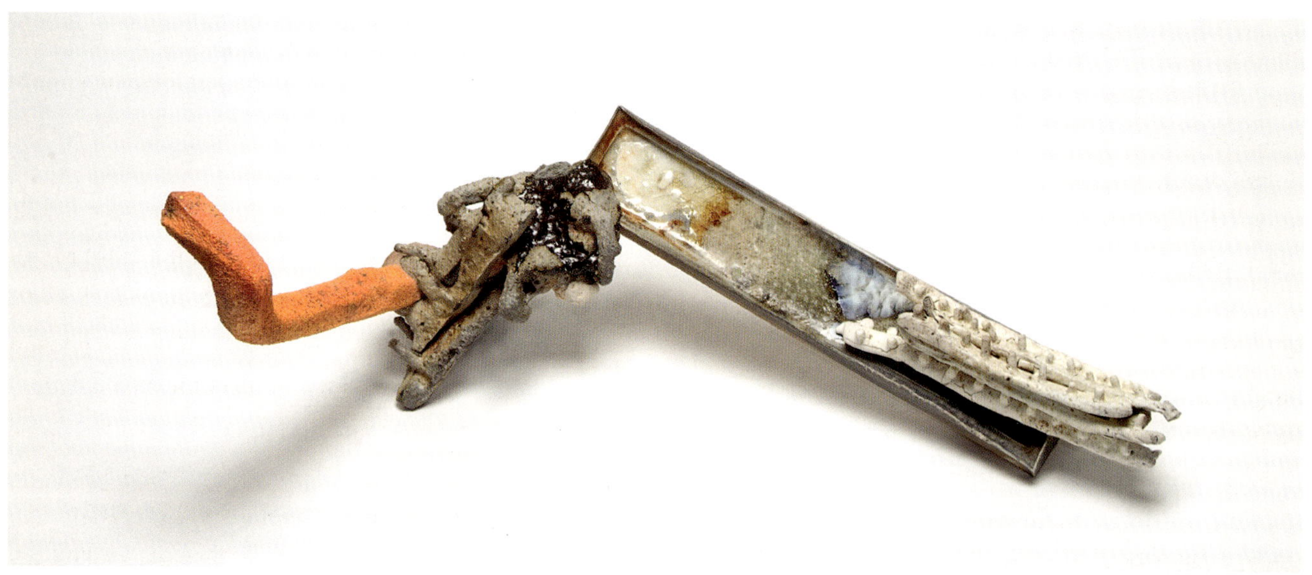

Waster (2007).
(Photograph by Guy Evans)

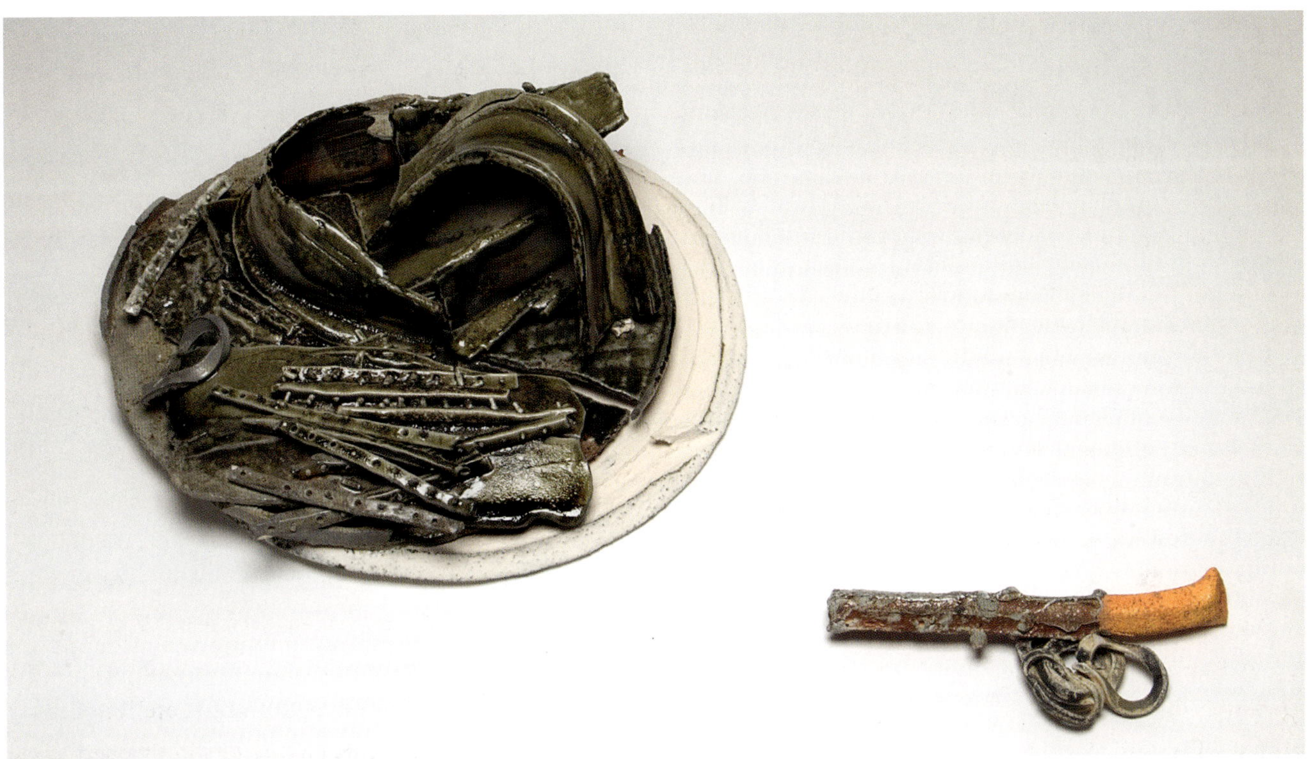

Crank (2007).
(Photograph by Guy Evans)

horizontal form of *Waster* looks like a sleep-prone body, an immovable lump that languishes across the surface. *Crank* appears more active, rougher, even angry. The gun-like sculpture seems to allude to the crank trigger mechanism of a semi-automatic weapon. The menacing crumple that is the central focus of the work looks akin to a disintegrated military uniform, perhaps a relic from battle, mounted on a platter for museumification. The titles of the works are in fact derived from the names of the derelict parts that comprise them. A 'waster' refers to an over-fired piece of ceramic; 'crank' is a device to hold flatware during the firing process.

As documents of the decline of ceramic manufacture in Stoke, these works are underpinned by a sense of loss. Yet, they are also brought new life by the collaging of relics into poignant works of contemporary ceramic art. As much as they are cenotaphs to

mass-produced ceramics in Britain, they also vibrantly respond to changing contexts. In the same way that the recycling of props in theatre performances attracts new associations as they are re-used in different contexts,[124] so Brownsword's works accrue meanings of history, loss and museumification, but also power, on-going relevance and cultural significance.

As the exhibition title suggested, the works included in *Poet of Residue* were documents of industrial processes threatened with extinction, a testament to the ephemeral nature of ceramic production. Parts could be salvaged from the ceramic factories of Stoke only because they were no longer used; the existence of these works was predicated upon the absence of a skilled workforce to activate them.

Brownsword explored the present absence of labour in subsequent work. For the 2017 British Ceramic Biennial, Brownsword took over the former

China Hall of the Spode factory in Stoke. His installation, *Factory* (2017), brought together films and performance-based exhibits to document and explore the threat of industrial decline to embodied knowledge. Brownsword collaborated with a number of practitioners to draw attention to the fact that certain ceramic production skills faced extinction.

One such practitioner, Rita Floyd, had been employed at numerous factories, including Royal Doulton, to make ceramic flowers. In Brownsword's installation, Floyd sat at a desk making these delicate forms. Instead of pressing them onto the body of a vase or passing them on for further use in a production line, they were simply discarded around her. A pile of redundant ceramic flowers blossomed around Floyd as the installation progressed. James Adams, along with Brownsword himself, used moulds to repair and remake damaged items found at the Spode factory. Paul Holdway created copper plate engravings for use in ceramic printing, and Anthony Challiner demonstrated his skills as a china painter.

Collectively, the installations foregrounded process of manufacture over finished object. Brownsword showcased the plethora of skills that Stoke industries relied upon, but also highlighted their fragility. As with *Poet of Residue*, there was the evocation of life (embodied skill) but also death (its neglect). Interestingly, Brownsword also featured visiting practitioners from Korea (*Factory* was first performed at the 2017 Gyeonngi International Ceramic Biennale in South Korea), where such skills are protected through their designation as Intangible Cultural Heritage. *Factory* drew attention to the blasé approach that Britain has taken towards its production history, and the lack of care in preventing embodied skills from dying out.

For me, Brownsword's decision to foreground processes of production as transient and threatened closely aligns his work with theatre performance. The focus on professional skills and behaviours evokes the notion of what theatre anthropologists call 'restored behaviour'. To restore something is to bring it back (e.g. as with furniture), to reactivate it in a different context for a new purpose. Actors do this as part of their stock in trade: they take observed behaviour (e.g. a person sitting in a café) and re-use it on stage as part of their performance as a character. Thus,

> Restored behavior is living behavior treated as a film director treats a strip of film. These strips of behavior can be rearranged or reconstructed; they are independent of the causal systems (social, psychological, technological) that brought them into existence. They have a life of their own. The original 'truth' or 'source' of the behavior may be lost, ignored, or contradicted – even while this truth or source is apparently being honoured and observed. How the strip of behavior was made, found, or developed may be unknown or concealed; elaborated; distorted by myth and tradition. Originating as a process, used in the process of rehearsal to make a new process, a performance, the strips of behaviour are not themselves process but things, items, 'material'.[125]

Actors do not 'invent' the behaviours they show on stage, rather behaviour is a kind of raw material that they select, utilize and re-deploy. In a similar way, Brownsword's acts of curation restored behaviour in *Factory*, redeploying the labour of ceramic producers such as Floyd as a different kind of labour, a wholly aesthetic one. Similar transformations – of utilitarian to aesthetic – can be found in *Poet of Residue*, but in *Factory*, ephemerality was a key means of communicating the fragility of embodied knowledge. The installation dealt with presence and absence; skill appears and disappears in front of us, deprived as it is of its industrial purpose. Performance and ceramic production converge as kinds of 'in the moment' process; once it is gone it can never be recovered.

In 2018, Brownsword participated in a residency at the Victoria and Albert Museum in London. He used the residency as an opportunity to explore the museum's collection of Staffordshire Chinoiserie ceramics. Brownsword subsequently amassed a collection of his own from online auction sites. By scanning the patterns through a digital scanner that purposefully disrupted the image, Brownsword produced a series of giclée prints, many with hand additions, that became *Pattern Book* (2018) – a reference book of designs held in ceramic factories. In each pattern, Brownsword highlighted the significance of cultural appropriation to British ceramics – a charge that hangs heaviest in the iconic British-designed willow pattern plate.

Brownsword seems to ask: how is East Asia re-imagined in Britain? How does the availability of material, techniques, and the need for efficiency and profitability alter the output? Brownsword's decision to digitize and manipulate Chinoiserie patterns draws attention to the acts of distortion and reinterpretation that underscored British representations of East Asian ceramics. They document the disfiguring effects of globalization, offering a reflective vantage point from which to examine the orientalist designs of the British past. In this sense, each pattern is a recorded strip of behaviour. It is behaviour that is, as noted above, 'concealed; elaborated; distorted by myth and tradition'. Acknowledgement of this distortion opens up the possibility for a critique of the imperialist impulse to profit from the exploitation of the exotic. Pattern books were referents for production, but as they are no longer in use, they are also collected and archived as works in their own right. Brownsword utilized this duality to conjoin industrial heritage with contemporary art, drawing attention to the cultural as well as economic role that the Industrial Revolution played in imperialism.

Process was once again foregrounded to highlight the displacement of one set of cultural practices

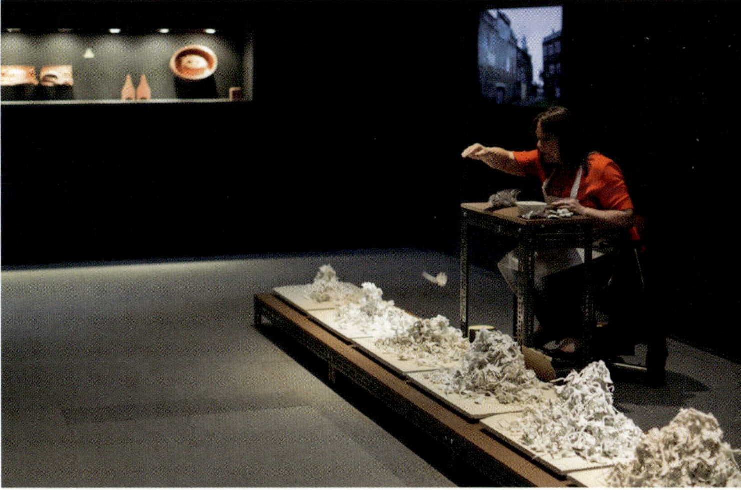

Factory (2017); Rita Floyd.
(Photograph by Une Kim)

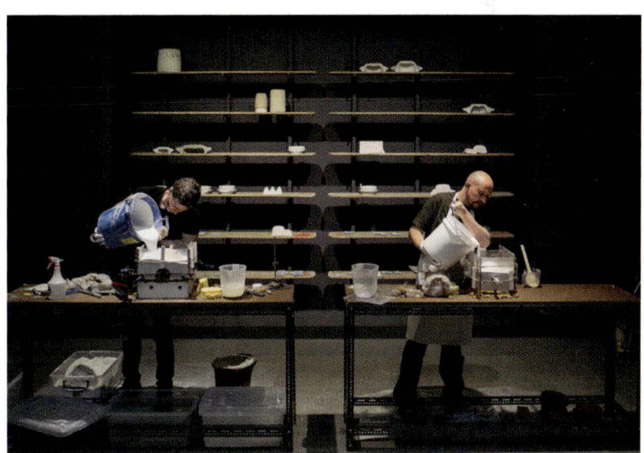

Factory (2017); James Adams and Neil Brownsword.
(Photograph by Une Kim)

(here, Chinese ceramics) into another (ceramic factories in Stoke). The notion of transference as process was key to a performance installation that accompanied *Pattern Book*. Brownsword asked Paul Holdway (who had also participated in *Factory*) to produce a copper plate of one of Brownsword's new pattern book images for use in ceramic printing. This act of re-inscription from one medium to another activated *Pattern Book* into an actual pattern book. In so doing, it also highlighted the skill of the engraver, whose own process of mapping the paper-based design into

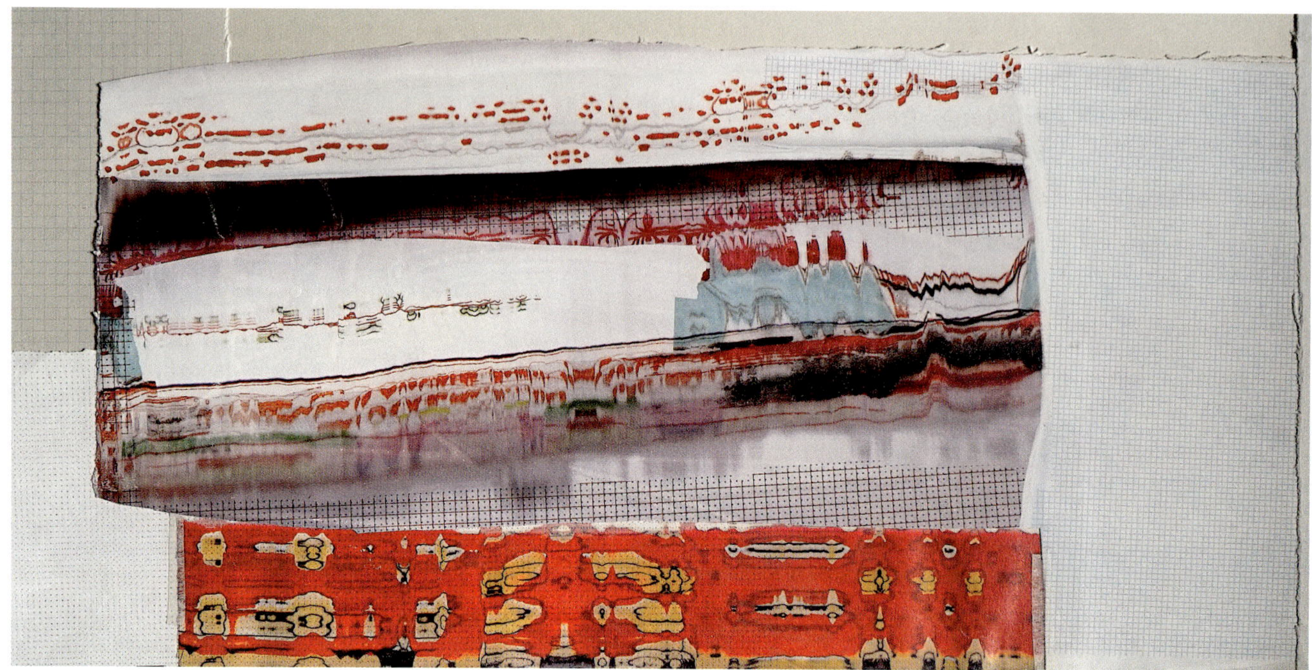

Pattern Book (2018).

(Photograph by Neil Brownsword)

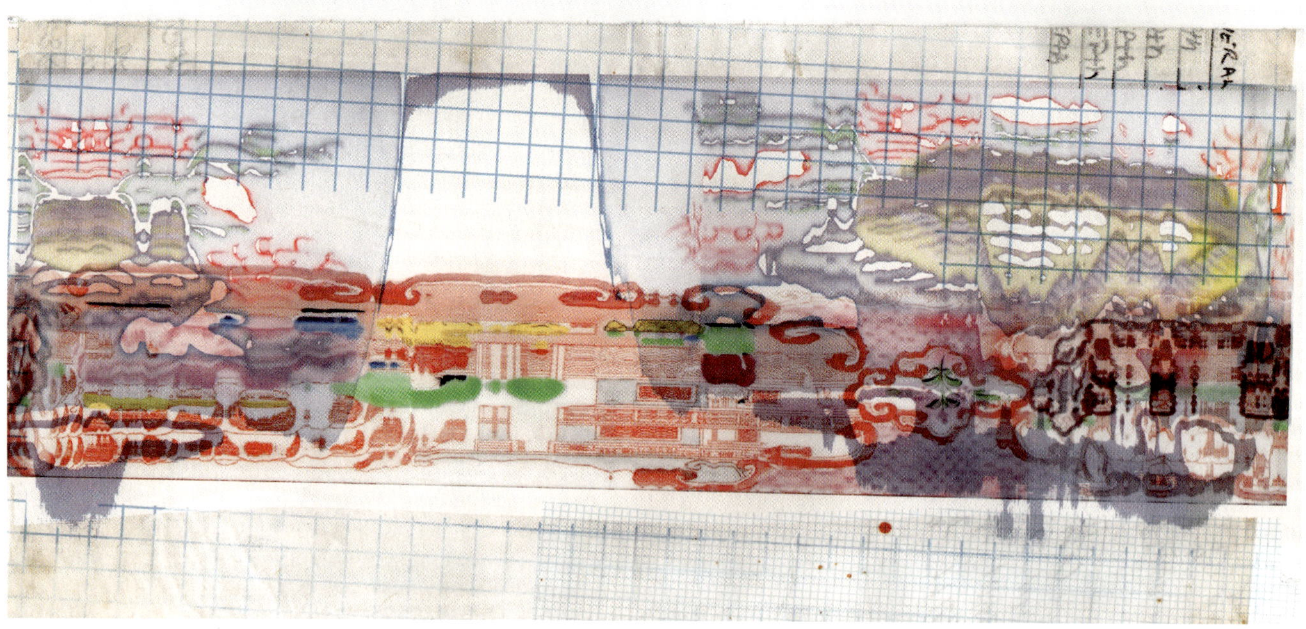

Pattern Book (2018).

(Photograph by Neil Brownsword)

copper echoed the translation upon which British responses to Chinese aesthetics depended.

For the 2019 British Ceramic Biennial, Brownsword showed an installation and archival project entitled *Externalising the Archive*. Eleven years earlier, in 2008, the Spode factory in Stoke had entered administration, leaving behind factory space that held some 70,000 moulds from the company's 238-year history. These moulds had not been archived. In fact, many were strewn across the factory and, if not already damaged, were critically at risk.

Early in 2019, Brownsword assembled a team, many from Staffordshire University where he is based, to produce an archive of the moulds. A process of Photogrammetry – using photographs as the basis for digital calculations of three-dimensional spaces – was deployed to create a digital archive of the moulds. Visitors were invited to see the Photogrammetry process at work, once again drawing the installation back to process over product. Indeed, there is an interesting parallel between mould-making and Photogrammetry: both are contingent upon a physical body to activate the mould and produce the work as part of a mechanized process. In effect, the act of digitization re-moulds the mould, transforming moulds into a virtual resource that can be recast into a 3D object by future generations. New castings taken from some of the available moulds were also exhibited as fragments, evoking the kind of work Brownsword showed in *Poet of Residue* in 2008 – interestingly, the year that Spode closed. Some parts of the factory could not be opened to the public but were made accessible as a virtual walk-through.[126] Thus, on multiple levels, the Spode factory was 'externalized' to the public in innovative ways.

From the above, it is clear that Brownsword has campaigned tirelessly for the preservation and systematic documentation of British ceramic history. However, this should not obscure his brilliance as a

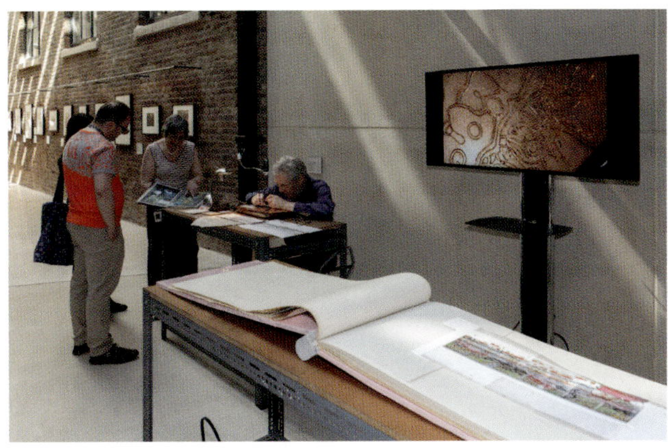

Paul Holdway etching a copper plate as part of the installation, *Pattern Book* (2018).
(Photograph by Peter Kelleher)

contemporary ceramic artist. His work is rigorously conceived and crafted, sourcing ideas derived from centuries-old 'craft' techniques as well as modes of contemporary 'art' installation. Brownsword trades in questions of performance: through 'artistic presentation' he highlights the skills needed in 'performing a task' to 'a level of achievement', the significance of 'efficiency', and the rise and fall of 'commerce' and 'profitability'. A unique voice in the field of British ceramic practice, he produces objects that place processes of production centre stage.

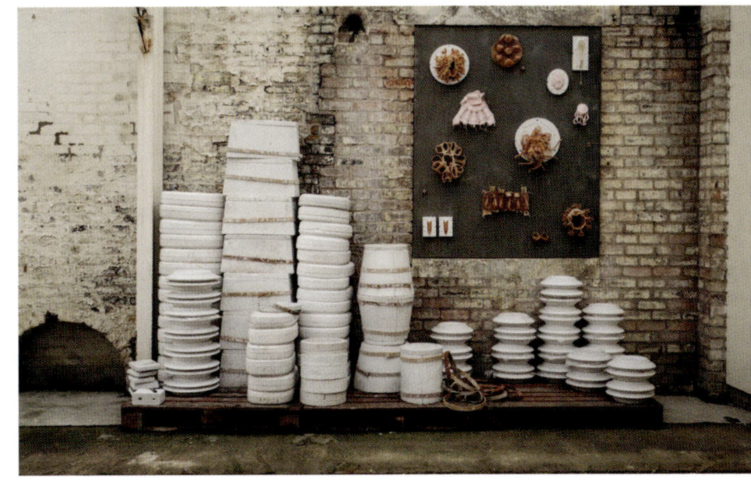

Externalising the Archive (2019).
(Photograph by Jenny Harper)

Afterword

Beneath the Surface

> How to treat this book. Is it a book. What would make a book of it. What is it to read this book. How to take it. Have I the right to say that it is beautiful. And first of all the right to ask myself that [...]
>
> [...] for example the question of order. A spatial, so-called plastic, art object does not necessarily prescribe an order of reading. I can move around in front of it, start from the top or the bottom, sometimes walk around it. [...]
>
> But a book. And a book of philosophy. If it is a book in the Kantian sense, hence a book of pure philosophy, one can in principle enter it from any point: it is a sort of architecture. [...] To be sure, the juridicial order supported by the foundations [that is, the chronological format of the book] does not coincide with the factual order: for example, Kant wrote his introduction after finishing the book and it is the most powerful effort to gather together the whole system of his philosophy [...] (Insertions in square brackets my own).[127]
>
> *Jacques Derrida*

Books appear to be prescriptively linear. You may well have read this book in chronological order from chapters 1 to 22. Yet, as I suggested in the introduction, it is not necessary to read it in this way. The volume has a very circular structure, and you could start in the middle and move chronologically to end up back where you started. In the quote above, Jacques Derrida suggested that when we observe a piece of art – ceramic art if you will – there is no fixed point of entry. Our eyes are free to enter and exit the work as we please. This observation about how we look at objects holds true even with two-dimensional reproductions of them, including those featured in this book. You may have flicked through the book to look at the images, some of which stood out over others, before reading it, perhaps even before buying it. Alternatively, you might have read the chapters in a totally random order. The essays were certainly written with this in mind.

Despite the apparent logic of chronology, Derrida suggests that a book is not so different from an art object because there is no fixed entry or exit point. As he observes, books are rarely written in chronological order. Certainly this one was not. Derrida's own example of Kant's *The Critique of Judgement* – explored in relation to Richard Slee's work in the first essay – was not either. While the structure of this book reflects the circularity of a vessel, it also attempts to replicate something of what it is to look at ceramic works.

Why do I collect ceramics? The simple answer is that I find it exciting. The malleability of the material and the variety of forms, textures, surfaces and treatments produce a seemingly endless variety. It is both a visceral and intellectual appreciation: each piece is an idea that has been generated with skill and confidence, but also risk and uncertainty. Something I find amazing has been achieved because the solution to the question each artist had set themselves was not obvious and required technical accomplishment to realize it. I recall a conversation with Ken Eastman in his studio on this subject. He told me that, even after decades of working, he still found clay in its raw form a strange material. To become comfortable with this strangeness is the process of making; to shape it to the point where a composition is discovered, an answer to a question is found, or a response to a feeling is materialized.

Then the piece is somehow 'ready'. Yet, paradoxically, at this point the work becomes strange again, as though someone else had made it. This separation enables critical scrutiny: is the work as like itself as it could be? Does it need more colour and another firing? Is it really ready to leave the studio? Although this is a reflection of Ken Eastman's own feelings about his practice, I feel it speaks to all of the artists I have featured in this volume. Processes and emphases vary of course, but there is a compelling sense of daring, challenge, intellect, instinct, fluency and, above all, emotion, in all of the work included. Collectively, these works make me feel something, and that is the impetus behind writing.

As I look back across the volume, I see the repetition of certain words: rhythm, composition, lines, tone, form. These are some – though by no means all – of the essential vocabulary for looking at ceramics. Yet, as critical words, they are equally at home in discussions of painting, drawing, sculpture, music and performance. Admiration for these ceramic artists comes from my belief that their practice is hardwired into interdisciplinarity. And like those other disciplines, ceramics trades in emotion, the belief that objects can be meaningful, and move us in our daily lives. To find this emotion, we just need to look beneath the surface.

Artist Biographies

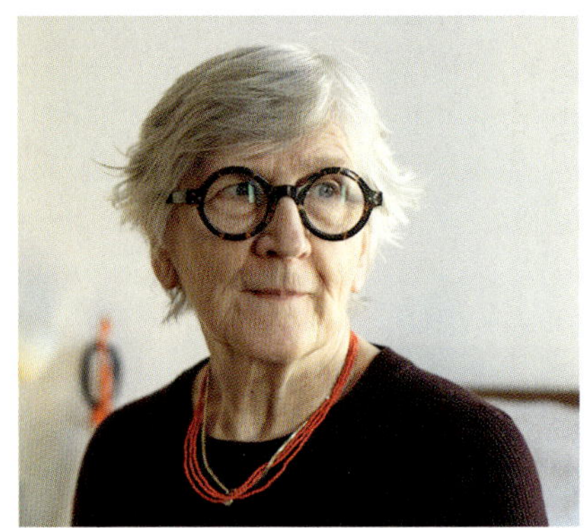

Alison Britton.
(Photograph by Toby Glanville)

Alison BRITTON, born in the London suburbs in 1948, was part of a group of radical RCA ceramics students in the 1970s, with David Queensberry as Professor. Working from London studios over four decades, she has an extensive exhibition history, here and abroad, showing in Tokyo in 1985 and often in the Netherlands in the first twenty years. She was awarded the OBE in 1990. Her retrospective that year toured the UK and concluded at the Museum Boijmans van Beuningen in Rotterdam. In 1996 a solo exhibition travelled to museums in Australia. *END* was a collaboration of ceramic artists from England, Norway and Denmark in 2007. Another retrospective, *Content and Form,* was at the V&A in 2016. *Things of Beauty Growing: British Studio Pottery,* at The Yale Center for British Art, USA, and the Fitzwilliam Museum Cambridge in 2017/2018, included her pots and the preface for the huge catalogue. Recent solo shows were in London, Oslo, Copenhagen and Geneva. She has consistently written in journals and catalogues, and Occasional Papers published her book *Seeing Things,*

Collected Writing on Art, Craft and Design in 2013. In the past decade she has lectured more, and in 2016 gave the twentieth Peter Dormer lecture. Britton was a selector for *The Maker's Eye*, a seminal exhibition for the Crafts Council in 1981. She curated, with Martina Margetts, *The Raw and the Cooked* in 1993, for Modern Art Oxford, which toured in the Far East and Europe. In 2009 she curated *Three by One*, from three public craft collections, for the Crafts Study Centre in Farnham, and also *Life and Still Life*, an exhibition that combined her work with her collected objects, in 2012. She now chairs the CSC trustees. She taught at the Royal College of Art from 1984 to 2017. For twenty years her London gallery was Marsden Woo, and she is now with Corvi-Mora.

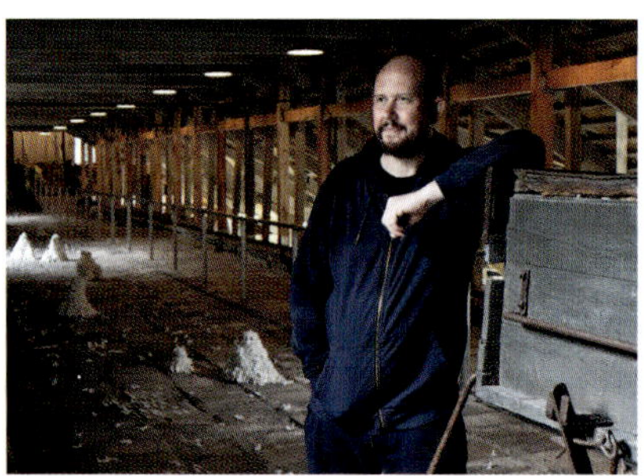

Neil Brownsword.
(Photograph by Austell Project and James Darling Photography)

Neil BROWNSWORD is an artist, researcher and educator who holds Professorial positions in Ceramics at Staffordshire University and the University of Bergen, Norway. Brownsword began his career in ceramics as an apprentice in the mid-1980s at the Wedgwood factory. His practice examines the legacy of globalization in relation to Stoke-on-Trent's ceramic manufacturing sector, and the impact this

has had upon people, place and traditional skills. Using film and performative installation, Brownsword deconstructs complex craft knowledge within industrial production to pose questions surrounding the value of inter-generational skill. His work is represented in public/private collections internationally, including the Victoria and Albert Museum, Korea Ceramic Foundation, Yingee Ceramic Museum Taiwan and FuLe International Ceramic Art Museum, China. In 2009 he was awarded the 'One Off Award' at the inaugural British Ceramic Biennial, and the Grand Prize at the 2015 Gyeonggi International Ceramic Biennale, South Korea. He was one of twelve finalists shortlisted for the 2017 Woman's Hour Craft Prize, held in collaboration with BBC Radio 4, the Victoria and Albert Museum and the Crafts Council, and in 2019 was awarded the Whitegold International Ceramic Prize Quartz Award.

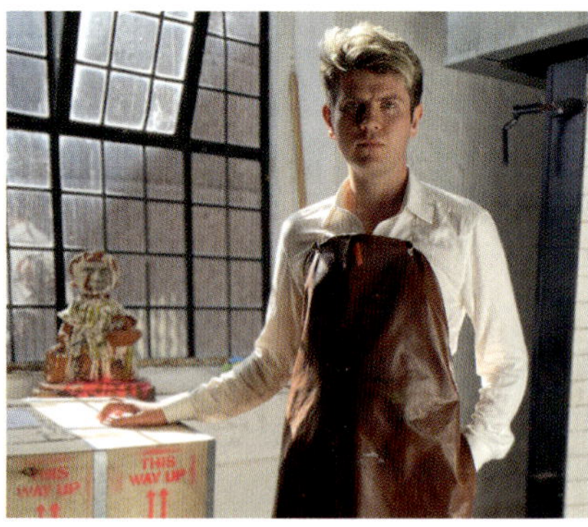

Connor Coulston.
(Photograph by Connor Coulston)

Connor COULSTON (b.1992, Oldham, UK) graduated from the Royal College of Art in 2017. Since graduating, he has shown his work nationally. His celebrated installation *Me, My Nan and Oldham* was shown at the Baltic Centre for Contemporary Art.

With this body of work, Connor has featured in documentaries for UK national TV, and has been shortlisted for numerous prizes. Connor is currently following in the footsteps of the renowned artist Gordon Baldwin, by teaching ceramics at Eton College, UK. In 2020, Connor won the prestigious Ingram Prize.

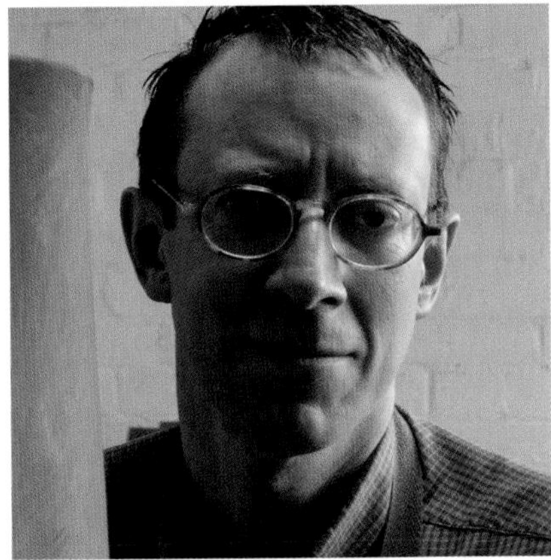

Ken Eastman.
(Photograph by Ken Eastman)

Ken EASTMAN (b.1960) studied at Edinburgh College of Art (1979–83) and at the Royal College of Art, London (1984–87). He exhibits widely and has won numerous awards in the field of the ceramic arts, including the 'Premio Faenza', Italy, in 1995, the 'Gold Medal' at the 1st World Ceramic Exposition 2001, Korea, the 'Primer Premio' at the 8th Internacional Bienal de Ceramica de Marratxi, Majorca, Spain in 2016, and the Primer Premio at the 8th Internacional Bienal de Ceramica, Talavera de la Reina, Spain. Eastman's work centres around the idea of the vessel. He uses the vessel as a subject to give meaning and form to an expression. Working through the medium of ceramics, Eastman can be both builder and painter; can handle shape and structure, as well as exploring tone and colour. Eastman's work is held in leading international public collections including the Victoria & Albert Museum, London; The Shigaraki Ceramic Cultural Park, Japan; The Powerhouse Museum, Sydney, Australia; The Museum of Fine

Arts, Houston, USA; Museum Boijmans van Beuningen, Rotterdam, Netherlands; Landesmuseum, Stuttgart; Musée des Arts Décoratifs de Montreal, Canada; The Fitzwilliam Museum, Cambridge; and the Museu de Ceramica de Manises, Valencia, Spain. In addition to his studio work, Ken Eastman has lectured and taught in many colleges and universities throughout the UK and is currently Associate Lecturer in Design Thinking and Creativity at the Open University. Ken Eastman, Behind the Gates of Clay, a monograph about the development of the artist's work, was published in 2004 by the Barrett-Marsden Gallery, London. With an analytical essay by Jane McCabe, the book explores recurrent themes in Eastman's work and the artist's approach to making ceramics.

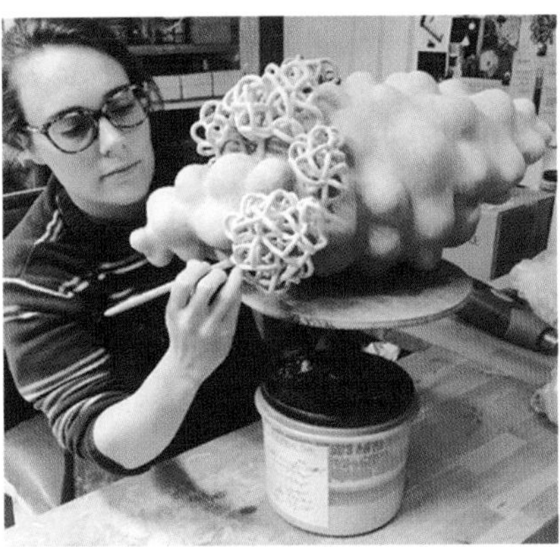

Tessa Eastman.
(Photograph by Tessa Eastman)

Tessa EASTMAN is an award-winning British ceramic artist with over twenty years' experience of working with clay. Her meticulously hand-built sculptures appear curiously alive with movement. Voluminous cloud-like shapes exploring the theme of space pushing outwards are juxtaposed with mesh structures revealing the internal. The tension between internal and external relates to receptacles where positive and negative space are equally valued, and also to the body where the void permits life. Tessa's work has been presented by the financial firms Abacus in 2003, Gresham Private Equity in 2006, and Clifford

Chance in 2019. She was shortlisted for The Cynthia Corbett Gallery's Young Masters Maylis Grand Ceramics Prize in 2017 and won the Craft Emergency Award in 2016, with a solo exhibition at Aspex Gallery in 2018. She has been exhibiting in the UK and abroad since 2005 and notable solo shows include 'Cloudspotting' with Jason Jacques Gallery in New York and 'Le désordre en délice de l'imagination' with Galerie de l'Ancienne Poste in France. Tessa's work has been selected for the British Ceramics Biennial at the Old Spode Factory, Stoke-on-Trent in 2015 and she received an honourable mention at the Gyeonggi International Ceramic Biennale Korea in 2017. Tessa has been teaching since 2005 and runs ceramic courses at the Kiln Rooms (open access ceramics studios providing professional development) and the Heatherley School of Art, one of London's oldest independent art colleges. She worked in London and France from 2002 to 2007 as an assistant to renowned ceramist Kate Malone. Tessa obtained a Bachelor of Arts Honours degree in ceramics from the University of Westminster in 2006, and in 2015 gained a Master's degree from The Royal College of Art. She set up her first studio in 2005 in West London in the Old Gas Works. In 2015 she joined Manifold, an East London collective founded in 2010 by a group of emerging artists and designers from the Royal College of Art. In 2017 she was granted a space at Cockpit Arts, the UK's only business incubator for craftspeople.

Elena GILEVA (b. 1992 in Russia; lives and works in London, UK) explores the decorative, historical and ornamental through the medium of sculpture. Gileva is trained in both ceramics and fine arts, with an MA in Ceramics and Glass from the Royal College of Art, and BFA from the Parsons Paris School of Art and Design. Her fascination lies with the language and history of objects. A myriad of references underpins the work but the artist's interest in Russian folklore is key to understanding her practice. Archetypal functional

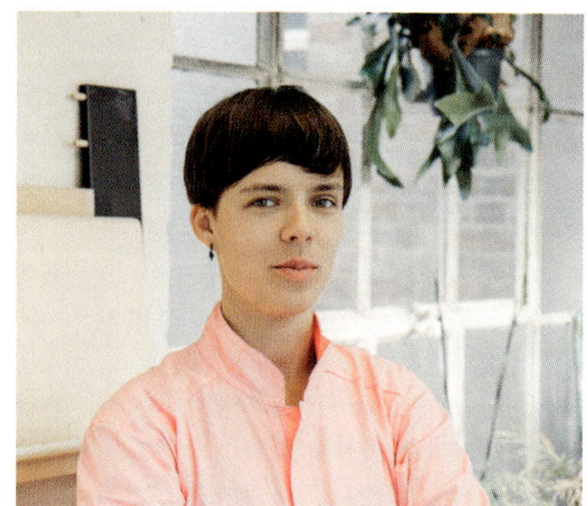

Elena Gileva.
(Photograph by Tania Dolvers)

objects – pots, jars, pillars – are reworked until they take on new colours, shapes and stories. Transmutation is a central motif in Russian folk stories in which frogs turn into princesses, boys into goats and women into swans. In Gileva's work this is a recurrent process; clay becomes form, craft becomes art, the past becomes present, the present past, and reality and fantasy flow in and out of each other. Recent projects include: La Borne, France 2020; Kleureyck: Van Eyck's Colours in Design, Design Museum Ghent, Belgium 2020; London Art Fair, White Conduit Projects, London 2019; FRACAS, Brussels, 2019; Nakanojo Biennial 2019, Gunma, Japan 2019; Cultural Lanscape part 2, Galerie de l'Ancienne Poste, Toucy, France.

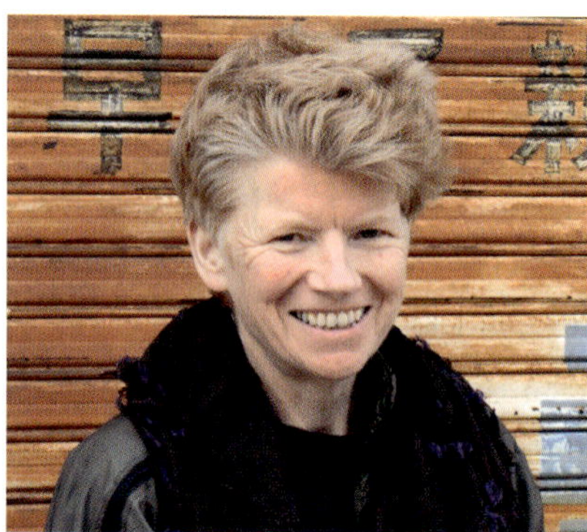

Jennifer Lee.
(Photograph by Jake Tilson)

Jennifer LEE (b. 1956 Scotland, 1975–79 Edinburgh College of Art; 1979–80 Andrew Grant Travelling scholarship to USA; 1980–83 Royal College of Art; lives and works in London, UK). Lee is a highly regarded ceramic artist who has been working in clay for more than forty years. She has won numerous awards and in 2018 her work was awarded the Loewe Craft Prize. Lee's work is concerned with the relationship of the materials in her studio. It is hand-built using the ancient traditional techniques of pinching and coiling and is made from basic elemental materials – clay, water and oxides. Her work involves a paring down of content from an assimilation of previous works. She has developed a method of colouring clay by mixing metal oxides into the clay before making. No surface decoration or glaze is applied. Colour runs through the pot and form and colour are integrated. Her work is represented in over forty-five permanent collections worldwide, including The Metropolitan Museum of Art, Philadelphia Museum of Art, Los Angeles County Museum, British Museum and Victoria & Albert Museum. Lee has had retrospective exhibitions in museums in Scotland and Sweden and in 2019 had a solo exhibition in Kettle's Yard, Cambridge, installation designed by Jamie Fobert. In 2009 Issey Miyake invited Lee to exhibit in *U-Tsu-Wa* with Lucie Rie and Ernst Gamperl at 21_21 Design Sight, Tokyo. The installation was designed by Tadao Ando and her pots appeared to float on a vast pool of water. On several occasions Lee has worked in Japan as guest artist in residence. Her travels include trips to Egypt, India, Australia, Japan as well as the USA and Europe. Lee regularly exhibits in London, Japan, South Korea and the USA. She was awarded an OBE in 2021 for services to ceramics.

Sam LUCAS (b.1967) creates contemporary ambiguous, figurative forms: conversation pieces with dark humorous undertones exploring the weight and awkwardness of being in the body. Describing how displacement is not only geographical, but can be within one's own skin, she takes some inspiration from her own lived experience as well as the observations of others. In exploring these notions, she also celebrates humour, beauty of diversity and issues of

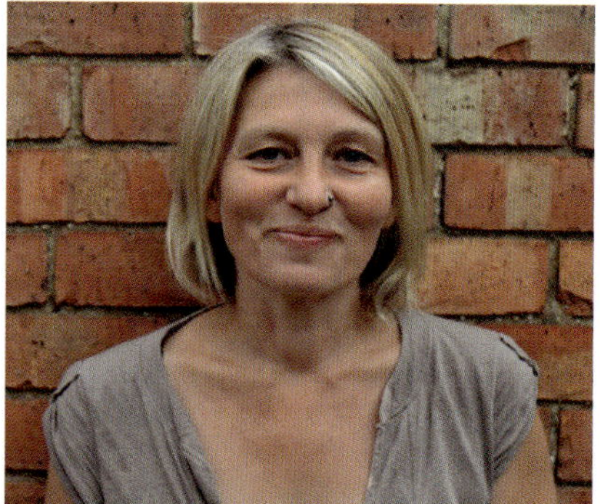

Sam Lucas.
(Photograph by Sam Lucas)

self-other-environment. Her work may at first appear careless but closer inspection reveals that there is an obvious skill in the making process, working with her own anxious demeanour and the immediacy of making at times as she allows the clay to collapse under its own weight. The results are roughly hewn hand-built forms with dry naked surfaces, which she frequently contrasts with the clean newness of slip-cast forms. Lucas explores different materials and textiles alongside clay in the hope of forming a tension and dialogue with the viewer. The surfaces of the work suggest emotion or expression and she also develops glaze techniques with different frits that emulate other materials or visceral bodily textures. Shortlisted for the British Ceramics Biennial AWARD in 2019, Sam Lucas lives and works in Britain.

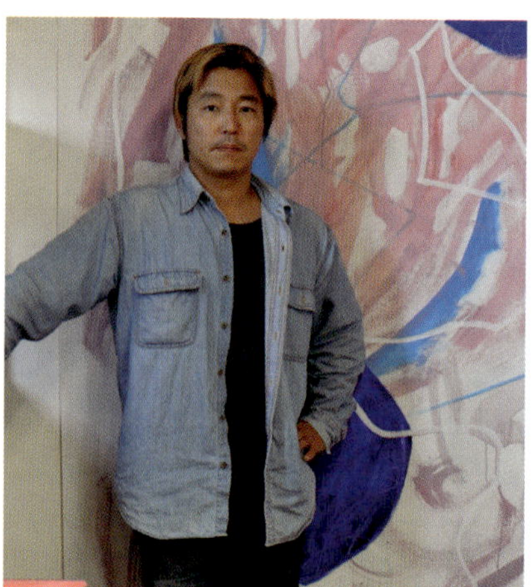

Nao Matsunaga.
(Photograph by Natsko Seki)

Nao MATSUNAGA (b. 1980) studied at the University of Brighton (1999–2002) on the 'Wood, Metal, Ceramic and Plastic' course, and completed his MA in Ceramic and Glass at the Royal College of Art in 2007. In 2013 he was the winner of the British Ceramics Biennial Award, and of the Jerwood Makers Open in 2012. Working with clay, wood and other materials, Nao Matsunaga makes sculpture imbued with a primal spirit. Its potency derives from a sense of the special, of objects beyond the everyday, charged with power. Cultural reference points are diverse, reflecting his Anglo-Japanese experience as well as a part-nomadic practice based around international residencies ranging from Arizona to Norway. His working processes respond directly to the material in hand. Often methodical and repetitive, these allow space for the subconscious to come into play, and for the material itself to guide the outcome. Matsunaga's work can be found in public collections including Crafts Council, London; Victoria and Albert Museum, London; Shipley Museum and the York Museum and Art Gallery, York. He has shown nationally and internationally in solo and group exhibitions.

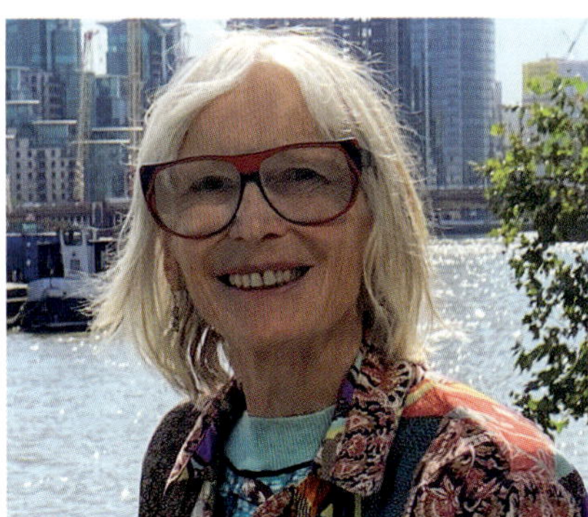

Carol McNicoll.
(Photograph by Polly Eltes)

Carol McNICOLL was brought up in the suburbs of Birmingham by parents who both loved to make. She learned clothes-making from her mother and DIY skills from her engineer father. She went to convent schools where you only did art if you were not seen as academic. She always wanted to be an artist. She did Physics, Chemistry and Biology A-levels and went to university to study Nutrition. She lasted a term and after dropping out got a job at Birmingham Rep as a Wardrobe Assistant. She moved to Stratford East when the Wardrobe Mistress got a job there. She realised that in order to progress in the theatre she would need to go to art school. In 1966 she did a foundation course intending to do a degree in theatre design and ended up studying Fine Art at Leeds. At Leeds she discovered ceramics, and after Leeds went to the Royal College to do an MA in Ceramics. While at the RCA she made stage costumes for Roxy Music, the most well-known of which was a jacket with feathers for Brian Eno, which is now in the V&A. After college she worked in a communal workspace. She made editions of functional domestic ware and eventually started making one-off pieces that were more sculptural but still always functional. In 1978 she had a son, and in 1981 was part of a group that bought an old piano factory where she created a living space and a studio. In 2003 she had a touring retrospective which was part of *show 5*. She became one of the Barratt Marsden gallery artists, now the Marsden Woo gallery, with whom she still shows.

Nathan MULLIS is a practising artist brought up in Gloucestershire and now living and working within Cardiff, Wales, channelling the topographies of the Welsh and South West landscapes respectively. Mullis's body of work is driven by material exploration and geological inspiration. The fabrication of Mullis's otherworldly fictitious landscapes represents the swirling junction of where his imagination, past environmental experiences and memories clash and morph to create objects where reality meets fantasy and fiction. The aesthetic and conceptual inspiration that underpins his practice is that of Chinese Scholar Rocks. Chinese Scholar Rocks could be described as geological wonders

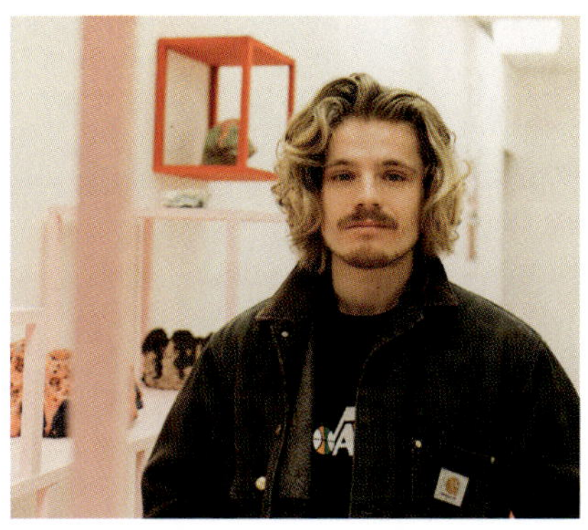

Nathan Mullis.
(Photograph by Nathan Mullis)

of the natural world in minuscule scale, a 1,000-year-old practice and cultural tradition of treasuring unusual natural form. It was a way for artists/scholars to obtain art in nature's image and acquire a slice of the environment's extended self-portrait in miniature, resembling mountainous landscapes, landforms, figures and *worlds within worlds*. Over time, the rocks began to be sculpted from clay and the art form manifested. In modern society the ready-made assists the sculpturally inspired form to craft a postmodern juxtaposition between original and simulacrum simultaneously; it is often hard to deduce natural from synthetic. Mullis sees his work as a modern counterpoint to the scholar rocks discussed above. A gestural tribute to the ancient art, you could say. For the artist the term natural is something that is masked in mysticism. The elicit nature of his work, much like the term natural itself, is shrouded in ambiguity to allow the audience to impose their own subjective feelings, sensibilities and ideas of what the work/compositions might be.

Aphra O'CONNOR is a British sculptor working primarily in clay. She was born in Whitby, North Yorkshire, and retains a strong link to her Northern industrial heritage through her three-dimensional collages. Aphra discovers pattern in discarded objects and casts them in plaster to create a unique visual library of sculptural design. She reanimates these forgotten forms by cutting, modifying and

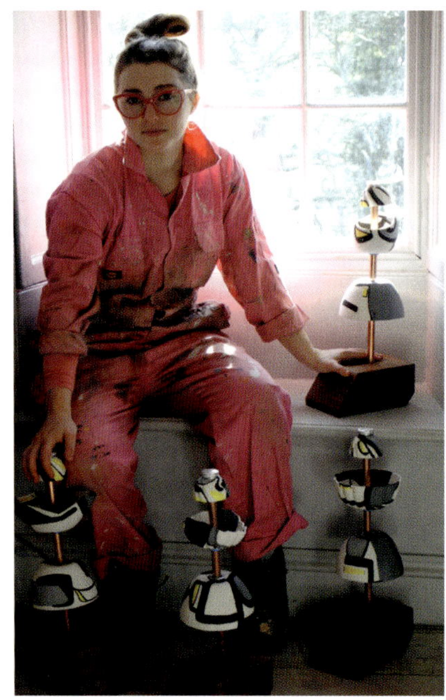

Aphra O'Connor.
(Photograph by Numi Solomons)

collaging moulded sections into new clay sculptures and in so doing, she imitates and reshapes everyday life, challenging the way we interact with and understand commonplace forms. She graduated from the Royal College of Art with a Masters in Ceramics and Glass in 2019, and from Wimbledon College of Art in 2014 with a BA in Sculpture. Having a sculptural background allows her to visualise clay in a manner that is outside the craft pathway and by assembling the forms with reclaimed metal and wood she aims to create a new way of experiencing ceramic sculpture. Aphra has now returned to Yorkshire to establish her studio and work with fellow artists to draw attention to the flourishing Northern art scene.

Benjamin PEAREY (b.1995) was born and raised in Essex, England. He received his BA from the University for the Creative Arts in 2018, before moving to London where he joined Studio Manifold. He has exhibited both in the UK and in China. Highlights include *All Work and All Play* at AIR Gallery, Manchester; *New Horizons*

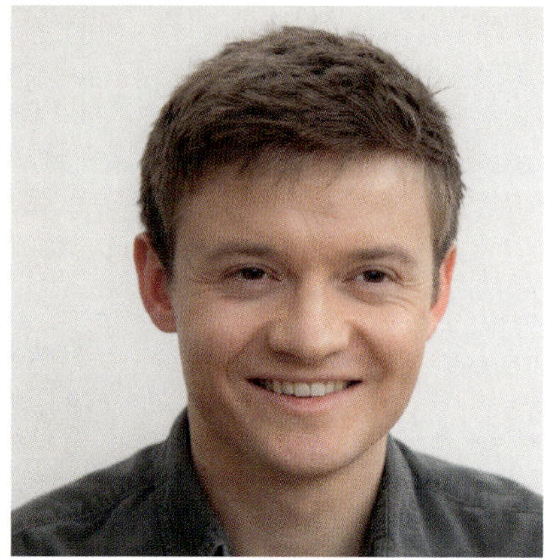

Benjamin Pearey.
(Photograph by Benjamin Pearey)

at Coast Gallery, Zhuhai; and *Play! Design* at Beijing Times Art Museum, Beijing. In 2021 he begins his MFA in Studio Art at the University of Arkansas.

Henry PIM (b. England, 1947) studied at Christ's Hospital School in Sussex, Camberwell School of Art in London and at the Gerrit Rietveld Academie, Amsterdam (postgrad). Pim started to exhibit ceramics in 1979. To date, he has had eighteen solo shows and taken part in seventy-four group shows. He has exhibited in the UK and in thirteen other countries. His work is represented in a number of private collections and in twenty-four public collections worldwide. These include the Victoria and Albert

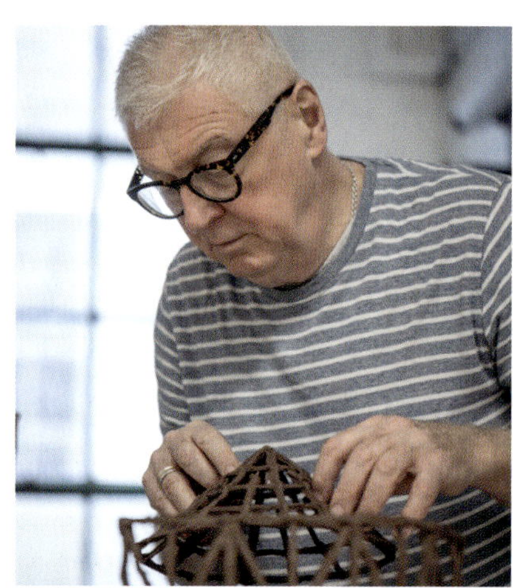

Henry Pim.
(Photograph courtesy of Henry Pim)

Museum in London, The Crafts Council collection (UK), the National Museum Collins Barracks in Dublin, The Ulster Museum, The Collection of The Irish Arts Council, The Los Angeles County Museum, The Stedelijk, Amsterdam, and the Museum of Western Australia, Perth. In 1990, Henry went to live in the Irish Republic, to take up the post of Lecturer in Ceramics at the National College of Art and Design. He remained in that job until his retirement in 2011, when he returned to live in Brixton. He now works at Vanguard Court Studios, in Peckham, where he has been developing the work featured in this book.

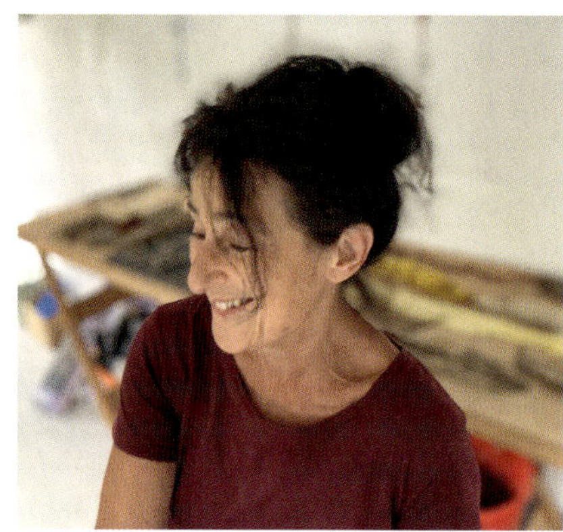

Sara Radstone.
(Photograph by Richard Stubbs)

Sara RADSTONE (b. 1955, London, UK) graduated from Camberwell School of Art and Crafts in 1979. She established her first studio at 401½ Workshops in South London, before becoming a founder member of Arlingford Studios in Brixton. Since the birth of her son in 1995 she has worked from her home in Greenwich. For over 40 years Sara has explored and sought to understand the possibilities and boundaries of clay. Her work is rooted in ideas concerning memory and human traces, frailty and absence; it continues to evolve, often drawing upon other materials to extend its language. Sara has taught at the University of the Arts, London as well as many other UK colleges. She has also been a visiting lecturer in Ireland, South Korea, Canada and the

USA, including New York State College of Ceramics at Alfred University, and in 1990 was Visiting Assistant Professor at the University of Colorado at Boulder. Since shortly after its inception she has been a tutor on the Ceramics Diploma Course at the City Lit in London. She has also contributed to a number of conferences, panel discussions and debates, and in March 2020 delivered the annual Henry Hammond Memorial Lecture. Sara's work has been shown nationally and internationally in numerous solo and group exhibitions, and in 2017/18 was the subject of a major retrospective at the York Art Gallery. Her work can be found in many public and private collections in the UK, continental Europe, America and Japan. Sara has received several awards, including grants from Greater London Arts, the Crafts Council and the Robert and Lisa Sainsbury Trust, as well as the inaugural Arts Foundation Fellowship. Since 1998 Sara Radstone has been represented by Marsden Woo Gallery.

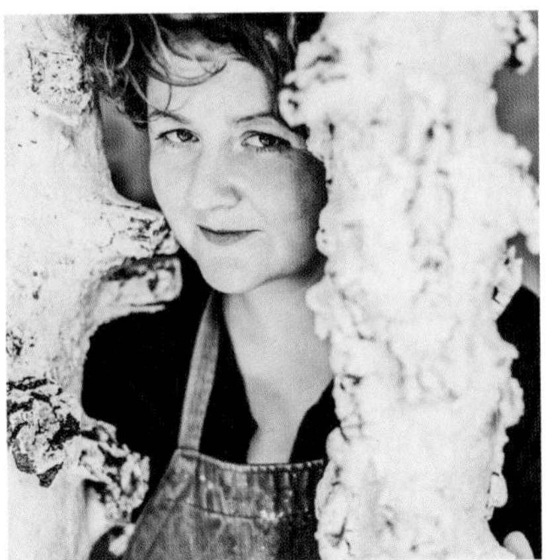

Aneta Regel.
(Photograph courtesy of Aneta Regel)

Aneta REGEL uses objects found in nature to convey her artistic vision. However, she seeks not only to capture the forms, energies and rhythms of these natural phenomena, but also to convey the emotional response they evoke in her. Growing up in Poland, she encountered large stones in forests; smooth round excrescences left behind by glacial action.

Endowed with anthropomorphic and seemingly magical powers, they are the subject of legend in her native country. Aneta Regel's work is informed by this same sense of awe in the face of nature and she has an openness to its transcendental dimension. However, preferring to not completely trust ideas, she puts her trust in material performance, from one state to another. This brings forward the unknown and presents a passage of time, a metamorphosis, a conflict and change that perhaps equates to our own ontology and the way we interact. Her resulting abstract sculptural forms convey a vivid sense of this intent, but also invite the viewer to participate in the dialogue. 'Forms that appear to imitate nature are immediately recognized as intruders in their new, unfamiliar surroundings. While they often mimic the real thing, they are, in fact, a hallucination of the real. Nothing it would seem is real anymore, nothing except the imagination.' Regel is a graduate of the Royal College of Art, UK (2006), and Westminster College (2003). Her work is part of international public collections, including The Westerwald Museum, Germany; Art Museum in York, Handelsbankens Konstförening in Sweden, and Carnegie Museum of Art in Pittsburgh. The artist has received several notable awards, was a finalist of the 2018 Loewe Craft Prize, was finalist of the British Ceramics Biennale 2016, Crafts Council Development Award and Excellence Award during World Ceramics Biennale in Icheon, Korea, 2020. She is a former member of the Royal British Society of Sculptors and is a member of Contemporary Applied Arts. She exhibited extensively in Europe, and US and is represented by Jason Jacques Gallery in NY, Sarah Mayerscough in the UK, and Taste Contemporary in Switzerland.

Mella SHAW makes thought-provoking objects and site-specific installations around environmental themes of balance, tipping points, fragility and loss. Her route into making has been circuitous; she

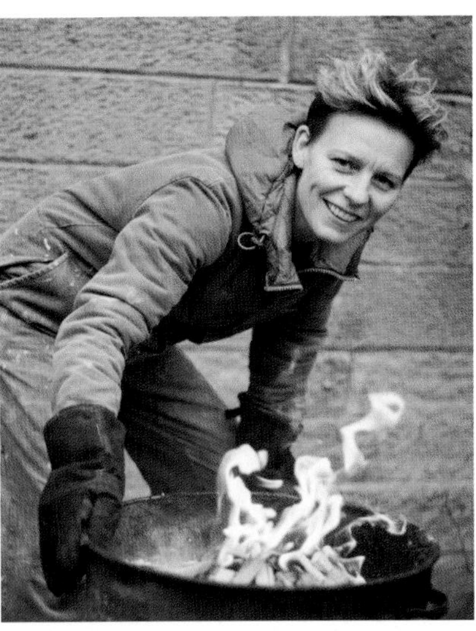

Mella Shaw.
(Photograph by Jo Spiller)

studied Anthropology at Durham University originally, where she obtained a First Class degree specialising in anthropology of art, critical theory and material culture. After a period making documentary films, she moved to London to pursue a career in museums and galleries and held various curatorial and exhibitions roles (including Head of Exhibitions at Dulwich Picture Gallery, London and Exhibitions Manager at the Fitzwilliam Museum, University of Cambridge). An interest in the way objects can be imbued with shared cultural meaning underpins her own ceramics practice. In 2009 she studied for a two-year Diploma in Ceramics at City Lit, London, and shared a studio at Vanguard Court, Camberwell. From here Mella went on to complete an MA in Ceramics and Glass from the Royal College of Art, graduating in 2013. Since then she has shown work nationally and internationally and has been selected for exhibitions such as AWARD at the British Ceramics Biennial in 2015 and Collect Open in 2017. Mella currently lives and works in Edinburgh where she combines her practice with teaching ceramics and freelance curation. She is a visiting lecturer on the BA Ceramic Design course at Central Saint Martins (London) and a board member of Visual Arts Scotland.

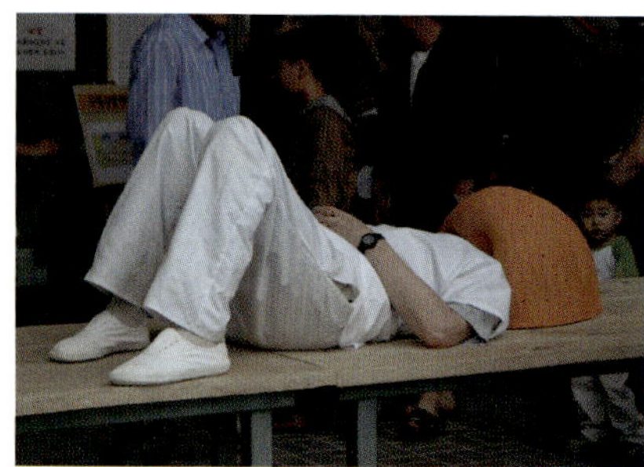

Richard Slee.
(Photograph courtesy of Richard Slee)

Richard SLEE (b. Cumbria, UK, 1946) studied at Carlisle College of Art & Design (1964–65) and studied ceramics at the Central School of Art & Design (1965–70). He graduated with an MA at the Royal College of Art (1988). Slee lives and works in London. His work attempts to challenge every conventional notion in ceramic art, transcending its utilitarian roots, whilst also sidestepping the self-indulgent aspects of the studio tradition that became ubiquitous in the late twentieth century. His works lie in contemporary debate and reference the current positioning of material specializations within visual creativity. For Slee, the objects he produces are intrinsically about the domestic interior and a love for the 'great indoors'. There are fabricated references in the work to the decorative, the ornamental and the symbolic both from past histories and within contemporary culture. These sources, often eclectic, are brought together to explore new meanings and dramas. For now they are resolved since the medium of ceramics permanently fixes them, but, as always, the drama of meaning is contingent and fluid. Selected group and solo shows include Studio Voltaire (UK); Tate St Ives; Tate Liverpool; Tramway (Scotland); Hales Gallery, London and New York; Barrett Marsden Gallery, London; Danish Museum of Art and Design; National Museum Sweden; Victoria & Albert Museum, UK; World Ceramic Center, Icheon (Korea); Museum of Modern Ceramic Art, Gifu (Japan). His work was included in *Postmodernism: Style and Subversion 1970–1990* (2011–12), Victoria & Albert Museum. Slee's work is represented in numerous collections worldwide, including British Council; Museum of Arts and Design, New York; Museum of Fine Arts, Houston, USA; Stedelijk Museum, Amsterdam; Victoria & Albert Museum, London. He is represented by Hales Gallery, London and New York.

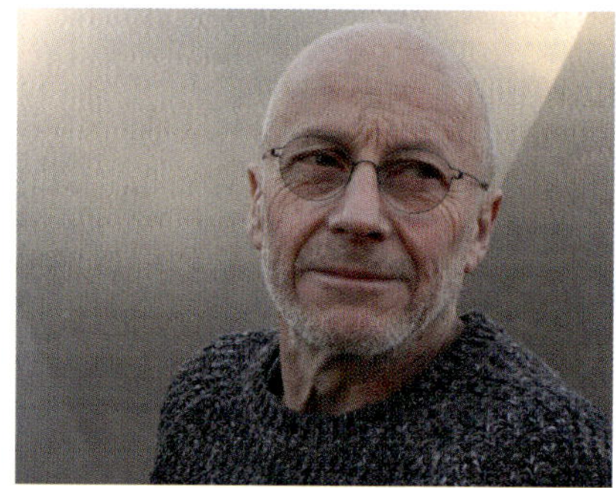

Martin Smith.
(Photograph by Judith Cowan)

Martin SMITH first studied Ceramics at Bristol Polytechnic before going on to the Royal College of Art, where he spent two years refining and developing the Japanese technique of Raku, graduating in 1977. The results of these investigations were shown in group exhibitions in Holland and Germany. He established his first studio in Suffolk but moved it to London in the early eighties, where he has continued to live and work in various spaces since. His first major solo exhibition was *Forms around a Vessel,* instigated by Leeds Art Galleries at Lotherton Hall, which had a national tour before concluding at the Crafts Council Gallery in London in 1982. Regular exhibitions followed in Holland at Gallerie de Witte Voet and the USA with Garth Clark. In 1996 the Museum Boijmans van Beuningen in Rotterdam mounted a twenty-year retrospective exhibition and in 2001 Smith produced *Wavelength*, a site-specific work for Tate St Ives. In 1998 he signed with Barrett Marsden Gallery, now Marsden Woo, and has held regular solo exhibitions since. Smith's work is represented in numerous international museums including the British Museum, Victoria & Albert Museum and the Sainsbury Centre in the UK; the Los Angeles County Museum of Art, Metropolitan Museum, New York and the Museum of Fine Art, Houston in the USA; the Stedlijk Museum and Boijmans van Beuningen in Holland; and the National Museum of Modern Art, Tokyo, Shigaraki Ceramic Cultural Park, and Mashiko Museum of Ceramic Art in Japan. Smith has also worked on exhibition design for York Art Gallery and in 2015 he designed the 'domestic' setting for the Anthony Shaw Collection for the Gallery. Alongside his creative practice Smith has held many senior teaching posts, including at Loughborough and Camberwell Schools of Art and then at the Royal College of Art where he worked from 1998 to 2018 and was Professor and Head of Ceramics and Glass from 1999.

Pam SU is an American artist working in the UK. She was born in Taiwan and grew up in the shadows of NYC in the United States. Su received her BA from Cornell University in Ithaca, NY where she studied film and had intended to be a filmmaker. Since then, she has trained and apprenticed in traditional Eastern pottery techniques and wood-firing kilns. In 2018, she received her MA in Ceramics and Glass from the Royal College of Art in London. Her foundation in pottery-making has enabled her

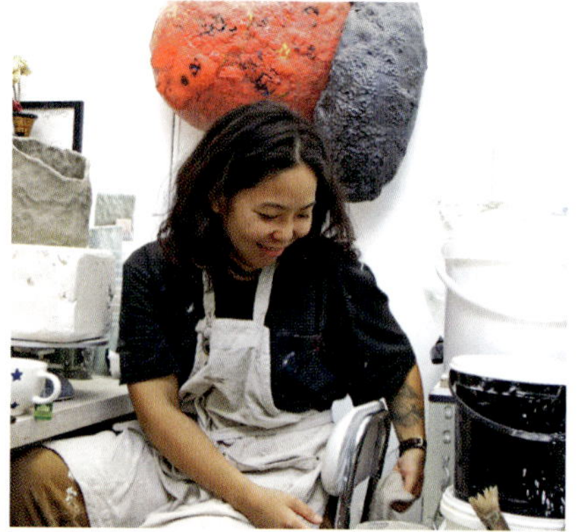

Pam Su.
(Photograph by Tom Griffiths)

to draw from the discipline and respect for the craft and, from there, take leaps into experimentation and challenge convention. Su's work is a contemporary offspring of the Abstract Expressionist and Beat Generation movements in 1950s America. Her practice is steeped in the personal and distant. It continuously strives toward inciting meaning and capturing the paradoxical nature and dualistic toil of existence. As such, her work is intentionally ambiguous and amorphous, embodying the sense of a liminal hyper-reality. On her days out of the studio, Su enjoys eating ice cream.

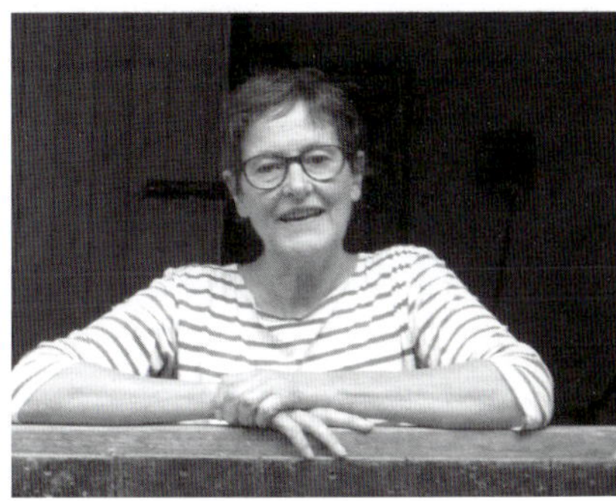

Annie Turner.
(Photograph by Steven James Will)

Annie TURNER was brought up in a small Suffolk village on the banks of the River Deben, where for many generations her family lived and worked. It has been several years since Annie went back to the river of her childhood and began to respond creatively to its landscape. It was always there in her mind of course, a period of gestation as she worked on other projects, a necessary distancing perhaps, but it was the water that finally drew her back and has guided her work ever since. In 1974, Annie obtained a place on the Foundation course at Suffolk College in Ipswich, where she discovered clay. Her BA Hons degree at Bristol in 3D Design ceramics (1976–79) was followed by a postgraduate MA from the Royal College of Art (1980–83). Annie has spent the last thirty-seven years primarily as a maker and in education. For nineteen years Annie taught part-time on the Foundation course at Wimbledon School of Art, inspiring many young makers who have gone on to be highly successful potters and ceramists. She is currently teaching on the Ceramics Diploma at the City Lit, London, and making in rural Suffolk in a converted blacksmith's forge. Annie has held solo exhibitions in London and Paris and was shortlisted for the LOEWE Crafts Prize Award in 2019.

Patricia VOLK was born in Belfast, Northern Ireland, and is a Fellow of the Royal Society of Sculptors and an RWA academician, confirming her position as an outstanding visual artist working in painted fired clay; a term she much prefers to 'ceramics'. Her sculptures feature in the collections of Swindon Art Gallery and Museum, best-selling author Anthony Horowitz, former BAFTA chairman Simon Relph CBE, the British Consul (Ivory Coast), Lord Carrington, and the television presenter Mary Portas. She was Regional Winner of the ING 'Discerning Eye' prize in 2007, has been shortlisted for the prestigious Brian Mercer Bronze Casting Residency in Pietrasanta, and has exhibited nationally and internationally at venues such as Chichester Cathedral and galleries including the Hannah Peschar Sculpture Garden, Arundel Contemporary, and the Beukenhof-Phoenix Gallery in Belgium. In 2017 she was invited by the Trustees of the Designer Crafts Foun-

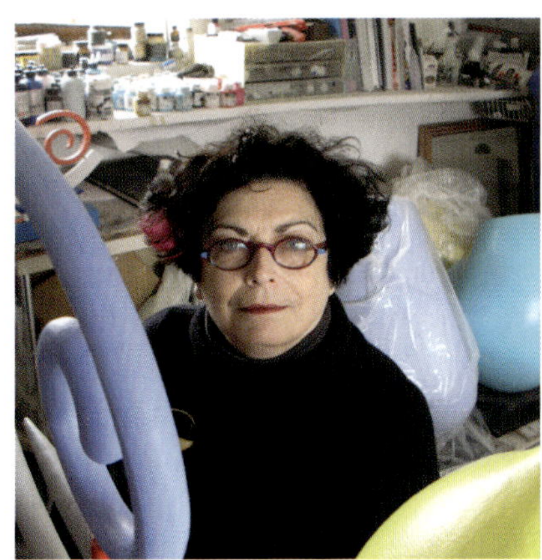

Patricia Volk.
(Photograph courtesy of Patricia Volk)

dation to visit Israel as one of their guest sculptors, speaking at the symposium in Tel Hai, lecturing both in Jerusalem at the Israel Museum and at the Bet Benyamini Centre in Tel Aviv. In 2019 she was commissioned by ITV as part of the prestigious 'ITV Creates' initiative, making her sculpture visible on screen to millions of television viewers. She has recently been included in *50 Women Sculptors*, the first book to give an overview of women sculptors from 1880 to today. It explores the work of 'extraordinary women artists who have forged a name for themselves in a male arena, as well as breaking rules, pushing boundaries and inspiring us with their visionary creations'. She lives and works on the border between Somerset and Wiltshire.

Notes

Introduction

[1] Sequoia Miller, *The Ceramic Presence in Modern Art* (Yale: Yale University Art Gallery, 2015), 20.

[2] See, for instance, Sainsbury's Centre for Visual Art, *Lucie Rie, Hans Coper, and their Pupils* (Norwich: SCVA, 1991).

[3] Miller, *The Ceramic Presence*, 46-7.

[4] Ibid.

[5] For analysis that places the work of Betty Woodman and Alison Britton in dialogue, see John Houston, *The Abstract Vessel: Ceramics in Studio* (London: Bellew, 1991).

[6] Britton's work was included in the exhibition *Lucie Rie, Hans Coper, and their Pupils*, held at the Sainsbury's Centre for Visual Art, Norwich in 1990 and the Fitzwilliam Museum, Cambridge in 1991.

[7] See, for example, Glenn Adamson, and Nigel Llewellyn, *Julian Stair: Quietus – The vessel, death and the human body* (Middlesborough: Mima, 2012); A.S Byatt, et al, *Edmund de Waal* (London: Phaidon, 2014); Emmanuel Cooper, and Amanda Fielding, *Walter Keeler* (Ruthin and Leicester: The Gallery Ruthin Craft Centre and The City Gallery Leicester, 2004); Claire Curneen, *To This I Put My Name* (Denbighshire: Ruthin Craft Centre, 2014); Jacky Klein, *Grayson Perry* (London: Thames and Hudson, 2009); Anthony Slayter-Ralph, ed., *Magdalene Odundo* (Aldershot: Lund Humphries, 2004); David Whiting, ed., *Gordon Baldwin: Objects for a Landscape* (York: York Museums Trust, 2012).

Chapter 1: Richard Slee

[8] Immanuel Kant, *Kant's Critique of Judgement*, trans. J. H. Bernard (London: Macmillan, 1914), 184. Italics in this, and the quotations that follow, are in the original.

[9] Ibid., 55.

[10] Ibid., 67.

[11] Ibid., 57.

[12] Ibid., 90.

[13] Ibid., 96.

[14] Grayson Perry, *Ceramics* (London: Birch and Conran, 1987); Klein, *Grayson Perry*, 17.

[15] John Houston, *Richard Slee: Ceramics in Studio* (London: Bellew, 1990), 32.

[16] Kant, *Kant's Critique*, 184.

Chapter 2: Alison Britton

[17] John Russell Taylor, 'Alison Britton – Playing with Clay', *Ceramic Review* (Nov-Dec, 1979), 6.

[18] Essays still in circulation at the time of writing can be found in: Crafts Council, *The Work of Alison Britton* (London: Crafts Council, 1979); Peter Dormer, *Alison Britton in Studio* (London: Bellew, 1985); Tanya Harrod, *Alison Britton: Ceramics in Studio* (Aberystwyth: Bellew, 1990); and Linda Sandino, *Complexity and Ambiguity: the Ceramics of Alison Britton* (London: Barrett Marsden Gallery, 2000).

[19] See Alison Britton, *Seeing Things: Collected Writing on Art, Craft and Design* (No. pl.: Occasional Papers, 2013).

[20] Victor Turner, 'Liminal to Liminoid, in Play, Flow, and Ritual: an Essay in Comparative Symbology', *Rice University Studies*, vol.60, no.3 (1974), 60.

[21] Dormer, *Alison Britton*, 22.

[22] Houston in Crafts Council, *The Work of Alison Britton*, 15.

[23] Sandino, *Complexity and Ambiguity*, 21.

[24] Alison Britton, 'Alison Britton', in Crafts Council, *The Maker's Eye* (London: Crafts Council, 1981), 16.

[25] Harrod, *Alison Britton*, 9–10.

[26] Dormer, *Alison Britton*, 26.

[27] Alison Britton, 'The Modern Pot', in *Fast Forward: New Directions in British Ceramics*, ed. by ICA, (London: ICA, 1985), 12. Britton's framing of contemporary ceramics via painting was developed from George Woodman, 'Ceramic Decoration and the Concept of Ceramics as a Decorative Art', *American Ceramics*, vol.1, no.1 (1982).

[28] Dormer, *Alison Britton*, 22.

[29] Charles Harrison, 'Notes on Ben Nicholson's Development and Commentary on Selected Works', in Tate, *Ben Nicholson* (London: Tate, 1969), 33.

[30] William Scott, cited in Norbert Lynton, *William Scott* (London: Thames and Hudson, 2007), 116.

[31] Ibid.

Chapter 3: Jennifer Lee

[32] Tanya Harrod, *Falls the Shadow* (London: Galerie Besson, 2011).

[33] Glenn Adamson, Alun Graves, and Edmund de Waal, *Signs and Wonders – Edmund de Waal and the V&A Ceramics Galleries* (London: V&A Publishing, 2009), 16.

Chapter 4: Carol McNicoll

[34] Sergei Eisenstein, *Film Form: Essays in Film Theory*, trans. Jay Leda, (New York: Harvest, 1949), 30.

[35] Ibid, 72-83.

[36] Tanya Harrod, and RosaLee Goldberg, *Carol McNicoll* (Leicester: City Gallery and Lund Humphries, 2003), 14.

[37] Ibid., 67.

[38] Glenn Adamson, and Jane Pavitt, 'Postmodernism: Style and Subversion', in *Postmodernism: Style and Subversion, 1970–1990*, ed. Glenn Adamson, and Jane Pavitt, (London: V&A Publishing, 2012), 33.

[39] Ibid.

[40] Victor Buchili, 'On Bricolage', in *Postmodernism: Style and Subversion, 1970–1990*, ed. Glenn Adamson, and Jane Pavitt, (London: V&A Publishing, 2012), 113.

[41] Harrod and Goldberg, *Carol McNicoll*, 100.

Chapter 5: Sara Radstone

42 Amanda Fielding, *Gillian Lowndes* (Ruthin: Ruthin Craft Centre, 2013).

43 Garth Clark, 'Rising Above the Polemic: Organic Abstraction in British Ceramics', *Pandora's Box*, ed. Crafts Council (London: Crafts Council, 1995), 19–20.

44 Directed by Waad al-Kateab and Edward Watts, produced by Channel 4 News / ITN News for Channel 4 and Frontline PBS.

45 Minghua Fan, 'The significance of Xuwu 虚无 (nothingness) in Chinese Aesthetics', *Frontiers of Philosophy in China*, vol. 5, no. 4 (December 2010), 565.

46 Ibid., 570.

Chapter 6: Pam Su

47 Paul Moorhouse, *Howard Hodgkin: Absent Friends* (London: National Portrait Gallery Publications, 2017), 16.

Chapter 8: Aneta Regel

48 Wislawa Szymborska, Vuyelwa Carlin, and Sylwester Cygan, 'Conversation with a Stone', *The Kenyon Review*, New Series, vol. 23, no. 2, *Cultures of Creativity: The Centennial Celebration of the Nobel Prizes* (Spring, 2001), 91.

49 Wislawa Szymborska, 'Rozmowa z kamieniem', https://poezja.org/wz/ Szymborska_Wisława/117/Rozmowa_z_ kamieniem., accessed: August 28, 2020.

50 Quoted in Anna Brzozowska-Krajka, 'The Folkloric Encoding of Meanings: Natural and Occasional Liminality in Polish Folklore', *Folklore Forum*, vol 32, nos.1/2 (2001), 49.

51 Ibid., 50.

52 Magdalena Wójtowicz, 'Etnografia Lubelszczyzny – ludowe wierzenia o drzewach', http://teatrnn.pl/leksykon/ artykuly/etnografia-lubelszczyzny- ludowe-wierzenia-o-drzewach/, accessed: August 29, 2020.

53 Ibid.

54 Jan Kochanowski, *Treny; The Laments of Kochanowski*, trans. Adam Czerniawski (Oxford: European Humanities Research Centre of the University of Oxford, 2001). For the text in Polish, see Jan Kochanowski, 'Treny,' http://www.staropolska.pl/renesans/ jan_kochanowski/treny/treny_07.html, accessed September 22, 2020.

Chapter 9: Nathan Mullis

55 Clark, 'Rising Above the Polemic', 15.

56 Ibid.

57 Michael Robinson, *Ewen Henderson: Recent Work* (London: Austin Desmond, 1998), 4.

58 Whiting, *Objects for a Landscape*, 11.

59 Clark, 'Rising Above the Polemic', 19–20.

60 Ibid., 16.

61 The original lines read: '苍然两片石，厥状怪且丑。俗用无所堪，时人嫌不取。' Translation by the author.

62 Juyi Bai, '*Shuangshi*', https://baike.baidu. com/item/双石/20154865, accessed: September 19, 2020.

63 The Editors of The Encyclopaedia Britannica, 'Agateware', *Encyclopaedia Britannica*, https://www.britannica.com/ art/agateware, last updated: July 10, 2019, accessed: September 13, 2020.

Chapter 10: Mella Shaw

64 Bonnie Kemske, 'Breaking the Taboo', *Ceramic Review* (Sept/Oct, 2009), 34.

Chapter 11: Tessa Eastman

65 Jacques Derrida, *Writing and Difference*, trans. Alan Bass, (London: Routledge, 2005), 352.

66 Ibid, 350-352.

Chapter 12: Annie Turner

67 A.D. Mills, *A Dictionary of British Place Names* (Oxford; Oxford University Press, 1991).

68 Kevin Crossley-Holland (trans.), *The Wanderer* (Wivenhoe: Jardine Press, 1986), n.p.

69 Claude Lévis-Strauss, *Structural Anthropology*, trans. Claire Jacobson and Brooke Grundfest Schoepf (New York: Basic Books, 1963), 62.

Chapter 13: Henry Pim

70 Raymond Williams, 'Structures of Feeling', in *Marxism and Literature* (Oxford: Oxford University Press, 1977), 132.

Chapter 14: Martin Smith

71 Juhani Pallasmaa, *The Eyes of the Skin: Architecture and the Senses* (Chichester: Wiley Academy, 2005), 41.

72 Ibid., 11.

73 Harry Holtzman, and Martin S. James, (eds. and trans.), *The New Art – The New Life: the Collected Writings of Piet Mondrian* (Boston: G.K. Hall and Co, 1986), 354.

74 See Museum Boijmans Van Beuningen, *Balance and Space: Martin Smith, Ceramics, 1976–1996* (Rotterdam: Museum Boijmans Van Beuningen, 1996).

75 See Leeds City Art Gallery, *Martin Smith* (Leeds: Leeds City Art Gallery, 1981); Tate St Ives, *Wavelength* (St Ives: Tate St Ives, 2001).

76 Deborah Norton, 'Perceptions and Illusions: Exploring Space with Martin Smith', *Studio Pottery: Ceramics in Society*, 31 (Spring, 1998), 40.

77 Pallasmaa, *The Eyes of the Skin*, 12.

Chapter 15: Aphra O'Connor

78 Holtzman and James, *The New Art*, 392.

79 Ibid., 27.

80 Ibid., 74.

81 V&A., 'Teapots, designed by Christopher Dresser, 1878-9', www.vam.ac.uk/content/articles/t/ christopher-dresser-teapots/, accessed: August 19, 2020.

82 Ibid.

83 Holtzman and James, *The New Art*, 354.

84-87 Ibid.

Chapter 16: Patricia Volk

88 Bridget Riley, quoted in Robert Kudielka, ed., *Bridget Riley: Dialogues on Art* (London: Thames and Hudson, 2003), 43.

89 Hazzlitt, Holland-Hibbert, *Barbara Hepworth: Drawings from the 1940s*

(London: Hazzlitt, Holland-Hibbert, 2005), 96.

90 Bridget Riley, *The Eye's Mind: Bridget Riley, Collected Writings 1965–1999* (London: Thames & Hudson, 1999), 201-02.

91 Elizabeth Fritsch, *Pots about Music* (Leeds: Leeds City Art Gallery, 1978), n.p.

92 Ibid.

93 Ibid.

94 Edmund de Waal, 'High Unseriousness: artists and clay', in *A Secret History of Clay; from Gauguin to Gormley*, ed. Tate Liverpool (London: Tate, 2004), 51.

95 See, for example, Bridget Riley's *Continuum [Reconstruction]*, 1963/2005, acrylic on aluminium.

96 See, for example, Barbara Hepworth's *Sculpture with Colour (Deep Blue and Red)*, 1940, in the Tate Gallery (collection number T03133).

97 Edward Lucie-Smith, *Vessels From Another World: Metaphysical Pots in Painted Stoneware* (London: Bellew, 1993), 11.

98 Philip Rawson, 'Empty Vessels', in ICA, *Fast Forward* (London: ICA, 1985), 17.

Chapter 17: Ken Eastman

99 Maurice Merleau-Ponty, *Phenomenology of Perception*, trans. Donald Landes (London and New York: Routledge, 2012), 69-70.

100 Ibid., 70.

101 Ibid., 70-71.

Chapter 18: Nao Matsunaga

102 Shigeru Uchida, 'Foreword', in Mira Locher, *Zen Gardens: The Complete Works of Shunmyo Masuno – Japan's Leading Garden Designer* (Tokyo: Tuttle, 2012), 8-9.

103 Jonathan Rutherford, 'The Third Space. Interview with Homi Bhabha', in *Identity: Community, Culture, Difference*, ed. Jonathan Rutherford (London: Lawrence and Wishart, 1990), 211.

Chapter 19: Sam Lucas

104 Hélène Cixous, 'The Laugh of the Medusa', *Signs*, vol. 1, no. 4 (1976), 893.

105 Cixous, 'The Laugh of the Medusa', 886.

106 Karl Abraham, 'The Spider as Dream Symbol (1922)', in *The Selected Papers of Karl Abraham*, trans. Douglas Bryan and Alix Strachey (London: Hogarth Press, 1927, 331.

107 Sigmund Freud, *The Standard Edition of the Complete Psychological Works of Sigmund Freud, Vol. XXII (1932–1936), New Introductory Lectures on Psycho-Analysis and Other Works*, trans. James Strachey (London: Vintage, 2001), 24.

108 Abraham, 'The Spider as Dream Symbol (1922)', 332.

109 Ibid., 331.

110 After Demeter discovers that Zeus had himself arranged the affair, she refuses to allow any crops to grow until her daughter is returned. As the mortal world plummets into famine, Zeus agrees to allow Demeter to enter the Underworld and collect her daughter. Unfortunately, Persephone has eaten pomegranate seeds, and any being that eats in the Underworld must reside there forever. Hecate enters the Underworld to console Demeter and her daughter, and Zeus decides that, to save humanity, Persephone will only stay in the Underworld for one half of the year and will return to be with her mother for the other half. This, the myth explains, is how the cycle of the seasons began.

111 Virginia White, 'A Study of Female Agency in *The Homeric Hymn to Demeter* through Word and Illustration'. PhD. Diss., Wellesley College, Massachusetts (April 2017). https://repository.wellesley.edu/cgi/viewcontent.cgi?article=1646&context=thesiscollection, accessed: September 17, 2000.

112 Carl Jung, 'The Psychological Aspects of the Kore', in *Collected Works: Volume 9*, 2nd edn. (Princeton: Princeton University Press, 1968), passages 306-383.

113 Ibid., passage 315.

114 Cixous, 'The Laugh of the Medusa', 893.

115 See, Sigmund Freud, *Beyond the Pleasure Principle*, trans. C.J.M.

Hubback (London: International Psycho-Analytical Press, 1922).

116 Ibid.

117 Kimberley Stratton, 'Interrogating the Magic – Gender Connection', in *Daughters of Hecate: Women and Magic in the Ancient World*, eds. Kimberley Stratton, K. and Dana Kalleres (Oxford: Oxford University Press, 2014), 28.

118 Cixous, 'The Laugh of the Medusa', 893.

Chapter 20: Elena Gileva

119 Nadieszda Kizenko, 'Feminized Patriarchy? Orthodoxy and Gender in Post-Soviet Russia', *Signs*, vol. 38, no. 3 (Spring 2013): 595-621.

120 Bertram Puckle, *Funeral Customs: Their Origin and Development* (Alexandria: Library of Alexandria, 1926), 46-7.

Chapter 21: Connor Coulston

121 Cited in Pilar Ordovas, ed., *Irrational Marks: Bacon and Rembrandt.* (London: Ordovas, 2011), 20.

122 Ibid., 26.

Chapter 22: Neil Brownsword

123 Discussions of earlier work can be found in Neil Brownsword, et al., *Neil Brownsword: Collaging History* (Stoke-on-Trent: Stone-on-Trent Museums, 2005).

124 Aoife Monks, *The Actor In Costume* (Houndmills: Palgrave, 2010), 140–142.

125 Richard Schechner, *Between Theater and Anthropology* (Philadelphia: University of Pennsylvania Press, 1985), 35.

126 To view the walk-through, visit: https://www.britishceramicsbiennial.com/externalisingthearchivetour/

Afterword

127 Jacques Derrida, *The Truth in Painting*, trans. Geoffrey Bennington (Chicago: University of Chicago Press, 1987), pp. 49-50.

Bibliography

Abraham, Karl. 'The Spider as Dream Symbol (1922)'. In *The Selected Papers of Karl Abraham*. Translated by Douglas Bryan and Alix Strachey. London: Hogarth Press, 1927, 326-332.

Adamson, Glenn, Graves, Alun, and de Waal, Edmund. *Signs and Wonders – Edmund de Waal and the V&A Ceramics Galleries.* London: V&A Publishing, 2009.

Adamson, Glenn, and Llewellyn, Nigel. *Julian Stair: Quietus – The vessel, death and the human body.* Middlesborough: Mima, 2012.

Adamson, Glenn, and Pavitt, Jane. 'Postmodernism: Style and Subversion'. In *Postmodernism: Style and Subversion, 1970–1990*, edited by Glenn Adamson and Jane Pavitt. London: V&A Publishing, 2012, 12-97.

Bai, Juyi. 'Shuangshi'. https://baike.baidu.com/item/双石/20154865. Accessed: September 19, 2020.

Britton, Alison. *Seeing Things: Collected Writing on Art, Craft and* Design. No. pl.: Occasional Papers, 2013.

-----------. 'The Modern Pot'. In *Fast Forward: New Directions in British Ceramics*, edited by ICA. London: ICA, 1985.

Brownsword, Neil, et al. *Neil Brownsword: Collaging History.* Stoke-on-Trent: Stone-on-Trent Museums, 2005.

Brzozowska-Krajka, Anna. 'The Folkloric Encoding of Meanings: Natural and Occasional Liminality in Polish Folklore'. *Folklore Forum*, vol. 32, nos.1/2 (2001): 43-56.

Buchili, Victor. 'On Bricolage'. In *Postmodernism: Style and Subversion, 1970–1990*, edited by Glenn Adamson and Jane Pavitt. London: V&A Publishing, 2012, 112–115.

Byatt, A.S., et al. *Edmund de Waal.* London: Phaidon, 2014.

Cixous, Hélène. 'The Laugh of the Medusa'. *Signs*, vol. 1, no. 4 (1976): 875-893.

Clark, Garth. 'Rising Above the Polemic: Organic Abstraction in British Ceramics'. In *Pandora's Box*, edited by Crafts Council. London: Crafts Council, 1995, 15–20.

Cooper, Emmanuel, and Fielding, Amanda. *Walter Keeler.* Ruthin and Leicester: The Gallery Ruthin Craft Centre and The City Gallery Leicester, 2004.

Crafts Council, ed. *The Maker's Eye.* London: Crafts Council, 1981.

-----------. *The Work of Alison Britton.* London: Crafts Council, 1979.

Crossley-Holland, Kevin (trans.). *The Wanderer.* Wivenhoe: Jardine Press, 1986.

Curneen, Claire. *To This I Put My Name.* Denbighshire: Ruthin Craft Centre, 2014.

de Waal, Edmund. 'High Unseriousness: artists and clay'. In *A Secret History of Clay; from Gauguin to Gormley*, edited by Tate Liverpool. London: Tate, 2004.

Derrida, Jacques. *The Truth in Painting.* Translated by Geoffrey Bennington. Chicago: Chicago University Press, 1987.

-----------. *Writing and Difference.* Translated by Alan Bass. London: Routledge, 2005.

Dormer, Peter. *Alison Britton in Studio.* London: Bellew, 1985.

Eisenstein, Sergei. *Film Form: Essays in Film Theory.* Translated by Jay Leda. New York: Harvest, 1949.

Fan, Minghua. 'The significance of Xuwu 虚无 (nothingness) in Chinese Aesthetics'. *Frontiers of Philosophy in China*, vol. 5, no. 4 (December 2010): 560-574.

Fielding, Amanda. *Gillian Lowndes.* Ruthin: Ruthin Craft Centre, 2013.

Freud, Sigmund. *Beyond the Pleasure Principle.* Translated by C.J.M. Hubback. London: International Psycho-Analytical Press, 1922.

Freud, Sigmund. *The Standard Edition of the Complete Psychological Works of Sigmund Freud, Vol. XXII (1932–1936), New Introductory Lectures on Psycho-Analysis and Other Works.* Translated by James Strachey. London: Vintage, 2001.

Fritsch, Elizabeth. *Pots about Music.* Leeds: Leeds City Art Gallery, 1978.

Harrison, Charles. 'Notes on Ben Nicholson's Development and Commentary on Selected Works'. In *Ben Nicholson*, edited by Tate. London: Tate, 1969.

Harrod, Tanya. *Alison Britton: Ceramics in Studio.* Aberystwyth: Bellew, 1990.

Harrod, Tanya. *Falls the Shadow.* London: Galerie Besson, 2011.

Harrod, Tanya, and Goldberg, RosaLee. *Carol McNicoll.* Leicester: City Gallery and Lund Humphries, 2003.

Hazzlitt, Holland-Hibbert. *Barbara Hepworth: Drawings from the 1940s.* London: Hazzlitt, Holland-Hibbert, 2005.

Holtzman, Harry, and James, Martin S., eds. and trans. *The New Art – The New Life: the Collected Writings of Piet Mondrian.* Boston: G.K. Hall and Co, 1986.

Houston, John. *Richard Slee: Ceramics in Studio.* London: Bellew, 1990.

Houston, John. *The Abstract Vessel: Ceramics in Studio.* London: Bellew, 1991.

Kant, Immanuel. *Kant's Critique of Judgement.* Translated by J. H. Bernard. London: Macmillan, 1914.

Kemske, Bonnie. 'Breaking the Taboo'. *Ceramic Review* (Sept/Oct, 2009): 34-6.

Kizenko, Nadieszda. 'Feminized Patriarchy? Orthodoxy and Gender in Post-Soviet Russia'. *Signs*, vol. 38, no. 3 (Spring 2013): 595-621.

Klein, Jacky. *Grayson Perry*. London: Thames and Hudson, 2009.

Kochanowski, Jan. *Treny; The Laments of Kochanowski*. Translated by Adam Czerniawski. Oxford: European Humanities Research Centre of the University of Oxford, 2001.

-----------. 'Treny'. http://www.staropolska. pl/renesans/jan_kochanowski/treny/ treny_07.html. Accessed September 22, 2020.

Kudielka, Robert, ed. *Bridget Riley: Dialogues on Art*. London: Thames and Hudson, 2003.

Leeds City Art Gallery. *Martin Smith*. Leeds: Leeds City Art Gallery, 1981.

Lévi-Strauss, Claude. *Structural Anthropology*. Translated by Claire Jacobson and Brooke Grundfest Schoepf. New York: Basic Books, 1963.

Lucie-Smith, Edward. *Vessels From Another World: Metaphysical Pots in Painted Stoneware*. London: Bellew, 1993.

Lynton, Norbert. *William Scott*. London: Thames and Hudson, 2007.

Merleau-Ponty, Maurice. *Phenomenology of Perception*. Translated by Donald Landes. London and New York: Routledge, 2012.

Miller, Sequoia. *The Ceramic Presence in Modern Art*. Yale: Yale University Art Gallery, 2015.

Mills, A.D. *A Dictionary of British Place Names*. Oxford; Oxford University Press, 1991.

Monks, Aoife. *The Actor In Costume*. Houndmills: Palgrave, 2010.

Moorhouse, Paul. *Howard Hodgkin: Absent Friends*. London: National Portrait Gallery Publications, 2017.

Museum Boijmans Van Beuningen. *Balance and Space: Martin Smith, Ceramics, 1976–1996*. Rotterdam: Museum Boijmans Van Beuningen, 1996.

Norton, Deborah. 'Perceptions and Illusions: Exploring Space with Martin Smith'. *Studio Pottery: Ceramics in Society*, 31 (Spring, 1998), 33-40.

Ordovas, Pilar, ed. *Irrational Marks: Bacon and Rembrandt*. London: Ordovas, 2011.

Pallasmaa, Juhani. *The Eyes of the Skin: Architecture and the Senses*. Chichester: Wiley Academy, 2005.

Perry, Grayson. *Ceramics*. London: Birch and Conran, 1987.

Puckle, Bertram. *Funeral Customs: Their Origin and Development*. Alexandria: Library of Alexandria, 1926.

Rawson, Philip. 'Empty Vessels'. In *Fast Forward*, edited by ICA. London: ICA, 1985, 15-17.

Riley, Bridget. *The Eye's Mind: Bridget Riley, Collected Writings 1965–1999*. London: Thames & Hudson, 1999.

Robinson, Michael. *Ewen Henderson: Recent Work*. London: Austin Desmond, 1998.

Russel Taylor, John. 'Alison Britton – Playing with Clay'. *Ceramic Review* (Nov-Dec) (1979): 6-8.

Rutherford, Jonathan. 'The Third Space. Interview with Homi Bhabha'. In *Identity: Community, Culture, Difference*, edited by Jonathan Rutherford. London: Lawrence and Wishart, 1990), 207–221.

Sandino, Linda. *Complexity and Ambiguity: The Ceramics of Alison Britton*. London: Barrett Marsden Gallery, 2000.

Schechner, Richard. *Between Theater and Anthropology*. Philadelphia: University of Pennsylvania ro Press, 1985.

Slayter-Ralph, Anthony, ed. *Magdalene Odundo*. Aldershot: Lund Humphries, 2004.

Stratton, Kimberley. 'Interrogating the Magic – Gender Connection'. In *Daughters of Hecate: Women and Magic in the Ancient World*, edited by Kimberley Stratton, K. and Dana Kalleres. Oxford: Oxford University Press, 2014, 1-37.

Szymborska, Wislawa, Carlin, Vuyelwa, and Cygan, Sylwester. 'Conversation with a Stone'. *The Kenyon Review*, New Series, vol. 23, no. 2, *Cultures of Creativity: The Centennial Celebration of the Nobel Prizes* (Spring, 2001): 90-93.

Tate St Ives, ed. *Wavelength*. St Ives: Tate St Ives, 2001.

The Editors of The Encyclopaedia Britannica. 'Agateware'. *Encyclopaedia Britannica*, https://www.britannica. com/art/agateware. Last updated: July 10, 2019. Accessed: September 13, 2020.

Turner, Victor. 'Liminal to Liminoid, in Play, Flow, and Ritual: an Essay in Comparative Symbology'. *Rice University Studies*, vol.60, no.3 (1974): 53-92.

Uchida, Shigeru. 'Foreword'. In Mira Locher, *Zen Gardens: The Complete Works of Shunmyo Masuno – Japan's Leading Garden Designer*. Tokyo: Tuttle, 2012, 8–10.

V&A. 'Teapots, designed by Christopher Dresser, 1878-9'. http://www.vam. ac.uk/content/articles/t/christopher-dresser-teapots/. Accessed: August 19, 2020.

White, Virginia. 'A Study of Female Agency in *The Homeric Hymn to Demeter* through Word and Illustration'. PhD. Diss., Wellesley College, Massachusetts (April 2017). https://repository. wellesley.edu/cgi/viewcontent. cgi?article=1646&context= thesiscollection. Accessed: September 17, 2000.

Williams, Raymond. 'Structures of Feeling'. In *Marxism and Literature*. Oxford: Oxford University Press, 1977, 128–135.

Wójtowicz, Magdalena. 'Etnografia Lubelszczyzny – ludowe wierzenia o drzewach'. http://teatrnn.pl/leksykon/artykuly/ etnografia-lubelszczyzny-ludowe-wierzenia-o-drzewach/. Accessed: August 29, 2020.

Acknowledgements

I would like to express my thanks to all of the featured artists for their support and assistance in preparing this volume. The welcome afforded me during studio visits, and the willingness to engage with my writing, have made the process of producing this book a genuine pleasure.

I would particularly like to thank Tessa Eastman, whose encouraging response to my first ever piece of writing on ceramics set me off on the journey that has produced this book. Her on-going engagement with my writing has been invaluable, and I am immensely grateful to her for the unstinting support she has offered.

I also wish to thank the numerous photographers who have given permission for their images to be reproduced in this volume. In particular, thank you to Sylvain Deleu, Michael Harvey and Philip Sayer for being so generous.

The following have also offered much appreciated assistance: Alison Britton, Claire Curneen, Tatjana Marsden and Siobhan Feeney at Marsden Woo Gallery; Grayson Perry and Hannah van den Wijngaard at Victoria Miro. Thanks to Teresa Murjas for pointing me in the direction of poetry. Sincere thanks to Greer Crawley for proofreading the manuscript. Last, but by no means least, thanks to The Crowood Press for believing in the project from the outset, and for seeing it through to completion with care.

Index